Washington
A Biography

Washington
A Biography

Noemie Emery

G. P. Putnam's Sons
New York

SBN: 399–11617–6

Library of Congress Cataloging in Publication Data

Emery, Noemi, 1938–
  Washington.

  Bibliography: p.
  Includes index.
  1. Washington, George, Pres. U.S., 1732–
1799.
E312.E43   1976   973.4'1'0924   [B]   76-6529

for my father
Francis Little Emery

my mother
Helen Touvim Emery

and
Colonel Moses Little
(8 May 1724–27 May 1798)

Author's Note

Washington as a subject presents a problem peculiar to himself. He is *known,* but what as? Very little, usually, and that little indeterminate and dim. Time has done little to reduce the image of the big man on the white horse, insufferably righteous, or the man who had such trouble with his teeth. Neither is much use to the scholar, seeking intellectual connections to history, or to the lay reader, seeking emotional connections to his life. Beyond this, the unacknowledged void between the needed fire of the soldier-president and the dim oddity we have been handed does something upsetting to our lives. It sets a dead echo at the center of American history, delegitimizing the first facts of our creation and nature, making revolution and government totter uncertainly, as if hanging in air. Washington's canonization has made orphans of us all. My purpose has been to locate him, to restore him to history, and to restore to him and to history the heat, struggle, and passion that are rightfully their own.

In the course of this exertion I have been the beneficiary of many people's aid. The New York Public Library provided the sources and then the facility—the Frederick Lewis Allen Room—in which this book was written. Harvey Ginsberg of Putnam's and Marilyn Marlow of Curtis Brown supervised the manuscript with care. Doris Speisman typed the final version with precision and speed. I am indebted to Richard B. Morris of Columbia University for the insights gained in his course on America Before the Revolution and for the others in his excellent books. I am also indebted to Michael Kraus, professor emeritus at City College of New York, and his wife, Vera, for their counsel, encouragement, and aid.

Countless people sustained me with continuing expressions of confidence that seemed at some moments premature and at others entirely misplaced. I am grateful to the other inmates of the Allen Room, especially Susan Brownmiller, Joan Goulianos, Ruth Gross, and Nancy Milford; to Joseph and Trude Lash, for help beyond all calls of duty; to my father and my grandparents for their strongly expressed encouragement; and to my mother, a Capricorn of the very first order, without whom this book, by a Pisces and about a Pisces, could never have been done.

22 February 1976
New York City

Contents

PART FOUR: THESE UNITED STATES

PART ONE:

King's Soldier 1732-1759

I

Beginnings

The habits, life, customs, computations & c. of the
Virginians are much the same as about London,
which they esteem their home.—HUGH JONES,
The Present State of Virginia, 1724

The enigma of George Washington has never been resolved. Remote, brooding, inaccessible, he stares down from the Houdon statue, bones massive in the nose and jawline, melancholy in the downturn of the mouth. The eyes, wide-set and solemn, look into the middle distance, skirting contact and comprehension, sealing their secret in themselves. The face presents a challenge that intrigues as it baffles and defies. In 1852, from the pit of a dissolving Union, Emerson took this stab into the mystery, seeking in that bleak moment solace from the source: "The heavy, laden eyes stare at you, as the eyes of an ox in pasture. And the mouth has gravity and depth of quiet, as if this MAN had absorbed all the serenity of America, and left none for his restless, rickety, hysterical countrymen." For two centuries, this strength has brooded over the American democracy in the tense attraction of born opposites: its balance, its counterpoise, its resource—and its reproach.

This strength has been a burden on America, and America has taken its revenge. No great man in history has a name so lifeless or a monument so featureless and blank.

13

Jefferson and Lincoln, adoptive saints of the democracy, dominate their own memorials; Andrew Jackson's very horse breathes fire; Washington's tribute alone reveals no warming touch of flesh. The lines describe the limits of the image: flawless aspiration—and what else?

More, apparently, than his countrymen have cared or dared to know. The reality is the inverse of the image, flawed and broken, violent, complex. Incident and irony weave strange and unexpected patterns in his life. He began a great world war when he was twenty-two years old, was branded an "assassin" in the courts of Europe, and chided for barbarity by Voltaire. In the war that followed, his pride, insolence, and insubordination were famous—and infamous—among British and colonial commanders in the skirmishes against the French. Eaten by a fierce ambition, he pursued fame relentlessly, missed it, and discovered later, when it came unbidden, that he had somehow lost the taste. He proposed to one woman while in love with another, married the first in a mood of almost bitter resignation, and found later that this, too, could change. Cool, aloof, and distant, he was known for the cold qualities of what Jefferson called his perfect justice, yet Jefferson, and others, sensed the hidden violence; portraitist Gilbert Stuart observed the lineaments of all the strongest passions and said that if he had lived among the Indians, he would have been the most fierce of all the savage chiefs. The results of those banked fires were apparent then and still endure: the army saved, the union soldered, the ambitions, flames, and talents of Hamilton, Jefferson, John Adams—the most contentious lot to coexist in any house of government—overmastered and subdued.

What happened, then, to blur this image, to make this man who tamed the fire-eaters of his lifetime seem so much the dimmest of them all? Sometime after 1775, with the vast portion of his public life before him, he passed into the hands of propagandists and mythmakers, more interested in imagery than in character delineation, more concerned with a totem to hang morals on than in the picture of a flawed and living man. Part was in the temper of the time: the need of a scrabble nation, fighting its own impending dissolution, for a presence to counter its centrifugal forces; something of mar-

14

ble, colder than flesh. Washington himself conspired in his own entombment, refusing to publish his recollections or to let those of the men who knew him see the light of day. "Any memoirs of my life," he wrote James Craik in 1784 when he was a world-famous figure, as well as the national hero of a state that was not quite a nation, "would rather hurt my feelings than tickle my pride whilst I lived. I had rather glide gently down the stream of life, leaving it to posterity to think and say what they please of me, than by any act of mine to have vanity or ostentation imputed to me . . . . I do not think vanity is a trait of my character."

In this disavowal lie two preoccupations that bordered on obsessions in themselves: Washington's social bias against self-aggrandizement and Washington's fear that any close inspection of his career and character could serve only to underline those deficiencies of temperament and training of which he was so painfully and so persistently aware. At first glance, these insecurities sit oddly with that serenity that impressed Emerson; at second sight they form a balanced pattern of anxiety and accomplishment that governed his emotional development and ruled the inner rhythms of his life. Without the doubts, the achievements would not have been so dazzling, each sense of his own insufficiencies driving him more surely toward his cold ideal. That stoic calm was a forced contrivance wrested out of inner turmoil; Washington had made himself, and then his country, from a tangle of disruptive forces in a prolonged and conscious effort of the will. The strains within the commonwealth are obvious, those within the man less clear. Yet they existed, and they too must come to light.

His family came from the north of England, the hard country near the Scottish border, known for the rugged nature of the landscape and the industry and purpose of the stock. Earliest records indicate that the first known member of the line, William de Hertburn, knight, came there from parts unknown in the train of the Count Palatine, Bishop of Durham, and was awarded the manor of Wessington, near the border of Westmoreland and Lancashire, around 1185. For four centuries thereafter the Wessingtons—or Washingtons—stayed close to their holdings, solid members of the upper middle classes, farmers, merchants and knights of the shire, pillars of the community and keepers of the peace. An attachment to order and stability was noted from their early days. One William Washington, the first of a long string of loyalists, backed Henry III against insurgents in the Barons' Wars. Another served as privy councillor of Durham, a third as justice of the peace. Finally, one Lawrence Washington of Grey's Inn, onetime mayor of Northampton and dealer in the Flemish wool trade, was given the grant of Sulgrave Manor in Westmorland by Henry VIII for fealty to church and crown of England on the dissolution of the monasteries in 1538. On this ascendant note the family moved still higher through the upper bourgeoisie into the lower reaches of the upper classes, advancing steadily in property and power through attachment to their country and their king. Another Lawrence Washington, also of Grey's Inn, became register of the High Court of Chancery, as did Sir Lawrence Washington, his son. A cousin, William Washington, soared higher still; he married Anne Villiers, half sister of the Duke of Buckingham, a favorite of James I. The Colonel Henry Washington who surrendered the city of Worcester to Puritans in 1647 was their son.

With their new allegiance to the Church of England, the family could have been no less than pleased when another Lawrence Washington, cousin to Henry and grandson to Lawrence the first, went down to Oxford for his master of arts in divinity in 1626, another tie in the connection to the established order that the family was forging link by careful link. Then, with devastating suddenness, the order snapped. Puritans and Parliamentarians rose against the increasingly repressive measure of the Stuarts and their allies in the church; by 1649 Charles I had been beheaded outside the halls of Parliament, Cromwell was supreme in Whitehall, and triumphant Puritans had ousted the Reverend Lawrence Washington from his living at Purleigh Parish, Essex, ostensibly on the grounds that he was a "common frequenter of Ale-houses, not only himself sitting daily tippling there, but encouraging others in that beastly vice," but more likely for the "malicious royalism" that his connections and his sense of order had led him to embrace. His sons, John and Lawrence, faced a grim decision: poverty, submission to the Ironsides, or emigration to America, the traditional refuge for the losers in England's internal quarrels since dissension had reached serious proportions around 1625. The sons, like their forebears, were stubborn and ambitious, geared to the pursuit of land and status; life without the hope of either must have seemed a prospect bleak in the extreme. What better choice than emigration; what better haven than Virginia—Anglican and so royalist that it had sworn allegiance to Charles II, then in exile in the Netherlands, as early as 1656? The brothers sailed in 1657. By the restoration year of 1660, which saw church and crown reclaimed in England, they were settled on the upper Rappahannock, with their private restorations well advanced.

Virginia, then defined as all the land from New England to the Carolinas and from the Atlantic to the "California Sea," was already touted as the refuge for the enterprising and embarrassed, with nothing wanting but industry and diligence to turn the beneficence of nature to a profitable life. A tract entitled *A Perfect Description of Virginia* published in England in 1649 (and which John Washington may well have read) described a lush and semitropic paradise, with the delights of "physick flowers," thirty sorts of fish, parakeets, and "one bird we call the mock-bird, for he will imitate all other birds' notes and cries, both day and night birds, yea, the owl and the nightengale." Deer abounded in this wilderness, along with bear and squirrel and "rackoons, as good meat as lamb." The soil delighted, being fat and rich and watered with mountain springs, ensuring abundance of the necessaries such as "bread, victual," and, important to an Englishman, "good beer." Tobacco, already the prime staple, was "much vented and esteemed," though selling only at the low price of three pence the pound, but hopes were high for profits from the silk industry and for trade with India and China, once a passage had been broken to the west. This, the pamphlet promised, was no more than a matter of time: "Sir Francis Drake was on the back side of Virginia on his voyage around the world, and now all the question is only how broad the land may be to that place from the head of the James River above the falls."

These prospects, along with the unsettled state of English politics, had already drawn a crop of settlers from among the younger sons and enterprising nephews of land-poor and well-connected families and people like the Washingtons, who found life among the Roundheads hard. By 1660 some of the great dynastic families were already present in the seed: John Carter; Benjamin Harrison I; Colonel Charles Lee at Paradise on the York River, where "faithful and useful to the interests of the commonwealth," he pursued a career in commerce, land, and politics as justice, burgess, councillor, and secretary of state. More would arrive in the years just after the coming of the Washingtons: William Beverley; Philip Ludwell; Charles Custis; William Byrd I. These could aspire, if diligent, to the status of one Captain Matthews, held up by the *Perfect Description* as the proper model for Virginia citizens, who:

> Hath a fine house and all things answerable to it; he sows yearly store of hemp and flax, and causes it to be spun; he keeps weavers, hath a tan house, causes leather to be dressed, hath eight shoemakers employed in their trade, hath forty negro servants, brings them up to trades in his house; he yearly sows abundance of wheat, barley &c., the wheat he selleth at four shillings the bushel, killeth stores of beeves, and send them to victual the ships when they come thither; hath abundance of kine, a brave dairy, swine great store, and poultry; he married the daughter of Sir Thomas Hinton, and, in a word, keeps a good house, lives bravely, and a true lover of Virginia; he is worthy of much honour.

John Washington settled on the Northern Neck, the uppermost portion of the colony, bounded by the Rappahannock and Potomac rivers, rich and thickly forested, dense with heavy growth of trees. There he moved quickly up the scale of colonial preferment, amassing land through purchase, marriage, and the bounty for the importation of in-

18

dentured slaves. To his settlers' fee of 1,000 acres he added 500 through a bargain struck with a shipmate and 700 the next year through his marriage to Anne Pope. More patents (and more marriages) followed, each adding its own portion: 600 acres in 1661; 600 more two years later; 595 in 1664. In 1670, as half interest on a shipload of servant-settlers, he acquired a grassy ridge on the Potomac called Epsewasson, or Little Hunting Creek. The land Mount Vernon would one day stand on passed into the family as broker's fee for human flesh.

Office followed land in the inevitable progression, stature rising with acquisition in an ascending pattern through the years: vestryman; county coroner; collector of tobacco taxes; justice of the County Court of Westmoreland County; colonel of the colonial militia; member of the House of Burgesses, 1666. There he served with diligence, if not with parliamentary brilliance, becoming a man at least as honored as the esteemed Captain Matthews, leaving a solid place in the colonial hierarchy and the neat sum of 10,000 acres to his heir in 1677. This was a time of vast territorial expansion, when "People flock'd thither apace; every one took up Land by Patent, to his Liking; not minding anything but to be Masters of great Tracts of Land." John's heir was the exception; a suave man, with more smooth and less grain than his father, he stayed content around his home plantation, gaining affection but no property, leaving a static estate to be shared among his three children, Lawrence, Mildred, and the blond sunny baby who was to be George's father, Augustine.

George's grandfather died in 1698 at the age of thirty-nine. His widow remarried two years later and followed her new husband to Cumberland in England, not far from where the Washingtons had first struck firm roots in British soil in the year 1185. There the children attended school at Appleby in Whitehaven with other scions of the lesser gentry and might have reverted to their origins if not recalled by relatives for lawsuits involving their paternal holdings in 1709. The children, uprooted for the second time in their short existences, were strangers to Virginia, English in everything but name. Doubtless, they noticed little in the way of

19

changes, but a practiced eye might have marked developments that cast their future in an uncertain light: the disappearance of open land below the fall line; the consolidation of those holdings into massive land blocs; the division of the map of the dominion into a series of interlocking demesnes of almost ducal size and scope. Patents in the tens of thousands were not uncommon; private holdings in the hundred thousands no longer rare. The Harrisons owned 125,000 acres on the York River, William Byrd II held 187,000 from the head of the James River to the Carolina border; Robert Carter, called King for his sway and arrogance, would control more than 330,000 acres of choice properties when he died in the birth year of George Washington, 1732. Against these, the Washington holdings, once the guarantee of gentle status, slipped to no more than a minor planter's share. Split, the portions would diminish even more: Lawrence, as the eldest, took the lion's share of 7,000 acres; Mildred, about 2,000; Augustine, the younger son's scant pittance of 1,750.

Augustine was rising thirteen, blond and ruddy, with his grandfather's temper and much of his reach. He came of a line obsessively ambitious, possessive, high-toned and high-tempered, who identified themselves with the prevailing social order and measured their own value by their standing on that scale. He was land-poor, but he was still place-conscious; his parents had been gentle, and he viewed his circumstances more as a setback to be struggled out of than as a permanent condition to be endured. John's grandson, like John himself, was prepared to fight his way from inconsequence back into the settled classes and would count himself in exile until he did.

His society, unfortunately, was not prepared to take him at his own estimation of himself. In the fifty years between John's death and his majority the colony had evolved into a strictly structured class society, marked by tight lines of social preference, in which a small clique of fifteen families, closely tied by bonds of blood and interest, seized control of property and public office, and held all power in a fine and close-knit web. By 1700 their ascendancy had been noticeable; by 1720 it was all but absolute. Royal governors from Francis

20

Nicholson in 1697 to Alexander Spotswood in 1722 railed against this hereditary faction of designing men who dominated the Council (or upper house of the legislature), stocked the lower house with their dependents and relations, intimidated the lesser orders by their control of the dominion's legal system, sent agents of their own to London to contest the governor's decisions (where they cut a wide swath through the city), and held the claims of both the crown and lesser planters well at bay. Lines within this "web of kinship" cut intricate patterns through the higher councils of the state: Benjamin Harrison, president of the Council at the turn of the century, was father-in-law to two other councillors, James Blair and Philip Ludwell II. Ludwell was uncle by marriage to William Byrd II, councillor and receiver general; Byrd was related to two other ruling families, Beverley and Parke. These alliances made them all but irresistible; when Spotswood complained to London of the intransigence and sway of the connection, he was referring not to a fleeting combination but to an entrenched web of blood and interest, root deep into the heart of the dominion, impossible to disturb or interrupt. Efforts to break the power of the faction ran head-on into the stone wall of class and family solidarity; governors had trouble finding men of means to fight the party or to fill the higher posts of government who were not parcel of the "family" themselves. Spotswood complained to London in 1713 about a vacant Council seat that "I know of no others so fit for that post, except some who enjoy places of profit in the government . . . or else others, who are related to one particular family, to which the greater part of the Council are already near allies." His efforts failed to end his problems; his successor, Hugh Drysdale, was writing home ten years later that connections foiled all efforts at securing unbiased personnel. The interlocking alliances of these families checked all efforts at externally imposed control. Spotswood's attempts to bring Ludwell up on civic charges were delayed endlessly; Ludwell's relations made the majority of almost every court.

To Spotswood, the powers of this "party" had reached the point of danger to the crown itself:

> His maj'ty must no longer retain in his Service at
> Home any one whom he thinks fit to Honour with the
> Chief Government of this Plantation, nor must he commit
> the Administration to a L' without incurring the Assent of
> the Party. . . . No Governor must reprove them on pain
> of having his Speeches and Messages voted Scandalous,
> and his modest Expostulations represented to his Sover-
> eign as a Crime.

If the appointees were vulnerable, the oligarchs were not:

> And lastly, none of this party must be removed from
> any office he enjoys, but his Conduct be never so irregu-
> lar, but a numerous Chain of Relations shall com-
> bine. . . . Upon the the Governor's refusal to concur
> therein he shall be sure to be Clamoured out of his Repu-
> tation and Post.

Spotswood's predictions were soon translated into fact.
His attempts to curb the land-grabbing sprees of the faction
in 1715 brought the tribe down on his neck. London listened
to the plaints of both parties, weighed the powers of one governor against those of an entrenched provincial gentry, and
took the one pragmatic course: Spotswood was requested to
resign.*

The new state of this aristocracy expressed itself in other
ways, as seductive as the Council powers and as tempting to
those lower down along the way. Beside the banks of the
great rivers "above where the great ships ride" you could
now see exquisite Georgian mansions, doubly impressive in
their wild setting, "Brick Houses of many Rooms on a floor
. . . their Stories much higher than formerly, and their
Windows large, and shast with Cristal Glass." Robert Carter
had begun Nomini Hall, the second of his great houses; his

---

*Whereupon he purchased vast land tracts in the western part of the
colony, built a mansion, an ironworks, and a model village, made fast
friends of all his former enemies, and founded what became one of "the
families" himself. His grandson, Colonel Alexander Spotswood, served
under Washington in the Revolutionary War.

son John was building Shirley; William Byrd was making plans for Westover, that gem of colonial architecture, to be erected in 1728. "Publick Times" at Williamsburg (when the Assembly was in session) were dazzling occasions, as noted with some astonishment by the Englishman Hugh Jones in 1724. There he found "as fine an Appearance, as good Diversion and as Splendid Entertainments as anywhere" (meaning no doubt London), attended by "handsom, well-dress'd and compleat Gentlemen," who "generally talk good English" and "discourse handsomely on most common subjects" (meaning dynastic politics, the science of Locke and Newton, the poetry of Pope and Dryden, and the journalism of Addison and Steele). "The habits, life, customs, computation &c. of the Virginians," Jones concluded, "are much the same as about London, which they esteem their home."

Culture flourished, through private, if not official, means. There was one college, and no public schools, but "King" Carter had a library at Corotoman of more than 1,200 volumes, running heavily to history, theology (for which he had a passion), and the law. Even the king was outmatched by William Byrd II, who had the largest collection in colonial America—nearly 4,000 volumes running from Homer to Hobbes and Descartes, from medicine to architecture, in seven languages, including Italian and Dutch. It was Byrd's habit to preface each day of land dealing, political infighting, and amatory dalliance with a predawn hour's reading in Hebrew or Greek. As a young man Byrd had been sent to England, where he met the playwrights Congreve and Wycherley and enjoyed the patronage of Sir Robert Southwell, Secretary of State for Ireland and president of the Royal Society for science and the arts. Portraits of Southwell and of Byrd's other friends—Lord Orrery, the Duke of Argyll, the Marquess of Halifax—adorned Westover's great hall.

This weave of culture with the gritty stuff of power made the upper classes irresistible to the outsider, especially the better type of young achiever to whom the blend of high purpose and high living held a double-edged appeal. With its tempering of grace and power, its roundness, its hunger for the best of all experience, it exerts a subtle fascination that

23

persists into the present day. Byrd himself defined the ideal (if not the total realization) of his society in this epitaph, somewhat idealized, to his long and picaresque career:

> Being born to one of the amplest fortunes in the country
> He was early sent to England for his education
> Where under the care and direction of Sir Robert South-
> well,
> And ever favored with his particular instructions,
> He made a happy proficiency in polite and varied learn-
> ing. . . .
> Thus eminently fitted for the service and ornament of his
> country
> He was thrice made Receiver General of His Majesty's
> Revenues here.
> Was thrice appointed Public Agent of Virginia to the
> Court and Ministry of England.
> And being thirty-seven years a Member,
> At last became President of the Council of that Colony.
> To all this were added a great elegance of taste and life
> The well-bred gentleman and polite companion
> The splendid economist and prudent father of a family
> With the constant enemy of all exorbitant power
> And hearty friend to the liberties of his country.

The spirit of leveling, noted an English visitor, so prevalent in many other colonies was all but nonexistent in Virginia, where the drive was not in the direction of equality but toward the definition of caste differences and the refinement of the ideal ruling class. The oligarchs, qualified in their own eyes by the dual claims of land and learning, were prepared to govern justly, but not to let their ascendancy diminish or their power be diluted by degrees. The names of the "accursed faction"—Byrds of Westover, Harrisons of Berkeley Hundred, Lees of Staunton, Carters of Corotoman and Nomini Hall—rang through the dominion in a harmony of land and power, a distraction to the royal governors, a lure to those families of like blood but lesser sustenance who had missed inclusion in the royal circle through mischance of timing or of luck. Of none was this more true than of the Washingtons, descendants of the possessors of Durham and of Sulgrave Manor, to whom the dual weave of status gained and service rendered had become the very stuff of life. Augustine, the first of the Virginian Washingtons to slip below the fringe of power, would feel his exclusion deeply and transmit his ambitions to his sons. The desire to instate themselves within the circle of preferment would become the ruling passion of their lives.

Still hopeful, still determined, still ambitious, Augustine celebrated his majority in 1716 with his first series of land purchases and his first marriage, to Jane Butler, the well-bred daughter of a local planter, a gentle woman with a sweetness and generosity that she transmitted to her sons. They settled at Wakefield, a farm on the upper reaches of the Rappahannock that had been part of the first land grant to John the emigrant in 1659. Augustine settled into his county duties on the moderate level to which his properties entitled him, while concentrating his main energies on plans to further his estate. It was not to be an easy or, in the end, a rewarding quest. His records of this period show a pattern of reach in excess of his resources, a steady, possibly nerve-straining effort to push himself beyond his means. His purchases showed enterprise but required more cash for development than he could put his hands on, and his lands lay largely unimproved. Some of the strain was reflected in the living quarters, as every spare coin was channeled to advancement; in a period of large house building, Wakefield remained a simple country farm. In one area, however, there could be no scrimping. His sons, Lawrence and young Augustine, were shipped to Appleby about 1725 for the cherished English education, a dazzling move for a minor planter and one that Augustine could ill afford. On this point he was immovable: his sons were to be trained as leaders and as gentlemen, reared to move among the class above them, to which Augustine in the recess of his mind belonged. This was followed by a new investment, in the Principio Iron Works, a foundry on his property where "Mr. Washington raises the ore and carts it thither for twenty shillings the ton of iron that it yields." Though "well-managed," the mines did not show a profit; in the early 1730s the colonial iron industry went into a precipitate decline. On top of this commercial disappointment a personal disaster struck. Jane Butler Washington died on 24 November 1729. For Augustine, the situation was intolerable; he needed a manager for his farms and his small daughter,* and, with his sons in England, lonely Wakefield would seem desolation itself. Practicality and loneliness would push him into a second marriage, which he made on 6 March 1731, to his Rappahannock neighbor, Mary Ball.

Mary herself held a tenuous position in society; she was the product of her father's second marriage, to a woman who was unfamilied and illiterate and may have been, as rumor said, his maid. Connections of this kind were not encouraged in Virginia, too close to the frontier to take conventions lightly and obsessed with the forming, not the flaunting, of social lines. William Byrd II spoke for the gentry on the subject of these mean alliances; at their worst they were prostitution, at their best, a prank. Since Joseph Ball was pushing sixty at the time of this adventure, it was probably regarded also as the last caper of an aging fool. Certainly, it brought no pleasure to his five grown children; there is a suggestion, from a deed of gift dated at the time of his remarriage, that he felt obliged to quiet their objections by turning over to them a large part of his land. Even this assurance that they would not be stripped of their inheritance by an adventuress did not increase their pleasure with their aging parent; the four Ball daughters appear to have dropped all connection with their father and with his new family after 1708. A brother, Joseph, like his father a man of independent spirit, relented to the point of corresponding with his half sister after he had moved to England some years hence. With this exception, all connections were broken by the marriage; Mary never knew her father's family or very many of his friends.

Mary's father died in 1711, when she was three years old, thus assuring that the only child of his second marriage would be brought up exclusively by the parent least

*This daughter, Jane, died in a riding accident in 1735.

equipped to do her good. Joseph Ball had left them money, but not his brain or his assurance; it was the narrow mind of Mary Johnson that shaped her daughter's world. The mother was a warm but not a wordly woman, and she may have transmitted her own sense of displacement in her upper-middle-class surroundings to the girl. Possibly they were viewed by others (and therefore by themselves) as intruders in unknown territories which they never understood completely and to which they did not properly belong. Mary grew, a small isolate atom inside an otherwise interwoven social fabric that seemed to have a classification in it for everyone except herself, deprived of the sense of place that might have eased her insecurities and the education that might have have given discipline to what was emerging as an iron, if erratic, will. A weaker girl might have been broken, but Mary was tenacious, like her father and half brother, and her anxieties surfaced in more complicated ways. She became both fearful and aggressive, defensive and defiant. Later she would cling fiercely to everything around her, to brake her sense of inner rootlessness, always clutching, always fearful, always certain that the rocks of her existence were deserting her, money vanishing, land going, children gone. In many ways her tensions were the inverse of her husband's: where the Washingtons suffered a sense of exclusion from the class that they were mentally attuned to, she suffered a lack of connection to the upper-middle-class society to which she so uncertainly belonged. Her new position as successor to a gentlewoman in a family obsessed with social standing would only aggravate her emotional strains. And the combined anxieties of Augustine and Mary would not make easy sailing for their sons.

For a slipped-down but still solid family like the Washingtons, the marriage was a monetary match, but a subtle comedown in class, reflecting Augustine's own weariness, his acceptance of a minor station for himself, if not for his two older children, and his own slippage in the marriage market since his schemes for advancement had failed to bear fruit. Less was to be brought to, and expected of, this second venture, the children of this marriage were not to share parity with those of the first. They would receive care, but not the special grooming; they would not be trained to crack the golden web.

If less esteemed, this second brood was soon more numerous; George, born on 11 February 1732 (old style) was followed by Elizabeth, 1734; Samuel, 1735; John Augustine, 1737; and Charles, 1739. Their quality was more than exceptionally uneven. Elizabeth had spirit; John Augustine was weak and charming; Charles, a drunk; and Samuel, a debtor, weak without charm. To these, George, with a calculation rare in childhood, gave what he believed their proper due. His love was for John Augustine and his half brother Lawrence, his affection for Elizabeth, young Augustine (and possibly his father); to the others, he was dutiful—no more.

All participated in the insular life of a planting family of the middle sort, on a series of farms on the Rappahannock and Potomac rivers, comfortable and inelegant, alike in everything but place. There were visits among family and neighbors (always on the same social level) but none of the commerce with the higher gentry that brought the grace (and arrogance) of the established upper class. What they did know of this world of space and power would come to them at first obliquely, in their father's talk of plans and disappointments, in their mother's odd defensiveness, in the hopes for their half brothers, in gossip of the doings of grandees. Later the sense of caste would have gone deeper, of a world of scope and influence they were unlikely to achieve. Washington's diffidence has baffled his biographers, who underestimate its intensity and depth. A peripheral position in a class-ridden society is not a recipe for self-esteem. Washington's birth and his Virginia background had given him both a goal and an initial disadvantage, and the stage for his first struggle had been set.

II

My Dear Brother

War is horrid in fact but much more so in imagination. We . . . have learned to live on ordinary diet, to watch much, and disregard the noise or shot of cannon—LAWRENCE WASHINGTON to his father, 1741

A Virginia childhood above the level of the "vulgar" often meant the pleasures of security both social and financial, followed by the steady, smooth ascension to the top. To George Washington, it meant the tensions of a family close to, but not of, the aristocracy, troubled by the frequent absence of a distant father and the attentions of an all-too-present mother, whose incursions had to be resisted and repelled.

Mary Washington by the middle 1730s had become a troubled woman, fretted by unnamed anxieties that centered on a desire to possess property when older and to possess her children when young. Later her letters would ring an endless plaint—"No Cornn in the cornn-house. . . . I should be almost Starved. . . . I never lived so Poore in my life"—hinging on the common themes of privation, insufficiency, and loss. She had not yet reached the dark tones of those years, but she was already both impressive and disturbing, intense in her preoccupations, backing her hesitant decisions with unchanging tenacity of will. These aberrations were neither tempered by young womanhood nor mellowed by old age. A veteran of the Revolution found her formidable when he met her, an enfeebled but still headstrong woman, in 1784. As for her effect on children, there is this testimony from George's cousin, written in retrospect in his own middle age: "When time has whitened my locks, and I am grandparent of a second generation, I could not behold that remarkable woman without feelings it is impossible to describe." He was, he confessed, "ten times more afraid than ever I was of my own parents," whether for general severity or excess zeal in the protection of her own children he did not say. Certainly, her efforts to protect these children—especially from things from which they did not always wish to be protected—were extensive and, for that rough society, severe. Many of the stories of George's childhood, unproved but disturbingly cohesive, ring with this repressive theme: George as a young child confined to the area around the farmhouse; George at nine, larger than most boys of eleven, riding to field school behind his servant because his mother would not let him ride alone; a fierce row among the elder Washingtons about the breaking of a wild horse. Did his courting of danger in his later years stem from this early disgrace? More factual is a letter from George to Governor Robert Dinwiddie in 1756 about a commission for his younger brother: "I have a brother that has long discovered an inclination to enter the Service; but has till this been dissuaded from it by my Mother, who now, I believe, will give consent." (He was wrong; she didn't; the brother stayed at home.) Her efforts to check his own military career were energetic, if less successful; each foray into the Ohio country was delayed and enlivened by maternal visits, maternal tantrums, and maternal tears. In April, 1755, George is writing to Robert Orme, aide-de-camp to General Edward Braddock: "The arrival of a good deal of Company (among whom is my Mother, alarm'd with the report of my attending your Fortunes) prevents me the pleasure of waiting upon you today. . . . "

These were not the protests of the usual protective parent; there was a mad quality to Mary's carping that precluded recognition, much less concern, for anything or anyone outside herself. It was her fear, not her children's welfare, that obsessed her; she showed all her life an inability to take pleasure in their achievements or their company or to recognize them in any way as personalities with identities and troubles of their own. Her total lack of interest in the honors that deluged her oldest child (which she lived to see, dying in 1789) is a peculiar chapter, but her sense of pleasure was as raddled as her eye for pain was keen. But her awareness of the rights of others was always shadowy at best. She wrote George, on campaign in the wilderness, for a Dutchman and butter, and her response to his travail in the Revolution was to dun him with complaints about her money troubles and finally to petition the legislature of Virginia for relief.

George was able, by the time of this last trial, to put the cause for these diversions where it rested, in his mother's own disordered mind. "Imaginary wants," wrote John Augustine in 1783 about what had long since become their common problem, "are indefinite; and sometimes insatiable, because they sometimes are boundless, and always changing." To Mary herself he wrote: "Happiness depends more on the internal frame of a person's own mind than on the externals of the world." But Mary, who had no acquaintanceship with happiness, was not about to form one now.

A child's resentment of a domineering parent is often of the love-hate variety, resistance overlaid with instinctive affection or the grudging admiration that strength pays to strength. George's own feelings show no such ambivalence: in childhood he was withdrawn; in youth, resistant; in maturity, resigned. His correspondence with (and about) his mother reveals no emotion except exasperation (and perhaps a saddened tolerance); his visits to her after childhood were infrequent, reluctant, unrewarding, and short. The conclusions to be drawn from this are inescapable: that he moved, as soon as it was in his power, to sever, or at any rate reduce, a connection that had brought him little comfort and a high degree of strain. Mary had her part in this estrangement, with her resentment of the outer world that drew him so compellingly and her rejection of all parts of his existence that did not directly touch on hers. George's realism prevented him from feigning an affection for which he recognized there was little hope of reciprocation. Later on he had another reason: she reminded him of the dry, stunted world of his childhood, the part of his life he wished most to forget.

His immediate reaction was insulation and emotional withdrawal. What harm this might have done without the later intervention of his half brothers is incalculable; at any rate, it left its scars. All his life he was to show reserve and a fine degree of distance, to have trouble, except in rage, in "letting go." His first portrait, as colonel of the colonial militia, shows a face wary and self-protective, well schooled in calculation and restraint. What else could have happened? His childhood was designed to produce a personality that was either guarded or destroyed. His father was preoccupied and often absent; his younger brothers were infants; his older brothers were away. The lack of any stable influence to work consistently against his mother's had thrown him back against himself. It was his good fortune that unlike his younger brothers, he had resources to call upon. These forces were turned inward, to caution, self-protection, and the gradual conception of escape. His background had taught him self-reliance—a trait that he would stand in need of—if not in the accepted ways.

The large gaps in the early story of George Washington (owing partly to his reticence and partly to the insignificance of his family) resulted, once his fame had been established, in a flood of legends of great vigor and uncertain truth. It was Mason Locke Weems, that itinerant peddler of nostrums and pieties, who deserves the credit (or the blame) for the most memorable and flamboyant; no sooner was his hero established in the realms of history and legend then Weems was spurring his wagon up and down the eastern seaboard, hustling his tracts to credulous audiences between Delaware and Maine. There is the enduring legend of the cherry tree, in which a six-year-old George barked the unhappy sapling to the displeasure of his father, Augustine:

"George," said his father, "do you know who killed that beautiful little cherry tree yonder in the garden?"

32

This was a tough question, and George staggered under it for a moment, but quickly recovered himself; and looking at his father, with the sweet face of youth brightened with the inexpressible charm of all-conquering truth, he bravely cried out "I can't tell a lie, Pa, you know I can't tell a lie; I did cut it with my hatchet."

—Run to my arms, you dearest boy, cried his father, run to my arms, glad am I George, that you killed my tree, for you have paid me for it more than a thousand fold. Such an act of heroism in my son is worth more than a thousand trees, though blossomed with silver, and their fruits of purest gold.

Another legend casts George in a less attractive light (though one Weems found appealing) as a tattler on his schoolmates, with whom he lived "in the spirit of a brother" although already acting out his historic role of paterfamilias, solving disturbances with Solomon-like aplomb. He would never permit violence, and if he could not disarm their "savage passions" through his reasoning, he would run to the master to inform him of their "barbarous intentions" by himself. Oddly, Weems tells us, this was not resented by the other children, who revered him all the more. Further, Weems assures us, "He was never guilty of so brutish a practice as that of fighting himself."

What can be made of these effusions? Seemingly, not very much. The first story is discredited by the character of George's father; the second by that of George himself, whose authority did not develop early, who showed all his life a marked distaste for easy moral judgments, and who made few shows of warmth in childhood to his own family, much less to assumed and assorted "friends." Weems himself gave the game away in a series of letters to his printer, Mathew Carey, that covered most of the years of their joint publishing ventures through the first quarter of the nineteenth century, or between the deaths of Washington and Weems. In June, 1799, a full seven months before the demise of his hero, Weems was hard at work collecting anecdotes for a work to be titled "The Beauties of Washington" enumerating the full list of his "Great Virtues" (including, oddly, his "Ven-

33

eration for the Deity") and embelished with the odd premortem frontispiece "Go thy way, Old George. Die when thou wilt, we shall never look upon thy like again."

In October, Weems wrote Carey that he was working on a story titled "The True Patriot," and, in January, 1800: "I have something to whisper in your lug. Washington you know is gone! Millions are gaping to read something about him. I am very nearly prim'd and cock'd for 'em. . . . "

He went on to inform Carey of his stories "curious and marvelous," his intentions to "hold up his great Virtues (as Govr McKean prays) to the imitation of our youth," and concluded, as ever, with his clinching argument: "We may sell it with great rapidity for 25 or 37 cents and it would not cost us 10."

From Washington's death until his own, Weems continued to press his printer for promotion and his audience for sales; his *Life of George Washington With Curious Anecdotes, Equally Honorable to Himself and Exemplary to His Young Countrymen* went through twenty editions between 1800 and 1825. These were the years when the country was changing from the Federal Republic to the Jacksonian Democracy; it would have been unusual if Weems had not made his stories progressively more sentimental, with the years. However much his fictions changed, his motives remained constant, as he reminded Carey in 1809: "You have a great deal of money lying in the bones of old George."

Weems never saw or spoke to Washington or had any known commerce with anyone who did. The first and, regrettably, the most renowned of all the Washington chroniclers was driven far more by a passion for the proceeds from the "bones of old George" than by any insight into old George himself, whose real character might have appalled the Weems constituency or at least raised puzzled frowns. Between the moral codes of tidewater Virginia and those of the emerging American democracy stretched a chasm deep and wide. Who was to explain to Weems or to his followers that the real greatness of Washington lay in his distance from this emergent culture, in his function as the check on the democracy, the cool corrective to its inherent flaws? The *Life* has far more to tell us about the fantasies of Americans of the

34

middle class in the first quarter of the nineteenth century than about the real life of a child of the displaced Virginia gentry, three-quarters of a century before, close, it would appear, neither to father nor to family, fighting a muted battle with his mother as he nurtured plans of independence and escape. Washington's own written memory does not begin until Belvoir and Mount Vernon, when for the first time he found himself in a life he cared to be a part of and his dream world and his real one merged. For his early childhood, his only comment was his silence: a mute and cogent judgment in itself.

George began his schooling sometime between the ages of six and ten. There is a tradition that he began at a school maintained by the farm community of Fredericksburg, presided over in haphazard fashion by a one-eyed ex-convict whose instruction consisted largely of stories of his past life in the Chelsea slums. There is another story, less picturesque but more reliable, that he attended a school in Fredericksburg, run by the Reverend Frederick Marye, a French Huguenot refugee. He may have attended another school, run by a Mr. Williams, when he stayed with his half brother Augustine at Wakefield around 1744. Some copybooks survive from his thirteenth year with the names of the British possessions in America and the laws of "physicks" detailed in his neat and graceful handwriting, but no indication of where he did them or for whom. The theory that he did attend some formal classes is given its most substantial backing in a letter to him from George Mason in 1755, requesting a commission in the army for "my neighbor and your old school-fellow, Mr. Piper," giving some evidence, since the Masons lived on the Potomac, for the theory of the Wakefield school. Whatever it was, it was rudimentary, supplying little in the way of belles lettres, much less the "Erudition in the Arts [and] Sciences" to which he referred wistfully in a letter to Alexander Hamilton in 1796. It was not the education of a gentleman, sufficient to mark him off in his own eyes from the children of the upper gentry, especially from his half brother Lawrence, the shining star of the family, who returned in 1738, the natural target for the adoration of an indrawn child, estranged by choice from his surroundings, who had found in the small world around him little to fix his fancies on. This blend of grace and vigor would attract a gauche and lonely youngster, already afflicted with the "consciousness of a defective education," and aware of both his size and silences as unbecoming social flaws. "My dear Brother. . . . " For the next fourteen years this star would hang over his horizon, the ideal for his emerging aspirations, a beckoning and benign light.

Lawrence's first stay was a short one; his arrival coincided with the breaking of the European peace. British fears of containment by the "family compact" of the French and Spanish Bourbons, dormant through much of the century, was roused again by trade disputes. Spanish ships waylaid an English slaver off Porto Bello in the Caribbean and carried off a crew of seamen; one, named Jenkins, lost his ear. This outrage set off a storm of protest among the members of the London trading party that the corrupt, pacific Robert Walpole, mentor and first minister to George II, found himself unable to control. Pitt roused the Commons with the first ring of what was to be his cry (and theirs) for half a century : "When trade is at stake, it is your last entrenchment, you must defend it, or perish." The colonies, feeling the pinch of Bourbon presence on their borders, joined in the clamor for defense. War was declared in October, 1739, to the sound of London's chimes. "They are ringing their bells now," said Walpole; "they will be wringing their hands." Britain tapped its colonial manpower for the first time in what was planned as a bicontinental attack on major Spanish trading bases, including forts in Cuba and Cartagena (now Colombia); Virginia was ordered to raise a party of soldiers for service under Admiral Edward Vernon with the British fleet. Domestic competition for these honors became strong. Lawrence, with his new friends and old connections, harangued the governor to the extent that he was hopped over the heads of nine other claimants to the post of first adjutant of the American brigade. What better for this white hope of the family, whose education already outran his expectations, than to add to his social luster through military prestige? Lawrence, like his half brother ten years later, was to find the military a sideways channel to the top.

It was the first experience of the family with service in a mixed force of British and colonials and of exposure to the genius of the War Office at Whitehall. The experience was neither promising nor happy; all of Lawrence's problems were to be encountered twentyfold by George. Delays beset the venture from the beginning; Lawrence fumed as the expedition, scheduled to sail in the summer of 1740, lingered on through fall. When it left, belatedly, his mood did not improve; complaints came back to Virginia about heat and illness, mistreatment of colonials, incompetence in the high command. The Americans, he told his father, had "not received the treatment we expected" but had resolved to persevere. At least one other colonial had his doubts about the undertaking. William Byrd II wrote Sir Charles Wager, "I have no great opinion of embarking landsmen on such distant expeditions. They will all be down with scurvy or something like gaol distemper."

For months the troops lay off the coast of Cartagena, then made an ill-planned lunge against the fortress, to be driven back with heavy losses to their ships. "The enemy killed of ours some 600 and some wounded, and the climate killed the greater number," Lawrence wrote his father on 26 July 1741. "Vast changes we have in each Regiment; some are so weak as to be reduced to the two-thirds of their men; a great quantity of officers amongst the rest are dead." The ships returned to Cuba for a year of idling while malaria cut into their troops' numbers and indecision ate into their nerves. Lawrence for one found the frustration worse than war itself. "War is horrid in fact but much more so in imagination. We there have learned to live on ordinary diet, to watch much and disregard the noise or shot of cannon."

The conflict petered out by 1744; the final showdown of the British and the Bourbon powers was still ten years away. The colonials took with them a profound disenchantment with the wisdom of the War Office and resentment at what they considered prejudicial treatment; Lawrence was to spend the next three years in prolonged haggling to get what he considered justice in the way of joint commissions for his troops. ("I hear Col. Gouge hath wrote to England," Lawrence's British agent informed him, "and accuses your Virginians of Cowardice, and that they are all or most of them back.") This did not however quell what had developed into a distinctly martial streak. "We have no great news that can be depended upon from England in a great while," Lawrence's neighbor John Lewis wrote him in his dismal Cuban stalemate. "I hope they will be in earnest now, for I think they have only been at play hitherto with the lives and fortunes of thousands of poor souls. . . . I cannot see what delight you take in such a life. I heartily wish you safe here with Honour, that so much wished for Title, so much described to be gained in the field of Battle, but I think may be as deservedly acquired at home in the service of his Country, County, Parish and Neighbourhood, in Peace and Quietness."

But for Lawrence—and the young half brother who had followed his exploits with such rapt attention—"Peace and Quietness" were not to be the chosen stars.

Lawrence was back in August, 1742, the grace of valor added to his luster, more than ever the star within the firmament, more than ever the model for a hero-starved small child to adore. With his full brother, young Augustine, who had returned the same summer from Whitehaven, they cut imposing figures in the parent family, bright starlings in a nest of wrens. The Washington position, since the start of the decade, could not be said to have improved. Since 1738 the family had been installed at Ferry Farm on the upper Rappahannock ("a very handsom Dwelling House, three store houses, several other convenient out houses, and Ferry belonging to it, being the Place where Mr. Strother lived") opposite the infant city of Fredericksburg, a remote town whose undeveloped stature matched the family's unpromising estate. The light and sandy soil of the Rappahannock Valley yielded little in the way of corn crops or tobacco; Augustine's account books registered only small returns. The ironworks had been the main reason for the move from the Potomac, but that too failed to prosper; the death of Augus-

38

tine's assistant and chief overseer in December, 1735, saddled the owner with added debt.

Records of the later years of George's early childhood show an increased work load for his father, increased preoccupation, increased periods away from his family; he was gone to England for eight months in 1738 and frequently spent days and weeks away from home. Considering the characteristics that undoubtedly had been coming to light in Mary Washington, these absences might not have been too unwelcome to Augustine. His interests in life beyond his business worries appear to have centered on the packet boat, with its dispatches from Whitehaven and the Caribbean front. For the younger children, this meant a lessening of the masculine and the paternal influence, less balance to the anxieties of their mother; for the father, it meant a weariness and a withdrawal of attention from the second family that had never engaged his interest fully and now held the miasma of defeat. One of George's very few mentions of his father in his later correspondence contains the notation that "my father died when I was only ten years old." Augustine in fact had died when George was past eleven; the remission of this age to a more vulnerable stage of childhood, plus the use of the word "only" in an age of early orphanhood suggests a sense in the child that he had in fact been deserted by his parent at a time preceding death.

The progress that did befall the family came more through the address of Augustine's accomplished older children than from the industry of Augustine himself. Young Augustine had married Anne Aylett, an heiress, and begun the transformation of Wakefield, on his plans and her money, from a farmhouse to a substantial country seat. Bigger things were in progress to the north. There the name of Fairfax had been one to conjure with, the much esteemed (and much resented) proprietary owners of 5,000,000 acres on the Northern Neck. Their line had begun in the 1640s with one John Culpeper of Wigsall, Kent, who had defended the interests of Charles I in the Long Parliament and followed him into exile in 1644. Culpeper displeased some among the entourage, among them Lord Clarendon, who called him "a man of no very good breeding, having never sacrificed to the muses or conversed in any polite company," but he did please the king, who made him first Baron Thoresway, guardian to the prince of Wales, and one of seven royalists to share in the patent for the lands "bounded by and within the heads" of the Potomac and Rappahannock rivers granted by Charles II in 1649. This lien passed into the Fairfax family in 1690 through the marriage of Culpeper's daughter to Thomas, fifth Lord Fairfax (ironically, the Fairfaxes had been Roundheads in the Civil War), and thence to their son, Thomas, sixth lord, in 1710.

To protect these interests the family depended on a string of local planters who acted as their agents, the last and most spectacular of whom was Robert "King" Carter, who made much of his fortune through taxes on the Fairfax quitrents, successfully settled a lawsuit that extended the proprietary by 3,000,000 acres, and no doubt as a self-assigned fee for service rendered, sliced from this a portion in six figures for himself. Slightly stung by what he considered a piece of too-cute management, Fairfax moved the agency within the family after Carter died in 1732. This agent was his cousin, Colonel William Fairfax, a longtime servant of the empire who had served with Marlborough in the Low Countries and enjoyed a diverse career as chief justice of the Bahamas, general of the port of Providence, and collector of the port of Salem in Massachusetts Bay. Driven south by the calls of kin and interest, he left Salem for the softer climate of Virginia, built Belvoir, an elegant brick mansion on the south slope of the Potomac, and moved there in 1737 with his six children and his second wife. Once installed, he assumed the prominence that fit his station, as controller for the Northern Neck, member of the House of Burgesses for Prince William County, member of the King's Council in 1742. He also fell into acquaintanceship, and then intimacy, with his neighbor, Lawrence Washington, four miles upriver, like himself a worldling and a veteran, who had taken possession of his father's Hunting Creek plantation and begun the building of his small estate, Mount Vernon, named after his commander in the Spanish wars. By early 1743, to

40

the intense delight of Augustine, Lawrence was courting Fairfax's daughter, Anne.

Against these triumphs, George's prospects seemed all the more remote, headed for the grim future of a younger son in a society as land-based as England's with none of the home country's convenient outs: there were no further colonies to go to; the church lacked distinction; the "army" was a citizen militia that convened at odd intervals for light drilling in the county courtyards and heavy drinking in the local pubs. He showed no talents, except a delight in mathematical precision, which seemed unlikely to win him either profits or prestige. There are some rumors, advanced in later years by George himself, that his father had planned to give him an English education, but this seems wishful thinking on his part. By 1743 he was eleven, well past the ages at which his brothers had been sent to England, and it is doubtful, on the later record, if his mother would have let him go. It is more likely that Augustine had shot his bolt on his two older children, lacked the energy and the resources to back a third, and that someone had decided that this awkward youngster was not worth the risk entailed. By the middle of the year the question had become academic: Augustine died in April, 1743, two months after George's eleventh birthday, after an illness of four days.

III

Ambition

My life is grafted on the fate of Rome.— JOSEPH
ADDISON, *Cato*

The loss of his nominal protector brought a further setback
in George's already unpromising estate. He was the oldest
child in a small and confined household, more than ever at
the mercies of a mother whose anxieties, now that she had
causes for them, were bound to deepen and increase. Fortunately, relief was at hand. Mary's regime of erratic discipline,
reduced rations, and lessened social contact brought alarm,
warnings, and, at last, intervention from Lawrence and
young Augustine. George gives no account of his mother's
part in the ensuing conflict, but a cryptic line dropped later
leaves no doubt that a struggle did take place. At length,
Lawrence, as titular head of the family, won the best bargain
he was capable of striking, and George, as the oldest of the
remaining children (and possibly the most in need of remedy), was packed off to a refurbished Wakefield, taking with
him his reserve and silence, his keen sense of his own shortcomings, and his desperate desire to improve.

George was now thirteen, a crisis age, placed by circumstances at a crisis of events, and the advice he later gave a
nephew might have fitted his situation now:

> At this crisis your conduct will attract the notice of
> those who are about you [he wrote George Steptoe Wash-

ington in 1789]. . . . Your doings now may mark the leading traits of your character through life. It is absolutely necessary if you mean to make any figure upon the stage, that you should take the first steps right. . . . The first great object . . . is to acquire, by industry and application, such knowledge as your situation enables you to obtain.

At Wakefield, now a graceful country mansion presided over in casual elegance by the fashionable Anne Aylett, he put these precepts into practice, trailing Augustine like a small and watchful shadow, studying his motions as the models for his own. His horizons widened, he attacked his studies with new energies; a cousin recalled his unexpected industry and assiduity at school. "While his brother and the other boys were at playtime," he remembered, George remained "behind the door, ciphering," preternaturally serious, except for "one youthful ebulition . . . romping with one of the largest girls." To guard against the threat of social error, he copied out in painful longhand 110 "Rules of Civility and Social Conduct," blending general advice for deference to those of greater station with such specific precepts as "Wear not your cloths foul, unript or dusty," and "In the Presence of Others Sing not to yourself with a Humming Noise, nor Drum with your Fingers or Feet."

Doubtless, these stood him to advantage when he was transferred to Mount Vernon in the spring of 1745, a sizable advance on his previous experience and a promotion both in quality and kind. Ferry Farm had been a backwater, Wakefield a pleasant country mansion; Belvoir and Mount Vernon were working factors in the web of empire that swung from Bengal to the Alleghenies, with London as its hub. Already, that small circle was an axis of some power; William Fairfax had moved to the Council in 1742, his son George William taking his place in the House of Burgesses; in 1744 Frederick had been detached from Prince William County, and Lawrence, with the Fairfax influence behind him, slipped into the created seat. Lawrence, Anne, and now George Washington were at Belvoir often, mingling with the swarm of notables who frequented the mansion's hall: William Byrd II,

John Mercer, John Taylor of Mount Airy, ex-Governor Spotswood, Governor William Gooch. There, George met the rising figures of his own generation: John and Landon Carter, George Mason, Richard Henry Lee. Also to Belvoir came his comrade in the coming wars, William Byrd III. High-strung and overspoiled, one of the few of his generation unable to stand the tumult of the coming decades, he would break beneath the strain of his conflicting loyalties. In 1777, perplexed by the defection of his social allies (among them George Mason and George Washington), he would put a bullet through his mouth. The constant influence at Belvoir, however, was George William Fairfax, then twenty-one (or halfway between George and Lawrence), old enough to be a guide and model, young enough to be a friend. His portrait shows a nervy, if harassed, intelligence; like most of the people George was drawn to, he was subtle, witty, ironical, complex (as was his bride, the black-eyed Sally Cary, whom he brought to Belvoir in 1748). This assemblage acquired added *ton* in the fall of 1747 with the arrival of Thomas, sixth Lord Fairfax, fleeing the rigors of London society and the memories (so rumor had it) of a traumatic jilting in his youth. Shortly, even Belvoir proved too much for his wearied social impulse. In 1749 he retreated sixty miles beyond the Blue Ridge into the protection of the Shenandoah, where he built a house at Greenway Court and kept modest table for his visitors (he slept in the cabin); George, on his surveying trips, made Greenway Court a second home. Later he recalled its owner as a reticent and oddly muted figure, redolent of both fatigue and mystery, an elusive stranger from another world.

Eclat, however, was only part of what Belvoir had to offer. Among the staples of its library was *Cato* by Joseph Addison (a London crony of Lord Fairfax), a post facto defense of the Bloodless Revolution that became the staple of the parliamentary party in both Britain and the colonies and the staple of their revolution when it broke. At Belvoir it was read often, performed frequently, taken with great reverence by all. George's part in these performances was a minor miracle of casting; he played Juba, an adoptive son and pro-

44

tégé of Cato, who fell in love with Cato's daughter, against his judgment and certainly against his will. ("I should think our time more agreeable spent, believe me," George wrote Sally Cary Fairfax in 1755, "playing a part in Cato with the company you mention, and myself doubly happy in being the Juba to such a Marcia as you must make.")

What did George take out of *Cato*, besides the memory of Sally Fairfax's black eyes? Cato was an enemy of Julius Caesar, and his strictures against the rising empire cast the line of values by which the self-conscious classicists lived. George, always one to take instruction seriously, absorbed through this painless medium the idea that civility was to be prized above the state of nature:

> A Roman soul is bent on higher views:
> To civilize the rude, unpolish'd world,
> And lay it under the restraint of laws;
> To make man mild and sociable to man,
> To cultivate the wild, licencious savage
> With wisdom, discipline, and liberal arts,
> The embellishment of life. Virtues like these
> Make human nature shine, reform the soul,
> And break our fierce barbarians into men.

reason over instinct:

> Let not a torrent of impetuous zeal
> Transport thee beyond the bounds of reason:
> True fortitude is seen in great exploits
> That justice warrants, and that wisdom guides;
> All else is tow'ring frenzy and distraction.

justice over laxity of standards:

> . . . this base, degenerate age requires
> Severity, and justice in its rigour. . . .
> This awes an impious, bold offending world
> Commands obedience, and gives force to laws.
> When by just vengeance guilty mortals perish
> The Gods regard the punishment with pleasure
> And lay the uplifted thunderbolt aside.

public service over private comfort:

> . . . what pity is it
> That we can die but once to serve our country. . . .
> I should have blushed if Cato's house had stood
> Secure, and flourished in a civil war. . . .
> My life is not my own when Rome demands it.

the great ideal of perseverance under pressure:

> . . . valour soars above
> What the world calls misfortune and affliction . . .
> The Gods, in bounty, work up storms about us
> That give mankind occasion to exert
> Their hidden strength.

the enduring fear of arbitrary power:

> Bid him disband his legions,
> Restore the commonwealth to liberty,
> Submit his actions to the public censure,
> and stand the judgment of a Roman Senate,
> Bid him do this, and Cato is his friend.

and, over all, the conviction that life without self-determination is worse than no life at all:

> . . . let us draw her term of freedom out. . . .
> A day, an hour, of virtuous liberty
> Is worth a whole eternity in bondage.

Here, distilled, is the credo of the Whig ascendancy, which echoes through his lifetime like a chime: honor, discipline, impartial justice, order, and relentless self-control. An austere doctrine, lifting values over human virtues, with solace for the fortune-stricken but no mercy for the weak. Seductive doctrine for an adolescent, high-minded and unfanciful, conscious of emerging powers, seeking a channel in which they could be at once released and controlled. In their own right, these ideas would have made an impression; backed and sponsored by the men he loved and looked up to,

46

they took a luster that would never fade. Washington would follow them, with the single-minded zeal of a religious postulant, from the first days of his awkward cubhood to his apogee as nationmaker and as head of state. For also in *Cato*, less noticed, in the beginning, but more telling for the end: "My life is grafted on the fate of Rome."

Belvoir would be to George, as it had been to Lawrence, the true north of his existence, as well as the high road to contact and position, of which the talented and land-poor brothers stood in need. To George, it was all this and something more: the acceptable substitute for the Continental education that he had always longed for and that he had been so arbitrarily denied. The library and ballrooms of Belvoir were just the things to rub the rougher edges from an earnest and adept apprentice, especially if the apprentice was at such pains to cultivate his craft. It was Belvoir, along with his own application, that gave him the depth and culture that made him a passable figure, first on the business of the colony, later on the universal stage. After his bleak childhood it came as an added blessing, benefits unexpectedly given and gratefully received. As victor and general, with the scales of power reversed between them, Washington did not forget his long debt to the Fairfax family or to the half brother, then long dead, who had been the willing bridge between them and added a special grace and kindness of his own. Fairfax properties remained untouched throughout the Revolution (though George William had gone to England); Lord Fairfax, then ninety, remained undisturbed at Greenway Court. A story ran that among the British taken prisoner at Yorktown was a naval officer who had been at school with Lawrence at Whitehaven. The general ordered the prisoner released.

This world, however, remained partially realized and only half possessed. The sessions at Wakefield, Belvoir, and Mount Vernon were hard-won, uncertain interludes, broken by forced visits back to Mary and to Ferry Farm. For five years the shifts continued, the shuttling making the contrasts the more painfully defined. Which would be his future métier, the wide and splendid or the narrow and confined? With his inheritance, the latter seemed inevitable; he would

47

have to make some drastic break or die. George was on one of his visits "home" in September, 1746, when the Fairfaxes crossed the Rappahannock on their way into their western territories; Robert Jackson, a neighbor of the Washingtons, saw them passing through Fredericksburg with a party of "surveyors. . . . valet de Chambre, and a numerous train of cavalry and Infantry," all of them "in fine spirits" with "Colonel Fairfax in particular as cheerful as I ever saw him," his mood perhaps enlivened by a conspiratorial glow. On his way the cheerful colonel had dropped Jackson some word about a common project: a plot among himself, Lawrence, and other friends and patrons of the Washingtons to send their unprofitable ward to sea.

This scheme, no doubt devised by Lawrence the last summer and entered into with some éclat by George, had the triple ends of circumventing George's landless situation, providing the proper blend of patriotic service and adventure, and getting the boy, still a minor, safely beyond his mother's reach. It may also have reflected Lawrence's memories, no doubt enhanced in recollection, of his life's one great martial adventure, plus the high-strung instinct of the Washingtons to prefer risk to stalemate and the open, stormy channel to the dull. Colonel Fairfax, himself a younger son and poor relation, might have reflected that his own career had started in the Royal Navy when he was thirteen years old. The impediment, as always, was Mary Washington herself.

> I have not yet seen Mrs. Washington [Colonel Fairfax wrote Lawrence on 9 September]. George has been with us and says he will be steady and faithfully follow your advice as his best friend. I have spoken to Dr. Spenser, who I find is often at the Widow's and has some influence, to persuade her to think better of your advice. . . .

This "influence" was transitory, as Jackson informed Lawrence the next week: "I am afraid Mrs. Washington will not keep to her first resolution. . . . She offers several trifling objections such as fond and unthinking mothers naturally suggest, and I found that one word against his going has more weight than ten for it." If Mary was looking for supportive evidence, she found all she needed from the one source she would listen to, *her* half brother, Joseph Ball:

> I understand you are advised, and have some thought, of sending your son George to sea. I think he had better be put apprentice to a tinker; for they will press him from a ship where he has 50 shillings a month and make him take three and twenty; and cut him and staple him and use him like a Negro, or rather, like a dog.

Then the helpful uncle added:

> He must not be hasty to get rich, but must go on gently and with patience as things will naturally go. This method, without aiming at being a fine gentleman before his time, will carry a man more confortably and surely through the world.

This last, with its cold-water emphasis on patience, place knowing, and submission to circumstance, was the last thing any of the Washingtons or the Fairfaxes could have cared to hear. Striving, audacity, and the pressing of the moment were the creed and code by which they lived. And they had another motive, one that Joseph might have been the last to realize or to acknowledge if he did: the necessity, now realized by all the Washington acquaintances, of removing George from the influence of Mary Ball.

From this debacle three things emerged: first, that Mary's eccentricities had increased to the point where she was regarded as a problem, not only by the friends of Lawrence, but by her own; second, that George had effectively cut all emotional ties with her and her establishment (if indeed he ever had them); third, that he had thrown his lot in with the Fairfaxes and his half brothers and was looking to them for protection and support. At the same time, they seem to have made a pact among them to protect the interests of this intense and painfully determined youngster and use the influence in their possession to open any doorways for his future. Thereafter, Ferry Farm became the place to get away from; his mother and the life she represented, a thing to rise above. Diverted by this temporary setback, his ambitions would go underground, but their innate force and fury would increase.

This was not his last battle with his mother, but it was the last one she would win. With his increasing age and independence, he would gain the right to make more of his own decisions, which would turn increasingly toward the greater stage. Soon, he would put that other life behind him, no more than the shadow of a threat. Then he would have the power to do what he had done always in the recess of his mind: listen, with a show of outward courtesy, and coldly and concisely shut her out.

George was back at Mount Vernon in the spring of 1747, back to the world of public times and private readings and the dazzling commerce of Belvoir. But how much was he really *of* it? He could not go on forever as the boarder in his brother's house. Into this dim picture stepped, again, the Fairfaxes; George was to be all his life astonishingly lucky in the fortuitous confluence of events. Lord Fairfax had decided to open his western territories for development; it was remembered that George had shone at school at calculations and had followed surveyors around Wakefield and Mount Vernon from the time that he was small. What better than to set their protégé, whose talents for one time seemed applicable, to the task they needed done? An exploratory force of seventeen, including guides, surveyors, George William Fairfax, and George himself, left Belvoir on 18 March for a four-week trip into the Blue Ridge passes, north along the Potomac into the western part of Maryland, and west again along the Chesapeake. George's account in his first extended literary effort had the self-conscious air of a boyish camping journey, in marked, ironic contrast with the dreadful marches of his later years. Characteristically, he revealed a penchant for industry, a keen appreciation of the land for both its beauty and market value; less for the settlers, whose standards of politesse and conversation did not approach the levels he was learning to appreciate at Belvoir.

We got our Supper [ran his entry of 27 March] and was lighted into a Room and I not being so good a woods-

50

man as the rest of my Company striped myself very orderly and went into ye bed as they called it when to my Surprise I found it to be nothing but a Little Straw-Matted
together without Sheets or anything else but only one
Thread Bear blanket with double its Weight of Lice Flease
&c. I was glad to get up (as soon as y. Light was carried
from us) I put on my Cloths and Lay as my Companions.
Had we not been very tired I am sure we should not have
slep'd much that night. I made a Promise not to Sleep so
from that time forward chusing rather to sleep in y. open
air.

The youthful acolyte at the shrine of aristocracy would never
find much enchantment in the ignorance or antics of the
poor. Congenial or not, however, he had found at last the
wedge to break his bind.

For the next four years he applied himself with all his
fierce attention to the one road that could lead him out of his
dependence into the foothills of his promised land. Backed
by the Fairfaxes, who sweetened the pot whenever George's
services were in question, he advanced steadily in both fees
and in proficiency; the swift appraisal of the tangible would
always be his mental forte. Much of his business was done for
the Ohio Company, a land development organization of Potomac planters and their London associates (among them
Robert Dinwiddie, future governor of Virginia), including
Fairfaxes, Carters, George Mason, and the brothers Washington. Lawrence became president in 1749, succeeding his
neighbor, Thomas Lee. Ironically, this profession he despised was to bring George the martial exploits that he
longed for; these forays of British colonists into the disputed,
vital Valley of the Ohio provoked a series of French counter-
thrusts that led to war in 1754. Fort Duquesne, of bitter
memory, was built on a spot first marked out by George
Washington; a storehouse of the Ohio Company was the first
post taken in the war.

Memorandum: "To Survey the Lands at the Mouth of Little Cacapehon and the Mouth of Fifteen Mile Creek for the
Gentlemen of the Ohio Company." . . .

To Thomas Fairfax: "My Lord: I went last Tues-
day . . . to see whether you had any further Commands or

directions to give concerning the Surveying of Cacapehon . . . a pity to Miss four or five Days of such weather as
we now have. . . ." Through it all his goal was coming closer; landed independence on an estate of his own earnings
that would place his claim to equity with his half brothers and
the Fairfaxes once for all beyond dispute. In 1748 he made
his initial land purchase, a 500-acre tract on Bullskin Creek
in Frederick County, bought with his first saved cache of his
surveying money, when he was slightly more than sixteen
years of age. Other purchases followed as the pistoles gathered, the reward for a grudged duty, the result of instincts
curbed and tastes denied; a cultivated farm of 450 acres
bought for 112 pounds in 1750, another tract of 550 acres
bought in 1752. That it *was* grudged business is seen in a letter to a friend from the back country in November, 1749,
"amongst a parcel of Barbarians and an uncooth set of People . . . in a place where no real Satis: [faction] be had":

> Since you recid my Letter in October Last I have not
> Sleep'd above three Nights or four in a bed but after walk-
> ing a good deal all the Day lay down before the fire upon a
> little Hay Straw Fodder or bairskin whichever is to be had
> with Man, Wife and Children like a Parcel of Dogs or
> Catts and happy's he that gets the birth nearest the fire.
> There's nothing would make it pass tolerably but a good
> Reward a Double-loon is my constant gain every day that
> the Weather will permit my going out. . . . I have not
> had my cloths of but lay and sleep in them like a Negro ex-
> cept the few Nights I have lay'n in Frederick Town.

It remained a time of calculation and constraint. The
tensions begun in early childhood did not entirely abate. The
affection of Lawrence and the Fairfax family had melted
some of the coldness he had brought with him from his
mother's house, but the vulnerable self-observation was a
habit too ingrained to leave. The few memoranda of his later
adolescence enforce this impression of control: he is seen
betting small sums at cards and billiards (and carefully recording both his gains and losses); drinking little (or carrying
it well); husbanding both his cash and his resources, circumstance inhibiting a native generosity or the expansive na-

ture of the Washingtons in conflict with the parsimony of Mary Ball. He was too insecure, in his own eyes and the cold ones of society, to lose a farthing or to relax his guard. He was still suspended too closely between the upper and the nether worlds of his mixed inheritance; his friends could give him opportunities, but he would have to expand upon them; he would have, at bottom, no more than his brain could win. This edge of present danger stood like a thin dividing line between himself and the Fairfax children and the other scions of the settled classes he was meeting, adding a strain of caution to his character and intensity and purpose to his goals. Excerpts from his later letters to his young relations, couched in the form of avuncular advice (but more likely recollection) throw light on his own tensions of this period, the eternal calculation of the rootless and the self-obsession of the insecure:

> One thing, however, I would strongly impress upon you . . . that when you have the leisure to go into company that it should always be of the best kind that the place you are in will afford; by this means you will be constantly improving your manners and cultivating your mind. . . .
> While a courteous behaviour is due to all, select the most deserving only for your friendships and before they become intimate, weigh their dispositions and characters *well*. . . .
> Of the young and juvenile kind let me advise you to be choice. It is easy to make acquaintances, but very difficult to shake them off , however irksome and unprofitable they are found. . . .

And through it all, the major theme, doubtless learned in the Belvoir ballrooms: "The more there are above you, the greater your exertions should be to ascend."

Did George cultivate the Fairfaxes? Certainly, but well within the permissible limits as defined by his society, and always with intentions of making suitable returns. There is no doubt that a strong affection was the final basis of their relationship, and there is no evidence that he would have cultivated men whom he did not admire or that he ever tried to push them beyond their chosen pace. That he was fully aware of his own role within this social two-step is established in his letter to his brother John Augustine when the younger man was living in Mount Vernon in 1755:

> I shou'd be glad to hear you live in Harmony and good fellow-ship with the family at Belvoir, as it is in their power to be very serviceable upon many occassions to us, as young beginners. I wou'd advise your visiting often as one step towards it; the rest, if any more is necessary, your reason will sufficiently dictate.

This extraordinary document reveals a typically Washingtonian streak of social realism; it was never his character to skirt the temper of a situation or to trim it to a softer, more appealing truth. Implicit also is the recognition of a compact mutually arrived at and mutually invoked; if it was in the power of great families to be "very serviceable" to "young beginners" it was the obligation of the protégés to turn the investment into good accounting through both personal accomplishment and service rendered to the state. That Washington was acutely conscious of his part in the understanding will unfold in the next stage of his career. Later he would repay his debt still further, acting as patron to the deserving and impoverished of the next generation, his extended protection of Alexander Hamilton being the most conspicuous of many cases to the point. Meanwhile, this sense of duty would add its spark to his own fires, making his drive toward accomplishment more dear.

The ordeal by discipline was beginning to yield its returns. Step by step, from the memorizing of the "Rules of Conduct" through the long study at Belvoir, the learning of the codes and customs, the lonely weeks and months on the frontier, he was edging his way into the golden circle, the small and guarded clique of influential men. But even this moderate acceptance was to have its angled edge: the culture that he was so assiduously absorbing was digressing sharply from the rest of the American experience, ordered where it was divergent, measured where it was spontaneous, patrician (and patronizing) where it was popular and close. There was no room in the Council rooms at Williamsburg for the town meeting of New England; Washington would suffer all his life from his efforts to impose the coda of his early training, first on the settlers of the Ohio Valley, then on all the thirteen states. The principles outlined in *Cato,* he would discover to his discomfort, were not universally admired in the colonies; "to civilize the rude, unpolish'd world" was not the idée fixe of New England or of Pennsylvania, much less of the emerging west. For Washington, the creed of Belvoir, colored in his mind by his youthful awe and by the first affection he had ever suffered, would become forever both the one true form of government and the scale by which all men were to be judged. Time would soften, but not entirely erode, this concept; if men failed him and his standards, it would be their fault and not his own. A touchy commander, perennially out of patience with his troops . . . his followers . . . his citizens, he would have trouble controlling his distaste and his temper when they slipped, as they did so often, below the levels he had learned to love. That he did learn to curb this temper (sometimes), under what he no doubt considered the extremes of provocation, would be another hard-won act of will.

George was twenty on what was now, new style, his official birthday—22 February 1752—a self-made creature of his own invention, headed toward a career of moderate consequence as a planter and landowner in the West. Then, within a year, his course was deflected sharply upward by war and tragedy, the latter from the last source he could have wished for—his brother Lawrence's declining health.

In his service on the Spanish Main, Lawrence caught tuberculosis; five years later its inroads had become severe. By 1747 his cough had become a constant trouble, and letters from this period strike a note of apprehension and concern. A neighbor wrote to him in September, 1748, expressing hopes for his recovery, but his health slid backward in the damp Virginia winter and by spring he was thinking of a trip to Britain to consult physicians there. "I hope your Cough is much mended since I saw you last," George wrote from Ferry Farm on 2 May 1749, "if so, likewise hope you have given over the thought of leaving Virginia," adding that he would be happy ("if its not too much trouble") to see him at the close of "publick times." In July, however, he was writing Anne Fairfax Washington of the "happy news of my Brother's safe arrival *in health* in England, and am joy'd to hear that his stay is likely to be so short."

By September Lawrence was back in Virginia, little better than he had started, to begin a grueling two-year fight against disease. In July, 1750, he was off with George to the springs at Berkeley for the first of a series of disappointing "cures." The gloom of the occasion must have colored George's impressions of the country, for he was later to recall it as a bleak and dismal place, "situated very badly on the west side of a steep mountain and inclosed by hills on all sides so that the afternoon's sun is hid by 4 o'clock and fogs hang over us until 9 or 10." Lawrence was so bad by the fall of the next year that he and George were off to Barbados in November, but that stay proved unrewarding; George caught smallpox, and Lawrence received little good. Sick and miserable, the brothers languished, hating both the heat and the monotony and longing for the keener airs of home. "I own no place can please me without a change of seasons," Lawrence wrote Lord Fairfax. "Our bodies are too much relaxed, and require a winter to brace them up. . . . I am obliged to ride out by the first dawn . . . for by the time the sun is half an hour high it is as hot as at any time of the day."

George was sent home at the end of December, and Lawrence, too, decided to move on: "The Climate has not afforded the relief I expected from it so that I have almost decided to try the Bermudas on my return." This decision proved misguided, for "though I was much mended and had lost some of the worst symptoms of my disorder, yet the Air being very keen brought all on again." In April, he was writing home:

> I have now got to my last refuge, where I must now receive my final sentence, which at present Dr. Forbes will not pronounce. He leaves me, however, I think, like a. criminal condemned, though not without hopes of a reprieve. But this I am to obtain by meritoriously abstaining from flesh of any sort, all strong liquors, and by riding as

much as I can bear. . . . These are hard terms, but what he further adds is still worse, that let me receive what benefits I may from this climate the next winter in Virginia will most certainly destroy me. . . . As my endeavour to overcome this cruel disorder has already cost me much money and fatigue. I should unwillingly give over the pursuit whilst any just foundation for hope remains. Six weeks will determine me what to resolve on. Forbes advises the South of France.

Later that month he added: "The unhappy state of health, which I labor under, makes me uncertain as to my return. If I grow worse, I shall hurry home to my grave."

Lawrence died at Mount Vernon on 26 July 1752. "My dear Brother." . . . He was thirty-six years old. There is a tradition that he took the hand of his half brother and prophesied a glowing future, taking the still-uncertain youngster by surprise. At any rate he passed on to him much of the wherewithal with which to make this happen: George was to come eventually into his seat in the House of Burgesses, his post in the colonial militia, and, finally, his home. In the terms of Lawrence's will (as in those of their father's) George was to take possession of Mount Vernon if he outlived Lawrence or his heirs. Six months later Anne Fairfax Washington married George Lee of Staunton in Westmoreland County, and George leased the house, which was to be his home forever, for twenty pounds tobacco by the year. Two years later Lawrence's last surviving child died, and the estate was his by right.

Much of George's affection for Mount Vernon doubtless stemmed from memories and from this litany of loss. It was as if Lawrence had bequeathed him the unfinished portion of his life. With this bequest, his interests would swing sharply eastward, the fierce and wild Shenandoah relegated to a second place. This, too, would have its future import; Washington, the westerner, might have become a different man. The focus of his life would shift to the Tidewater, Anglophile and aristocratic, which would make him more entirely its own.

The other agency of advancement would have a more external source. After years of an uneasy respite the long quarrel of the French and British empires was about to stir again. From their strongholds in Canada and along the long spine of the Mississippi the French edged south and east into the heart of the Ohio Valley; they had penetrated halfway from Lake Erie to the western ridge of the Alleghenies by summer, 1753. Robert Dinwiddie, as new governor of Virginia and old stockholder in the Ohio Company, sensed the threat to both his interests and moved to guard them. On 16 June he sent a letter to the Board of Trade in London, warning of a possible invasion, asking for assistance and advice. Dispatches dated 28 August from the Earl of Holdernesse, secretary of state for the plantations, bearing the seal of George II, reached Virginia at the end of the next month:

> Whereas we have received information of a number of Europeans not our subjects, being assembled in a hostile manner, upon the River Ohio, intending by force of arms to erect certain forts within our territory on the said river, we do hereby strictly enjoin you to make diligent enquiry and if you shall find that any number of persons, . . . shall presume to erect any fort within the limits of our province of Virginia you are first to require of them peaceably to depart . . . and if not withstanding your admonition they still endeavor to carry on such unlawful and unjustifiable designs, we do strictly charge and command you to drive them out by force of arms.

Dinwiddie relayed these instructions at an emergency meeting of the Council at Williamsburg on 8 October 1753. He would draw up the message, he informed them, but he needed a bearer, familiar with the frontier country, strong enough to endure the journey, sufficiently well mannered to impress the French. William Fairfax said nothing, but his nomination already had been made. He posted back to Belvoir when the session ended; consultations undoubtedly were held. About noon on 26 October, George Washington, adjutant general of the militia of Virginia, rode up to the Capitol at Williamsburg with his offer to carry the king's message through the Ohio winter to the French.

58

IV

Force by Force

I have heard the bullets whistle, and believe me,
there is something charming in the sound.—
WASHINGTON to John Augustine, 29 May 1754

The new arm of empire had a brisk induction into the travail of public life: a grueling trek through the Ohio winter to Fort Le Boeuf within fifteen miles of Lake Erie; diplomatic duels with both the French and Iroquois; and a nightmare journey back through sleet-glazed forests in which he skipped death by narrow margins twice—once through the misplaced fire of a French-allied Ottowa Indian, once through a fall into the Ohio River, where he barely saved himself from being staved against the rocks. On the way the French had entertained him with genial accounts of their designs. "They told me," he wrote later of one wine-soaked supper, "that it was their absolute Design to take possession of the Ohio, and by G-- they would do it: For that altho' they were sensible the English could raise two men for their one; yet they knew their Motions were too slow and dilatory to prevent any undertaking of theirs." Nonetheless, he kept both his patience and his temper, opened his ears to the reports of traders and his eyes to the array of boats and cannon at Le Boeuf, and returned to Williamsburg on 15 January, husbanding three things—the stiff reply of the French commander to the summons from Dinwiddie, the certainty that the French planned a spring offensive, and his own desire to play a part above the common order in the coming war. Delicately, George began a subtle push for preference among the line of notables that circled around Belvoir. Could Richard Corbin, a councillor and Fairfax intimate, mention him for promotion at the appointment of the officers in March? He would be sincerely grateful, and would try to conduct himself "without censure" if awarded command. Here, in his own words, was his first expression of his controlling passions—the drive for distinction and the enduring fear of blame. They would rule him for the remainder of his life.

Major Washington was brevetted lieutenant colonel sometime before 20 March and dispatched to Alexandria to recruit, supply, and train 300 soldiers to reinforce a company of 100 who were already garrisoning an ancient storehouse of the Ohio Company at the forks of the Ohio and Monongahela rivers, a key point to the center of the continent, which commanded the flow of waters to the south. If his destination was clear, however, his instructions from the governor were tantalizingly obscure. He was to act on the defensive, Dinwiddie had written him, but "in case any Attempts are made to obstruct the Works or interupt our Settlem'ts . . . You are to restrain all such Offenders, and in case of Resistance . . . kill and destroy." What in this case was "defensive," and what was an "Attempt"? Dinwiddie's letter to Governor Hamilton of Pennsylvania hit a more martial tone: "My Orders to the Com'd'g Officer shall be to take Possess'n of all the Lands to the back of our frontier settlem'ts . . . and if any foreign Force appear to interupt them . . . he is in that case to repell Force by Force."

As disturbing as this studied vagueness was the fact that corresponding instructions, alike almost to the word in their ambiguity, were being given by the Marquis Duquesne, governor-general of Canada, to his agent on the Ohio, Contrecoeur.

The war George had looked to as the glory road began on a note of discord and disarray. Personal grievance was complicated by professional malaise. An unexpected cut in

60

pay from the £15 allowed a lieutenant colonel on the British roster to a major's pay of £12/6 hurt his pride and brought a nasty run-in with the governor and the first of many offers to resign. Enlistment and supply went slowly; his nerves and temper suffered badly as pressures to beat the French to the forks of the Ohio ran head-on into obstacles that conspired to keep him rooted to the spot. At last, undermanned and ill supplied, he left on 2 April with 150 men (half of the force specified) on a "march" that consisted mainly of hacking a pathway through the tangled underbrush wide enough to permit the hoped-for wagons and artillery to pass. (Colonel Joshua Fry, his direct—and only—superior, remained at Alexandria to collect the second column of the Virginia regiment and bring them up when equipped.) Axing trees and hauling stumps, he did not reach Wills Creek, a storehouse twenty miles distant, until 14 April, when he received another typical surprise: the packhorses he had ordered for fast, light marches up the valley were nowhere to be seen. Nothing remained but to wait for more supplies. He was still waiting on 20 April when an Iroquois runner arrived with the news he had been half expecting: three days previous the French had swept down from Lake Erie with 900 men, 300 canoes, and eight six-pound cannon, turned the British from the fort they had been building, razed the half-completed storehouse, and begun the erection on the point 200 yards upriver that George had recommended in his December report to Dinwiddie as a perfect place for a fortress of their own garrison, Duquesne.

George now moved sixty miles northwest to the Great Meadows to wait for reinforcements to allow him to attack. There new discontents drew him into a second quarrel that made relations between Dinwiddie and himself more strained. A further drop in pay, on top of the arduous and unmartial task of road clearing, wore tempers to the quick. The men sent Dinwiddie an irate protest, and George, instead of cooling them, jumped into the fray himself. Angry letters flew between George and the governor, the former insistent upon two counts: he was grievously insulted by the pay reduction; he would quit and serve as a volunteer. Dinwiddie tried to calm him down, in all the wrong ways—he misread his wounded pride as an appeal for money—ending one letter on a scolding note: "I have no complaint of this kind from Colo. Fry." To Fry himself, he sent an urgent letter, asking him to hurry to Great Meadows and to look into the affairs of the first column on the sly. ("There is some discontent crept into the detachment under Colonel Washington, and I think it is not well-founded," Dinwiddie wrote, asking him *"by all Prudent Methods"* to douse the fires George had fanned.) Washington had meanwhile damped matters himself, complaining that he had been forced to act the hypocrite, and warning that only duty held his soldiers in their posts. Not a graceful way to make obeisance. Meanwhile, events in the forest had turned his thoughts to more tangible concerns.

Isolated in the woods with his truncated regiment, George had begun to receive disturbing news. Reports reached him of French movements in the woods below Duquesne, penetrating in some cases to the plantation of Christopher Gist, a woodsman and longtime employee of the Ohio Company (who had gone with George on the Le Boeuf mission) only fifteen miles north of George's camp. Who were these French? Washington was sure he knew—spies sent out to reconnoiter his position and call a party down upon him from Duquesne. If so, his position would be desperate—the French could choose among 1,200 soldiers, while "I have not above 160 Effective Men." His Iroquois allies in the area had been feeding him disturbing warnings, and on 25 May he received a warning from their leader, the Half-King, warning him of a "freench armey" and a message oddly spelled but frighteningly concise: "I deesir you to be awar of them for deisin'd to strik ye forist English they see."

George fortified his stockade at Great Meadows (now aptly christened Fort Necessity) and dug in to await a siege. Four days later Gist himself arrived, with the news that fifty Frenchmen had descended on his plantation the day previous, "would have killed a cow and broken everything," and were presumed loitering in parts unknown. Some Iroquois runners were about the camp; at this point another aspect of the future leader came into light. Gist had told Washington the French had asked about the Half-King's whereabouts;

George leaked this information to the braves. *"I made them understand that* the French wanted to kill the Half-King," he wrote to Dinwiddie later. "Immediately, they offered to chase after the French with our men. One of these young Indians was sent out toward Mr. Gist." The italics were his own, and underscored his sense of their importance: the executive—the man who uses others—was already in the bud. At eight that evening the messenger returned: the Half King had discovered the tracks of the French ten miles north of the Great Meadows and traced them to a hollow in the woods.

Washington was on the edge of a decision of monumental scope. France and England were nominally at peace. He was ordered to act only on the defensive, yet to counter any threat by arms. He *assumed* the French meant to attack him. Was this enough to justify the prime point of British policy, and counter "force by force"? George was on edge from his fracas with the governor, thwarted in his quest for honor, underemployed and overtired, frustrated since mid-March. "That very moment," he wrote later, "I . . . ordered my ammunition to be put in a place of safety . . . left a guard to defend it, and with the rest of my men, set out in a heavy rain, and in a night as dark as pitch."

About dawn they reached the camp of the Half-King, who agreed to join them in an attack. Trailing the Indians singlefile through the underbrush, they found the French secluded in a gloomy hollow, rising and at breakfast, then (as George and the English were at pains to have it) reaching on the hurry for their guns. The English, on the rim around the hollow, raked the bowl with fire; one story had the commander, Coulon de Jumonville, caught by surprise still standing by his bedroll, bayoneted, and then scalped. Twenty minutes later all was over, the survivors, protesting loudly they had come about an embassy, lined up for a march to Williamsburg as prisoners of war. Behind, in a hollow sprayed with blood and brain matter, lay the bodies of ten French—the first dead of a war that was to howl through three continents and drop corpses from Bengal to Quebec.

George's mood was manic, almost dangerously high. "I have heard the bullets whistle," he wrote John Augustine in a quote that would raise roars through Europe, "and believe me, there is something charming in the sound." He talked now of a march through Duquesne into Canada: "If all are like these chosen soldiers, I have no doubt we shall chase them to the d----- Montreal." Ecstatic letters from his friends and relatives did nothing to deflate his mood. "I heartily congratulate you all ye brave gentlemen," wrote Colonel Charles Carter, who should have known better. "From this happy beginning I am led to hope you will soon make those cruel men know that numbers can't support an unrighteous cause." Bryan Fairfax and John Carlyle each told him of the "Great Rejoycings of Your Good Success," and Sally Carlyle (Brian's sister and John's wife) chimed in with a grace note of her own: "As God has blessed your first Attempt, hope he may Continue his blessing. . . . And on your return, who knows what fortune may have reserved you for sum unknown She, that may recompense you for all the Tryals past."

This euphoria was far from founded; he was now in greater danger than before. Contrecoeur had greeted the news of the attack with fury; Coulon de Villiers, brother of the slain commander, was already begging him for the privilege of leading the reprisal force. Dinwiddie had finally pried loose the promise of a detachment from Maryland and two independent companies from New York and one from South Carolina (British companies in the colonies unattached to any regiment), but their arrival was less a matter of certainty than hope. "I hope the good Spirits of Y'r Soldiers will not tempt you to make any hazardous Attempt against a too numerous Enemy," Dinwiddie cautioned Washington on 1 June. "When Colo. Fry's Corps and Capt. Mackay's Compa. join You, You will be enabled to act with better Vigour." To Mackay, making slow progress through Maryland, he was more candid: "As Colo. Washington is in a very dangerous Situation, I can't help beseaching · Y'r most expeditious Efforts to join him." The delay of Fry's troops in leaving Alexandria harassed him, too. "You cannot believe the uneasiness and Anxiety I have had for the Tardiness of the Detachment," he wrote George on 4 June, signing himself in an excess of anxiety "your real friend."

What remained of Washington's elation was doused rapidly in a succession of disasters in which frustrations mount-

64

ed and every blessing seemed to hide a hook. Supplies dwindled dangerously; he and John Carlyle (in charge of stores at Alexandria) began to suspect their contractor of fraud. Joshua Fry's detachment came up on 9 June, but without the colonel; he had died on 29 May of injuries suffered in a fall from his horse. The Iroquois arrived on 7 June, trailing forty squaws and children, who added nothing to the defense of Fort Necessity but demanded to be fed. Colonel James Mackay's company arrived on 10 June, bringing 100 soldiers and a touchy question of command—who was to take precedence, the colonel, who held his rank from a provincial governor, or the captain, who held his directly from George II? Mackay and Washington got on personally, but neither would give way. "For want of proper instructions from your Honor, I am much at a loss to know how to act," George wrote Dinwiddie on 12 June. "At present, I assure you, they will rather impede the service than forward it, for . . . they look upon themselves as a distinct body, and will not incorporate and do duty with our men." Unable (or unwilling) to resolve this, he took his own "poor fellows" off to break the road north to Red Stone Creek. "That the first Column of the Virginia Regiment has done more for the Interest of the Exedition," he wrote Dinwiddie in some petulance, "than any other Company or Corps that will hereafter arrive, will be obvious to all."

Action relieved his nerves but not his problems. Supplies and men remained distant: Carlyle and Fairfax, waiting at Alexandria to review the independent companies, fretted as weeks passed without a sign. When they did appear, they were disappointments: paltry and in miserable shape. Colonel James Innes of the Carolina Independents arrived at Winchester, but his troops, alas, did not. In these circumstances, George's plunge into the forest caused some uneasiness at home. "I wish you had suspended going to Red Stone Creek till you was joined by the other Forces," Dinwiddie wrote him on 25 June, "being much afraid of a Surprize." Fairfax, ever the bellwether, tried to gentle his impatience with avuncular advice: "It will yet require long time before They can join You—till then You can do little but Guard." From Belvoir, 10 July, he cautioned George again. "What a

Tedious Suspense to You that Languish for Strength enough to undertake some Notable Action against an Enemy that now Seems to Dare Your Meeting in the Field." And, he added gently, "You will remember, in the campaigns of the D. of Marlbro, many wise Retreats performed that were not called Flights."

By the time this note was written, its words of caution were already six days out of date.

Washington's contingent of 300 had hacked its way to Gist's plantation on 28 June, when an Iroquois sped into camp with the intelligence that a party of 1,200 French and Indians was on its way down from Duquesne. George called Mackay up from Great Meadows for a hurried conference; at a council of war the next morning it was resolved to fall back to the fort. Back by the road they had just broken, they walked the fifteen miles to Great Meadows, loading their baggage on their horses and dragging their artillery by hand, arriving exhausted on 1 July. All day, all night, and into the evening of 2 July they threw up stores and trenches; about eleven in the morning of 3 July the first signs of French fire broke through the woods.

After an attempt to storm the fort the French retreated and settled down into a constant fire from behind every hillock, tree, and bush. In the afternoon torrents drenched the stockade and the arms cache, turned the trenches into quagmires, and left the British squatting in their stations knee deep in misery and mud. After six hours of this sodden interchange a voice broke through the darkness, "Voulez-vous parlez?" astonishing the Virginians who expected, from their later comments, to be pressured to the death.

Coulon de Villiers at first claimed to be acting from charity but admitted later in his journal he was running short of ammunition and his Indians had threatened to desert. At length, Jacob Van Braam, a translator who had gone with George on the Le Boeuf mission, was dispatched to the French commander; he waded back two hours later with the terms "in a bad Hand, on wet and blotted Paper, so that no Person could read them but Van Braam." Squinting through the drizzle, listening to Van Braam's mangled English, they found the terms more tolerable than they had dreamed.

66

They were to withdraw from the Ohio, destroy their arms, confess to the attack of 27 May and to what they read as the "killing" of Coulon de Jumonville. Somehow, between the dark and the dampness, *assassinat,* the word used by the French, was overlooked.

Wet and wretched, the Virginians departed the next morning, Adam Stephen, Washington's subordinate, in an altercation with a Frenchman who had tried to steal his clothes. Seeing a man run off with his satchel, he had dashed after the offender, "kick'd the fellow back side" and returned. Stunned by such "pertness" in the ragged Stephen, the French denied he was an officer till the outraged major dragged out and donned his regimentals ("which in those cheap days cost thirty pistoles"), his fiery coat and lace trimmings contrasting oddly with his hands and face, black with powder, and his bare and filthy legs. Beguiled, the French fell into cheerful banter and begged to be made prisoners. "They were very desireous of going to Virginia," Stephen recounted, "as they understood there were great many Belles Mademmoiselle."

George took the proceedings with less ebullience, his humiliation compounded by resentment at having defeat pushed upon him by circumstances largely out of his control Grimly he went about his duties, his mien as downcast as his mood a month before was high. Later he traveled the 160 miles back to Williamsburg in total silence; Mackay, who went with him as far as Wills Creek, recalled that he uttered not a word.

He rode back into the middle of a storm. He had turned a war of nerves into a shooting one, lost the first real battle (and the last British post west of the Alleghenies), and confessed, as he discovered to his horror, to the "assassination" of Coulon de Jumonville. Varied versions of his share in all these matters poured in on him from all sides—from London; from his critics in the colonies; above all, from the French. Contrecoeur wrote Duquesne an infuriated letter, accusing the British of the murder of a party of ambassadors, heaping scorn on the journal Washington had written to vindicate himself, and closing with a blast at George himself:

You will see that he is the most impertinent of men . . . as clever as he is crafty. . . . Besides, he lies a great deal in order to justify the assasination of Sieur Jumonville, which had recoiled on him and which he was stupid enough to admit. . . . There is nothing more unworthy, lower, or even blacker than the opinions and the way of thinking of this Washington! It would have been a pleasure to read his outrageous journal to him right under his nose.

In London, Horace Walpole (diarist, gossip, and son of the late prime minister) took note of the encounter in a witty letter to a friend:

The French have tied up the hands of an excellent fanfaron, a Major Washington, whom they took and engaged not to serve for a year. In his letter, he said, "Believe me, as the cannon-balls flew over my head, they made a most delightful sound", adding in his journal: . . . On hearing this letter, the King said sensibly, "He would not say so, if he had been used to hear many."

Dinwiddie wrote a plaintive letter to the Earl of Albemarle, British ambassador to France, explaining among other things that the "embassy" had been a military party and that George had been deceived. "Washington not knowing Fr. was deceived by the Interpreter. If he had not, he declares y't he w'd not have agreed to it, tho' then in great Straits. The Interpreter was a Poltroon, and tho' an Officer with us, they say he has joined with the French." Albemarle in Paris was only partially appeased and wrote an angry letter to the prime minister at home—"Washington and many such may have courage and resolution, but they have no knowledge or experience in our profession; consequently there can be no dependence on them"—and said British regulars must be sent to America before the French could be repulsed. This and more—including an attack on George's character—was contained in a critique from William Johnson, the colonies' foremost expert on frontier fighting and Indian affairs:

I wish Washington had acted with the prudence and circumspection requisite in an officer of rank, and the trust at the same time reposed in him, but I can't help saying he was very wrong in many respects and I doubt his being too ambitious of acquiring all the honor or as much as he could before the rest joined him. . . . He should rather have avoided an engagement until all our troops were assembled, for march in such a close country and by detachments will never do.

Desperately, George tried to clear his name. The mission was not, as the French had claimed, an embassy, but a scouting party sent to draw a larger mission that would imprison or annihilate his troops:

They, finding where we were Incamp'd, instead of coming up in a Publick manner, sought out one of the most secret Retirements . . . moved back two miles, sent off two runners to acquaint Contrecoeur of our Strength. . . . Now 36 Men w'd almost have been a retinue for a princely Ambassador, instead of a Petit. Why did they, if their designs were so open, stay so long within 5 Miles of us?

Charges of panic in the aftermath of Fort Necessity, spread in an account by Coulon de Villiers, were "extraordinary . . . inconsistent . . . absolutely false." He had brought off his wounded and his colors (except "a large flag of immense size and weight") and later camped within three miles of the French. "Mr. Villiers pays himself no great compliment in saying, we were struck with a panic . . ." he concluded acidly. "We surely could not be afraid without cause, and if we had cause after capitulation, it was a reflection on himself." Above all, he denied that he had ever confessed to an "assassination," laying the fault on the rain, the darkness, the confusion, and Van Braam: "Whatever his motives were for doing so, certain it is, he called it the death, or the loss, of the Sieur Jumonville. . . . That we were willfully, or ignorantly, deceived by our Interpreter, I do aver, and will to my dying moment."

He wrote to friends and other officers in other parts of

the colonies to quench the rumors, the scope of his correspondence revealing the depth of his anxieties and the extent of his fears. Mackay reported from Baltimore the suppression of a mild clamor, and Adam Stephen broke into print on 29 August in the *Maryland Gazette*:

> Our conduct is blamed by a busy world, fond of finding Fault without considering Circumstances, or giving just Attention to Reasons which might be offered to obviate their Clamours. . . . Let any of these brave Gentlemen, who fight so many successful engagements over a Bottle, imagine himself at the head of 300 Men, and laboring under all the Disadvantages above-mentioned, and would not accept of worse terms?

That George was still uneasy surfaced in his next step—he took the extraordinary measure of writing to the governor of Maryland, Horatio Sharpe, who confirmed and then comforted his fears. Wild stories had swept the colony, Sharpe reported, but refutals by Mackay and others had been effective, and his sinking reputation had revived. Sharpe closed his letter on a kindly note, meant no doubt to soothe the younger man's anxieties, but more prophetic than either could have dreamed: "I have no doubt but that your future Behavior will convince the World of the Injustice done you by the Suspicions they have entertained."

Eventually, the storm blew over, in the public mind, if not George's own. Whatever his failings, they touched too closely to the grain of his society to allow for a general censure; whatever his problems with Dinwiddie, the governor was roped too closely to the Fairfax interest to alienate his chief supporters through a blow against their protégé. To George, the stain was not so easily erased—another goad to his excessive sensitivity; another thing to be made up for; another bad impression to excuse. His "honour" would be more than ever precious, his ambitions more embattled, his suspicions all the more acute.

This was not the ending of his troubles. He had barely straggled back to Winchester with the tattered remnants of his column than Dinwiddie ordered him back on the ready for another go against Duquesne. Ever the realist, George shot a letter to William Fairfax, outrage in every line— French advantages in men and money would make an expedition suicidal and inane: "We should be harassed and drove from place to place at their pleasure . . . and to what end . . . I cannot see." His troops had rioted at the whisper of a new campaign. Dinwiddie had ordered him to recruit new forces, yet had sent no money, and his own troops were nearly in rags. "I have orders to compleat my regiment, and not a 6d is sent for that purpose . . . scarcely a man has either shoes, stockings, or a hat." No money had been sent to pay the Indians, without whom an expedition would be doomed. "This, with the scarcity of provisions," he concluded acidly, "would induce them to ask, if they were to join us, if we meant to starve them as well as ourselves."

Stubbornly, he fought Dinwiddie through the remainder of the summer, resisting the governor's increasingly annoyed demands. "I sent You Orders to Recruit Y'r Regim't, with all possible Diligence," Dinwiddie wrote him on 3 August. "I repeat my orders now." George wrote to Innes, begging him to use his influence to beat some sense into the governor, meanwhile larding his own letters with sarcasm and a barely throttled rage. "What Men we can, we do enlist," he wrote, "but to Send Officers into different parts for that purpose would be unavailing, as they have neither money, nor can get any." Meanwhile, he poured cold water on the governor's plans to send the regiment to a settlement above Wills Creek: "I fear we cannot, were we to attempt it and at that place, for want of proper conveniences, we could not remain."

At this impasse the Assembly took him off the hook with a "clog" on the governor's war budget that caused Dinwiddie to prorogue them in a fury and drop his further war plans in disgust. "A governor," he wrote a colleague, "is really to be pitied in the discharge of his duty," and to another, "Such wrong-headed people, I, thank God, never had to do with before."

George had barely recovered from his relief at this development than he was shattered by a crushing blow—all colonial regiments were to be broken into ten companies of 100 each, to be commanded by officers not above the rank of captain. This was the brainchild of Sharpe and Dinwiddie, who feared that a replay of the spat between Mackay and Washington might paralyze the army in case of war. To George, this was half of a two-part disaster. He would be dropped below the rank he had held during the summer. Also, Fort Cumberland, the new outpost being constructed at Wills Creek, was on the territory of Maryland, which would tend to tip the scales of power from the Virginians to Mackay. Sometime before the end of October, George threw in his commission, this time for good. "I think the disparity between the present Offer of a Company, and my former Rank too great to expect any real satisfaction or enjoyment in a Corps, where I once did, or thought I had a right to command," he wrote to Governor Sharpe, who had tried to ply him with a soothing letter. "I should be reduced to a very low command, and subjected to that of many who have acted as my inferior officers . . . every Captain, bearing the King's commission, every half-officer . . . would rank before me." How could Sharpe insult him with the offer of an honorary colonel's post? "If you think me capable of holding a commission that has neither rank nor emolument affixed to it, you must entertain a very contemptible opinion of my weakness, and believe me to be more empty than the commission itself."

In mid-October came the thanks of the House of Burgesses for the valor of his detachment in the "late and unsuccessful Engagement with the French." In view of the intervening circumstances, it had an acid edge. It did not stop him from retiring to the Potomac, as threatened, with a cutting answer on the next campaign to Sharpe's aide: that the next year's endeavor would "meet with my acquiescence in everything except personal services" as far as the colonial establishment was concerned. In a memoir written in 1787, long after the scores might have been expected to have been settled, the memories were still alive. He attributed his abrupt retirement to:

> Some new arrangement of Rank by which no officer who did not *immediately* derive his commission from the *King*

could command one who did. This was too degrading for
G.W. to submit to; accordingly, he resigned his military
employment, determining to serve the next campaign as a
Volunteer.

How did George come out of his initiation, his tempering by fire, rumor, and intrigue? Some things augured well.
He was brave. He was cool in crisis. His judgment on tactical
matters was sound. Even the debatable rashness of his attack
on the French party vanished on afterthought—what choices
would have been left to his colony or empire if his column
had been captured or wiped out?

Other aspects were less promising. He was still frightful-
ly unsure of his own status, and his preoccupation with
advancement had bred a veritable obsession over rank. Self-
justification had become a passion; inhumanly fearless
against cannon fire, he could become terrified at the threat
of a cross word. One letter, in the middle of his second fight
with Dinwiddie, opens a revealing window on his mind.
Rather than accept a pay reduction (and therefore have his
value cheapened), he would work for no pay at all. "But let
me serve voluntarily; then I will, with the greatest pleasure in
life, devote my services. . . . I would rather prefer the great
toil of a daily laborer, and dig for a maintenance, . . . than
serve upon such ignoble terms." Here is a fixation verging on
the irrational, that could divert him from his duties and lead
to a confusion of perspectives in his mind. Before he told
Dinwiddie of the attack that would bring war upon three
continents, he devoted five full pages to his troubles with
Mackay.

George withdrew to the familiar axis of Belvoir and
Mount Vernon, nursing his grievances in the sympathetic
company of the Fairfaxes and John Augustine, pondering
means to recoup his losses and regain his hoped-for state.
From his viewpoint, the year had been disastrous; "honour"
had gone glimmering, and advancement had been taken
from him, retreating behind a series of trick doors. In his
hurt he had closed his mind to further work within the colonial establishment, but not yet upon the war. If opportunity
appeared in other guises, he would put himself within its

path. "It was to obey the calls of Honour, and the advice of my Friends, I declined it," he explained later of his lost commission, "and not to gratify any desire I had to leave the military line. My inclinations are strongly bent to arms."

V

Braddock

They began to Ingage us in a Half Moon and still Continued Surrounding us . . . if we saw of them five or six at one time it was great sight and they either on their Bellies . . . or Running from one tree to another almost by the ground.—BRITISH BATMAN, with Braddock's expedition, 9 July 1755

Sparks from George's shots had jumped the ocean to light strange fires: the home government was now convinced that war was inevitable for North America and that the colonies could not fight it on their own. On the day (4 September) that news of Fort Necessity reached London, the Cabinet went into extended and tumultuous session, centering first on the Duke of Newcastle, then prime minister, Lord Chancellor Hardwicke, Sir Thomas Robinson of the Southern Department (in charge of the colonies), and the Earl of Halifax of the Board of Trade, then, at last resort, upon their enemy but needed adjunct, the Duke of Cumberland, the king's second son and first favorite, head of all the armies of the empire, always brave, sometimes brutal, stubborn almost to a fault. Within three weeks Cumberland had dunned them all into adoption of his grand design: a plan to oust the French from all their water fortresses by a march up the Ohio to Duquesne, west to the Lake forts of Crown Point and Niagara, then north to Acadia in Canada by fall. William Shirley, governor of Massachusetts and self-designated military mastermind, with a body of provincials, was to hit Niagara on Lake Ontario; William Johnson, with another northern muster, was to attack Crown Point at the head of Lake Champlain. For the Ohio arm of this adventure, Cumberland tapped a career soldier, Major General Edward Braddock of the Coldstream Guards, with a reputation (like Cumberland's) for obstinacy and courage. Serving under Braddock would be two frayed arms of the British infantry, Halkett's 44th and Dunbar's 48th, disgraced at Prestonpans in 1745, now wintering at Cork in Ireland, whose past exploits and future prospects did not augur well. Demoralized and understaffed, they were down to fewer than 400 men apiece; when fleshed out on orders by drafts from other regiments, the donors, themselves short of manpower, happily gave up their worst. Both troops and general had experience entirely orthodox and European, unprepared for what Washington would later refer to as "difficulties to which they had never been accustomed in regular Service, in Campaign Country, and of which they seemed to have had very little idea." Halifax was the only one to show reservations at the prospect of a standard European baggage train, complete with howitzers and twelve-pound cannon, winding its way through 300 miles of uncut forest and sheer mountain drops: "as all the Convoys . . . must be brought . . . thro' a country full of Woods, it is sufficiently obvious how liable they would be to be interrupted." It was obvious, unfortunately, to Halifax alone. Cumberland, with the king behind him, was immovable; Newcastle lacked the brain, the stomach (and the influence) to make objection; Henry Fox, the secretary of war, was in Cumberland's pocket; Pitt, paymaster of the House of Commons, hated Newcastle, the king, *and* Cumberland, disliked their strategy and their appointments but was swept along on the tide of his two overwhelming passions: his concern for the safety of trade and of the colonies and the need to cut and humble France. Accordingly, there was no overt dissension when Fox rose at a packed joint session of Parliament on 14 November to announce the departure of the regiments and their commander to defend the possessions that fed the imperial wealth.

76

Halifax, however, was not the only one to brood. The wretched Irish regiments showed no enthusiasm, nor did the general himself. He had only harsh words for the colonials; secretly he was disheartened at the task. Strangely, for one of his mundane temperament, he indulged in a piece of melancholy prophecy his last night in London to the actress George Anne Bellamy, his ward:

> Before we parted [she recounted in her memoirs] the General told me that he should never see me more; for he was going with a handful of men to conquer whole nations, and that to do this they must cut their way through unknown woods. He produced a map of the country, saying at the same time: "Dear Pop, we are sent like sacrifices to the altar." . . . On going away, he put into my hands a piece of paper, which proved to be his will.

Nonetheless, Braddock and his military family (including his secretary, the eldest son of Governor William Shirley of Massachusetts, and his aide-de-camp, Robert Orme) docked at Hampton Bay, Virginia, on 20 February, to an ecstatic reception from Dinwiddie, a curious one from the population, and a politic letter from George Washington, congratulating them on their safe passage and offering his services to the campaign as volunteer. Despite the moral bruising his name had taken, he still held one asset that was to prove invaluable: he had gone on foot over the wild country that was *terra incognita* to the rest. Sensing the value of this offer, Braddock bent backwards in his efforts to appeal. If disputes over rank had caused past troubles, Orme delicately wrote Washington, a special appointment as private aide would solve all problems. If divorce from private business should prove distracting, he would be allowed the month of April to settle the affairs of Mount Vernon on John Augustine. It sounded promising, the balm to his sore spirits, the obverse of the bruising he had taken from the colonials the year before. The one objection came from Mary Washington, who arrived at Mount Vernon at the end of March to stage a brief and unsuccessful tantrum before returning, unappeased and unheeded, to Ferry Farm. Concern from a more stable source might have proved equally unwelcome.

Connected at last to the established army, in the good graces of a ranking general, in a venture of historic moment, he seemed poised at the beginning of his real career.

Having made his commitment, he was at pains to justify his choice. He had turned down provincial service to take an imperial appointment; would men see sordid motives in his move? Through March he issued streams of protestations to his friends: "I can very truly say I have no views either of profitting or rising in the Service, as I go a Volunteer, without rank or Pay."

The protests, reflecting both his enduring sensitivity and the lingering tenderness from the assassination rumors, were factually honest but morally untrue. He had not recovered from his ordeal by rumor; this campaign, blessed by the aegis of official London, must prove the means to quell the whispers and redeem his honor beyond murmur or reproach. Second was the matter of career. Braddock might have no commissions, but Braddock was not the army. If Duquesne fell (as was expected), service in the triumph might commend him to the establishment and push open now-closed doors. His pleas for experience took on new meaning, which he was the last one to deny. "To be plain, Sir," he confessed to Orme in one of his first letters, "I wish for nothing more earnestly than to attain a small degree of knowledge in the military field. . . . I am not a little biass'd by selfish and private views."

The experiment in cross-Atlantic cooperation was not off to a glowing start. The soldiers, docking limp and seasick after an appalling ten-week crossing, were nonplussed to find themselves in a wild country with vast stretches of untenanted landscape and villages of seven houses, one tavern, and a cow. Used to the flat landscape of Ireland, they found the mountains frightening and spent their spare time in the grog shops, getting drunk. The officers, on a higher level, expressed a disenchantment that not even the attentions of the doting gentry could allay: "I was invited to supper by a rich planter," wrote one disaffected officer, "and the heat of the climate, the dim light of the wax myrtle candles, and the number of black, half-naked servants that attended us made me think of the infernal regions, and that I was at supper with Pluto," and another added: "I reckon the day I bought my commission the most unhappy in my life." Like the enlisted men, they were awestruck by the mountains and by the dense and brooding presence of the woods. Penetration of this wilderness seemed daily less inviting, and their notes and journals took on an apprehensive tone. They had not yet seen the Allegheny hills.

Braddock himself, in temporary headquarters in John Carlyle's brick house in Alexandria, was having troubles of his own. Early in January he had dispatched Sir John St. Clair, quartermaster general for the expedition, to the colonies to commission supplies and transport, contract for a supply road from Philadelphia to the Ohio, and enlarge the camp at Wills Creek to a suitable fort and base camp for the march. Under St. Clair's relentless prodding, Fort Cumberland was rising at Wills Creek, but elsewhere little had been done. Maryland and Virginia were in endless hassles over preferment in the way of transportation, the Pennsylvania road remained unbroken, and the several assemblies refused to vote supplies.

At a meeting on 14 April at Alexandria, the provincial governors—Dinwiddie, Sharpe, Shirley, Morris of Pennsylvania, Glen and Dobbs of North and South Carolina—tried to introduce Braddock gently to the facts of life among the colonies: inter- and intranecine suspicions; trade and other rivalries; stubborn and faction-ridden assemblies that used their powers to wreak vengeance on their enemies as they held onto the powers of the purse. Morris in particular was in the middle of a squeeze between rebellious settlers and the Penn proprietors and was hampered further by a large infusion of Germans, cool to the idea of war with France to help the British empire, and Quakers, cool to the idea of war. In that case, Braddock queried gently, was there any prospect of a *common* fund? None, they told him; the colonies would stand no regimentation. The Albany Congress, held the year before to forge a wartime union, had foundered on the shoals of apathy and fear.

At the same time Braddock broke to them his staggering conceptions of a train: four eight-inch howitzers, four twelve-pound cannon (that he had inveigled from the battleship *Norwich,* now at anchor in Hampton Bay), twelve cohorns, thirteen caissons, numerous six-pounders, twenty gun carriages, and seventeen wagons to haul the ammunition. He had also procured from Admiral Augustus Keppel and the *Norwich* block and tackle to haul the brass guns over the mountains and thirty seamen to operate the gear. Keppel himself expressed strong doubts about the project: "I own I have my Fears that the heavy Guns must be left off this Side the Hill." If the governors had similar misgivings, they kept silent. Braddock was a British regular, backed up by the Duke of Cumberland, and the plans at any rate were too advanced to change.

Dinwiddie wrote Sir Thomas Robinson that the expense was monstrous but made no comment on its sense. Still, something odd was brewing that the more astute could sniff at but were unable or afraid to name. The purpose of joint efforts was to pool strengths of systems; this was pooling disabilities instead. British coordination, plus colonial knowledge of topography, might have formed a working combination, but this linked colonial chaos to British ignorance and compounded the chances of catastrophe threefold. Each part in the grand design was working from its weakness, and the result was to be a bitter crop.

Irritated at his inconclusive meeting with the governors, vexed at lack of wagons, and frustrated by his contacts with the colonials, Braddock left Alexandria for Frederick in Maryland on 18 April, shooting off an irate letter on the way:

> I have been greatly disappointed by the neglect and supineness of those assemblies of those provinces . . . they promised great matters and have done nothing. . . . When I get to Wills Creek I will send you . . . whatever information or intelligence I shall get there, it being impractical to get any here, the people of this part of the country laying it down for a maxim never to speak the truth upon any account.

At Frederick, there was new disenchantement: neither the food supplies nor wagons had arrived. Sharpe, who came

80

up the day after, pleaded problems with his assembly and suggested Braddock contract for supplies himself, occasioning delay and confusion and putting the army at the mercy of the local farmers, many of them Swiss or German with no martial spirit, who took advantage of the emergency to push their prices up. Braddock, anxious to reach Duquesne before reinforcements bolstered its slim winter garrison, was forever writing home to London to apologize for expense and delay. ("The Duke [Cumberland]," wrote Horace Walpole cheerfully, "is much dissatisfied at the slowness of General Braddock, who does not march as if he were at all impatient to be scalped.") Braddock raged, and St. Clair, on a mission to Fort Cumberland, had an unexpected run-in with James Croghan, the Pennsylvania commissary, that Croghan related to his governor with awe:

> He is extremely warm and angry at our province. . . . He would not look at our draughts . . . but stormed like a lion rampant. . . . He said our commission to lay out the road should have been issued in January last upon his first letter, that doing it now is doing of nothing, that the troops must march on the first of May, that the want of this road and the provisions promised by Pennsylvania has retarded the expedition, which may cost them their lives . . . that he would tomorrow write to England by a man of war, . . . represent Pennsylvania as a disaffected province; . . . and hang an arse (as he phrased it) on this occasion and told us to go to the General if we pleased, and he would give us ten bad words for every one that he had given.

Alarmed, Morris dispatched Benjamin Franklin to Frederick to smooth things over. He accomplished the joint miracles of calming Braddock, deflecting at least some of his wrath at the colonies, and persuading the reluctant farmers of the Pennsylvania countryside to "donate" (for recompense) their wagons to the expedition through a series of well-placed public notices that contained ingenious mixtures of the carrot and the club:

> If this method of obtaining the wagons and horses is not likely to succeed, I am obliged to send word to the

general in fourteen days; and I suppose St. Clair the hussar, with a body of soldiers, will immediately enter the province for that purpose, which I shall be sorry to hear, for I am sincerely and truly your friend.

Now in the rare good graces of the general, Franklin took the opportunity to size up Braddock, who confided to him his plans to go through Duquesne after three or four days' passage to the French forts on the Great Lakes. More acquainted than Braddock with conditions in the backcountry and the dangers from nature and the Indians, Franklin urged caution, but the general demurred:

> He smil'd at my ignorance, and reply'd, "These savages may, indeed, be a formidable enemy to your raw American militia, but upon the king's regular and disciplined troops, sir, it is impossible they should make any impression." I was conscious of an impropriety in my disputing with a military man in matters of his profession, and said no more.

George joined Braddock at the end of April, riding with him to Fort Cumberland along a land route whose location in Maryland had pained the Virginia contingent for some months.

Once at the fort he slipped easily into the suave airs of the official family, where he found the company agreeable and his new rank as private aide to Braddock very to his taste: "I am hereby freed from all commands but his," he wrote happily to John Augustine, "and give Orders to all, which must be implicitly obey'd." But not even this, or acceptance by the likes of Orme and Shirley, could cover his disquiet at the tensions, tardiness, and disarray. As the weeks dragged on, the wagon train blossomed in its unwieldy glory, and irritations grew among the staff. Jealousies flourished between the regulars and the colonials, between staff members and officers of the line. "I saw myself a slave," Orme confessed to Washington, "constantly engaged in keeping peace." Like Franklin, George was too shy in front of regulars to confess his mind completely, but he had increasing run-ins with the general, and his letters to his brothers and the Fairfaxes began to sound the old impatient note. "I see," he wrote on 15 May, "no prospect of moving from this place." Similar doubts infused the other officers as the problems of supply continued and the promises extracted by St. Clair in the winter melted in the suns of May. Flour ordered from Pennsylvania was never delivered; beef bought in Maryland turned out to be rotten, and a committee of the Virginia Assembly refused to confirm a contract to buy 500 head of beef. Vanishing edibles were not the only source of grief. Dutch settlers on the Blue Ridge Mountains had promised St. Clair in the winter to furnish wagons and horses to carry provisions from Fort Cumberland; when the time came for performance, the settlers changed their minds. On 20 May the artillery arrived, having been stranded two weeks at Alexandria through lack of transport, and made their way at last through the expedient of impressing horses from the farms around—a temporary palliative as most of the horses were recaptured by their owners or wandered off into the forests by themselves. Orme concluded that they lost their horses as fast as they collected them, and lost ground in their project every day.

As frustrations mounted, Braddock's temper, never genial, reached explosive heights:

> You will [he wrote Governor Morris] be informed of the situation I am in by the folly of Mr. Dinwiddie and the roguery of the Assembly, and unless the road of communications from your province is opened and some contracts made . . . I must inevitably be starved. . . . Sir John St. Clair (who by the way is ashamed of having talked of you in the manner he did) has employed, by the advise of Governor Sharpe . . . one Cresap, who behaved in such a manner in relation to the Pennsylvania flower that had he been a French commissary he could not have acted more to their interest. In short, in every instance but my contract for the Pennsylvania wagons, I have been deceived, and met with nothing but lies and villainy.

Washington was as enraged as Braddock at the repeated duplicities, but the general's lack of composure under pressure had begun to raise his doubts.

The General [he wrote to William Fairfax] by frequent breaches of Contracts, had lost all degree of patience, and for want of that consideration and moderation which shou'd be used by a Man of Sense . . . instead of blaming the individuals as he ought . . . charges all his Disappointments to a publick Supineness; and looks upon the Country . . . as void of both Honour and Honesty; we have frequent disputes on this head, which are maintained with warmth on both sides, especially on his, who is incapable of Argument with't; or giving up any point he asserts, let it be ever so incompatible with Reason.

Washington was not the only aide to show disquiet at Braddock's inability to control the chaos that was enveloping the camp. Young Shirley, less discreet or more distracted, sent off a heartsick letter to Governor Morris (whom he had befriended in Alexandria) that limned the disintegration in detail:

We have a general most judiciously chosen for being disqualified for the service he is employed in almost every respect. He may be brave, for aught I know, and he is honest in pecuniary matters, but as the King said of a neighboring governor of yours when proposed for the command a year ago . . . "A little more ability and a little less honesty upon the present occasion might serve our turn better." . . . I am greatly disgusted at seeing an expedition (as it is called) so ill-conceived originally in England, and so ill-appointed, so improperly conducted since in America—and so much fatigue and expense incurred for a purpose which if attended with success, might better have been left alone.

Supplies and troops at last collected, they pushed off into the forest at the end of May, an advance guard of 300 hacking a roadway through the trees and underbrush for the great brass cannon to pass through. A batman in the advance guard left a record of the march: "This day we marched about seven miles, and was 8 hours of marching it . . . the Rocks being so large that we were Obliged to Blast them several times . . . the great Quantity of Wagons delayed us, and the Roads being all to Cut." As the main body of the army followed, Orme took up the plaint. It once took them seven hours to move the wagons past an incline a quarter of a mile long, then six hours more to pass another steep ascent. Then came a chain of steep and rocky mountains, with barely enough land or water to pitch camp. Together, regulars and seamen from the *Norwich* hauled the caissons over the hills with ship's tackle, blocking their wheels at every station on the descent to prevent a wild downward plunge. While painfully time-consuming, this was not totally successful, time after time wagons slipped the blocks to career downward, lose their wheels or axles, or have their precious cargo smash against the rocks. "What was looked on at home as easy is our most difficult point to surmount," St. Clair wrote. "I mean, the passage of this vast track of Mountains . . . we are obliged to blow the Rocks and lay Bridges every Day."

The heat, the strain, and the frustration were wearing down the spirits of the company. George, edgy and already sickening with typhoid, was in a controlled rage about the wagons and the slow pace of the march. "I ac'd you," he wrote John Augustine in a cryptic shorthand when he was almost too weak to write, "that unless the numb'r of Wag'ns were retrenched and the carr's Hs. [carrying horses] Incr'd, that we never sh'd be able to see Duquesne . . . they had often a rear of 3 or 4 Miles of waggons; and . . . the sold'rs guarding them were so dispersed that if we had been attack'd either in Front, Center or Rear the part so attack'd must have been cut off and totally dispersed."

To his delight, the train broke down in Little Meadows, and Braddock, in one of those sudden shows of humility that made it impossible for George to turn against him totally, came to the Virginian for advice. His counsel, which had doubtless been brewing since Fort Cumberland, was a compound of his temperament and experience: to move in light, forced marches before French troops could reinforce Duquesne. "I urg'd it in the warmest terms that I was Master of, to push on; even if we did it with a chos'n Detach't . . . leaving the baggage and other Convoys with the Remainder of the Army to follow by slow and regular Marches . . . while we were advanc'd in the Front."

Braddock accordingly split the army and marched off

with Burton, Halkett, Gage, and a party of 1,200, leaving Dunbar (with the baggage) furious and Washington "with the most infinite delight." British and colonial ideas of speed, however, were not precisely in accord. "This prospect was soon overturn'd," Washington reported, "and all my sanguine hopes brought very low when I found, that instead of pushing on with vigour . . . they were halting to level every Mold Hill, and to erect Bridges over every Brook; by which means we were 4 Days getting 12 Miles, where I was left by the Doct'r's Advice."

Violently ill, he remained by the roadside to wait for Dunbar's van, having first wrung from Braddock the solemn promise that he would be brought up to the main army before the assault on Duquesne took place. Two weeks' forced rest reduced the fevers, but contact with the slow motion of the baggage train brought on another round of his sarcastic gibing and a nerve strain almost as trying as disease. "I have been now 6 Days with Colo. Dunbar's Corps," he wrote John Augustine on 28 June, implying it had been six days too many, "who are in a miserable Condition for want of Horses, not hav'g more than one half enough for their Wag'ns, so that the only method he has of proceedings, is to March on himself with as many Waggons as those will draw, and then Halt till the Remainder are brought up, which requires two Days more; and I believe shortly he will not be able to stir at all."

Dunbar might not stir, but George was determined. On 7 July, with the baggage train some fifteen miles south of Gist's Plantation, he had himself lifted to one of the forward baggage wagons and brought up to reach Braddock on the near shore of the Monongahela twelve miles south of Duquesne. *He* had lost the first race for the Ohio; *he* had lost Fort Necessity (whose remains he was now passing); *he* must be present at the moment of revenge. Reaching the camp at sunset on 8 July, he found the aides and Braddock jubilant. "We hugged ourselves with joy at our good luck in having surmounted our greatest difficulty," wrote one soldier, "and too hastily concluded the enemy would never dare oppose." In full battle dress they advanced the next morning. George was to recall them later as they crossed the river, scarlet

86

against the blue and green, sun striking flares of fire from the spires of their bayonets.

Strapped onto a cushioned saddle ("much reduc'd and very weak"), he had crossed the Monongahela with Orme and Braddock when they heard the first sounds of conflict from the front. Then sharp bursts of rapid firing, more confusion; then St. Clair pounded down the road to the advance guard, blood pouring from a wound in his right shoulder, shouted something about ambush and collapsed. They flew ahead into a hell of smoke and fury—Gage's advance had run into a detachment of Indians from Fort Duquesne. As Gage fired into the center, the Indians dispersed into the trees around them and began a scathing fire from three sides. In confusion, Gage's men fell back upon St. Clair's detachment, which piled into Burton's wagons in the rear. Within minutes, a line of 1,200 soldiers, blinded by smoke and terrified by the incessant fire, had been impacted into a roadway twelve feet across at its widest and no more than a quarter of a mile long. "Such was the confusion," recounted one survivor, "that ye men were sometimes 20 or 30 feet deep . . . all this time the Enemy kept up a continual fire, & every shott took place."

The officers plunged into the welter. Braddock roared at Burton to assault a hillock at the right, from which entrenched Indians were pouring fire. The men had reached it when three were wounded, and they fled. The Virginians broke for the trees to fight guerrilla-style; the regulars, mistaking them for French or deserters, fired point-blank at their backs. Dazed, the survivors staggered back into the center, while the officers, sobbing with fury and frustration, shouted unheard and unobeyed commands.

Braddock was everywhere, raging at the regulars and flailing at them with the flat end of his sword. George was beside him, weakness overcome by anger, shouting above the shots and screams of dying horses in an icy frenzy of disgust. Nothing helped. Trapped inside a closing noose of fire, packed so tightly that the dead remained wedged between the living, the troops broke after about three hours of relentless slaughter. In minutes the remains of Cumberland's grand army were in full flight down the road to the Monongahela, tossing rifles, shot, and clothing by the roadside, staining the river with their blood.

Washington would later rake the regulars for their part in this debacle, both before and after flight, blaming them for the appalling tolls among the officers and the members of the Virginia regiments, then for running like "the wild Bears of the Mountains" or, in another scathing metaphor, like "Sheep before the Hounds." He was supported on both points by accounts from the British. Robert Orme wrote: "The Officers were absolutely sacrificed" and an unnamed British officer confirmed that "The greatest part of the Men who were behind trees were either killed or wounded by our own people, even one or two Officers were killed by their own Plattoon." An aide to the wounded John St. Clair added to the condemnation: "Scandalous as the action was, more scandalous was the base and hurried Retreat. . . . We carried with the sweat of our Brows, a pretty Train of Artillery up to the french, which they never could have obtain'd otherwise."

The indictment of the regulars was true, but still conditional. By all accounts, it was the fact that they could not *see* the enemy that raised the deadly terror in the troops. A dispatch from a batman in Gage's detachment, which took the brunt of the first impact, conveys the sense of sightless terror: "They began to Ingage us in a half Moon and still Continued Surrounding us more and more . . . if we saw of them five or six at one time it was a great sight and they either on their Bellies . . . or Running from one tree to another almost by the ground. . . . "

Washington himself, with the tempering of maturity, absolved them at least partially in a short memoir written in 1785, laying the confusion to "the unusual Hallooing and whooping of the enemy, whom they could not see . . . seeing no enemy and themselves falling every moment from the fire, a general panic took place among the Troops." For George, it was an object lesson in the follies of excessive reliance upon "*regularity* and *discipline*" at the expense of adaptability, especially in "opposing compact bodies to the sparse manner of Indian fighting, in woods. From thence forward," he noted, "another mode obtain'd."

The battle of the Monongahela falls irremediably into that class of battles less won by the victors than tossed away by the opposing side. The French were as surprised as anyone when the small force they had sent out to harass the invaders ended by destroying them. Contrecoeur's note to a colleague had an uncharacteristic note of stunned humility, ending with the subdued reflection that "God put himself on our side." Braddock was prepared, European fashion, to march an army to assault a fortress, according to the rule books and his own experience, but Indians and *coureurs de bois* were not European soldiers, and the Alleghenies were not European terrain. Ironically, the disregard of orders by the regulars (which brought down universal wrath upon them) was nothing if not incidental. Targets as they were within that deadly circle, all sense suggests that if they had kept their heads enough to be deployed in regulation units, it would have brought them little more than the honor of being mowed down in proper order instead of in a melee.

The British had probably tossed it away in the beginning when they assigned a parade ground general to a terrain unlike parade grounds anywhere, with no effort made in any fashion to school him or his underlings in the conditions they might encounter on the way. As it was, the regulars were terrified from the beginning, and the ambush in the forest only wakened their already-present fears. The officers, who kept their heads, were betrayed not only by the regulars but by their own training, which prompted them to expose themselves to utmost danger in ways that ran against all mother sense. Vast changes were to be demanded and made in the British concept of effective warfare before England could fight for, and win, the wild continent that was about to drag the old world behind it into war.

Nothing was left to the shattered British officers but the organization of retreat. The carnage among them had been appalling, sixty-three dead or wounded out of eighty-six. Gage, Burton, and St. Clair were wounded; Orme was bleeding from a bullet in the thigh. Halkett was dead, as was his son, James, who had run to rescue him—their intertwined skeletons, one atop the other, were discovered by their elder son and brother when Duquesne fell to the English in 1758. At least two grim prophecies had fulfilled themselves: young Shirley, whose letters had breathed doom from the beginning, had been killed in the first minutes; Braddock, whose last night in London was haunted by visions of sacrifice, took a bullet in the shoulder that tore through his right lung.

The one exception to the role of slaughter had been George himself. Protected, as Orme teased him, by unearthly spirits, he had charged into the thick of fire, taking four bullets in his hat and jacket, emerging magically unscathed. With some difficulty, he had Braddock lifted to a covered wagon and conveyed under heavy fire to the other shore. Some reports insisted Braddock begged to be allowed to die upon the battlefield, one account had him seizing Croghan's pistols in an attempt to shoot himself. On the far bank the wounded made a temporary campsite, but George himself had twelve more hours before he could find rest. Braddock sent him to Gage to help him quell the panic, then to Dunbar, forty miles to the rear, to have supplies and doctors sent up to Gist's Plantation to succor the wounded on retreat.

Sundown was now passing into a sultry summer night. For a time, rage had masked George's weakness; now, compounded by fatigue and horror, it came flooding back, blowing nightmare to grotesque proportions, etching each strain on his nerves. Desperately weak, he clung to his saddle, wracked by the screams from the dying men who lined the roadside, as his aides, blind in the pitch blackness, groped for the pathway on their hands and knees. Exhausted, he reached Dunbar at midmorning, and collapsed, staying semiconscious through the day and night after, while the survivors straggled in by twos and threes, to die horribly of fatigue or infection, or watch their wounds turn gangrenous and maggot-ridden in the heat. Braddock was brought up in a litter 11 July (Orme, to his disgust—and Washington's— had to bribe the men to carry him) and, in great pain and intermittently conscious, gave his last commands: to break the great brass cannon left with Dunbar to prevent their capture by the French.

On 12 July the battered party began its slow procession south. Great Meadows, the scene of one dim memory for the

British and for Washington, received another grim memento. At eight that evening the tormented Braddock died. Stoic to the last, he had been silent through the day, murmuring only (as Orme told Franklin), "Who would have thought it?" and "We shall know better how to deal with them another time." It was left to George—on whom all things were devolving—to select the gravesite, conduct the ceremony, and, since the chaplain had been wounded, read the services himself. A shallow trench was dug in the middle of the high road, and Braddock's body, cradled in two blankets, was lowered into the pit.

Later George drove the army and the train of wagons back and forth across the gravesite until not a trace remained. There was a macabre reason for this ritual; he feared Indians might unearth and mutilate the corpse. Orme, ever the Coldstream regular, had only good words for his general; George's judgment, rendered in print only thirty years later, was perhaps more balanced and astute: "Thus died a man whose good and bad qualities were intimately blended . . . brave even to a fault." He might have meant that Braddock had courage without mutability or that all-important factor, "sense."

For some time, George had been subjecting his superiors—military and civilian—to intense scrutiny, mining their defects and assets for an equation of his own. Braddock, determined but impolitic, had supplied him with another puzzle to study. Thoughts of the blending of purpose with imagination, stubbornness with sensibility, and fixity of purpose with flexibility of means, as regards both states and armies, were to concern him for the remainder of his life.

Ill and exhausted, he brought the survivors to Fort Cumberland 16 July and went home to a dominion stunned with horror and just beginning to assimilate the impact of its loss. "From our first inexpressible affecting intelligence of the total defeat of our Forces," William Fairfax wrote him, "we have been in torturing suspense . . . now You are by a kind Providence preserved and returned to us, we can say the Catastrophy might have been worse." One thing remained if he cared to think about it: he was back in the good graces of the colony, the empire, the world. Orme could not say enough about his courage; Philip Ludwell talked him up to Dinwiddie; Charles Lewis wrote from Williamsburg to tell him of the "good Opinion the Governeur, Assembly, &c entertain of Yr. Conduct . . . scarce anything else is talked of here . . . I think it is unanimously agreed, you shall command our Forces in the next Scheme."

"Who is Mr. Washington?" asked Halifax some months later in a turn that laid waste forever last year's gibing. "I know nothing of him, but they say he behaved in Braddock's action as bravely as if he really loved the whistling of bullets."

For George, still sickened by his first full dose of slaughter, the mood was the now-familiar one of exertion having come to nothing and valor expended in defeat. Though his own conduct had been exemplary, he still felt tainted by his connection with the debacle; his score stood at the dismal record of two outings and two routs. "Shameful" was the most that he would say about it: "so scandalous that I really hate to have it mentioned . . . had I not been witness to the fact on that Fatal Day, I s'd scarce give credit to it now."

The experience he longed for had been a cram course in disaster; Braddock's death had cut his one tie to the establishment; he was no closer to preferment than he had been in the spring. Any new command that he could hope for would be provincial and colonial, under grim and all but hopeless circumstances, with both advancement and victory beyond all expectation and survival as his only hope.

Cumberland's master plan had failed almost all along the continent; Monckton had reduced Acadia, but Johnson and Shirley (thanks partially to plans found by the French at the Monongahela) had been halted before Crown Point and Niagara. There would be no hope of succor from the north. Dunbar, who had gone to pieces the day after the massacre, pulled his troops into winter quarters at Philadelphia ("where the inhabitants can protect him") on 2 August, leaving the frontiers of the middle colonies open to the rain of blood and fire that the triumphant French and disaffected Indians could inflict.

"Common sense would have prevailed not to leave the frontiers exposed after having opened a road over the mountains to the Ohio, by which the enemy can easily invade us," Dinwiddie wrote, ". . . to march off all the regulars, and leave the fort and frontiers to be defended by four hundred sick and wounded, and the poor remains of our provincial forces, appears to me to be absurd." In the last weeks of Braddock's march, when the fall of Duquesne seemed imminent, hostile Indians had begun to ravage the Virginia border settlements. Now the new commander could count himself fortunate if he could prevent the frontiers from being pushed into the sea. On whom this new command would settle was becoming clearer by the day. "The brave Colonel Washington," by default and by virtue of his rage of coldness, had become the first soldier of the Old Dominion and the first choice to defend its fragile safety in its low and bitter hour of the war. Full command—the thing that he had always wanted—was his almost for the taking, but scarcely terms to warm his heart.

Defending a frontier of nearly 400 miles with less than one whole regiment was not a recipe for fulfillment, much less for honor or prestige. His drive was now taking him in directions he did not really wish to follow, and ambition was taking on the aspect of a vise.

VI

The Reign of Blood and Fire

Nothing is to be seen or heard of but Desolation and Murder . . . . The Smoke of the Burning Plantations darken the day, and hide the neighbouring mountains from our sight.—ADAM STEPHEN to Washington, September, 1755

This time there was no begging for preferment but an anxious, half-willed effort to escape an obligation being pressed upon him that interest and ambition urged him to avoid. Compliance in this hopeless task, he wrote his colleagues, would sink his reputation and open him to censure and abuse. Cannily, his friends in the Assembly hit hard on his other key: the sense of obligation to the commonwealth that he had absorbed from his older brothers and from his adored patrons at Belvoir. Through August the debate continued—with the one note sent *against* his going cast perhaps as the deciding vote:

> Madam [he wrote to Mary Washington]: If it is in my power to avoid going to the Ohio again, I shall, but if the Command is pressed upon me by the genl. voice of the Country . . . it wou'd reflect eternal dishonour upon me to refuse it; and that, I am sure, must, or ought to, give you greater uneasiness than my going in an honourable Com'd.

94

"Honour," the old obsession of his childhood, was upon him again, but this time in its colder guise: the sense of duty at the expense of self and comfort that was the centerpiece of Roman virtue and the heart and standard of its creed. Could the protégé of Belvoir ignore his country's need? On 17 September he was reinstated as "Colonel of the Virginia Regiment, and Commander in Chief of all the Forces that now are, and shall be Raised." Titles aside, his third foray started on a downcast note. Something more than his customary self-deprecation ran through a parting note to a cousin : "Be not deceiv'd. I am unequal to the task."

His grim presentiments were too soon translated into facts. By early fall, Indian parties from Duquesne had begun to claw at the frontier settlements conjunct to the Ohio and west of the Blue Ridge. "Nothing is to be seen or heard of but Desolation and Murder," Adam Stephen wrote George from Fort Cumberland. ". . . The Smoke of the Burning Plantations darken the day, and hide the neighbouring mountains from our sight." While the Assembly wrestled with emergency measures for a draft of £40,000 in paper money to bring the regiment up to muster, George began a frantic swing through the 400-mile border, rallying militia, inspecting county units, and installing makeshift fortresses, hampered as always by disorganization, scant materials, and the low state of the provincial forces, decimated at the Monongahela and still piteously undermanned. ("No Officer shall list any Men under Sixteen, or above Fifty years of Age," ran his instructions to the county captains. "Nor . . . under five feet Four Inches high. . . . Neither are they to list any men who have old Sores upon their legs, or who are subject to Fits.") In all, he took his charge with admirable dexterity, revealing both the capacity to assimilate a wealth of.detail and an executive passion for control. Attached to his orders to the more than thirty local units was some variation of a common theme: "You are to send me an Account from time to time of your Proceedings. . . . You are to transmit me weekly Returns of your Company . . . and a Return the first Day of every Month."

None of his moves came soon enough. The second week

in October a raiding party fell upon the lower Shenandoah, killed or kidnapped seventy of the settlers, devastated their plantations, and sent the survivors flying down the roads to Winchester with a vale of smoke and ruin at their backs. Halfway on a circuit round to Alexandria, George rode back into a scene of panic: "Crowds of People, who were flying as if every moment was death," he reported, "firmly believing that Winchester was in flames." Cool as ever in the midst of chaos, he was into action like a whirlwind, sheltering the stricken, calling up the militia of outlying counties, sending scouting parties back into the field—undercut as ever by failures of organization and morale. Militia units failed to appear or do their duty, citizens foundered in their own confusion, and his own plans to chase the Indians up into the mountains were discarded in some fury when only twenty men appeared to back him up. Terror among the settlers was an endemic problem. He was twice called out by alarms from a frantic plantation owner, which he traced on investigation to "3 drunken Soldiers of the Light Horse, carousing, firing their Pistols, and uttering the most unheard-of imprecations" while "the party of Indians . . . proved to be a Mulatto and a Negro, seen hunting of Cattle by his Son." This run-in with panic left an indelible impression. The future general and politician would always appreciate the importance of confidence and/or illusion and would never underestimate morale.

Morale, unfortunately, had been the most of what he had to give. His presence of mind plus the onset of the winter season put a momentary check to the ravaging, but all his blend of fixity and fire could not counter the flaws within the scheme. Without a martial law to control the militia he could enforce no security, and as long as he was tied to a defensive policy, he could offer no more than a post facto binding of the wounds. Thoughts about the draft, lax discipline, and the follies of defensive warfare were to concern, occupy, and obsess him for the rest of the campaign.

Winter brought a welcome respite for garrisoning the border fortresses and pressing the Assembly for relief. Despite his plaintive and repeated protests, they turned down his appeals for stronger measures, appointed a committee of "volunteers" to oversee his conduct, and cut his request for a draft of 2,000 men to patrol the borders to a less-than-minimal 1,400. None of this was encouraging either to George or to his friends in the Assembly. His old fear of failure, stemming from a cause he could not alter, appeared more than ever real.

One ray of hope remained. If he could attach his regiment to the established army, he might bring it under British regulation, hold out the prospect of advancement to himself and his beleaguered officers, and bring some semblance of order to the whole. Opportunity came in the guise of a disruption. A captain at Fort Cumberland, his head turned by a king's commission, disputed Washington's authority, argued with his underlings, and made matters more chaotic than before. Infuriated, George obtained permission to travel to Boston to lay his grievance before Governor Shirley (temporary commander in chief of the colonial forces since the death of Braddock). Shirley, who had lost one son to the French at the Monongahela and another to camp fever at Albany, received him kindly, granted him authority over the disruptive captain, but on the larger matter backed into a corner and could not be moved. (Shirley's own position was ambiguous; now in trouble with both William Johnson and the ambitious Governor James De Lancey of New York, he would be superseded by midsummer to make way for another misplaced Cumberland appointment, Lord Loudoun.) George returned in March with only one part of his goal accomplished and a disturbing pattern as regards his future taking form inside his mind: Braddock dead and Shirley powerless—on the crucial matter of establishment, his connections had a way of fading into mist.

Spring began, as he expected, with another murderous assault—a wave of blood and fire that swept through the valleys west of Winchester, pushing the frontier miles eastward and leaving the plains a barren wasteland of the dead. The sufferings of the miserable survivors whipped him into helpless anger, and his letters back to Williamsburg hit a pitch of anguish that they never reached again. "Desolation and murder still increase and no prospect of relief," he wrote Dinwiddie after one blood-drenched week. "The Blue Ridge is now

97

our frontier, no man being left in this country, except a few that keep close with a number of women and children in forts. . . . If such a torrent as this has been . . . should press upon our settlements, there will not be a living creature left."

He ended with a bitter reference to the limitations that he labored under in his attempts to stem the tide of blood: "For a man to have inclination, and not power, he may as well be without either, for the assistance he can give." His ranging parties went into the valley daily, but their small numbers curtailed their effectiveness, and he had no powers to increase their force. By mid-May he had restored some order, but his mood remained uneasy—lacking troops, he could do little more than tend the wounded and ply the suffering with promises he knew could not be kept. The laggard support of the Assembly and the vague directions of the governor compounded his anxieties, and his correspondence with the capital took on a taut and edgy tone. His complaints upset the governor, and some in the assembly replied in kind. Fairfax wrote him in mid-April that some in the legislature found his bearing a shade too martial: "Appointment of an Aide-de-Camp is thought extraordinary . . . the Committee will not allow pay." John Robinson sent news of terrible reports about the conduct of his officers, followed four days later by word from Dinwiddie of the Burgesses being inflamed by tales of immorality and drunkenness (countenanced presumably by the commander), and discipline neglected at the front. George's reaction was galvanic—*discipline* neglected, when his every breath had been a plea for martial law? Fatigued and infuriated, he sent his friends a rash of angry letters: if abuse was his reward for effort, he would leave the service now. Appalled, Landon Carter sent him a stiff letter, urging him to grow another skin upon his feelings and warning that his defection at this juncture would be interpreted as fear by his enemies and bring immense troubles on his friends. "If I expostulate with you so warmly," he concluded, "it is only to save myself and your other friends from such difficulty that must attend our efforts to justify yr. Conduct. . . . Rather let Braddock's bed be your aim than any thing that might discolour those laurels that I promise myself are kept in store for you."

George succumbed, but with a difference: his note now was iron and not gold. Ambition, hope, and joy in battle had long since vanished, eaten down by disappointment and the endless tides of blood. He would stay, but under duress. Only duty and the fear of censure could keep him in his post. And talk of "laurels," kindly as Carter might have meant it, must have seemed a bitter joke.

Nothing that happened in the remainder of the summer improved his mood or his morale. Prodded by the French, detachments of Catawba and Iroquois slipped between the border fortresses, descending on the homesteads to scalp and murder, fading back into the forests to bring their grisly cargo to Duquesne. "Indians are only match for Indians, and without these, we shall ever fight upon unequal terms," he wrote to John Robinson. "Their cunning is only to be equalled by that of the Fox, and like them, they seize their prey by stealth. They will travel from pole to pole, depending upon *chance*, and their own dexterity for provision." Train them as he would in the Indian fashion of warfare, the drafts from the regiment were no match for the invaders, and the ranging parties he sent out after them could do little more than wade though the rubble, collect what remained of the livestock and fodder, attend to the wounded, and bury the dead. Maddened by his lack of powers, George pelted the Assembly with proposals that were inevitably and invariably turned down. Could the government compel the settlers to live in towns for the duration, providing shelter for children and women and freeing the men for scouting service with the troops? Sensible, but no member of the Assembly was willing to commit such vast infringements on freeholders' rights. Repeatedly, he begged to be allowed to go on the offense: "until an attempt is formed against Duquesne, so as to remove the fount of all our disturbance and trouble, we may never expect a peaceable day." But Virginia on its own could not raise an offensive, Loudoun turned down an embassy from Philip Ludwell for outside assistance, and the neighboring colonies remained, in Dinwiddie's phrase, "a Sleep." George appealed for new laws to draft and to control his army—enlistment terms as they stood covered just enough time to train the men before their terms were over, and the militia came and went at will. But the Assembly rejected his pleas in a classic clash of frontier and Roman values, and his pressures continued to awaken fears. On 3 September an anonymous writer in the *Virginia Centinel* unleashed a blast—a scathing picture of a corrupt and monstrous war effort, fueled by influence and bought commissions, in which a corps of debauched and venal officers executed numberless atrocities, sent their underlings into the line of battle, and tyrannized citizens and the enlisted men alike. Influence, debauchery, *and* cowardice? This time George truly threatened to resign. His friends again were desperate, and his brother Augustine, in a dash to Williamsburg, sent back (16 October) a letter that set him back to rights. Whatever his feelings, he could not quit now. It would devastate the colony—"It will in some measure be giving up your Country"—and it would do infinite damage to himself:

> Consider if you resign, what will be the consequences. All the officers . . . will follow your example, & the common soldiers will all desert. . . . Our Country then left defenseless to a barbarous & savage Enemy. . . . I am sensible you will be blamed by your Country more for that than every other action of yr. Life.

There was no answer to this last appeal. Everything that had gone to make him—concerns for the past and future, instincts of generosity and self-interest—converged to seal him in the grip of duty, in a service as impossible to drop as to fulfill. The worse it got, the more he was locked into it; he might leave in a quiet moment with both his conscience and his reputation; defection at this time would ravage both. The only hope, for his colony and his own escape, lay in establishing some measure of stability, which his sense informed him that the restrictions placed upon his service never would allow. Tied more than ever to the pursuit of the policies that

100

he detested, he added a new fury to his rage against the governor and Council, a new urgency to his appeals for change.

Worse was coming with Fort Cumberland. For months Washington had begged to be allowed to evacuate that structure, now miles beyond the line of settlers, whose upkeep drained the frontier of men and subsidies and which was now too far distant to be of any help. Dinwiddie vacillated in a way that maddened him, answering his persistent queries with all but indecipherable replies. At last, he capitulated, to George's immense relief. "You may call a Council of Officers," he wrote Washington on 30 September, "& consult whether to keep or to demolish it. . . . I desire you to be very explicit in your Arguments . . . as they must be laid before Lord Loudoun."

George was happily supervising the transfer of stores to Winchester when he received another note. Dinwiddie had gone instead to his Council and overrruled the decision made on the field. "I hereby order you to march 100 Men to Fort Cumberland from the Force you have at Winchester," he now wrote Washington. "You are to remain at Ft. Cumberland to make the Place as strong as you can, in Case of an Attack." What had caused this change became apparent in a letter that had been sent to him by Lord Loudoun and that he later enclosed to George. The lord could not agree with Colonel Washington. Washington was to replace the provisions he had removed to Winchester, and to garrison Fort Cumberland at once. ". . . if he leaves any of the stores behind, it will be at his own door. These proceedings, I am afraid, will have a bad effect as to the Dominion, and will not have a good appearance at home."

George exploded at this joint betrayal—of himself by Dinwiddie and of the country by Dinwiddie and Loudoun. What would this do to the defense of the southern settlements and to the people he had promised to protect? "To encourage them all my little help has been administered . . . but the late command reverses, confuses, and incommodes everything, to say nothing of the extraordinary expense." Another round of caustic letters went off to his friends in the assembly—he now distrusted Loudoun and Dinwiddie and

suspected collusion to benefit Maryland (on whose territory
Fort Cumberland was stationed) on the part of Dinwiddie
and Sharpe. Gritting his teeth as he set about the business of
refortifying what he now referred to as the "eye Sore," he
poured out his outrage into John Robinson's paternal ear:

> Whence it arises, or why, I am ignorant, but my
> strongest representations relative to the safety of the fron-
> tiers are regarded as idle and frivolous: my propositions
> and measures as partial and selfish; and all my sincerest
> endeavours for the service of my country perverted to the
> worst purposes. My orders are dark, doubtful, and uncer-
> tain; *today approved, tomorrow condemned.* Left to act and to
> proceed at hazard, accountable for the consequence, and
> blamed without the benefit of defense. If you think my sit-
> uation capable to excite the smallest degree of envy, or
> afford the least satisfaction, the truth is yet hidden from
> you, and you entertain notions very different from the re-
> ality of the case.

He and his party set their hopes upon Loudoun. In a
long, detailed, and painful letter he spelled out his woes—his
wish to go on the offensive; his frustrations in office; his troubles with the governor himself. It is a measure of his desperation that he should unburden himself to a man like Loudoun
(from whom he had received the letter on Fort Cumberland)
and still more so that he would attack Dinwiddie to another
servant of the crown:

> We are under no government at all . . . there is a
> jumble of laws that have little meaning or design. . . . -
> The orders I receive are full of ambiguity. I am left, like a
> wanderer in a wilderness, to proceed at hazard . . . an-
> swerable for my consequences, and blamed without the
> priviledge of defense. . . . It is not to be wondered
> at . . . I should be sicken'd in a Service which promises
> little of a Soldier's reward.

His efforts came to nothing; he received no answer from
Loudoun. Then he came to a last-ditch conclusion: he must
address the general himself. That he trusted no one (least of
all the governor) is evident in his insistence that *he* meet Lou-

doun in Philadelphia, though Dinwiddie himself was to travel there for a convention of the southern governors on 7 March. Some of this, with Dinwiddie's growing annoyance, is present in his reply to Washington's request for leave: "I cannot conceive what Service You can be of in going there, as the Plan concerted will in course be communicated to You. . . . However as You seem so in earnest to go I now give you leave."

Nothing came of this. Loudoun proved consistently elusive; George was kept waiting three weeks in the city for an audience that lasted twenty minutes. No one made a record of that stiff, truncated meeting, Loudoun from possible unconcern, Washington from probable disgust. Loudoun was thinking of more pressing matters, notably his foredoomed and harebrained design to attack the rock fortress of Louisburg by sea. Not only would he not give Virginia the troops to conduct an offensive, but he would draw troops away from the borders to advance his northern schemes. Doubtless Loudoun (on the evidence of Franklin and others) had sealed his plans beforehand, but Washington had also been the victim of his own emotions for neither the first nor last time in the campaign; if Loudoun had already marked him down as rash and insubordinate (as seems likely), then George had done himself and his party no favor when he allowed himself to rip into the governor in print. He had gone around Dinwiddie to John Robinson and others, but Loudoun was an outsider, prone to favor another crown servant in all contention and to regard criticism from a provincial colonel in a less than grateful light. For George himself, he was left to face another season of drift and indecision: there would be no help from "home" this year. The war that he had started in the Ohio Valley had gone north to the lakes and coasts of Canada, leaving Virginia to shift for itself. He could do no more than return to his neglected colony, depression now compounded by despair.

He was back in Winchester by early April, his mood sullen and downcast. "I have been posted . . . upon our cold and barren Frontiers [where] I am become in a manner an exile," he wrote one correspondent, and, to Dinwiddie, "I am tired of the place, the inhabitants, and the life I lead." Only one light note lit the landscape: Fort Cumberland, having reverted to Maryland in May, was no longer in his charge. The burgesses had passed new war funds and a bill to bring the regiment (never near its complement) to a strength of 1,275. But the draft law, framed to enlist vagrants and stragglers, reaped a crop of terrified indigents, and George, more a jailer than a commander, spent most of his energies arresting flight. Despite threats, whippings, and a few judicious hangings, the regiment was down to 600 by mid-July—at which point 200 were dispatched to South Carolina under orders of the helpful Lord Loudoun. At least partially because of the reduced number of inhabitants, Washington had kept the borders relatively quiet, but he and the few remaining settlers lived in constant fear of new incursions. The frustrations of defensive warfare were an incessant strain. Sense prevented him from pressing offensive plans on the Assembly when his resources were so limited, but he was tormented by the thought of what he could do, if only "they" would let him, and he could not stop himself from making schemes. A force of 3,000, he wrote one of Loudoun's aides, under efficient officers and backed by engineers and by artillery, could block the passes to the Ohio, cut communications between Duquesne and Canada, and take possession of the fort. No one replied. Troops, engineers and artillery, much less the lost and longed-for "regulation," were missing from the colonies that year.

Nor were they present in the empire at large. Now formally at war with France (as of February, 1756) Britain was embroiled on three continents by a complex host of foes. Dragged by Hanover—the ancestral domain of its royal family—into the cockpit of European conflict, it was embattled with Russia, France and Austria, as India, another scene of uneasy Anglo-French hegemony, took flame. Disaster followed disaster, Britain's ministry vying with its adversaries in sinking the country in disgrace. Cumberland, in Hanover with a band of German mercenaries, was forced to disband them on the orders of his government, to the rage of Prussia, Britain's only ally, and much against his will. Barely home, he was inundated with abuse from the king and ministry—"Here is my son, who has ruined me and disgraced himself" were his father's first words upon seeing him—for the measures they had ordered him to take. On 15 October Cumberland resigned as commander on the European front.

The prime minister was the Duke of Newcastle, immensely rich, with a fortune of £30,000 a year and an intricate skein of political connections, hysteric, ignorant and vastly jealous of his empire of patronage and of incursions into his terrain." A desperate attempt at coalition in late 1756 to harness Pitt's talents to his influence broke in weeks on the twin rocks of Pitt's ego and Newcastle's petulant devotion to intrigue. At year's end the country had been handed back to Newcastle again. "We are no longer a nation," wrote a despairing Lord Chesterfield, " . . . undone both at home and abroad."

It was at Minorca in the Mediterranean that the nation reached the nadir of demoralization and disgrace. The French besieged the island fortress, and a British fleet, under Admiral George Byng, was sent to drive them off. Through inexplicable confusion in instructions, the rescue failed, the island tumbled, and a key to the Mediterranean basin passed into the possession of the French. Byng was brought back to Britain under guard. Next came an outcry from London and eight counties for a thorough inquiry, the nature of which, however, was foreshadowed by Newcastle himself who blurted out, "Indeed he shall be tried immediately, and he shall be hanged." The admiral, said Walpole, was "marked for sacrifice by a set of ministers, who meant to divert on him the vengeance of a betrayed and enraged nation." Byng was shot.

Things were no better in America, where confusion crippled effort after effort and sent fortress after fortress tumbling to the dominion of the French. Shirley, undercut by backbiting among his supposed allies, was replaced in the summer of 1756, leaving a series of plans for attacks on Crown Point and Ticonderoga that Loudoun discarded unread. Inspired anew by the sight of yet another regular, the colonials hoped for leadership, but Loudoun was a chronic procrastinator, forever preparing to get ready to begin.

While he spent July and August in protracted squabbles with the New England officers over points of rank and plans to fortify Oswego, the French General Louis Joseph de Montcalm swept down on that undermanned fortress, took the fort and its vast stores of artillery, and sent tremors of invasion fever down the colonies from Albany as far south as New York.

The next year, if possible, outdid the first. Loudoun had made his mind up in midwinter to bypass both the lakes and the Ohio for an assault on Louisburg by sea. With unusual, if misplaced, energy he laid an embargo on colonial shipping that crippled the commerce of six provinces, preempted the coast defenses for an escort fleet, and, for purposes of security, detained all outbound ships for weeks. Benjamin Franklin, en route to Britain, where he was to stay for eighteen years, was detained six weeks in New York Harbor, then five weeks more trailing Loudoun up the seacoast before he was at last permitted to depart. "The other two paquets he still detained, carried them with him to Halifax, where he stayed some time to exercise the men in sham attacks upon sham forts," Franklin reported, "then alter'd his mind as to besieging Louisburg, and returned to New York with all his troops." In this interim the French and their Indian allies swopped down on Fort George on the border of New York and Canada, captured the garrison, and, after capitulation, put the defenders to the sword.

Loudoun had waited five weeks at Halifax, first *for* Admiral Francis Holbourne to arrive from England with eighteen ships of the line, then *with* him, to check rumors that a massive French armada, strong enough to forestall all challenge, had reached Louisburg some weeks before. On 4 August word arrived that the reports were true: the rock fortress, formidable to start with, was now guarded by a supplement of three naval squadrons and 20,000 men. Loudoun returned to New York and ignominy; Holbourne, in a wistful effort to divert some of the French convoys, sailed up the coast of Canada, where he was caught in a late-summer hurricane and all but blown to bits. Montcalm again had seized the moment, roaring down on Fort William Henry at the gates to Lake Champlain, chasing the English out of all their lake positions, and edging the colonies in an unamiable embrace. Panic once more seized the colonies, this time commingled with despair. Four years after they had begun their first harassments of the British traders on the subwaters of the Ohio, the French had extended their hold from Canada to the frontiers of the Carolinas, circling the seabound colonies in an ever-closing noose. The new world had not escaped the cyclone blowing through the British empire; their efforts to help themselves had miscarried with distressing frequency, and help from Britain had gone farcially awry. No one appeared to have learned anything from past disasters; in a campaign based on misconceptions, each motion brought them closer to the brink.

On the edge of the dissolving empire, the colonel of the Virginia regiment was working out the second year of his ordeal. He had now spent twenty months commanding men in crisis; what had it revealed of him? The seeds dropped at Belvoir had now come into full flower; his first address to his troops at Fort Cumberland was a roll call of the Roman virtues: duty; the subordination of interest to the common welfare; the concept of self-mastery as the coin paid for command. A neighbor, friend, and now a military subordinate, with a drinking problem, received a kind, but iron, warning: vices tolerable in the social framework were out of line in the public arena, where they could jeopardize the lives of others or the well-being of the state.

Troops found pillaging private houses received severe reprimands—"They are intended to relieve, and not add to, the distresses of the people"—and fifty lashes with a rawhide whip. There was a rebuke to a county captain for recruiting men through torture, a practice "unjustifiable" in a British army, as "they not only cast a slur upon your character, but reflect dishonour upon mine." There was also the case of the wife of one captain, who hung about the post, causing trouble. "If she is not immediately sent from the Camp," George warned the husband, "I shall take care to drive her out myself." Deserters reaped the most terrible punishment of all. "Any Soldier, who shall desert, though he return again, shall be hanged without Mercy," he declared, through an aide, and had built a forty-foot gallows to loom ominously above

107

the entrance to the post. Nor did it suffer from lack of use. A two-time deserter, who had tried to make off with his whole company, was hanged in front of his assembled regiment, including the entire corps of new recruits, as a "good warning" to them all. "Your Honor will, I hope, excuse my hanging, instead of shooting them," he wrote to Dinwiddie. "It conveyed much more terror to the others, and was for example made." The colonel, who was learning every day the value of appearance, could use fear as well as comfort for effect.

None of it seemed enough to put him on an even footing with chaos or to stem the tides of dissolution that threatened to undo his efforts as he made them and render all exertions nil. The basic cynicism he had learned at Belvoir was hardened at each exposure to men in groups as they behaved in settings military and political and took on an ever sharper edge. His developing ideas on the things needed to regulate society are reflected in an astounding portion of his letter to Lord Loudon, scolding those "prone to censure and condemn all proceedings that are not *strictly lawful,* not considering what causes may arise." Hence also this sentiment in a letter to the governor, detailing the maturing of his mind:

> I must assume the Freedom to express some surprise, that we alone, should be so tenacious of our Liberty, as not to invest a power, where Interest and Politicks so unanswerably demand it; and from whence so much good must consequently ensue. Do we not see that every Nation under the Sun find their acct, therein; and without it no Order, no regularity, can be observed? Why then should it be expected from us, (who are all young and inexperienced) to govern, and keep up a proper Spirit of Discipline with't Laws, when the best, and most Experienced, can scarcely do it with?

Here was a strain of iron, bound to bring him into difficulties with those holding notions of unbridled liberty and freedom from supervision and control. His growing contact with a wide range of humanity had left him with grave misgivings about what most people, left to their own devices, would use their liberty to do. Order and discipline were needed to check the trends to chaos and to self-destruction;

energies existed to be channeled, passions existed to be controlled. Despite his troubled relations with the governor, he was already looking to the state as the agent of morality, working to impose order on chaos and enforce the greater interest over selfish goals. For these ends, the state must, of course, have means—"If a man have inclination, without powers, he may as well lack either, for the good that he can do." This was assuming, as befitted the protégé of Belvoir, that the state would choose to perform good. What happened when the state itself became disordered was the problem of another day.

The fall of 1757 brought a new cascade of woes. Indians reappeared and killed ten settlers within twelve miles of Winchester; two weeks later a party of 100 took off twelve more. William Fairfax died in September, the last of his great father figures, an irreparable loss. A few weeks before he had received a letter from an aide in Williamsburg that set off another row. The aide had heard, thirdhand, that Richard Corbin had talked down George's pleas for aid the year previous, claiming that "there was not an Indian in the neighborhood" and that the appeal was part of a scheme of Washington's to garner glory for himself. "This piece of deceit," the aide continued, "has lessened the Governor's and some of the leading men's esteem for you, or at least they make use of it as the reason for the worse opinion (they say) they have had." Off went another irate letter to the governor, heavy with grievance and excuse. "Did I ever send any alarming account, without also sending the original papers (or their copies) which gave rise to it?" he asked pathetically, ending with the aggrieved cry, "I conceive it would be more generous to charge me with my faults, and let me stand or fall according to evidence, than to stigmatize me behind my back."

Dinwiddie's answer took off on a soothing note. He had never heard the Corbin story; George had never sent reports without foundation; George was urged not to credit "idle stories" for his own peace of mind. At the end, he could not prevent an explosion of his own ire: "My conduct to you from the beginning was always friendly, but you know I had good reason to suspect you of ingratitude, which I am convinced your own conscience and reflection must allow." George's reflection admitted nothing, and he told the governor that interested parties had maliciously misinterpreted his views.

In his agitation, he had evolved a double standard: his circumventions of the governor amounted to concern for the commonwealth, while criticisms of himself evoked the insidious working of cabals. Convinced anew of plots against him, he begged to be allowed to go to Williamsburg to settle some accounts with the governor and the Assembly in the only way he trusted, man to man. Dinwiddie's answer ended that remaining hope:

> I cannot agree to give you leave. You have been frequently indulged with leave of absence. You should not be absent when daily alarmed with the enemy's intentions to invade our frontiers, and I think you are in the wrong to ask it. You have no accounts that I know of to settle with me, and what accounts you have to settle with the country may be done at a more proper time.

This rebuff seemed to doom his last attempts to clear his name. With his other ills, the slap took on exaggerated meaning. It was a bad ending to a painful season, and Fairfax, who might have soothed his mind, was dead.

George had stopped the incursions at the mountains' edge; but the Shenandoah was now desolate, and he could see no hope for the future years. "While we pursue defensive measures, we pursue inevitable ruin," he insisted. "There will be no end to our troubles . . . and every year will increase our expense." To John Robinson, he confided his desperation for the colony, the settlers, and himself. "I do not know on whom these miserable, undone people are to rely on for redress. . . . If you conclude the Assembly have done what they are able, and the recourse must be had elsewhere I am determined . . . to apply to Colonel Stanwix. . . . Through these means, perhaps, we may be able to draw a little of Lord Loudoun's attention to the preservation of these colonies."

As he wrote, he must have sensed that it was hopeless; the Assembly was in no mood to listen to his urgings, and Loudoun had proved a broken reed. At any rate, affairs in the capital would be in temporary abeyance. Dinwiddie, health broken by fatigue and labor, had put in for retirement, having served a troubled, if dramatic, tenure and having brought both courage and confusion to his task. "We have not yet heard who is to succeed him," Robinson wrote George on 3 November. "God grant it may be somebody better acquainted with the unhappy business we have in hand, who . . . may dispell the heavy cloud at present hanging over this distressed and unhappy country. Till which happy event, I beg, dear friend, you will bear, so far as a man of honor might, the discontents and slights you have too often met with, and continue to serve your country, as I am thoroughly convinced you have always hitherto done."

Cold comfort, and taken coldly, too. There was an added reason for Washington's malaise. He was sickening, and had been for weeks, with the violent dysenteric ailment called the flux, the classic battlefield disease of dirty lodgings, stale food, bad water, and no rest. He fought it off as long as possible before reaching John Carlyle's house at Alexandria on 18 December in a state of near collapse. There he wrote a neighboring physician to "aske the favor of a visit, that I may have an opportunity of consulting you. . . . It is too painful for me to write, Mr. Carlyle will say the rest." Carlyle finished the letter, and it was an aide of his who wrote to Dinwiddie later in the week:

> For upwards of three Months past Colonel Washington had labour'd under a Bloody Flux, about a week ago his Disorder greatly increas'd attended with bad Fevers; the day before yesterday he was seized with Stiches & violent Pleuritick Pains. . . . This complication of Disorders greatly perplexed the Doctors as what is good for him in one respect hurts him in another; the Doctor has strongly recommended his immediately changing his air and going some place where he can be kept quiet. . . . The Colonel objected to following this Advice before he could procure Your Honour's Liberty but the Doctor gave him such reasons as convinced him it might then be too late.

For the second time he would be put out of action at a crucial moment, cashiered for reasons of his health, but this time in a bleaker season and for a longer stretch of time. It would take four months of rest and careful nursing before he would be allowed to see the wars again. In that time, changes would have swept across his universe; he would return to a new command, a new governor—and a new regime in the home government, this time made of grit and iron and girding to reverse the war. But in the December depths of his retirement both he and his cause seemed to flicker at the near edge of extinction, and health and victory seemed very far away.

VII

Breakdown

*Colonel Washington's behavior has been in no ways
like a soldier . . . consult Colonel Washington,
though perhaps not follow his advice.*—GENERAL
FORBES to Colonel Bouquet, 1758

Four years of battering from India to the Ohio had at last
had their effect at home. The king and Newcastle, backed to
the wall by the rain of terrors, had turned again to Pitt. This
time there was no room for temperament: in a series of negotiations as delicate as those between two foreign powers,
the princes of Parliament and Patria agreed upon a sharing
of the wealth; Newcastle in the Treasury to revel in "the
boundless power of appointing agents, commissaries, victual-
lers, and the whole train of leeches," Pitt at State to plow
through the War Office, overturning the establishment of
old boys, textbook generals, and ne'er-do-well first cousins
for the men, wild, tough and indefatigable, to flesh out and
enforce his schemes. Paying Frederick to maul the French in
Europe, he drew off the strength of England to save its dying
empire, reinforcing troops in India, sending a new group of
fledgling generals for another three-pronged effort in the
west. Wolfe and Amherst, jumped from the ranks to lieutenant and to major general, were to hit Louisburg as the pro-
logue to an invasion of Canada. General Robert Abercromby, dim and aging but backed up by the dazzling Lord Howe,

113

was to attack Ticonderoga and Crown Point. And Brigadier General John Forbes, onetime aide to despised and deposed Loudoun, was to lead a mixed force of 7,000 Highland guardsmen, Royal Americans (German émigrés inducted into the British army) and provincials from the middle colonies in another blow against Duquesne. Whether fiery like Wolfe or methodical like Forbes, all had two things in common: devotion to Pitt's ideal of total conquest and the ability to temper tactics to events. (This adaptability was to produce odd sights: guardsmen traipsing through the woods in short-cut buckskin, living off the contents of their knapsacks, cooking their own dinners of bear meat and rabbit, and doing their own laundry in the streams. "No women follow the camp to wash our linen," wrote one dazed member of the Ticonderoga expedition. "Lord Howe has already shown an example by going to the brook and washing his own.")

Pitt was out to reverse the tide of dissolution that had hobbled British efforts in the Americas, sending men to command who could learn the forest and checking what he could of colonial administrative confusion by gathering the reins into a single fist, his own. The dilatory provinces were relieved summarily of all functions, save the levying, clothing, and pay of their men. One more step was taken to ease the meshing of disparate gears: colonial officers were to be put on a straight line with British regulars, with authority over those under them in rank. Ecstatic at the prospect of salvation, the Assembly at Williamsburg voted a war chest of £26,000 to equip two regiments of 1,000 each, to be trained at Fort Cumberland and brought up to rendezvous with Forbes. William Byrd III, elevated to his father's rank of colonel, would lead the second regiment. Colonel Washington, of course, would have command.

Pitt's switch to action from "ignoble lethargy" had come in the nick of time to save the empire. It had come at least two years too late to save George's spirits and ambitions from a deep and ongoing decline.

Nothing in the spring of 1758 could rouse Washington from a lethargic depression of his own. Ill and irritable, he brooded at Mount Vernon, fighting off the last of his attack of dysentery, venting his spleen in notes like this response to a query from Colonel Stanwix about a certain Major Shaw who had approached him with a new idea for the capture of Duquesne: "Pray, does not his *plan* sufficiently indicate the man? Can there be a better index to his abilities than his scheme for reducing the enemy on the Ohio? and his expeditious march of a thousand men to Detroit? Surely, he intended to equip them with wings?" News of Pitt's plans brought at best a mixed response. George was part, at last, of an offensive, but reduced from supreme commander to officer of the line, no more or less than four other company commanders with layers of aides and adjutants between himself and the top. His letters of introduction to Forbes' aides reflected the muted tone: no pleas for preferment or experience, only a plaintive wish to "be distinguished from the *common run* of provincial officers . . . as I understand there will be a motley herd." Pride alone remained out of that first ambition; fatigue, frustration, and the exposure to unending misery had chilled the enchantment of the military life. Gone too was the old place seeking to be replaced in turn by a trace of damn-your-eyes perversity that would press his superiors to the limits of their patience, as if daring them to think and do their worst. There was only one thing left they all could give him—the chance to fulfill his wish to leave with honor, a wish that he had cherished since the fall of 1756. He would see it through and then be done with it. For one time, his protestations that he served from selfless notions rang sadly true.

He was already making motions to cover a retreat into civilian life. There had been a previous, abortive effort at an entry into politics, described by George in a letter to John Augustine from Braddock's camp about his prospects for a vacant seat in Fairfax County in 1755.

> Major Carlyle mention'd it to me in Williamsburg in a bantering way and asked how I shou'd like to go, saying at the same time he did not know but that they might send me when I knew nothing of the matter. . . . I shou'd be glad if you cou'd discover Major Carlyle's real sentim'ts . . . w'ch I hope and think you may with't disclosing much of mine. . . . If you do anything in this pray let me know by the first opportunity how you have succeeded in it; and how these Gentlemen stand affected. If they

seem inclinable to promote my Interest . . . you may then declare my Intentions and beg their assistance. If on the contrary you find them more inclin'd to favour some other, I w'd have the Affair entirely dropped. . . . Conduct the whole . . . with an air of indifference and unconcern.

Despite (or because of) the brothers' efforts at subtlety and intrigue, the affair fell through. The twenty-three-year-old one-term colonel lacked the experience and weight. By 1758, however, the moment and the man were ripe. Waging an absentee campaign from Fort Cumberland (absent on the splendid and impressive grounds of duty), paying a team of hired campaign managers, accepting the helpful intervention of Lord Fairfax (whose Greenway Court was in his district) and footing the bill for a staggering assortment of libations (40 gallons of rum punch, 34 of wine, 43 of beer and "strong beer," 6 gallons of the best Madeira, and a hogshead of Barbados rum), he swept the field to become burgess for Frederick County for the session starting January, 1759. His thanks to his managers contained the line "I hope no exception were taken to any that voted against me . . . and that all had enough"—a curious notation, considering his skill at mathematics and the fact that the freeholders voting in his election totaled no more than 355. For his part, the grateful victor vowed to repay the voters' confidence by "Making their Interest (as it really is) my own." What mattered was that he had laid a base for advancement in a life outside the army. Government, not warfare, would be his new point of focus, his obligation to the state. The campaign had slipped into its place as a stepping-stone between his past and future; the year—what remained of it—would be an entr'acte.

The entr'acte itself was off to a bad beginning. Not even the best of brains and purpose could make more than partial headway against colonial confusion, disorganization, and intrigue. "No sergeant or quarter master of a regiment is obliged to look into more details than I am," Forbes wrote Pitt from Philadelphia, "and if I did not look into everything myself, we should never get out of this town." Despite his resolution to work with the local talent, his allies came as

116

something of a shock. His opinion of the Indians was abysmal, and his opinion of the provincials—"an extream bad Collection of broken Innkeepers, Horse Jockeys & Indian traders"—even worse. Henri Bouquet, the adroit Swiss-born engineer he had picked out of the Royal Americans and made his second-in-command, sent back a train of ominous complaints from the field: reports of bad roads and broken contracts, illness, and a spirit of malaise. Forbes sympathized and sent a few words of advice: "I am sorry you have met with so many cross accidents to vex you, and have such a parcel of scoundrels as the provincials to work with, but the *vin est tiré,* and you must drop a little of the gentleman, and treat them as they deserve." Bouquet confessed that the expedition had encountered innumerable difficulties, and Forbes himself was writing Pitt of his misgivings that delay and factional jealousies could pitch his army into insurmountable distress.

George, drilling the Virginians at Fort Cumberland, was suffering "distresses" of his own. He had secret reasons for disquiet, but the overt troubles furnished cause enough. The campaign was taking too long to get moving. He was unhappy in his new role as subordinate. There were the usual problems with discipline and drafting. And there was the matter of the road.

Bouquet and Forbes, with their unending scrutiny into the source of Braddock's failure, were having second thoughts about his route. "I am told that Braddock's army went three days without finding grass for the horses, which made them unable to carry provisions, and he would have been likely to die of hunger if he had beaten the enemy," Bouquet reported back to Forbes. "I think as you do that you cannot accept Cumberland until you have it in your power to demonstrate the impossibility of finding another road." In mid-July, Bouquet dispatched a party through the Allegheny and Laurel mountains to explore the chance of blasting a direct route from the advanced post of Raystown west. They came, returned, and in two weeks Bouquet was able to report that they had found "a gap which no one here had the slightest knowledge. . . . It appears that with a great deal of work a road much more satisfactory than the other could be built."

117

This prospect of a free channel to the fat, untapped Ohio raised happy cries from Pennsylvania merchants and screams of rage from the Virginians, including, and especially, George, whose personal stake in the road and the Ohio went back to his dreadful trip of 1753 and, by association, to the plans of the Fairfaxes, Augustine, and his beloved Lawrence in 1746. "Colonel Washington," Bouquet wrote Forbes, "writes me that from all he heard . . . our route is impracticable even for pack horses . . . and that Braddock's road is absolutely the only one to take."

The storm blew into a hurricane as the Virginians, whipped on by Byrd and Washington, launched a campaign against the General and his harassed and harried aide.

> All the letters I have from Virginia [Bouquet wrote Forbes on 11 July] are filled with nothing but the impossibility of finding a passage across Lawrel Hill, and the ease of going by Braddock's road. This is a matter of politics between one province and another, in which we need have no part; and I have always avoided saying a word on the subject, as I am certain we shall find a passage, and that—in that case—we should for many reasons prefer this route.

Ten days later, as Bouquet indicated, neither side had budged:

> The Virginia party in regard to your route is continuing in full force, and though the secret motive animating them appears to me to smack of partiality, it seems to me, however, that this is a motive for acting with double caution . . . in order that we may answer their outcries convincingly in case of an accident, which they would not fail to attribute to the choice of a new route.

As Bouquet remained imperturbable, the Virginians hammered on three themes: Braddock's road had been already broken, its dangers were familiar to at least some of them, and the delays expected in the opening of a new route would bring them to the Ohio too late in the season to attack Duquesne. Bouquet kept his peace with admirable composure, even when the furor had become the gossip of the Raystown camp. "The Virginians are making great interest that our route may be by Fort Cumberland," wrote one James Young on 23 July, "but I hope they will not succeed." Forbes himself made a first attempt to stay above the battle. But he too flew into a fury when Byrd turned up at his doorstep with the information that sixty warriors would consent to accompany the expedition—if, of course, it went by Braddock's route. "A new system of military discipline," Forbes exploded to Bouquet, "and shows that my good friend Byrd is either made a cats-foot of himself, or he little knows me if he imagines that sixty scoundrels are to direct me in my measures."

If a cat's-foot, then to whom? George, in the grip of one of his obsessions, never quite knew where to draw the line. Bouquet and Forbes laid the fret to "partiality," and so it may have started, but the mania suggests a deeper root: strained nerves, the fixing of this point as the focus for years of frustration, the fear of yet another failure as the weeks of summer ticked away. There is something irrational in his insistence to Bouquet that the horrors of the Braddock road (itemized by Bouquet as the lack of forage, the length, the narrow passes, and the river crossings) were too trivial to be worth mentioning, and in the obsessive note of persecution and impending catastrophe that tied up his correspondence from now on:

> God knows what's intended [he wrote a friend on 29 July] for nothing seems ripe for Execution; backwardness, and I would (if I dared) say more, appears in all things. Tomorrow I am summoned to a Conference with Col. Bouquet on the Rays Town Road, when I shall warmly urge the Advanced Season and every other Argument that the Important Matter requires to hurry things forward and still endeavour to obtain leave (if possible) to advance on with the Virginians to the crossing ahead. . . .

Called before Bouquet for a last chance to refute the drawbacks of the route up from Fort Cumberland, he was less than convincing, as Bouquet later reported to Forbes:

I had an interview with Colonel Washington to find out how he imagines these difficulties can be overcome. I learned nothing satisfactory. Most of these gentlemen do not know the difference between a party and an army, and find everything easy which agrees with their ideas.

Still, he could not leave bad enough alone. On departing from Bouquet (who can be imagined to have had enough of him), he sent six pages of incessant argument, more insistent than ever, working up to an apocalyptic pitch. Next he wrote to Francis Halkett, Forbes' aide aide-de-camp, blaming Bouquet for everything and asking him to intervene with Forbes against Bouquet: "If Colo. Bouquet succeeds in this point with the General, all is lost! All is lost, by Heavens! Our Enterprize Ruin'd; and we stopped at the Laurel Hill this Winter, not to gather Laurels, by the by." To Francis Faquier, who succeeded Dinwiddie in June as governor, he sent a blow-by-blow account of the encounter, finishing, "I said, and did, everything to avoid a mischief that seem'd to forebode our Manifest Ruin, this is the light it appears to me." To a civilian acquaintance, he confided, "They have already work'd on the Road to be open'd from thence to Fort Duquesne, and flatter themselves with getting a better than Genl. Braddocks, they may do so, and I shall believe it when I am an eye witness to it." And to Bouquet himself, who laid down the law at last on 5 August, he was stiffly uncontrite: "The General's Orders . . . will, when once given, be a law to me . . . but till the order came out, I thought it incumbent upon me to say what I cou'd."

From this beginning his fortunes, temper, and repute careered steadily downhill. He was ordered to break a fake road from Fort Cumberland, to divert the French at Duquesne, not only rubbing in the pain of having his advice disregarded but relegating him, whose itch was always for the center of action, to make work, far from the main event. Forbes had come across the Halkett letter and was now in a rage. "By a very unguarded letter of Col. Washington that Accidentally fell into my hands, I am now at the bottom of their Scheme against this new road, a scheme that I think was a shame for any officer to be concerned in."

120

To Abercromby and others he described Washington's behavior as "insufferable," "ridiculous," and "in no ways like a soldier," and counseled Bouquet, on a matter of tactics, to "consult Colonel Washington, although perhaps not follow his advice." None of this had much effect on Washington, who was now referring to Bouquet and Forbes as "d-ps or something worse to P-s-v-n Artifice," and urging his friends at Williamsburg to intervene at home.

> If you are surpriz'd to find us still Incamp'd at this place [he wrote Faquier from Fort Cumberland on 2 September] I shall only remark that your surprize cannot well exceed my own. . . . The Pennsylvanians . . . had prejudiced the General absolutely against the Road, made him believe we were the partial people . . . to them as Instigators may be attributed the misfortunes of this miscarriage, for I think *now* nothing but a miracle can procure success.

This information, "of which any use may be made that you think proper," was followed by a letter to John Robinson that hit a more impassioned note:

> How is it to be accounted for? Can G-l F-s have Orders for this? Impossible: Will then our Injur'd Country pass by such abuses? I hope not. Rather, let a full representation of the Matter go to his Majesty. Let him know how grossly his Hon'r and the Public Money have been prostituted. I wish I was sent immediately home as an Aide to some other on this Errand, I think I cou'd set the Conduct of this Expedition in its true colours, having taken some pains, perhaps more than any other, to dive to the bottom of it.

And he could not stop himself from tormenting Bouquet when the endemic problems of supply and weather caught up with the Raystown Road: "In all human probability, we might have been in full possession of the Ohio, if Braddock's road had been followed. . . . But I ought to give you an apology, as all has been decided, and it is too late to go on about this head."

Bouquet's response was in keeping with his character. Reports from the advance guard found "every other thing answering our expectation" and the route itself in shape.

> I cannot therefore entertain the least doubt that we shall now all go on hand in hand and that the same zeal for the service that has hitherto been so distinguishing a part of your character will carry you by the Rays Town Road over the Allegheny Mountains and to Fort Duquesne.

Bouquet's brave reply had more face than fact about it. The campaign was beset through the fall and summer by all the common problems of forest fighting, plus some new ones of its own: Forbes' debilitating illness (which threw more burdens on Bouquet's shoulders) and the incessant and road-killing rains. Adam Stephen with the advance guard complained of the "numberless, damned petryfyd old logs as hard as iron" that tore the heads off of the axes, and John St. Clair agreed. "Send me as many men as you can with digging tools," he wrote back to headquarters, "this is a most diabolical work, and whiskey must be had."

Forbes reached Raystown in a litter in the middle of September, drained by his sickness and the unending trials of coping with his putative allies. "The Catawbas have left us like scoundrels," he wrote about the breakdown of his carefully nurtured Indian relations, "after bringing us in one scalp, which was recognized by the Cherokees as an old scalp, which they themselves gave them in the spring." To Bouquet, he complained of troubles with his staff: "Mr. Gordon the Engineer has either gone off at the nail, or is turned so dilatory in every measure . . . that it is almost impossible to get any one thing done to the purpose where he is concerned. If a triffle is to be done, he makes it a labour to man and horse, and if a work of consequence, makes alight of it." He had also had his difficulties with St. Clair: "The immense confusion of the Wagg'ns and roads are intirely Sir John's creating, who by a certain dexterity has you in fresh Dilemma's every day, and with his solemn face will tell you when he has done the worst, that he really acted for the best."

Bouquet crossed Laurel Hill to Loyal Hannon on 7 September, finding the advanced post in confusion and the guard in terror from guerrilla parties from Duquesne. Two soldiers who had run away were both arrested, "to put an end to such cowardly conduct at once." It was not a happy omen for the forerunners of a force that might—like Braddock's—come face to face against the French and Indians, at or near Duquesne.

Washington and Byrd, disgruntled and in a vicious temper, brought their troops to Raystown on 22 September and walked straight into a dressing down from Forbes, who related to Bouquet:

> I told them plainly, that, whatever they thought . . . we had proceeded from the best intelligence that could be got . . . and added that those two gentlemen were the only people I had met with who showed their weakness in their attachment to the province they belonged to, by declaring so publickly in favor of one road without their knowing anything of the other.

Even this failed to end the trouble; a Briton wrote on 3 October that George had been "sanguine and obstinate," and George himself had written back to Francis Faquier—after having followed the despised route to Loyal Hannon—that the choice of the Raystown route had doomed the expedition and that the road itself was incredibly bad. En route too, he heard a dreadful story that increased his doubts about the British regulars and sank his spirits to new lows. On 12 September a Major Grant of the Highlanders, with a detachment of 800, had marched to Duquesne from Loyal Hannon "to annoy the Enemy and gain Intelligence," a project that was accomplished the same night. The next day, however, the deranged major sent an engineer and a covering party up almost to the doors of the fortress, accompanied by an immense blare of reveille, that brought an answering round of musket fire and the French upon their necks in droves. Grant was saved only by a party of Virginians, who dashed up from the rear to cover his retreat, until themselves driven into the Ohio, where vast numbers drowned. The major was found by the river in stunned desolation. "My heart is broke," he told the Virginian who discovered him. "I shall never outlive this day." Forbes was horrified. "I cannot believe that such an attempt would have been made without my knowledge," he wrote Pitt on 29 September. "There are two wounded Highland officers just now arrived who give me so lame an account of the matter that one can draw nothing from them, only that my friend Grant most certainly lost his wits." Nearly 270 men were then still missing, lost in the forest, dead of exposure, or drowned. George himself was heartsick for a special reason: the Virginians, who had saved the party, sustained proportionally the greatest loss. "62 killd, this is a heavy stroke upon the Regiment, who had only 8 Officers, 166 Men there."

On 12 October, French and Indians surrounded a British outpost nine miles northwest of Loyal Hannon, penned the British up through the day and evening, and retired at last at nightfall, taking all the horses as they left. For reasons of morale, Forbes declared the French "retreat" a British "victory," but his real thoughts agreed more with Bouquet's: "A thousand men keep more than 1500 blockaded, carry off their horses, and retire undisturbed with all their wounded, and perhaps ours, after burying their dead. This enterprise, which should have cost the enemy dearly, shows a great deal of contempt for us, and the behaviour of our troops in the forest justifies the idea only too well." Nor could they move if they had wanted to: rains washed the roads out almost nightly, and Forbes, uncertain of the true strength of the French garrison, refused to risk the carts and cannon on the forty-mile trek to Fort Duquesne. Reaching Loyal Hannon on 2 November, he had begun a grim assessment of his state: the cold coming; the draftees ready to leave on 1 December; the rumors of 1,000 French at Fort Duquesne. Some rash souls may have encouraged action, but Bouquet and Forbes demurred. They had not come so far, so painfully, to risk all on a sudden plunge. On 11 November a convocation of the officers agreed that an attack would be delayed till spring.

All transpired as George had feared—the campaign stalled; the French still on the Ohio; himself pursuing Indian marauders through the woods. One of these forays led to an appalling incident: a group of Virginians, sent out to repel

124

the raiders, fired on their supporting party (led by Washington) and cut them to pieces. George, "between two fires, knocking up with his sword the presented pieces," found his life "in as much jeopardy as it had ever been before or since." His own luck held—again—but there were others not so fortunate. Fourteen were dead and twenty-six were wounded by the time they straggled back to camp. His response, predictably, was bitter: "After a Month's further Tryal, and the loss of many more Men by the Sword, Cold, and perhaps Famine, we shall give the Expedition over as impracticable this Season, and return to the Inhabitants, condemned by the World, and derided by our Friends." What an ending to his five-year war: sick, discouraged; in disfavor (for good reason) with his superiors; condemned to do the one thing that he most hated—wait. Under strain, the edge had gone off the carapace he had tried to build around him, reflecting both his difference from the marble image and the distance that he had to go. He was never stoic; it was all a mask; he was high-strung, impatient, vulnerable as to his reputation, endlessly tormented by his nerves. He was tenacious, and he was ice-cold under fire, but endurance on the long haul was something different; shows of patience through long sloughs of inaction were a fiercely executed fraud. How fiercely executed had been the lesson of the year. Through his command, responsibility had been a checkrein on him; with authority transferred and lifted, the backwash of the four years past emerged, taking their toll in brutal fashion, warping his judgment, sending his sense of proportion out of joint. Four years of frustration, shame, and broken promises—and now this venture, halted forty miles from Duquesne.

He had another reason for his torment, as hopeless as the rest. By the fall of 1758 he was, by all evidence and by his own admission, in love with his best friend's wife.

VIII

Sally Fairfax

I confess myself a Votary to Love. . . . .
—WASHINGTON to Sally Fairfax,
12 September 1758

Not all fires have an open flame. It was a secret, and it stayed one, until a letter unearthed in the effects of Mrs. George William Fairfax at the bottom of a trunk at the resort of Bath, in England, appeared to transfix a generation that had learned to treasure the notion of the stone-cold general in the year 1877.* Even at this late date, the exposure might have enraged the general, who treasured eccentric notions of his right to privacy and clung all his life to the belief that "the world has no business" to probe the recess of his inner life "when I wish it conceal'd." This affair touched other qualities, deeper even than his reticence, whose implications he had special reasons to conceal from prying eyes: disorder; ingratitude; a humiliating failure of control. Confusion, anxiety, and the torment of conflicting loyalties were doubtless also high upon his private listing of those things that "the world had no business" to know.

His torment grew from his source of happiness, Belvoir. George had been sixteen, a gauche and awkward sometime

*In the New York *Herald,* under the heading "A Washington Romance."

126

visitor when George William had brought home a dark, witty, and enchanting girl, two years George's senior, a generation beyond him by virtue of her status, ages older in erudition and élan. No written descriptions survive of Sarah Cary Fairfax, but her one portrait, a stilted, if charming, primitive, shows a dark changeling of the Anne Boleyn fashion, face fined down by a startling intelligence, too close to the bone for contemporary beauty, leaning more to challenge than repose. But George always took to "edge" in both men and women—and the family at Belvoir were his gods. How could the marginal half brother, almost mute before his social betters, fail to be drawn to this paragon, at home in library, salon and ballroom, who bantered with the governor and quoted Juvenal and Locke?

The new Mrs. Fairfax was drafted quickly into the cadre that was self-assigned to induct George into the mysteries of gentilesse—in her case, most likely in the social graces, in which he stood in greatest need. The instruction appears to have been extended and at least partially successful. In his first years at war, George was to write to "you . . . to whom I stand indebted for so many obligations." About women also he had much to learn. The records of his early years show him split between painful and foredoomed approaches to his social betters and the traditional riot of the backwoods and barracks, including (according to a letter from another celebrant) indulgence in "Charms even stranger to the Cyprian Dame" with an otherwise unmentioned "Mistress Nel." Socially, the early Washington appears in three fragmented and unconnected roles: as thwarted suitor, barracks rake, and—at Belvoir—the eternal little brother, tutored, groomed and cared for by the Fairfax coterie, including, and especially, Colonel Fairfax, George William, and his wife. It was in the very last of all these cases that his set of differentiated relationships had begun to overrun its stated lines. None of his other "tutors" was an enchanting woman to whom response to men was almost second nature. None of his other women had such wit or worldliness or the high sheen of social and intellectual eclat. The scattered pieces had begun to come together as his disparate drives and aspirations drew toward a common focus of their own.

By the start of 1755 there were indications that the sibling relationship was edging into something else. Leaving for Braddock's camp in late April, George had written Sally begging to "deserve a corrispondence" while away: "It will be needless to expiate on the pleasures that communication will afford me . . . and that none of my friends are able to convey more real delight." When May passed with no sign of the "corrispondence you had partly promis'd me," he wrote again:

> You express'd an Inclination to be inform'd of my safe arrival at Camp . . . but at the same time desir'd it might be communicated in a Letter to some body of your acquaintance. This I took as a gentle rebuke and polite manner of forbidding my corrisponding with you and conceive this opinion is not illy founded when I sifted it thus. . . . If on the contrary these are apprehensions only, how easy it is to remove my suspicion . . . and make me happier than the Day is long.

Do brothers write their older sisters thus? (Or do, for their part, sisters lead them on?) When a month had passed with no mail coming, George sent an urgent express back to Braddock's rear guard, asking after lost or missing packets, "for I have been greatly surprised at not receiving any Letter's from my Friends since I came out, and must impute it to miscarriage somewhere, for I am certain it cannot be owing to their not writing." And to his confidant, John Augustine, he wrote: "You may thank my F'ds for the L't'rs I have rec'd w'ch has not been one from any Mortal since I left Fairfax, except yourself. . . . It is a piece of regard and kindness which I sh'd end'r to acknowle was I able and suffer'd to write. . . . Make my Compliment's to all." His return from Braddock's debacle yielded a note from William Fairfax that Sally was about to walk from Belvoir to Mount Vernon, "desirous . . . with loving Speed to have an ocular demonstration of your being the same Identical Gentln. who lately departed to defend his country's Cause," and (the only words from her to George surviving) a postscript from Sally herself:

> After thanking Heaven for your safe return I must
> accuse you of unkindness in refusing us the pleasure of
> seeing [you] this night. I do assure you that nothing but
> our being satisfied that our Company would be disagree-
> able should prevent us from trying if our Legs would not
> carry us . . . but if you will not come to us to Morrow
> Morning very early we shall be at Mount Virnon.

Sally was doubtless as good as her word, but when George went back to Winchester in October all correspondence ceased. Did Mrs. Fairfax satisfy her interest through third parties, or did she prefer at this moment to withdraw? It was at this point that George made an effort to divert himself. On his way to Boston the next March he stopped at New York with John Robinson's son and paid brief court to Susanna "Polly" Philipse, sister of Mary Philpse Robinson and heiress to 5,102 acres of Hudson Valley land. Whether Polly or the acres were the main attraction, George stayed ten days, taking Polly to the plays, museums, and the most sensational exhibit of the city, the "Microcosm of the World." But Polly was unimpressed (or George was unenthusiastic); he lost out to Roger Morris ("you know him," wrote one of George's friends, "a Lady's man, always something to say,") who had the graces George was still so sadly lacking and the prestige of a British regular as opposed to that of a provincial field command. By the next spring Roger and Polly were a settled thing—though not quite so settled that George's informant did not advise a last-ditch assault. "I think I should have made a flying march of it," the friend wrote in early 1757, "if it had been only to see whether the works were sufficient to withstand a vigorous attack." George did not attack, his heart was not in it, and Polly and her acres slipped away. (Later George took revenge of a sort on the Morrises—their splendid house was one of his New York headquarters in 1776.) For the present, the attempt had been enough to keep him safely single through the two years of border war—undiverted by fiancée or family and unattached to anyone in the eyes of society, if not quite in his own.

Perhaps no move was possible until he had come to terms within himself. Just as he might have given up hope forever, Sally reappeared in the blameless role of helpful neighbor, offering to oversee his absentee and bachelor household in such matters as the mending of his shirts. "Sorry to give you the trouble," the soldier answered, "if Miss. Nancy will do me the favour to get thread and buttons suitable it will oblige me much. I have really forgot to procure them myself." This show of concern revived his confidence. Returning home in the fall of 1757, he threw himself upon her mercies for his nursing and the exotic diet that his doctors had prescribed: "I have no person that had been used to making these kinds of things and no directions, I find myself under a necessity of applying to your Acct. Book for a little while. . . . Please also lend me a bottle or two of Mountain or Canary Wine."

Doubtless, Sally was at Mount Vernon frequently, dispensing soup and sympathy; the absence of George William on business in England for the early part of the winter may have freed some of her time and her attention and left her at loose ends. No records remain of what transpired, but George's later letters imply that Mrs. Fairfax had infused her neighborly solicitude with a spark of something else, something of that blend of response, withdrawal, and those things that "you did one time partly promise." Sally was a flirt by nature and more than something of a tease. But would even she have drawn a man who was something more than family into a skein of insoluble emotions if the web had not enmeshed her, too?

If Sally herself now felt the fires, what had sparked the change? Some clue may be found, ironically, in "corrispondence"—not in that of George to Sally, but in that of George with all the Fairfax *men*. In 1754 and 1755 (the time of his unanswered letters) George is still very much the protégé and coddling, lifted to his place through Fairfax influence, held there largely through Fairfax counsel and advice. By 1756 (the time of Sally's silence) the advice is still forthcoming, but elsewhere there has been a subtle change. While still ministering to George's tender ego, William Fairfax is coming to him with *his* troubles, speaking to him man to man about his travail with Bryan, his unstable second child, enlisting his aid as confidant and equal in his attempts to instill "a little Taste of Fortification" in his son. He uses George's name in an effort to curtail Bryan's gambling—enlisting him as guardian in Bryan's brief military employment—confiding in him his fear, despair, and final anguish when Bryan vanished for two weeks in the spring of 1757 to be discovered under an assumed name in a jail in Annapolis and brought home by John Carlyle to reform. Fairfax wrote sadly, "I hope he will return compos'd with Mr. Carlyle . . . and submit to God's Disposal and the best manner we can assist." Earlier, when Bryan had dropped out of the army for a winter on the social circuits, Fairfax had written Washington plaintively of "a Life that does Honour to the Worthy and generally rewarded with one's Country's esteem." The message was unmistakable: George was harvesting the laurels that the Fairfax young were not. If this was not enough, George William, then occupied in the Assembly, had written George in 1756 after a particularly atrocious raid, "I beg that you'll freely command me, being willing and always desirous of serving under so experienced a Commander" as the "brave Colonel Washington," eight years his junior, who had been his little brother for most of their joint lives.

If George William sensed the shift between them, what about his wife?

Something had to be done. In early 1758 George had a chance meeting on his way to Williamsburg with a plump and creamy little widow, eight months his senior, with two children, two mansions, vast tracts of tempting river country, and a history of purpose and surprise. Ten years previous, Martha Dandridge, the daughter of a county clerk of no distinction, had astonished everyone by marrying the well-off Daniel Parke Custis from under the thumb of his erratic and evil-tempered father, who had terrorized his son and a succession of better-bred but less-resourceful would-be brides to the extent that the ranks of the wealthy eligible had been long since decimated, and Custis himself made a nerveracked and unwilling bachelor at the then unheard-of age of thirty-eight. Tentatively presented to the elder Custis, Martha triumphed through a combination of ingenuity and prudent speech. "He is more enamored of her character than you are of her person," an intermediary wrote the quaking

131

Custis, "hurry down immediately for fear he should change." Having pulled this coup, Martha then pulled off another, slipping from the social nadir to the heights of Williamsburg society with a steady head, good humor, and an earthy common sense. Doubtless, she now lost no time in turning these assets on the colonel, so much more appealing than the pliant Custis, so completely his own man. Four days later on his circuit back George stopped in at the Custis mansion and left with an understanding—he would marry the widow at the end of the campaign.

Was the engagement a beginning or an end? On his return to his base at Fort Cumberland, his private correspondence takes an unexpected turn. Scarcely a word to anyone about his nuptials or their object, but a spate of letters to carpenters and masons (and George William, who had offered his services as overseer) about the business of restoring Mount Vernon from its ramshackle condition to a dwelling for a family of four. ("You will perhaps think me a crazy fellow," he wrote to his distracted business agent, "ordering and counterordering goods almost in a breath.") Only two letters of that year reveal the private tone, one to Mrs. Custis on 20 July:

> We have begun our march for the Ohio. A courier is starting for Williamsburg, and I embrace the opportunity to send a few words to one whose life is now inseparable from mine. Since that happy hour when we made our pledges to each other, my thoughts have been continually going to you as to another Self. That an all-powerful Providence may keep us both in safety is the prayer of your ever faithful and affectionate Friend.

And one to Mrs. Fairfax on 12 September:

> Yesterday I was honour'd with your short, but very agreable favour of the first Instt.—how joyfully I catch at the happy occasion of renewing a correspondence which I feared was disrelished on your part—In silence I now express my Joy—Silence which in some cases—I wish the present—speaks more Intelligibly than the sweetest Eloquence. . . .

Sally had doubtless twitted him, on both his whirlwind courtship, and his anxiety to end the war. Did unbridled passion for the widow spur him on?

If you allow that any honour can be derived from my opposition to our present system of management, you destroy the merit of it entirely in me by attributing my anxiety to the animating prospect of possessing Mrs. Custis— When—I need not name it—guess yourself. . . . 'Tis true, I profess myself a Votary to Love. I acknowledge that a Lady is in the Case—and further I confess, that this Lady is known to you—Yes Madam, as well as she is to one who is too sensible of her Charms to deny the Power, whose Influence he feels, and must ever submit to. I feel the force of her amiable beauties in the recollection of a thousand tender passages that I could wish to obliterate till I am bid to revive them—but experience, alas! sadly reminds me how impossible that is. . . . You have drawn me, my dear Madam, or rather I have drawn myself into an honest confession of a Simple Fact—misconstrue not my meaning—'tis obvious—doubt it not, nor expose it— the World has no business to know the object of my Love—declared in this manner to—you. When I want to conceal it—One thing, above all the things in this World I wish to know, and only one person of your Acquaintance can solve me that, or guess my meaning—but adieu to this, till happier times, if I shall ever see them. . . . I dare believe you are as happy as you say—I wish I was happy also.

Sally sent back an oblique answer to the "one thing, above all things" he had asked to know. "Do we still misunderstand the true meaning of each other's letters?" George wrote in a letter following the one of which no misunderstanding was conceivable, "I think it must appear so, But I'll say no more, and leave you to guess the rest." At this remove the lessons of Belvoir still held them: impulses existed to be channeled; passions exist to be controlled. Sally had her reasons, and George most certainly had his: George William was not just another husband, he was the emotional legatee of Lawrence and of William Fairfax; to betray him would be the height of that unnatural and sordid vice, ingratitude; moreover, it would be unjust. As for the "animating prospect of

possessing Mrs. Custis," it was another step in the accomodation of desire to necessity, the recognition that some conditions did not yield to human will. "Love may and ought to be
under the guidance of reason," George later wrote to a
young relation, "for though we cannot avoid first impressions, we can assuredly place them under guard." Easier said
by the general in 1795 than by the colonel in 1758, and
another instance of the still awesome distance between his
unruly feelings and his ideals of control.

Curious too in this context is this assertion, tossed off
with breathtaking assurance in 1785, that "I have always considered marriage as the most interesting event of one's life,
the foundation of happiness or misery"—a strange reflection
for one who took his own marriage with supreme indifference and spent the year of his engagement rattling between
dementia and despair, as if his own ideas of happiness had
not been reduced to the expedient of putting up with Mrs.
Custis while keeping Mrs. Fairfax as a friend. For the rest,
reason would induce him to accept what he could not
change. And as for passions, those disturbing elements, they
would stay, as any draftees of his regiment, firmly "under
guard."

George Washington married Martha Custis on 6 January 1759, most likely at St. Peter's Church in New Kent
County, near the Custis home. Martha, in white quilted silk
and satin, arrived at the church in a coach drawn by six
horses, while the colonel, stiff in regimental regalia, rode his
best horse alongside. Some of the more reflective of the wed-
ding party might have sensed a note of repetition, of adherence to the patterns of the past. George was following the
paths of Lawrence and young Augustine in allying character
to settled property, and Martha, who had once done well for
herself in marrying her way out of a dim and landlocked future, was about (though nobody could sense the true dimensions) to do well for herself again. With her children, they
went to Williamsburg for the winter session of the assembly,
then back in March to Mount Vernon, where they resumed
the familial commerce with Belvoir that had existed in unbroken fashion since Lawrence had come under the Fairfax
wing in 1743. "I have just quit a Military Life," George wrote

to a cousin on 7 May, "and shortly shall be fixed at this place with an agreeable Partner, and . . . be able to conduct my own business with more punctuality than heretofore." Sally Fairfax saved his letter of 12 September, took it with her when she left Virginia sixteen years later, and kept it with her for the remainder of her life.

The marriage marked a turning point in Washington's development, heavy with the sound of closing doors. Along with parallel events in his career (he resigned his commission in December) it marked a turn from high to homely aspirations, from sky staring to a focus on the earth. Duquesne had fallen at last on 23 November, more with a whimper than a bang—the scouting party that had almost killed him had scooped up three prisoners who told a startled Forbes that the French had withdrawn the great part of their garrison, leaving fewer than 200 to defend the fort. Forbes at once moved forward with a light detachment of 2,500 men. George and his companions reached the forks in time to see Duquesne go up in smoke and fire as it was destroyed by the retreating French—an anticlimax typical of his war experience and, as he might have been forgiven for thinking, of the pattern of his life.

Other celebrants were more ecstatic. The *Pennsylvania Gazette* thanked God for the happenstance that "fixed us on the Banks of the Ohio . . . in the quiet and peaceable Possession of the finest and most fertile country of America lying in the happiest Climate in the Universe":

> It deprives our Enemies of the Benefits they expected from their deep laid schemes, and breaks asunder the Chain of Communications betwixt Canada and Louisiana, a Chain that threatened this Continent with Slavery. . . .
>
> The Twenty-sixth of this Month was observed, by the General's Orders, as a Day of Publick Thanksgiving to Almighty God . . . and To-day a great Detachment goes to Braddock's field of Battle, to bury the Bones of our slaughtered Countrymen . . . lying above Ground ever since.

The fall of Duquesne ended both his goal and obligation. He had no further part in the string of victories that swept the French from the Lakes and Canada, climaxing in a tableau of dreadful glory when Wolfe and Montcalm died within hours of each other on the Plains of Abraham on 13 September 1759. That year was England's "Year of Miracles," the bells of London never silent as Pitt's fury reaped its final harvest and Canada . . . Gibraltar . . . India dropped into the British net. George, his vision now turned inward, took no more than a passing note. It was of a time that he had put behind him, and it was not his practice to look back.

The army was done with; his inclinations were no longer bent to arms. A scanning of his correspondence from the war years 1754–57 shows the slow slide of ambition to its grave:

[1754]   I have heard the bullets whistle, and believe me, there is something charming in the sound. . . . If all are like these chosen soldiers, I have no doubt we shall chase them to d--- Montreal.

[1755]   I wish for nothing more earnestly than to attain a small degree of knowledge in the military field. . . .

[1756]   Desolation and murder still increase, and no prospects of relief. . . .

The number of little paultry forts along the frontier, render the forces very difficult and expensive to be supplied. . . .

[1757]   I exert every means in my power to protect a much distressed country, but it is a task too arduous. . . .

I do not know on whom these miserable, undone people are to rely on for redress. . .

Summed up at last in his cry to Loudoun: "It is not to be wondered at . . . I should be sicken'd in a service which promises little of a soldier's reward."

Add to this the Sally Fairfax trouble. He had twice let his emotions lead him and they had led him into dead ends, a hopeless passion, and a miserable command. What was to be salvaged from it? The general, in 1781, had some comments for the colonel to heed: "We ought not to look back, unless it is to derive useful lessons from past errors, and for the purpose of profitting by dear bought experience . . . and to steer clear of the shelves and rocks we have struck upon, is the part of wisdom."

His last five years had been a battering. Time to change his course.

What were his new objectives? Moderation and tranquility, a predictable existence that would skirt the shoals of passion and despair. What sadder than this note from the recent bridegroom, from Mount Vernon on 20 September: "I am now . . . fixd at this seat with an agreable Consort . . . and hope to find more happiness in retirement than I ever experienc'd amidst a wide and bustling World." Retirement, at twenty-seven, from the world and from himself, from the wars and the internal rages, from the dying soldiers and the homeless men, from peril and the "charming" play of bullets, from the capacity to suffer—and to kill. Children of destiny had need of this acquaintance. Planters in retirement did not.

Once before, he had come to a decision to direct his course, to fight his way out of his mother's house into the world beyond it, to grow, to prove himself, expand. Now he was changing once again, but to the opposite direction; to draw in, to reduce his line of vision, to bring his reach to a level somewhat lower than his grasp. Perhaps both shifts were part of the same instinct: to save and then protect himself. His new career would draw on very little. But that perhaps was all he cared to risk.

His other side—the part of pain and fire—would stay coiled for the season underground.

PART TWO:

Our
Lordly
Masters
1760-1775

IX

Our Lordly Masters

*That no man should scruple, or hesitate a moment,
to use a-ms . . . is clearly my opinion . . . yet
A-ms, I wou'd beg leave to add, should be the last
resource.*—WASHINGTON to George Mason,
1769

George was home, in the first that he had ever known, reveling, it seemed, in his new role as lord of land and manor, retired, as he was to tell Lafayette in a revealing note some twenty-four years later, "not only from the world, but within myself." In the chorus of comment that greeted this abrupt reversal, one voice at least rose to approve. "I have had much trouble since I saw you," Mary Ball Washington wrote her half brother. "There was no end to my trouble when George was in the army, but now he has given it up." From the army came notes of dismay at this sudden loss of what at least some of the officers under him had come to think of as a great man, expressing doubts that the placid rounds of crop rotation could distract what had appeared heretofore as an encompassing ambition and an intelligence both restless and obsessed.

For his part, George showed an extreme awareness of how far from glory he had gone. "Dull" was his most frequent word to describe his own existence. More than once in the years following he made apologies to correspondents for

living what appeared—to him, at least—a period of protracted and perhaps shameful lull. One slip alone revealed discordant tensions: a note in 1760 that he had wished to visit
London, but "am now tied by the Leg," indicating tremors of
internal discord, signs that the flight from struggle may have
involved a struggle of its own.

One overt strain emerged to interrupt the placid tenor
of the days—a long and, in the long run, losing effort to in-
ject the virtues of his breed and background into John Parke
Custis, his stepson and unrewarding ward. For twenty years
(from his marriage to Jacky's death from fever on the eve of
Yorktown) the appointive parent, with the aid of Jacky's tutor, the Reverend Jonathan Boucher, conducted an ongoing
guerrilla action to cure the young heir to the immense Custis
fortunes of "lazyness," "indolence," and what Boucher later
described, as Jacky entered adolescence, as "a Propensity to
the Sex, which I am at a loss how to judge of, much less to describe." Advice, indulgence, and outright bribes failed in
turn to inculcate the heroic virtues, and a downcast Boucher
was forced at last to make this sad report to the hero: "I never did in my Life know a Youth so exceedingly Indolent, or
so surprizingly voluptuous; one wd. suppose Nature had intended him for some Asiatic Prince."

George himself took this setback with an odd degree of
resignation, conditioned by fatalism, his deference to the
Custis family, and his sensitivity to the limits of his situation.
Guardians, as he wrote repeatedly to Boucher, were subject
to strictures and suspicions not operative on parents, and his
accounts of some meager discipline often ended with the
comment "Farther than this I did not think myself at liberty
to decide." Strange conduct for the future leader and past
taskmaster of the battlefield, but consistent with his early shyness before the rich and powerful and his new mood of re-
trenchment and retreat. Consistent too with another trait of
character—a strong vein of social tolerance regarding human lapse and excess, combined with a sense of impropriety
of trespass beyond a certain point. In all areas that did not in-
fringe on the public welfare, there were distinct limits
beyond which he did not think himself "at liberty" to go.

In public also the submission held; the prima donna of
the battlefield made no effort to shine front and center in the

House. For nine years after his first election he sat twice yearly on the long wooden benches that lined the Burgesses' Chamber of the exquisite Capitol, silent in the play of oratory, serving on obscure committees, barely opening his mouth. Stranger still, he made no efforts to use his war record or his impressive friendships to give him a hand up into the ruling classes, to raise himself, as he had wanted in his worst days in the army, above the common run. Even his legislative acts were uniformly unspectacular; bills to keep pigs from the water troughs of Alexandria were his maximum efforts on the parliamentary front. To all outward views, the original Washington, all calculation, nerve, and purpose, had sunk into the epitome of the commonplace, as unexceptional a self-creation as effort could produce.

What had caused this transformation of fire into earth? This was no ordinary "retirement," but something deeper and more strange—a retreat from character so total that for more than an eight-year period all outward traces of personna disappeared. This was the first, but not the last time this would happen; in 1783, after the ordeal of the Revolution, he would make another effort at submersion, this time astonishing not just his friends but a world and nation that had come to regard him as a universal fixture and the soul and center of the state. These swings between withdrawal and intense activity sprang not from whim, but from internal rhythm, the shadow side of his intense involvements, the coin paid for control. Each spell of activity had its backlash in the need for retreat and self-repletion, to repair frayed nerve ends and restore resources drained. In time, his energies regained their normal level and reached out for strain again. Washington in 1760 was twenty-eight years old. How long could he have remained "in retirement," living on the top tenth of his character, all shadow and no sun? More germane to this than his own decisions were the problems of another, who came to power the year after George bowed out of it, who also suffered from the pull of nerves and duty, and who also gloried in the title "Farmer George."

George II, the reluctant immigrant who had presided with dutiful disinterest over the tripling of the British empire, dropped dead in his dressing room on 25 October 1760

143

without a warning and without a sign. About seven in the morning (related Walpole) his valet heard a tumult in the chamber and, running in, found his master on the floor, groaning, with a great gash (from falling) on his head. The old king made some feeble speaking motions, then expired on the spot. Walpole was also present at the requiem ("I had never seen a royal funeral") and found it "absolutely noble," the grandeur of the great hushed abbey abated only slightly by the Duke of Newcastle, who made the demise of his royal patron the occasion for an excessive scene. Entering the chapel, he collapsed in a pew as the archbishop hovered over him with smelling salts, then dashed in and out among the titled company, alternately eavesdropping, sobbing horribly, and peering at the mourners through his glass. Later, as the fall chill came up through the marble floors of the abbey, the old king's son, the obese and ailing Duke of Cumberland, felt his movements impeded and, turning, discovered Newcastle standing on his train.

George III, the old king's heir and grandson, was ill equipped to open a period of imperial grandeur. Conscientious by temperament but slow by nature (he did not read till he was past eleven), the clash between his sense of duty and his knowledge of his limitations had begun to breed a fierce anxiety before he left his middle teens. Two years before his accession his tutor, Lord Waldegrave, noted the presence of a "kind of unhappiness" deep within his nature, and the prince himself was revealing an obsession with the difference between the "indolence, inattention, and heedlessness that reigns within me" and the ideal of the perfect ruler, paternal, just and resolute, that he must force himself to be. A pathetic pattern of failure, disgust, resolution, and failure again began to appear with dreadful frequency in his letters to the one man in the world he trusted, his guardian, Lord Bute.

> As I have chosen the vigorous part, I will throw off that indolence which if I don't soon get the better of will be my ruin. . . . I will take upon me the man in every thing, and will not show that indifference which I have as yet too often done. . . .
> I despise myself as every body else must, who knows

how I have acted. . . . I am resolved in myself to take the
resolute part, to act the man in everything, to repeat what
I have to say with spirit, and not blushing and afraid.

There was a twin danger in the prince's character, in
both his "indolence" and his attempts to root it out—the
threat that the swing from "inattention" to the "resolute
part" might overshoot the mark into a rigid stubbornness
that could not bend without bringing down the whole. Waldegrave had already noted that his resolution when it appeared was compounded with stubbornness, that he had
"strong prejudices" and "too correct a memory" for slights—
traits that could lead to political catastrophe and create unwitting harm. As Waldegrave noted with a touch too much
perception, this king "Will seldom do wrong, except when he
mistakes wrong for right."

The king's first efforts to "do right" ended in predictable
disaster: The despised duo of Pitt and Newcastle became the
trio of Pitt-Newcastle-Bute; then Bute and Newcastle; at last
(1762) Bute alone: "My D. Friend . . . whom I shall always
follow . . . on whom everything depends." Eight months
later the "D. Friend" was out, trailing the fumes of a vast incompetence and the rumors of a scandalous connection with
the princess dowager, and the king was thrown back on
George Grenville, "the ablest man of business in the House
of Commons" and a master of finance, if not precisely of
finesse. Estranged from Pitt (who was his brother-in-law, but
who detested him) Grenville fell in with the "Bloomsbury
Gang"* at the far right wing of the emerging scale of factions, who matched him line for line in his passions for order
and economy and, sadly, in his lack of politesse.

In short order, their harangues had driven them into
schisms with the king and into violent conflict with Pitt and
Newcastle over their attacks on free speech and free shipping and a general odor of constraint. General warrants
against sedition became staples of politics; trade was "cor-
rected" (to the distress of the traders); control pervaded ev-

*A reactionary faction headed by the Duke of Bedford, often acting in
alliance with Lord Bute.

ery portion of the state. What hope for the colonies, distant and disorderly, to escape the iron hand? Search-and-seizure was extended to their customshouses; molasses imports were curtailed from the French West Indies (cutting painfully into the rum business); men-of-war patrolled the coasts, giving to revenue an aura of coercion and to the colonies the subtle scent of force. While they had begun to twitch uneasily in the air of threat and hardship, Grenville introduced his American Act in February, 1764, including a new line of trade restrictions and a scheme to raise revenues through affixing stamped papers to deeds of commercial and legal transactions and most deeds of sale. It had the virtue, which Grenville noticed, of being cheap and self-enforcing, and the fault, which he did not, of cutting across that creed of the unwritten constitution that men could be taxed only by assemblies in which their elected representatives directly sit. Grenville gave the colonies a year to set the wheels in motion and sat back to await his revenue. Instead, he reaped a storm.

Warnings came first in apprehensive letters from the governors, telling of touchy tempers and financial distress. Parliamentary taxation, warned Francis Bernard of Massachusetts, was foreign to the colonists and hinted at a range of power both uncharted and disturbingly diffuse. Next came a stream of petitions from the colonial assemblies, asserting that direct control of the taxing power was a staple of the British constitution, applicable to Britons in America as well as to those at home. These words, and others, broke against an iron wall. Parliament refused to hear protests against its own prerogatives, and these, against a bill on money, were twice refused. Condescending at last to meet a delegation of agents* on 2 February, 1765, Grenville told them coldly that he had pledged his administration to the Stamp Act and would brook no disruption of his plans. At least one noncolonial found much to object to in this mishandling of affairs. Edmund Burke charged later that Grenville had con-

*The colonies hired representatives to lobby for them in Parliament, sometimes Americans like Franklin, sometimes sympathetic Englishmen like Burke.

146

cealed the protests to avoid a challenge on the floor. "They were suppressed, they were put under the table," he wrote later. "The House proceeded to its business . . . without the least regular notice of the objections that were made."

This innovation was to take place on 1 November. But the colonials had other plans.

From the colonies came rumors of appalling violence as the dreaded date drew near. Bernard reported in mid-July that the Boston mob had hung Andrew Oliver, his confidant and stamp consignee, in effigy, paraded the totem around the State House three times, razed the stamp office, and burned the "body," fittingly enough, in timbers pulled from the debris. Dire as this was, the next developments were worse. Two weeks later they turned on Thomas Hutchinson, the lieutenant governor and symbol of crown order, in an orgy of appalling rage—stripping the walls from his mansion and the tiles from his roof, dismantling all except his kitchen furniture, and destroying his priceless collection of state papers and historical manuscripts, the loving work of more than thirty years. Tragic and impressive, Hutchinson stayed on to confront his foes in the assembly, while Bernard took off with the cache of stamped papers for Castle William (an island fortress six miles out in Boston Harbor), where he stayed behind a screen of British warships, firing off infuriated letters to the ministry that scourged both the mob and Grenville at extreme and equal length.

Nor was this the only scene of tumult. In Virginia, Governor Faquier had to walk George Mercer, stamp consignee and Washington's old comrade-in-arms, through a hostile mob on Duke of Gloucester Street and in an all-night session at the Palace (attended by Mercer's terrified relations) persuaded him to resign. Faquier, too, moved the stamps beyond water, to a warship eight miles up the York.

Riots brewed in all the provinces. In October representatives from nine colonies held an unprecedented Stamp Act "Congress" in New York. The first of November came around with the stamps cashiered, the courts shut, commerce at a standstill, and the crowds chanting for redress in the streets. In New York, center of the British army (where mobs had almost stormed the garrison), Thomas Gage, another Braddock alumnus and the commander in chief of His Majesty's forces in America, was draining the inland posts to move troops to the cities and dropping broad hints to his superiors at home. "No Requisition has been made of me for Assistance, which I must acknowledge, I have been sorry for," he wrote London. "I confess, I should be glad of a legal Pretence to collect all the Force I could into one Body, which might Check in some Measure the Audacious Threats of taking arms."

For London, the impasse produced a choice of woes: to enforce the unenforceable or to appear to have caved in under force. "If they relax, their Predecessors will reproach them with giving up the Honour, Dignity and Power of this Nation," Franklin wrote his son in America, "yet even they, I am told, think they have carried things too far."

Happily, the administration had undergone a change. George III had dismissed Grenville on 10 July, after a succession of incessant arguments, the last of which, over a Bill of Regency, had been at least partially responsible for the first attack of royal madness, in spring, 1765. After a try for Pitt, who had lapsed again into temperament, the king fell back on the Newcastle faction, headed this time by the Marquess of Rockingham, a vastly rich Whig landholder, gentle and amiable, but hideously reticent and (to the relief of the king, if not his party) almost too shy to speak at all. Only a very strong military, warned Burke (Rockingham's mouthpiece and secretary), could enforce order while the Act prevailed. Unhappily, this was what the Grenvillites appeared to crave. "They are for taking vigorous . . . I call them violent, measures," wrote the Whig Lord Chesterfield. "No less than *les dragonnades*."

After some haggling, Rockingham dragooned the king into grudging support for his policies. "Modification was my constant," the king noted in a memorandum of 6 January 1766, "but if the differing parties were too wild . . . I clearly declar'd for Repeal." "This hour is the most critical ever known in this country, but I hope Providence will steer me through it with honour," the harassed king wrote to his lord

148

chancellor, "my headache is not abated, nor the feverish complaint."

The "wild parties" clashed in mid-December, when Parliament convened. Grenville ("a little out of his head on the Article of America") opened with a great blast at the colonies, vociferating at the demonstrations and urging military force. This performance drew complaints from Lord Shelbourne, Rockingham's aide and Pitt's satellite, who complained to the latter, "I felt attaching the name of *rebellion* . . . to the Americans . . . dangerous, and perhaps imprudent, and unjust." Pitt himself emerged after Christmas recess in a bravura daylong performance, engaging Grenville in a debate of some hours, insisting on the right of the colonies to resist taxation, lashing the administration with his scorn.

Burke made his debut on the seventeenth of the month. Presenting a petition from the merchants of Manchester, he became possessed. "I know not what struck me, but I took a sudden resolution to say something about it. . . . I did say something; what it was, I know not upon my honour, I felt like a man drunk." He, too, rowed with Grenville, then resumed, "still giddy, and affected with a swimming in my head." Others spoke more kindly of this onset of a great career. Dr. Johnson said that he had astounded London, and he had the rarer kudo of a tribute on the floor from Pitt—a rare spark between exotic commoners not always to see eye to eye.

Grenville suffered, on and off the floor. Merchants, enraged at their lost trade profits (and whipped into a frenzy by the Rockingham clique), packed the outer chamber till all hours, cheering at the sight of Pitt or Rockingham and howling at Grenville so unmercifully that he plunged into the crowd after one of his tormentors and had to be pulled back by a colleague by his coat. Merchants, agents, and representatives of colonies and the trading interests were paraded before the House of Commons in brisk profusion, to tell appalling stories of impending ruin and collapse. Star of the hearings was Franklin, who sat through a two-day session, baited by Grenville and led on by the Whigs, answering with the pragmatism that was totally his own.

149

Q. If the act is not repealed, what do you think will be the consequences?

A. The total loss of the respect and affection the people of America bear to this country, and of all the commerce that depends.

Q. Would the Americans . . . pay a moderated tax?

A. No, never . . . unless compelled by force of arms.

The position of the king was piteous, caught between his hatred of Grenville and the rightward drift of Lord Bute and his friends. When Newcastle begged him to rein in his allies, his reply was pathetic. What could he do, when they told him they could not vote in conscience for repeal? To Bute he spoke frankly of his dislike of Rockingham and his intention, once the crisis was over, to cast him and his party adrift. To Lord Egmont, his floor leader in the House of Lords, he sent a chillingly explicit note: "Pray see Lord Rockingham . . . and *keep him steady,* for I fear lest the Secretaries should stagger him; all I desire is that they will act firmly until the arduous business of the American colonies is over, then I can stand on my own feet."

In the end, repeal carried, but only after the Declaratory Act—reaffirming the right to tax the colonies—had gone over to wash down the bitter pill. The colonials celebrated in a rain of rum and revels. Boston capped a day of feasting with a great display of fireworks, in which pyramids, obelisks, and fantastic creatures burst brilliantly above Boston Common, scattering sparks on the ecstatic crowds below. Washington's reaction was more circumspect (as had been his involvement), showing ambivalence, mixed feelings, and the signs of inner war. As befitted his new position "in retirement," he stayed away from all contention, speaking not at all and writing little and keeping an unbroken silence in the House. The debate, he wrote in one (rare) letter, "engrosses the conversation of the speculative part of the colonists"— keeping his pose of calculated distance in good order and drawing careful lines of difference between the "speculative" party and himself. Not quite in the line of his retirement was a strain of iron. Had Parliament persisted, he wrote gravely,

150

"the consequences, I conceive, would have been more dire than is generally apprehended" to the colonies and to Parliament itself.

Also not in the line of his retirement was his growing friendship with George Mason, an austere, acerbic scholar very much of the speculative part who had taken a large part in the agitation and whose suspicions had not been totally allayed. "There is as yet no Cause our Joy shou'd exceed the bounds of Moderation," he wrote to friends in London. "Such another such experiment as the Stamp-Act wou'd produce a general Revolt." George doubtless shared this bit of skepticism, as well as Mason's next comment: "Some Bungler in Politicks will soon, perhaps, be framing Schemes."

As it happened, they had less than one year to wait.

George III had never liked the Rockinghams, and when they wavered of their own inherent weakness, he felt no compunction about setting them adrift. The marquess was out by early 1767, and Pitt was in, having been placated at last with a promise to concoct a ministry from the tag ends of all parties (except the Rockinghams, with whom he had been feuding) to free the king from his terror of concerted pressure and Pitt from the annoyance of having to listen to anyone's opinions but his own. "He did not cultivate men because he thought it an incumbrance," said Pitt's friend Shelbourne, "and thought he could act more to advantage without the encumbrance of a party." Burke, as one of those excluded, had a more jaundiced point of view:

> He made an administration so chequered and speckled . . . so crossly indented and whimsically dovetailed . . . here a bit of black stone, and there a bit of white; patriots and courtiers, king's friends and republicans; whigs and tories, treacherous friends and open enemies—that it was indeed a very curious show. . . . I venture to say it did so happen that persons had a single office divided between them, who never spoke to each other in their lives until they found themselves, they knew not how, pigging together, heads and points, in the same truckle bed.

"Pigging together" were Pitt's friends Conway, Grafton, Camden, and Shelbourne; Barrington and Northington, protégés of Grenville's friend the Duke of Bedford; and Charles Townshend, a brilliant and eccentric scapegrace who had rattled in and out of a dozen stands and parties, dazzling all with his eclectic genius as he appalled the thoughtful with his lack of base. As Burke had it from his brother William: ". . . great abilities put it in his power always to do mischief. . . . From Constitutional habit he seemed unable to form an opinion . . . and consequently could never argue from a real sense of right or wrong." Pitt had allowed Grafton to foist this peacock on him under the impression that his austere fires could harness Townshend's scattershot exuberance and hold it on a settled course. This theory never had the time to stand the test.

Pitt had knocked this government together to checkmate itself through its own diversity and disintegrate without his guiding hand. Five months after its formation Pitt fell into a "Dejection and flutter," retiring to Somerset in an intense depression while his allies foundered and his enemies closed ranks. "The Earl of Chatham* is still at Bath and consequently the King's Administration has got the gout and hobbles terribly," Grenville noted happily. "Mr. C. Townshend indeed seems to wish to move a little more nimbly and to try to walk without crutches." He did, indeed.

In January, 1768, he had shown signs of imminent conversion, coming down on the side of the Bedford-Grenville faction on a vote to cut taxes after two days of intense debating (much of it his own) in which he argued by turns on both sides of the question, and was cheered in rotation by every party in the House. Flushed with success, he was back the next day to take up a charge that *he* could do what had eluded Grenville—collect an American tax. All parties were stunned. "What he means," said an astonished Shelbourne, "I do not conceive." Neither, apparently, did Townshend, who "seemed to create knowledge, instead of searching for it," and gave the appearance of having concocted the proposal on the spot. Shelbourne tried to rouse his stricken master:

*Pitt was created Earl of Chatham by George III.

152

"I believe Your Lordship will think the speech I have just mentioned to you is not the way to make anything go down well in North America"; but Pitt remained too ill for combat, and his friends were too inert or stricken to protest. "No one in the Ministry had sufficient authority to advise the dismission of Mr. Charles Townshend," Grafton wrote, adding later, "His behavior on the whole is such as no Cabinet will, I am confident, ever submit to." Shelbourne concurred. "Excessive on every occasion," he confided to Pitt. "It appears to me impossible that Mr. Townshend can mean to go on."

He could, and he did. Townshend, now the adored darling of the Bedford faction, appeared daily in the House of Commons, heaping scorn on administration personnel and policy as he chatted with Grenville arm in arm. Grafton made frantic efforts through the spring to contact Chatham but was always turned away. Pitt's solicitor, one of the few allowed entrance, found the lost leader white and trembling, murmuring pieces of distracted nonsense as he sat with his head between his hands. Grafton got through at last on May 7 but found Pitt incoherent and incapable of counsel or advice. By that time it scarcely mattered—on 13 May Townshend introduced his program, which went the Stamp Act two better by adding insult to injury and civic coercion to economic strain. Taxes were to be levied on all paint, glass, lead, and tea imported to the colonies, with the monies used to pay the salaries of judges, transferred thus from colony to crown control. The hated courts of admiralty, in which disputes between crown and colony were tried by a strictly British judge and jury, were expanded to five courts instead of one. Of all, the last provisions seemed the most offensive, as they struck at the soul of judicial integrity and turned the courts into political hammers and instruments of crown control. Burke, Isaac Barre (a Whig M.P. who had traveled widely in America), and a tattered clique of Pittites fought the program fiercely, but Townshend had the backing of the Bedford-Grenville faction, wounded in both pride and pocketbook and avid for revenge. Parliament debated in May in a savage session, highlighted by Grenville's fierce attack on Conway, his insistence that Pitt and Rockingham encouraged sedition in the colonies, and his suggestions that dissenting members be impeached. Helpless without the shield of Pitt's fierce presence, the opposition was trounced easily, and the acts passed on 30 May by heavy votes. "Absurdity itself," Burke said later, "never devised such a plan of taxation as the one proposed in 1767," and the whole, from start to finish, had some elements of farce. But the colonials, once burned, had no taste for humor, and their response was to lead to blood.

Contentious Boston, center of all tumult, took the lead in the orchestration of revolt. First came news of a boycott of taxed items, then, a bid for continental action, a circular letter to the other twelve colonies, urging a general embargo and a united front. Shelbourne had been ousted from his post in the Colonial Department for Lord Hillsborough, a Bedford puppet, who commended himself to his employment by the statement that he would give nothing to the colonies that they did not ask for with a rope around their necks. Hillsborough was alone in London when the circular letter arrived. Consulting no one, he sent back his *own* letter, ordering the other colonies to disown Massachusetts and Massachusetts to rescind its letter on pain of having its Assembly dissolved. The results were predictable (to anyone but Hillsborough); hitherto-hesitant colonies dashed to support their sister colony as one. The Massachusetts Assembly flung his demand in his teeth by a vote of 92 to 17 and was prorogued, as promised, while toasts to the "Glorious Ninety-two" were drunk up and down the seacoast and a forty-five-pint punch bowl, lovingly designed by Paul Revere with the names of all naysayers inscribed on its silver surface, was passed about under a huge elm in South Boston, a gathering place for patriots known as the Liberty Tree. The customs commissioners, tangible symbols of harassment, were the objects of unending riot. Mobs massed about their houses almost daily, while the upper house of the Assembly (whose consent was needed for military intervention) blandly deflected Bernard's timid efforts to call Gage and the British army from New York. "The Commissioners have asked me what Support I can give them, if there should be an insurrection; I an-

154

swer none at all," Bernard wrote London sadly. "I have promised them an Asylum at the Castle, & possibly may want it myself."

The decision was taken out of Bernard's hands forever on 10 June, when the man-of-war *Romney* pulled in the *Liberty*, a ship belonging to the vocal patriot John Hancock, ostensibly for smuggling wine into the colony, and nearly set off civil war. Mobs set on the customs officers, sending them flying to the *Romney* (and thence to Castle William) maimed and battered and in terror of their lives. Hillsborough had already alerted Commodore Hood at Halifax to have his ships in readiness. Now he browbeat Grafton into acquiesence, and sent (30 July) this dispatch to Gage:

> His Majesty has thought it fit that the Hands of Government in his Colonies should be further strengthened by the addition of two Regiments from Ireland . . . and . . . the 64th and 65th Regiments . . . should be augmented by Draughts to 500 Men each, and sent immediately to Boston. . . . Transport Vessels are preparing with all possible Dispatch, in order to take on board the Troops at Cork.

"Ready and ripe for open revolt," was Hood's opinion, as he embarked the transports from Halifax, and Gage, preparing to join the troops at Boston, sent these words back home: "You cannot act with too much vigour. . . . Quash this Spirit at a Blow."

At high noon on 1 October the flotilla moved into Boston Harbor, guns pointed at the city as if for a siege. Seven hundred soldiers, with a great train of artillery, trailed in full parade to Boston Common, where the array of tents, incessant drill, and harsh calls of parade orders (plus the whipping of deserters in full view of the public) rapidly gave the impression of the invaded province and the military state. Citizens were soon insulted by armed sentries, arrested and detained without warrants, and harrassed as they passed the city gates. In conscious insult, Faneuil Hall, the meeting place for colonial dissidents, became a barracks for the British officers; cannon pointed directly at the council chambers gave ample comment on the change. "The town is now a perfect garrison," wrote the Boston *Post* in indignation, "administering justice under the points of bayonets." To the occupiers, the new air of stunned tranquillity seemed to prove that a dose of arms was what the doctor ordered to quell sedition and bring the population back to rights. Hood told Grenville that troops should have been called at the first sign of trouble, and Gage sent this note to Hillsborough from Boston on 8 November:

> Every thing now has the appearance of Peace and Quiet. . . . The Presence of the Troops has already produced some good Effect, and it appears very necessary for his Majesty's Service, that both his Land and Sea Forces should be strong in North America for some time to come.

Boston's ordeal roused a continental measure of response. Pamphlets, blending fire and exquisite logic, kept resistance at a ready pitch. New York and Philadelphia, the two other leading seaports, joined Boston in nonimportation, signing covenants on 31 December 1768 and 2 February 1769. And in Virginia a colonel "in retirement" sent this note to George Mason at Gunston Hall:

> At a time when our Lordly Masters in Great Britain will be satisfied with nothing less than the depredation of American freedom, it seems highly necessary that some thing should be done to avert the stroke. . . . That no man should scruple, or hesitate a moment, to use a-ms in defense of so valuable a blessing, on which all the good and evil of life depends, is clearly my opinion; yet A-ms, I wou'd beg leave to add, should be the last resource.

The swing from withdrawal to violence was typical, as was the period of prolonged thought before the move. Moderate and calculating as to measures, the iron colonel was a creature of extremes.

One course remained open, short of "a-ms"—the extension of the boycott begun in the northern cities into the pastoral, plantation economy of the South. In April, 1769, George took the floor in the House of Burgesses to present proposals drafted by himself and George Mason for a colony-wide network of associations of planters and merchants to restrict the importation of proscribed British goods. It was his first address on any point of substance in his ten-year presence in the House. The colonel "in retirement" was yielding to the man of thought and action, under the inexorable pressure of events.

The next year and a half produced the engaging sight of the two Georges and other staples of the local gentry riding out at all hours to comb through shipments from Britain for proscribed material, including one incident near the end of the association when they were called aboard a ship from Glasgow to inspect a suspect silver shipment and discovered only a parcel of hats. Hampered considerably by a lack of common standards among the colonies and a lack of real power within, the associations managed nonetheless to dig large holes in the British revenues and render the duties ineffective as a money-raising scheme. The infliction of pain on the mother country had become their one claim to justice in the presence of intransigence and force.

Events in the mother country gave small immediate encouragement for the prospects of détente. Following the lapse made by Pitt's fall into depression, his enemies launched an attack on the administration that his shattered heirs were unable to combat. Shelbourne, Camden and Conway were talented but unaggressive (they could not have been Pitt's friends otherwise), and the Rockinghams, who could have helped them hold the line, were out. Pitt's de facto successor was the Duke of Grafton, at thirty-one a languid and reluctant premier-designate, who, in the sad words of Horace Walpole, "gave himself up to Lord Bute's influence; rushed into an alliance with the Bedfords, whom he hated, against his interests and at last permitted them to betray him, not without suspecting, but without resenting it." No one protested when the Bedfords pushed their way into the Cabinet, installing their puppets Gower at Admiralty, Weymouth in the Treasury, and the bellicose Sandwich at War, or, in 1768, when they split Shelbourne's Southern Department in two, tossing control of colonial policy to Lord Hillsborough, their protégé. "The Administration, since Lord Chatham's illness," Camden wrote Grafton on 24 September, "is almost entirely altered, without being changed and I find myself connected with persons to whom I am scarcely known. . . . I am truly, my dear Lord, distressed."

He was more distressed than ever when Hillsborough, outraged at the reception of his orders, dug up (8 October) a statute of Henry VIII, "passed in the dotage of his understanding, and the last year of his reign," to extradite dissident colonials to Britain to be tried for treason in a British court. "It was brought here without a father, without anyone to own it," Burke told the House in an outburst of sardonic fury. "They took this little foundling, this Oedipus, this riddle, they laid it on your table, and you accepted it." The "foundling," though never used, caused new flurries in America and did more than anything to convince the colonials that Parliament was determined to meet protest with the sword. Nor could they find much comfort in the king, who appeared to take all appeals as insults to his dignity and went to special pains to impress on his subjects that no amount of pressure could make any alteration in his course. He accepted petitions with studied discourtesy; receiving a plea (March, 1769) from the city of Westminster, he turned his back on the plaintants and passed the paper to a lord-in-waiting, who handed it to another, who at length passed it down to a groom. Later that month, receiving a delegation from London, he read it a lecture on obedience, then turned to his courtiers and laughed. Doubtless, he believed he was living the code he had defined to Lord Bute years earlier: "I am resolved to act the man." Franklin for one had different views of what acting the man—and king—entailed:

> When I see that all petitions and complaints of grievances are become so odious to government that even the mere pipe which conveys them becomes obnoxious, I am at loss to know how peace and union are to be maintained. . . . Grievances cannot be redressed unless they are known; and they cannot be known but through complaints. . . . If these are deemed affronts, and the messengers punished as offenders, who will henceforth send petitions? And who will deliver them? It has been thought

a dangerous thing in any state to stop up the vents of grief. Wise governments have therefore generally received petitions with some indulgence, even when but slightly founded. Those who think themselves injured by their rulers are sometimes by a mild and prudent answer convinced of their error. But where complaining is a crime, hope becomes despair.

Despair was growing very thick among the Whigs in Britain as the impasse settled in. "Our severity has increased their ill behaviour," Burke told the Commons of the dispute with the Americans. "We know not how to advance; they know not how to retreat. . . . Some party must give way, and there is a willingness in that country to meet us. . . . The disposition of the administration, with regard to America, must have a change." Franklin described the dilemma in a letter to a friend in America: "The Majority really wish the Duty Acts had never been made . . . but they think the National Honour concern'd in supporting them, and they say it is of great importance to the Nation that the World should see it is Master of its Colonies. . . . On the other Hand they really are afraid of provoking the Colonies too far."

The solution was a session of "empty terrors and idle menaces"—bluster followed by a tactical retreat. "It was several times suggested," Burke reported, "that it would be a wise thing to repeal these obnoxious acts. The answer was Never! We will not give them an iota; we will not give them a peppercorn; we shall shortly have them at our feet."

One week after Parliament adjourned, Hillsborough himself dispatched a letter to the colonial assemblies that "His Majesty's present administration have at no time entertained a design to lay any further taxes upon America . . . and that it is their intention to take off the duties upon glass, paper, and colors, upon consideration of such principles have been laid contrary to true principles of commerce." As Burke pointed out with some malice, it had taken them a long time to discover where "true principles" lay. But as he himself acknowledged, principles that conceived the Townshend duties were readily dispensable when they embraced neither equity nor sense.

There remained the problem of "face." Like repeal before it, the volte-face could not go forward without some gesture to the Bedford party and its pride. "I am clear there must always be one tax to keep up the right, and as such I approve the tea duty," said George III later, and the ruling clique of Bedfordites and King's Friends agreed. The few Pittites in the Cabinet fought them fiercely but were worn down by fatigue and attrition, losing by a vote of 5 to 4 on 5 March 1770, the deciding vote being cast by the new prime minister, the King's Friend Lord North. North and his patron congratulated themselves on having come through another debacle with the tag end of their "dignity," but their triumph stood on shaky ground. The tea tax had reduced a solution to a mere expedient, and Britain had saved its "honour" at the price of its enduring peace.

"Honour," however, had become the heart of the affair. George III, champion of prerogative and of the manly front, would never waver in his conviction that sovereignty and accommodation were incompatible, that the first concessions to a subordinate would snap the ties of awe and empire apart. Pitt and Burke, together with their allies, had different notions of where the nation's interests lay. They knew Britain needed America for trade and as an ally in case of a renewed war with the Bourbon powers and they watched it cede the fact to the façade of power with rising anguish and despair. Ironically, as often happened, it was the weak demanding what the strong were willing to concede. Bute and Grenville, who had called Pitt's French war too expensive, were foremost in the less demanding battle for prerogative, while Pitt, fighting the effects of gout and melancholia, would drag himself to Parliament time and time over to urge conciliation: in times of impasse, the stronger should give way. The extended preference of pride to interest would never cease to confound the Whigs. Walpole would profess amazement at the sacrifice of substance to sovereignty. Franklin at the infatuation with compounded error, and Burke would burst out in the Commons, after honor had led them into war with both America and France.

> They tell you, Sir, that your dignity is tied to it. I
> know not how it happens, but this dignity of yours is a ter-

rible encumberance to you, for it has of late been ever at war with your interest, your equity, and every idea of your policy. Show the thing you contend for to be reason . . . and then I am prepared to allow it whatever dignity you please. But what dignity is derived from perseverance in absurdity is more than ever I could discern.

Despite the second reversal, the settlement had seemed to come three years too late. Deep divisions had been sown already, between Americans and Britons, among Britons themselves. Three portents had survived the new accommodation to raise shadows of prolonged unease: the tax on tea remained, the token of ill will to the colonials, and the sign that the quarrel could arise again. On the very day of repeal (5 March 1770) members of the Boston garrison, harassed beyond endurance by an equally beleaguered mob, fired into their tormentors and shot five dead, sending jolts of horror through the colonies and sealing enmity in blood. And last, though least noticed, this disturbing fact: a former soldier of the king, who had once seen his life in terms of service to the empire, himself a perplexing mixture of restraint and violence, had begun to write, in the cryptic terms that denote a sense of the barely thinkable, of recourse to the use of "a-ms."

X

The Die Is Cast

*The people are ripe for mischief . . . we must
either master them, or totally leave them to
themselves.*—GEORGE III to Lord North,
19 November 1774

The colonial tumult subsided into torpor following this second settlement, both sides in a balance between pride and terror that neither appeared willing to upset. "Thus has the winter, which set out with such big black clouds, concluded with the prospect of more serenity than we have seen for some time," Walpole wrote a friend in the spring of 1770. "You may compose yourself to tranquillity . . . and take as good a nap as any monarch in Europe." Events seemed likely to prolong this happy state. "Indolent" was his word for the new prime minister, a pliant creature given to passivity in council and catnaps in the House of Commons, where he was famous for extended dozes in the most ferocious of debates. One bemused member recalled a session in which Burke halted a diatribe in mid-torrent, "looked directly at Lord North, who was asleep, and said, in the Scripture phrase, 'Brother Lazarus is not dead, but sleepeth,'" enchanting everyone, including North, "as soon as he was sufficiently awake."

Three years later the spell was broken—by an intended act of peace. North had aroused himself in 1773 with a new

162

answer to a chronic problem: a plan to ease the mammoth debts of the East India Company by shipping its surplus teas to America for disposal there at bargain rates. Sadly, tea was the one remnant of the hated Townshend duties and the one item still proscribed. Cargo ships bearing the detested product were turned back in New York and Philadelphia. In Boston the governor insisted that they land. The ministry had letters first of a stubborn impasse, then news of a bizarre revolt. Citizens, faces blackened with coal dust and arrayed grotesquely in Indian feathers, had swarmed aboard the ships and "made a Tea-Pot of the Harbour," disposing of the tea with suspicious precision before slipping back into the side streets of South Boston as the gutted tea chests bobbed along the docksides and the now brown and brackish water gently washed along the wharves.

"Notable and striking," said John Adams. ". . . the most magnificent moment of all." The administration had a different point of view.

London responded with a legislative riot of its own. "There is an ostrich egg laid in America, where the Bostonians have canted three hundred chests of tea in the ocean, for they will not drink tea with our Parliament," declared Walpole, adding with some foresight, "Lord Chatham talked of conquering America in Germany; I believe England will be conquered someday in New England or Bengal." For the ruling Bedford faction, it was the grand chance for revenge and power, to make Boston, as Burke told his New York clients, "an Example of Terror to the other Colonials" and the showcase for imperial prestige. Dartmouth and the languid North tried to stem the tide of fury but were always overborne. The Coercive Acts, reported on 2 February, were three counts of fury: the port of Boston was to be closed on 1 June; councillors and judges, under popular control since the birth of the colony, were to be replaced by appointees of the royal establishment; and Gage, with an army of 5,000 and the backing of the fleet from Halifax, was to invest the city as military governor (under a new act to exempt the soldiery from civil justice), to keep order, and to enforce the new regime. "I have seen Lieutenant-General Gage," George III wrote

North. "He says they will be lyons, whilst we are lambs; but if we take the resolute part, they will undoubtedly prove very meek." A tattered clique of Whig survivors, lacking all but vocal power, continued to warn that force would aggravate the sore. Pitt, surfacing from a long trough of depression, appealed for a "more gentle mode of governing America . . . for I sincerely believe the destroying the tea was the result of despair." George Johnstone, one time governor of Pennsylvania, warned the Commons that the repressive measures would weld the colonies in a rebellious union, and Burke wrote his clients in America, "This sort of unhappy Conflict may bring on Effusion of Blood."

All were helpless in the tide of rage. "The torrent is still violent against America . . ." Franklin wrote of the Coercive Acts. "There is little hope they will not pass." Pass they did, by wide margins, at the end of March. "Be assured," Burke warned his clients, "That the Determination to force Obedience . . . seems as strong as possible, and that the ministry appear stronger than ever I have known them. . . . I am full of trouble. . . . My advice has little weight anywhere."

Guns deployed at every porthole, the men-of-war reached Boston on 17 May, disgorging battalion on battalion of King's soldiers, as the fleet sealed an iron ring around the harbor, making the bay a forest of hostile masts. Redcoats, at the ratio of one to every four Bostonians, patrolled the streets, keeping order and breaking up seditious gatherings—or meetings not permitted by the governor, in writing in his hand. Defiant as ever, the Assembly was prorogued on 17 June (forever, as it happened) pushing through resolutions for a mass boycott, a trained militia, and a general congress of the colonies as Gage's messenger banged at the barred door. (All were adopted into the program of colonial resistance when the Congress met, as urged, in September, but it was the last Assembly ever held within that state.)

Beyond the range of British rifles, chaos reigned. Mobs toting muskets, rakes and pikestaffs met royal judges, councillors, and court officials at the locked doors of their courthouses and sent them flying into Boston and the shelter of the guns. Courts were closed riotously in Berkshire, Taunton, and innumerable other townships; in Worcester, fifty miles out of Boston, an infuriated mob of 5,000 made a lane and forced the court officials to pass between them, hats in hands, and disavow the acts of Parliament no less than thirty times. Gage wrote Dartmouth that he found conditions intolerable, the general spirit of sedition making it almost suicidal for his troops to venture beyond Boston Neck. Nothing but wholesale occupation, he insisted, could restore order under the conditions that prevailed. "I hope you will be firm, and send me a sufficient Force to command the Country, by marching into it, and sending off large Detachments to secure obedience thro' every part," he warned London. "They talk of fixing a Plan of Government of their own, and nothing less than the Conquest of almost all the New England Provinces will secure Obedience to the Late Acts of Parliament for regulating the Government of Massachusetts Bay."

Boston's travail hit a continental note. County, town and colonial assemblies sent infuriated petitions; shipments of food (including herds of sheep from Brooklyn and Connecticut) came pouring through the narrow pass of Boston Neck. And from the Virginia burgesses (prorogued and reassembled in the Raleigh Tavern) came an anguished, almost incoherent letter from George Washington to George William Fairfax at Belvoir:

> The Ministry may rely on it that the Americans will never be tax'd without their own Consent that the Cause of Boston the despotick Measures in regard to it I mean now and forever will be considered the cause of America . . . and that we shall not suffer ourselves to be sacrificed by piece meals, though god only knows what is to become of us, threatened as we are by so many hoverg. evils . . . since the first settlement of the Colony, the minds of the People in it were never more disturbed.

Frustration, intransigence, and the shade of unchecked power had wrung this at last from the conservative, the order lover, the onetime servant of the crown. With the other members of the dissolved Assembly he observed a day of prayer and fasting, voted to send food to Boston and to put Virginia, county by county, in a posture of defense. When the order keepers became the order breakers, what answer but the sad resort to force? Or, as he wrote the unconvinced and troubled Bryan Fairfax: "What reason is there to expect any thing from their justice? . . . I am convinced, as much as I am of my own existence, that there is no relief but in their distress."

"Distress" for Britain had become the center of the case. With six other Virginians, George arrived at Philadelphia on 3 September to concert schemes for the relief of Boston to end the rule of decree and bayonet. Typically, he made no notes of the star-packed assembly, of the debates in chambers, or the bibulous lobbying out of doors. Still, he did not go unnoticed in the accounts of others. Silas Deane, the chatty envoy from Connecticut, remarked favorably on his youthful air, the firm countenance and military manner— the compelling blend of diffidence and power that was the basis of his mystery and magic and the source of his appeal. "Speaks very modestly, and in cool, but determined style," said Deane of his private address—a reading that was both the sum and prophecy of his impact on his continental peers.

John Adams said that Washington never spoke in public in this first meeting of continental minds. If so, he had much to listen to. On 5 September came rumors of an appalling rupture—Gage and the "country people" had come to blows outside Boston; Boston had been shelled by warships in the harbor; 10,000 men from Connecticut and western Massachusetts were reported on the march. For three days Congress waited in hideous suspense. It was not until the afternoon of 8 September that the rumors were dispelled. A British detachment had marched out quietly to Cambridge to fetch some powder that had been sold to them and just as quietly returned. The rumor, however, set the background for the next event. On 16 September an express came roaring in from Suffolk County (Boston) with nine resolves of resistance to the occupation, asking the endorsement of Congress for three explosive schemes: to withhold taxes from the crown and pay them to a provincial congress; to raise, arm and train a colonial militia; and to ask the Congress to back the province if it came to blows with Gage. That night, John Adams wrote this passage in a letter to a friend: "The Congress will support Boston and the Massachusetts, or perish with them. But they earnestly wish that Blood may be spared."

Congress was committed to a defensive war.

Backpedaling from this drastic measure, the delegates drafted a last petition of rights and grievances to Britain, adopted plans for a continental boycott to be enforced by associations elected by the towns and counties, and left on 29 October in a glow of Madeira and amity, having first made plans to reconvene, if necessary, the next May. Before departure, John Adams had a chat with Patick Henry in an apprehensive meeting of their minds. "Waste paper," was the best that they could say of the spate of appeals and petitions, "necessary to cement the union of the colonies" and "expected by the people at home." What people "at home" could expect later was detailed in a letter Adams passed to Henry that had been sent him by a Massachusetts friend. The time had not come for a break with Britain. The colonies should avoid all shows of violence; they were not yet strong enough to win them, and premature encounters would lead to crushing and permanent defeat. Negotiations with Britain were useful, to let strength and determination mature within the colonies and convince both the world and the Americans that they had done all possible to skirt a break. As for the future, the letter was both prescient and grim: "Either an effectual non-consumption agreement or resistance of the new government will bring on hostilities very soon. . . . Fight we must finally, unless Britain retreats."

Britain responded, not with retreat, but with a roar. "The die is now cast," George III wrote to Lord North when reports of the Congress reached London. "I do not wish to come to severer measures, but we must not retreat." Shortly after, North introduced a three-part program: to declare New England in rebellion; to request the king to reduce it to obedience; and to close the fisheries of the seditious colonies, cutting off their central source of foodstuffs and of trade. "This most infamous Bill for famishing the four provinces of New England," Burke exploded, ". . . my Soul revolts."

Few shared his feeling as the angry days wound on. The

revised goverment (now stocked with King's Friends and loyal Bedfordites) quashed all opposition in an orgy of splenetic rage. "Long days make small sensation when the majorities are very great, and always on the same side," wrote the disheartened Walpole in his diaries. "The Houses go on fulminating against America." Nor were the ruling powers friendly to dissent. The petition of the Continental Congress, Franklin reported, "came down with a great heap of papers and intelligences from the governors and officers in America . . . the last on the list, and was laid upon the table . . . undistinguished by any particular recommendation of it to the notice of either House." Pleas from Franklin and Arthur Lee to be heard in support of the petition were disallowed in the House of Commons; remonstrances from the merchants of London and Briston were consigned to what Burke referred as "the committee of oblivion," as the machine ground on its course. Opposition leaders scorched the air but could not find the votes to match their fires. Pitt's plea for the recall of the troops from Boston, Franklin said, "was treated with as much contempt as they could have shown to a ballad offered by a drunken porter"; Camden joined him, "but all availed no more than than the whistling of the winds." Much the same befell Burke on his magnum opus, the first Speech on Conciliation, offered in the Commons on 22 March, destined for the ages, if not the North ministry, and less remarkable for the impress it made upon the ministers than for the fleeting peace it gave his mind. "He began at half-past three," wrote his brother, "and was on his Legs, until six Oclock . . . such performance, even from him, was never before heard in that House. . . . America was not on his mind only as a Politician, it hung on his Conscience as being accountable for his Actions and his conduct. That is now satisfyed—it will be highly necessary that he should."

There was little comfort other than in conscience in a climate bending more and more to force. The king himself came out firmly on the side of "vigour" in a February letter to Lord North; he would meet violence with resolution (his old obsession) and bring the seditious colonies to heel. More disturbing than this compulsive rigidity was a note of callous rancor creeping into ministerial debate. The Earl of Sand-

168

wich (later a disastrous head of Admiralty) prayed for an extensive rebel army: "The more the better, the easier would be the conquest; if they did not run away, they would starve themselves into compliance . . . the very sound of a cannon would carry them off."

Franklin himself was losing taste for reconciliation in these high and bitter winds. His breaking point came at a soiree in March when a certain General Clarke said within his earshot that he and 1,000 grenadiers would go from one end of America to the other and "geld all the males, partly by force and partly by a little coaxing." Franklin left the next week on the New York packet and was in Philadelphia in time to serve on the Pennsylvania delegation to the second Continental Congress on 2 May.

The news from London gripped the provincials in renewed despair. "I think we have little hopes of a Speedy Redress of Grievances," George Mason wrote Washington on 14 March, "but on the contrary we may expect to see coercive and vindictive measures still pursued." From Britain came other words for Washington, from an old friend removed there the year before:

> It is reported in London that you are training the People of Virginia to the Use of Arms. I hope you do not find those of your own County the most deficient, or that they misbecome their new uniform. . . . God grant you your Privilages and a happy and speedy Reconciliation upon Constitutional Principles, is the daily Prayer of
> Dear Sir [sic]
> Your Affect: and most Obliged humble Servt:
> G:W: FAIRFAX

George had been training an army since the summer previous, dipping into his own (and Mason's) pockets for arms and powder, riding the circuits to drill militia on their twice-weekly turnouts on the county squares. That winter he had wined, dined, and picked the brains of two local veterans of the British army, Horatio Gates (now resident at Traveller's Rest in Virginia) and that peripatetic oddity and late ornament of the court of Poland the scrawny and eccentric

169

Charles Lee. Doubtless, George was deferential to this odd duo, leading perhaps to misconceptions that brought endless difficulties in later years. Before his sojourn at Mount Vernon, Lee had gone to Boston on a self-devised inspection tour, stopping on his way back to fire off a letter to Burke in London, warning in his flamboyant manner of the coming immolation of the British empire, and ending finally on this extraordinary note:

> I find it inserted in a paragraph of an English paper . . . that I had offered to put myself at their head; but I hope it will not be believed that I was capable of so much temerity and vanity. To believe myself qualified for the most important charge that ever was committed to mortal man, is the last stage of presumption. Nor do I think that Americans would, or ought to, confide in a man (let his qualifications be ever so great) who had no property among them . . . my errand to Boston was mere curiosity . . . and I had likewise an ambition of being acquainted with some of their leading men. . . . Our ingenious gentlemen . . . therefore very naturally concluded my design was to put myself at their head.

Did Washington, eminently propertied, entertain such notions for himself? Silent as ever, he went about his new-found duties, methodical and supremely competent, the emerging military expert in a time of rising tension and the focus of all eyes. Then, at the tag end of a workday letter to John Augustine (praising him for raising his own independent company) he let drop this momentous line: "It is my full intention to devote my Life and Fortune in the cause we are engaged in, if need be."

Beleaguered Boston, besieged and besieging, prepared to write new chapters in the military scene. British fortresses, bristling with abatis, stood on Beacon Hill and Boston Neck, almost within shelling distance of the militia drilling in the western suburbs. Beyond the Neck the province was in an ingenious scheme of military government. The Provincial Congress ran committees of supply and safety, secreting stores of arms and powder, drilling militia and an elite corps of minutemen, ready to march out at a moment's notice if Gage

170

took one step beyond the Neck. Proof of their determination occurred on 1 April, when a party of light infantry went four miles into Cambridge, and almost immediately returned—shadowed all the while by silent crowds of armed militia, who dogged their steps until they repassed the Neck. Happily, there were no incidents—owing partly to their peaceable demeanor and partly to the fact that they had gone out without heavy guns. Joseph Warren, the elegant young surgeon who had become president of the Provincial Congress, wrote a grim forecast to a friend. "Had they gone out eight or ten miles . . . not a man of them would have returned."

Two weeks later the truce was shattered for all time. Gage had been receiving warnings of an arsenal at Concord of cannons and powder and on 18 April ordered out 800 crack grenadiers and light infantry with these orders to Major John Pitcairn and Colonel Francis Smith: "You will March . . . with the utmost Expedition and Secrecy to Concord . . . where you will seize and destroy all the Artillery and Ammunition you can find."

To further secrecy they went off by night, ferried after dark across the Charles to wade through the salt marshes of Charlestown and wait an infuriating three hours for supplies. But the movements of troops and boats had roused suspicions, and riders, including the indefatigable and legendary Paul Revere, had gone out before them. Parading wet and miserable through the blackened roads, the troops saw signs of an intense activity, and shortly after 5 A.M. the advance guard under Pitcairn came upon 100 militia facing them across Lexington Common in the graying light of early dawn. There was a swirl of smoke, cloaking everything, from which horses' heads reared grotesquely; a militia man saw a wall smoke with the bullets hitting it and blood puddle near the foot of the rebel station and trickle six or eight feet into the road. "Isaac Muzzy, Jonathan Harrington, and my father, Robert Munroe, died near the place where our line was formed," one militiaman wrote later, "Samuel Hadley and John Brown were killed after they had gotten off the common. . . . Caleb Harrington was shot in attempting to leave the meeting-house, where he and some others had gone." An infuriated Pitcairn reined in his troops and pushed them on

171

the road to Concord, after some delay. Militia, on the hills outside the village, saw them coming as the sun rose behind them, touching the blood red of their scarlet jackets and striking fire from their bayonets. Watched silently by armed minutemen, the British passed into Concord proper, leaving three companies to guard North Bridge against a growing cluster of militia that had formed on a hill opposite and were now looking down at them ominously from the heights. In Concord they discovered no cannon, but several hundredweight of bullets were rolled out and dumped in the millpond. Vast clouds of black smoke billowed skyward as gun carriages were hauled out of the town house and set on fire in the green.

Convinced the town was burning, the militia began to push across the bridge. The British let off a dropping shot that splashed into the Concord River, then were lost in a melee of bullets that cracked into the compacted columns or kicked up the river in fine sprays. Two Americans and four Britons died, almost on the top of one another, dropping their blood onto the wooden planks beneath them or into the river underneath the bridge. The British position had been mangled by an idiotic colonel, and the columns, pressed behind each other, were pushed back from the bridge. The rebels did not follow but fell back along the road to Lexington; the Reverend William Emerson saw a party of 150 cut through a back pasture and line the road, crouch behind walls and fences, and wait with rifle barrels fixed. For some moments there was calm. The British column, massed and visible, had come back half a mile out of Concord when the Americans caught them in a crossfire that swept the line from start to finish and sent the flankers flying back to the main body in a melee of confusion and distress. There was no shelter from the deadly rain. "All the hills on each side of us were covered with rebels," said one survivor later of the dreadful march. "When we arrived within a mile of Lexington our ammunition began to fail . . . a great number of wounded, scarcely able to get forward, made a great confusion . . . so that we began to run, rather than retreat."

At three that morning Colonel Smith had sent a rider

172

back to Boston when the first signs of trouble started to appear. Now, the First Brigade, under Hugh Percy, heir to the Earl of Northumberland, came into Lexington from the east as the column fell into it from the opposite direction, staggering under the rain of fire that had followed it for eight miles past. From a hill looking down upon the village, a lieutenant in the relief column saw a sweeping panorama of the rebels investing all parts of the countryside, scattered in small groups of twos and threes, picking off the highly visible regulars from sequestered perches behind rocks and trees. Reinforced, the column rested, then resumed its march. Again, there was relief for half a mile. Again, the deadly blast began—this time hotter, for hundreds had flocked in from outlying counties, many on horseback, the better to harass the column in its path.

At Menotomy (now Arlington) the fighting reached new depths of desperate barbarity. The rebels raked the streets unmercifully from garrets and upper-story windows as bullets shattered glass about them, and regulars forced and fired the houses, strafing the terrified inhabitants with rifle fire or impaling them on bayonets. Street fighting was intense and violent. Percy saw rebels come within ten yards to fire at him in the very teeth of British guns. Looting was rampant, houses plundered, furniture hacked to pieces, walls and windows wantonly destroyed. It was after seven when the troops staggered back past Charlestown Neck, to collapse exhausted upon Bunker Hill and wait for the transports back—a lengthy process; the last boats did not recross the Charles until twelve at night.

The next day a shaken Percy wrote a somber note to Gage: "Whoever looks upon them as an irregular mob will find themselves much mistaken. . . . You may depend upon it, that as the rebels have now had time to prepare, they are determined to go through with it. Nor will the insurrection turn out so despicable as it is perhaps imagined at home." Among those depending on it was Gage himself, who sent back pickets to guard Charlestown and threw up new batteries and a great ditch at Boston Neck. "It appears that the general is apprehensive the rebels will make some des-

173

perate attempt," wrote an aide, ". . . the numbers which are assembled . . . and their violent and determined spirit, make it prudent to guard against what they may do."

The Americans had not gone home. Stopped at the deathtrap that was Charlestown Neck, they had swung back south and east into the outer suburbs, falling at last into Cambridge Common and the nearby grounds of Harvard Yard. In the next five days the "camp" was swelled by a steady stream of recruits, camping out in two halls of Harvard College and tents spread over Cambridge Common, feeding on donations and hijacked shipments to the troops in Boston, cooking their dinners in the Harvard mess. An improvised cadre of veterans and militia captains, scarcely less disorganized themselves, were shaping them into makeshift regiments, stationed on strategic hill sites overlooking Boston from Prospect Hill near Charlestown to Dorchester to the south and east. On 23 April the Provincial Congress authorized troop enlistments through the end of December, issued orders for the formation of twenty-four regiments, and commissioned officers through the rank of major general, including Henry Knox of Boston, John Sullivan of New Hampshire, Joseph Warren, and that unexpected, if exemplary, soldier, the Quaker blacksmith from Rhode Island, Nathanael Greene. By the end of the month 7,500 soldiers of the New England Army were entrenched in an arc around Boston, and Gage, now besieged, was barricading Boston Neck with ten twenty-four-pound cannon, spiked abatis before the bastions and a triple row of the chains of spikes of iron known as cheveaux-de-frise. The city itself was unutterably chaotic, shut off completely from the outer province, with the inhabitants battening their houses against siege or invasion or huddled miserably beside their portables, waiting for rare and erratically distributed passes out. "Beyond description," said a Tory of the wretched city, and a patriot wrote in his diary: "Boston shut up. No persons allowed to come oute & our army at Roxbury Suffer'd none to go in . . . from these terable times, Good Lord deliver us"

The Second Continental Congress convened on 2 May at Philadelphia, with Boston at the center of all eyes. The

174

Virginians were back with two substantive changes: the continental debut of Thomas Jefferson (who replaced the ailing Peyton Randolph in mid-session) and the appearance of George Washington in his militia uniform, a splash of martial purpose among civilian drab. The silent colonel had a sense of drama all his own.

This time he surfaced in a more impressive guise, being named in quick succession to four committees concerned with military preparation and defense. "Col. Washington," wrote John Adams, "appears at Congress in his Uniform, and by his great Experience and Abilities in military Matters, is of much Service to us." Who but the veteran of seven years of border warfare could call the tune on the pressing issues of deployment and detail? The familiar blend of special portions of a rare experience, allied to the default of others, was drawing him into a vacuum of power by the pressures of necessity and force.

Nothing now could stop the torrent of events. On 16 May Congress learned that forces under the joint command of Ethan Allen and Benedict Arnold had swooped down on Ticonderoga, the British fortress at the foot of Lake Champlain and captured it lock, stock, and cannon in the early morning of 10 May. The dazed commander had been routed out of bed in his nightshirt and then asked to surrender, in the graphic words of Allen, "In the name of the Great Jehovah and the Continental Congress (the authority of the Congress being very little known at the time)." Later the joint command became chaotic; a visitor one month later found the fort a heap of rubbish and the commanders at each other's throats—Arnold and Allen were barely speaking, and Arnold had twice been threatened with a gun. Behind the clash of temperaments was a more dangerous confusion of command—Arnold, a resident of Connecticut, had been commissioned by the Massachusetts congress to strike a fort in New York's territory; Allen, from Vermont, had been commissioned by Connecticut, had a price on his head in New York for his part in a border dispute between that province and New Hampshire, and was in danger of imminent arrest. In all, it seemed to point up to the need for union and the cool touch of the iron hand.

Nor were things peaceful in Boston itself. On 25 May the *Cerebus* entered Boston Harbor with reinforcements for the besieged garrison and a present of a sort for Gage—three more major generals, Sir William Howe, Sir Henry Clinton, and the theatrical part-time playwright ("General Swagger," in Walpole's description) Sir John Burgoyne. This ill-assorted trio was to prove an odd complement to the demoralized Gage (as to one another), but the presence of four generals in a city of 20,000 seemed a grim measure of intent. And on 2 June came an urgent plea from the Provincial Congress to adopt the army around Boston and establish it on a continental scale.

Congress was not yet ready to oblige. John Adams, frantically canvassing the delegations, found an immense suspicion of New England and a scheme to table all talk of armies, pending a second appeal to the king. Hideously wracked, he sat through debates on the petition "full of anxieties . . . and apprehending daily that we should hear very distressing News." His "anxieties" increased at the end of one stormy session when John Dickinson, leader of the conciliatory faction, chased him out into the courtyard and cornered him with an appalling threat: "If you don't concur with Us, in our pacific System, I, and a Number of Us, will break off from you in New England, and We will carry on the Opposition by ourselves."

"I was determined," wrote Adams, "to take a step which should compel them and all the other Members of Congress, to declare themselves for or against something." Shortly thereafter, he revealed what "something" was. On the morning of 15 June, he took a stroll in the courtyard with his cousin Samuel and said, "I am determined this Morning to make a direct Motion that Congress should adopt the Army before Boston and appoint General Washington Commander of it." Seconding his proposal an hour later, Adams saw something from the corner of his eye: "Mr. Washington, who happened to sit near the Door, as soon as he heard me allude to him, from his usual Modesty, darted into the Library Room."

The nomination, when it crossed the water, received a fatalistic and subdued response. "I hear that Congress have

176

named General Washington *generalissimo*," wrote Walpole, who had followed his career from the beginning, noting with approval and some apprehension that he had turned down a proferred salary of £2,000 a year. "If these folks will imitate both the Romans and Cromwellians in self-denial and enthusiasm, we shall be horribly plagued." "Washington himself is a man of good Military experience, prudent, and Cautious, and yet stakes a fortune of about 5000 a year," wrote Burke, with the slight awe of the unlanded. "God knows they are very inferiour in all human resources. But a remote and difficult Country, and such a Spirit as now animates them, may do strange things."

Strange things were already under way. On 17 June, as Congress was taking the steps to clear the appointment of General Washington, Boston suffered the greatest bloodletting ever to happen in the eight years of the war. At dawn Gage and his trio had been awakened by cannonading from the river—the British ships *Lively* and *Somerset* bombarding rows of rebels who had entrenched themselves overnight on Breed's Hill in Charlestown, an eminence within splendid strafing distance of the British posts in Boston and all the water traffic in the bay. At high tide (1 P.M.) 2,000 of Gage's crack troops were rowed across the Charles to regroup in formal lines of battlefield precision at the foot of the hill. Bayonets fixed, they began a slow march to within fifty feet of the redoubts—when the walls erupted in a blast of smoke and fire that ripped the lines from side to side, flinging the men back in the faces of the lines behind them or spinning them sideways to slip into the shallow water of the inland beaches or to drop in bloody parcels on the grass. "A continued sheet of fire for near thirty minutes," said one bloodied officer. "Most of our Grenadiers and Light Infantry . . . lost three-fourths, and many nine-tenths of their men. Some had only eight or nine men a company left; some only three, four and five."

Howe, standing alone for one terrible minute in a field of the fallen, had, as he wrote George III later, "*a moment that I never felt before.*" Twice he sent his forces back to pick their way up the blood-spattered hill. Twice the cannonade resumed. It was five in the evening when the third charge carried, the regulars pouring into the redoubts with bayonets flashing as the Americans, bullets gone, fired nails and scraps of metal and hurled rocks into the sea of blades. "They kept up this fire until we were within ten yards of them," wrote one shaken officer, ". . . knocked down my captain close beside me, after he had got into the ditch." At length the rebels, parrying bayonet thrusts with their muskets, made a dash past Bunker Hill and into Cambridge, via Charlestown Neck, leaving behind a scene of awesome carnage, the bodies hanging over the deserted redoubts or strewn grotesquely on the bloody field.

Joseph Warren lay a few feet from the last redoubt (from which he had been "walking away, slowly"), his forehead pushed out grotesquely by the ball that shattered the back of his skull. The smoldering wreck of Charlestown, blazing horribly where shells from the men-of-war had struck houses from which rebels had been picking off the British soldiers, scattered a fine rain of ashes on the ghastly scene. Into the morning the boats were busy, ferrying the wounded back to makeshift hospitals in Boston, where their moans made a hideous cacophony in the streets. More than 1,040 British had fallen of the 2,200 engaged. "A dear bought victory," said Clinton, as the ghastly salvage work went on. "Another such would have ruined us."

Bunker Hill (as it was called mistakenly) became the byword for the Pyrrhic victory: Gage had won an outpost at the cost of one-fifth his total army and one-half the men engaged. Howe in particular never recovered from the sight of the grenadiers going down around him; he remained gunshy of rebels entrenched behind a barricade for the remainder of the war. "When I look to the consequences of it, I do it with horror," he wrote the king later. "The Success is too dearly bought." Gage had his own words on the matter: "The loss we have sustained is greater than we can bear. . . . I wish this cursed place was burned."

Gone also were the last faint hopes that the impasse could be settled short of war. In London, Burke wrote sadly, "All our prospects of American reconciliation are, I fear, over . . . the sluice is opened—where, when or how it will be stopped, God only knows."

178

At the far end of the sluice stood Washington, very much the unknown quantity, to the world, and largely to himself.

Why Washington? There was nobody else. The other veterans of the last war were old, or dead, or had gone back into the establishment, like Gage. As his critics pointed out, and he acknowledged, he had not fought in fifteen years, he had never won an open-field battle, and he had never handled more than 800 men. In his favor were his demeanor—the reassuring diffidence, the flash of elemental iron, and the air of competence and character that he could maintain under external pressure in all but the fiercest kind of stress. The rest was fortune, which made insurgency respectable, and geography, which changed the struggle from New England's battle to a continental war. "I do not believe that in knowledge or experience he is so far superior" wrote Silas Deane of Washington, "but he removes all jealousies, and that is the main point." That *was* the point. George and the Congress knew it, and if it was a slender point on which to pledge their futures, it was all they had.

Nonetheless, he was catapulted to the peak of chance and danger, as John Adams acknowledged in a letter to Abigail, his wife: "I hope the people of our province will treat the General with all the Confidence and Affection, that Politeness and Respect, which is due to one of the most Important Characters in the World. The Liberties of America, depend upon him, in a great degree."

The "Important Character" took his elevation in a strangely muted way. Friends found him subdued and solemn, awed by the sudden impact of an obligation which, if he did not actively campaign for, he had done nothing consequential to avoid. That he was under no illusions about the real reasons for his elevation is revealed in a letter of 20 June to John Augustine: "The partiality of the Congress, joined to a political motive, really left me without a choice." He ended with this odd, if typical, disclaimer: "I have the consolation of knowing, if I act to the best of judgements, that the blame ought to lodge upon the appointers . . . as it was by no means a thing of my seeking, or proceeding from any hint of my friends." Four days later, his acceptance speech (if one could call it that) hit the same extraordinary note: "Lest some unlucky event should happen unfavourable to my reputation, I beg it may be remembered by every gentleman in the room, that I this day declare with the utmost sincerity, I do not think myself equal to the command."

He was back where he had bowed out fifteen years earlier, at the dead center of world history, this time not in the press of an imperial adventure but at the vortex of upheaval and of awesome and unprecedented change—pulled there by forces he had half made and half resisted, but which had at the finish proved stronger than his own divided will. Perhaps, despite all his talk of green fields and domesticity, it was where he had belonged all the time. In this context, even his retirement fell back into its true perspective: the breathing space between endeavors, the lull between storms. It would all begin again, the strain and the unending torment, this time without the comfort of establishment or of legality. There would be nothing behind him but an improvised and half-formed semination and no one to fall back on but himself—adrift, as he wrote John Augustine, "on a wide ocean, boundless in its prospects, and in which perhaps, no safe harbor is to be found."

PART THREE:

The Archrebel Washington 1775-1783

XI

Trial and Terror

If I were to put the bitterest curse to an enemy this side of the grave, I should put him in my stead with my feelings. . . . I was never in such an unhappy, divided state since I was born.—WASHINGTON to Lund Washington, September, 1776

Washington slipped into Cambridge shortly after noon on 2 July, without ceremony and so quietly that for some hours many of the troops did not know he had arrived at all. First impressions did not augur well. "Dirty and nasty" was the best that he could say of the New England regiments, disordered, slovenly, and painfully indifferent to the necessities of subordination and of rank. Disciplinary measures made him momentarily unpopular—"I expect . . . to render myself very obnoxious to the greater part of these people"—fed a growing sense of isolation, and bred tensions between himself and his men. His own strains surfaced in a spate of letters, by turns anxious, angry, and despairing, to his friends. To Richard Henry Lee, a Virginia neighbor now in Congress, he sent (a bad sign) an anguished letter signaling the return of his prime anxiety—he feared he would be blamed for the result of problems that he could not totally erase. George had so far come in contact only with Virginians and with British regulars in his experiences in the military line. New England came as an unpleasant shock. What was he to make of "these people," whose officers hobnobbed as a matter of course with the common soldiers, and where one captain was even discovered giving shaves and haircuts to his men?

Worst of all, he felt himself alone. Philip Schuyler, a soul mate and the owner of vast tracts of land in New York's Mohawk Valley, might have been a comfort, but he had been shipped north to take command of the lake and border fortresses, incommunicado save for letters in which the generals shared troubles and exchanged their woes. His two immediate subordinates—wished upon him by the will of Congress—were with him in Cambridge, but there was small comfort there. Gates, pale and pudgy, with a woolen cap pulled over his ears beneath his tricorn, was alternately sly and ingratiating, with conscious camaraderie to the common soldiers that contrasted in too politic a fashion with the air of distance George felt obligated to inculcate in camp. Nor was Charles Lee appealing, thin to the point of emaciation, with a stream of wit and malice in his conversation and a spattering of soup stains on his shirt. "An odd genius," wrote the historian Jeremy Belknap, "full of fire and passion . . . a great sloven, wretchedly profane, and a great admirer of dogs." Belknap accepted Lee's invitation to dinner one evening at his house in Cambridge and was astounded to find himself seated between two hounds at table, "one of them a native of Pomerania, which I should have taken for a bear had I seen him in the woods."

George wrote later that he had detested Gates from the beginning, and Lee's eccentricities must have raised some tremors of alarm. Wary and isolated, he kept them at arm's length, drawing closer to Knox and Greene among the younger officers and to his adjutant general, Joseph Reed. Still missing were many of the great names to develop in the course of the revolution and to become his solace and support—William Alexander ("Lord" Stirling, from a disputed Scottish title), florid, brave and bibulous, to join him in New York in 1776, and Anthony Wayne (to join him in Pennsylvania in 1777) a beguiling firebrand of dash and spirit whose exploits were to give him great delight. Missing, too, were the "boys" to become his aides and part of his extended family

184

and fill some vital void within his soul—John Laurens, son of the president of the council of South Carolina (later president of the Continental Congress), gentle, brave and greatly gifted, and the young man with pale skin, flaming hair, and a small head bobbing oddly on his long, thin body, Marie Joseph Paul Yves Roch Gilbert de Motier, Marquis de Lafayette, who had left his vast estates in France, stolen aboard a ship to South Carolina, and appeared, aflame and bedraggled at camp outside Philadelphia, in August, 1777. And, the odd third leg to this high-toned trio, Alexander Hamilton, a small and slender émigré from the West Indies, a student of law and military tactics, with pink cheeks and eyes so deeply blue that they were almost violet and an expression alternately fierce and vulnerable on his face. Now drilling his company of artillery in the Battery in New York City, he was to trade his cannon for a quill pen in the beginning of 1777, becoming George's secretary, voice, and sympathizer in his fight for order and cohesion and his premier aide-de-camp.

Laurens and Lafayette were the real thing, born into positions of security and power the younger Washington had looked up to with longing and in his own eyes never totally achieved. Hamilton, however, an "alien" and by his own confession an "exotic," had a deprived and deeply troubled background that cast long shadows on his future life. Born in Nevis in 1755, the child of a common-law union between the ne'er-do-well son of a solid Scots family and the daughter of a French émigré who had left her husband in scandalous circumstances, he had been reared in poverty and deserted by his father before he reached the age of ten. At thirteen he was forced to stand in court at at the probation of the meager estate of his dead mother to hear himself and his brother described as her obscene children and put to work the same year as a clerk in a shipping company before being sent—a precocious youngster and a collector of patrons—to school in America on funds raised by neighbors in 1773. He never spoke of what those years had done to him, but the effect was doubtless present, adding a grim strain to a buoyant temperament, honing an already-fierce ambition and infusing added tensions into a character already dangerously high-strung. In 1769, a wretchedly unhappy assistant in a shipping office, he had written an astounding letter to a friend in America, baring his soul with appalling candor: ". . . to confess my weakness . . . my Ambition is so prevalent that I contemn the groveling condition of a Clerk . . . to which my Fortune &c. condemns me, and would willingly risk my life tho' not my Character to exalt my Station," ending in that endemic cry of the romantic climber "I wish there was a War." Most of George's wartime intimates reflected some part of his own character—Schuyler the impatience, Wayne the fire, Greene the calculation and control. What nerve did this touch in Washington, the onetime climber, who had sought out patrons, found the sound of bullets "charming," and scaled the social ladder step by step? His accord with Hamilton, always close and often troubled, was to be among the most momentous of his life.

Nothing could have been more trying than the situation into which he had been sealed—an endless stalemate vis-à-vis the British, they unable to move beyond the gates of Boston, he without the means to push them out. Through the summer, fall, and winter he was held fast in forced inaction as campaigns up and down the continent brought cascades of disturbing news. An American invasion of Canada ended in disaster in the narrow streets of Quebec City in the early morning of the first day of the new year, leaving the American dead piled in the snowbanks of the walled city and the survivors to straggle south, tormented by hunger and disease (mass graves marking each stop on their journey) until they staggered into Ticonderoga in July. Concurrent with the start of this dismal venture, British regiments sailed from Cork in Ireland to begin a massive siege of Charleston, queen city of the South. By the start of the year they had been joined by Sir Henry Clinton and a fleet of warships; George was forced to send Charles Lee down in February to direct the American defense. Neither escapade was likely to encourage Washington, who was beginning to sense the dimensions of his bind. Beyond the strains inherent in his staff and army, he was starting to nurture grave doubts of the defects of order within the confederation and the implications of its slapdash rule. There was one week in September when

186

his supply of powder dwindled to thirty barrels (or barely enough for five shots per man), the calculations of his ammunition having failed to take into consideration the depreciations made at Bunker Hill. A frantic secret search of the neighborhood brought his stores up to the bare minimum but tied new tangles in his nerves. "No man perhaps since the first institution of armies ever commanded one under more difficult circumstances than I have done," he burst out in anguish to John Augustine. "Many of my difficulties and distresses were of so peculiar a cast, that in order to conceal them from the enemy, I was obliged to conceal them from my friends."

Worse still were his problems with his troops. Enlistments made in April ran barely through the start of winter; the Connecticut troops went off in mid-December, with the others preparing to depart on the new year. "I tremble at the prospect," George wrote to Joseph Reed. "Our lines will be so weakened, that the minute-men and militia must be called up for their defense." A quickly assembled parade of green militia marched on the barricades through two months of hysterical recruiting, until February, 1776, when by grace of pleading, threats and bribery, the lines again were filled. From Cambridge to Virginia and Philadelphia went the usual spate of anguished cries—what was he to do without arms or men or power, and what would people think? "Which is mortifying. . . . I cannot stand justified to the world, without exposing my own weakness, and injuring the cause . . . which I am determined not to do." The tormented note of his correspondence reveals a rising note of fear. Cash, cohesion, discipline—all were missing from the union. He would have to bind the army by himself.

Britain, meanwhile, had prepared for total war. George III had been direct and brutal: "Every means of distressing America must meet with my concurrence, as it tends to bringing them to feel the necessity of returning to their duty," he wrote North on 15 October, eleven days before the crucial fall session of Parliament began. Although efforts to buy troops from Catherine of Russia had fallen through, he had managed to hire no less than 7,000 recruits from the

German principalities, mainly Brunswick and Hesse-Cassel. More to the point was the cashiering in November of the unhappy Dartmouth for the violent and bellicose Sir George Germain—an old soldier given to fierce tirades upon the floor of Parliament and intricate designs in the Colonial Office for master stratagems to beat the rebels to their knees. Already, his plans were taking form and shape: an immense force—German mercenaries, Scots Highlanders, and Royal Guards—was to sail in a fleet of transports under Admiral Richard Howe (William's brother) in the spring. The prevailing mood was summed up neatly in this "savage sentence" of Lord North: "If we suffer . . . we shall at least have the satisfaction of making the Americans suffer more."

Ingenuity must atone for governmental slackness and the appalling scarcity of arms. Late in winter came the fruits of a secret coup. Henry Knox returned from a 400-mile circuit in Ticonderoga bringing sixty cannon, dismantled, and pulled on sledges over an icy wilderness of steep mountains, deep ravines, and four crossings of the Hudson, frozen with a six-inch glaze of ice. On 1 March Howe woke to a huge array of guns and barricades, circling Boston in a giant arc from above Charlestown on the northeast angle to a point just over Boston Neck. At nine the cannon began a racketing barrage, splintering houses and sending soldiers and the dazed inhabitants spilling out into the streets in a shower of falling timbers and flying glass. One British soldier saw several houses collapse under the cannonade, then watched in horror as a cannonball tore through the 22d Regiment, killing eight soldiers who had dashed into the street. British guns on Beacon Hill began an answer, in an earsplitting exchange of fire that appeared by daylight as a rain of huge black bullets and as a storm of meteors at night. "Sheets of fire seemed to come from our batteries," wrote a British colonel, "some of the shells crossed one another in the air, and then bursting, looked beautiful. . . ."

On 5 March, after a night of exceptionally ferocious bombardment, the British found another terrible surprise: two huge batteries had appeared "like majick," aiming down into Boston on the southern angle from the steep slopes of Dorchester Heights. Poised on the barricades were twenty cannon and a weapon of a novel sort—barrels filled with earth and stones, ready to roll downhill into the face of an advancing enemy, breaking columns altogether, and piling them in a heap of mangled bodies at the base—displaying, in the words of Howe's aide, Charles Stedman, "that fertility of genius in expedients, which strongly characterized the Americans during the war." British cannon, from Boston Neck and the shipping in the harbor, opened a tremendous fire, in what everyone expected was the prelude to a grand attack. "During the forenoon, we were in momentary expectation of witnessing an awful scene," wrote one American, "nothing less than the carnage of Breed's Hill."

Washington had hopes of a climactic showdown, and Howe seemed ready to oblige. Small boats loaded down with arms and men had begun to cross the river to the mainland when a sudden storm of intense violence blew up sheets of wind and water, overturning some ships in midchannel and driving others back in wreckage on the shore. The next day, when Howe recovered, the American lines had become an iron ring. On 8 March a messenger approached the lines at Cambridge, carrying a flag of truce.

Howe's conditions were simplicity itself: the safety of Boston in return for his safe passage out. Washington, infuriated at the loss of Howe's army, could do nothing but agree. Howe embarked in haste and tumult, troops and Tories (terrified and alerted at less than six hours' notice) jammed in transports helter-skelter, and two hospital ships filled with the sick and wounded "and the utmost horror and confusion amongst them all." On 17 March the last of the ships sailed out past Castle William, minutes before American forces ran over Charlestown Neck and into the forts on Bunker Hill, arms waving wildly, and another corps of 500 tumbled down from the heights near Roxbury and broke open the gates at Boston Neck. Washington himself entered hours later, riding silent through the debris and clutter, all disheartening and much of it obscene. Burgoyne had turned the South Meeting House into a riding academy and quartered horses in the pews. Cannon, shot, and shell were scattered everywhere; shattered carts and wagons, smashed against the docksides, had been washed up on every shore.

Boston had ceased to be his problem. That same day he had sent General William Heath with five regiments of foot and two companies of artillery to follow the rifle battalions already marching for New York. Upwards of 5,000 soldiers from the New York and New Jersey companies had been there since January, frantically entrenching along the miles of exposed coastline. Charles Lee had supervised them briefly before leaving for Charlestown in March.

New York, the seabound strategic center of the colonies, seated at the foot and entrance to the Hudson, control of which could sever New England from the southern provinces and split the colonies in two, was the logical destination of the British navy, the new troops from Britain and Hesse-Cassel, and the troops from Boston that Howe would bring back from Nova Scotia in the spring. "The object worthy their attention," George himself had written, ". . . the place that we must use every endeavour to keep them from." At this stage (as will appear later) he had considerable doubt about his capacity to much more than delay the inevitable when his unseasoned army met Lord Howe's navy and the hammer thrust of European troops. Numbers and topography, which had been his friends in Boston, would now become his enemies and make his defects—supply and discipline—more damaging than they had shown themselves before. In this context his Boston "victory" appeared chimerical and his new crop of honors—a gold medal from Congress and an LLD from Harvard College—the tantalizing symbols of a reputation that might plummet to the depths. On 4 April he joined his troops in the long, extended trek across Connecticut for an encounter he had every cause to dread.

One look confirmed his fears. New York lay between the East and Hudson rivers, a long, extended arm of steep rock faces and deep woods, with the tiny city clustered at the southern end in a jumble of parks, mansions, steep-roofed Dutch houses and atrocious slums, open on all sides to naval power, with coves and inlets vulnerable to attack. At the

190

north there was a pass at Kingsbridge, where ships could trap a captive army; on the east lay the high crest of Brooklyn Heights, where cannon could bombard lower Manhattan, turning the terrain of hills and pastures to a bloody marsh. Reinforcements were there from New York and New Jersey, but they were small encouragement, being diverse, undisciplined, and painfully untried. "I don't like your situation," Robert Morris wrote to Joseph Reed. "You had better give up that city to the enemy, than let them get behind you, and pen you up . . . as they were cooped in Boston last year." Washington, for his part, was at least half wary of his plight. He complained later that he had been forced into it by Congress, which had begun entrenchments early and against his will. This was half true. He had sent Lee to start them four months previously, and he had been shy of fighting Congress when the crunch came between his military judgment and its will. What was wholly true was his distress at being forced into untenable positions and his resentment of armchair generals, with their propensity for wishes over truth. Political illusion and military fact were to clash in the island city and nearly bring the dissolution of the cause.

Manfully, he did his best. Six weeks' work with pick and shovel produced a spate of makeshift wood and mud entrenchments—mud forts on the small harbor islands; five forts overlooking the East River on Brooklyn Heights; on Manhattan, barricades along the convoluted coastline (with small redoubts on every street leading to the rivers), capped by a great stone fortress at the Battery, a monumental work of rocks and fretwork which the soldiers were energetically topping off with turf. Sadly, these sand castles did little to relieve American malaise. "Our whole force," Washington wrote sadly to Congress on 28 June, "is but small and inconsiderable when compared to the extensive lines they are to defend, and most probably, the Army he brings. . . ."

The "Army" arrived with a vengeance on 1 July, three tense days after this apprehensive note. A private from Connecticut, in an outhouse on a hill high above the harbor, had the first view of Howe's armada when he peered out a window and saw the masts fill the river, "something resembling a wood of pine trees trimmed. . . . In about ten minutes the whole bay was full of shipping. . . . I declare, that I thought all London was afloat." Manning their mud forts with their mismatched muskets, the Americans watched in horror as the ships spilled their cargo into Staten Island in a dazzling and ominous parade: grenadiers; kilted Highlanders; and, in their unfamiliar white and gold-braid uniforms, the German troops from Hesse-Cassel. Nor was this the end. "We have Ships now popping in, which we suppose . . . to be part of the expected reinforcement," Washington wrote his brother days later. "When this arrives . . . the Enemy's number will amount to at least 25,000 Men; ours to about 15,000. . . . If they will stand by me, the place will not be carried without some loss, notwithstanding we are not yet in such posture of defense as I could wish. . . ."

His plight was made more desperate by a piece of awesome news. America and the mother country had come to the parting of the ways. An express from Philadelphia brought the report that independence had been declared by Congress on 2 July. In New York the army responded with cannonades, fireworks, and riots, including the demonstration in which a statue of George III on horseback was hauled from its moorings by a crowd armed with ropes and crowbars and melted into bullets with which to pelt his troops. Washington for his part was restrained and practical: "I have never entertained an idea of an accommodation, since I heard of the measures which were adopted in consequence of the Bunker Hill fight." The reaction was characteristically pragmatic: facts produced their own reality; proclamations altered nothing and were useful only to influence morale. James Thacher, a physician with the army, had another point of view: "When we reflect on the deranged state of our army, the great deficiency of our resources . . . and at the same time contemplate the prodigious resources of our enemy, we may view this measure of Congress as a prodigy." He also told a story that had come from Philadelphia concerning two signers, the rotund Benjamin Harrison of Virginia and Elbridge Gerry of Massachusetts, a wizened creature half his size: "Mr. Harrison said smilingly to Mr. Gerry, 'When the hanging scene comes to be exhibited, I shall have the advantage over you. . . . All will be over with me in a minute, but you will be kicking in the air half an hour after I am gone.' "

For Washington, independence was followed by a diplomatic minuet. Was he the first general of an emerging nation or, as British propaganda had it, "the arch-rebel Washington," outlaw leader of a guerrilla band? The Howes, Whigs in Parliament, had come with pre-independence powers to make terms. Their first approach—a letter from Lord Howe to "Mr. Washington"—was formally refused. "Sir," said Joseph Reed to the aide who delivered the offending message, "we have no person in our Army with that address." Another note, addressed now to "George Washington, Esq., &c. &c. &c." met the same response, Henry Knox recording the exchange between Howe's emissary and George. To the aide's insistence that &c. "implied everything," George's answer was succinct: "It does so," said the general, "and any thing."

The terms were likewise quietly refused. To the Howes' assurance that they would pardon the Americans, George replied that he knew of nothing the Americans were guilty of. With that, efforts at rapprochement ceased. "General" Washington had his paper nation—for as long as he could keep it whole.

Cautious as ever, the Howes waited into August as the slow accumulation of men and sail built up. Nothing was to be wanted for the hammerblow that was to crush the insurrection once for all. Through the month the harbor filled with transports—on 16 August Clinton arrived from Charleston, "as unexpected," wrote Reed in horror, "as if he had dropped from the clouds." On 22 August came the dreaded move—the massive shipment of men and cannon across the Narrows, then a swift advance through the flat plains of Brooklyn, driving back the American pickets in a trail of gutted farms and burning wheatfields, finally facing Sullivan and Stirling, posted between Flatbush and the forts along the heights across a slope, steep and all but perpendicular, traversed by three guarded pathways, cut with ravines and thick with undergrowth and knotted, gnarled trees. Washington was in an agony of apprehension, torn be-

193

tween fears of forfeiting Long Island and leaving Manhattan open to a sudden strike. Anxious letters to Congress from his headquarters in Manhattan explained the temper of his bind: he would send reinforcements to Brooklyn as he judged expedient, but he would not send the whole of his detachments (barely enough to give even a show of minimal resistance) while the possibility existed of a feint.

Still torn, he returned to Brooklyn in midmorning on 26 August and found a scene of rage and dread. Howe had made a roundabout through the Jamaica Pass (an unguarded cow path ten miles northeast of the encampment) and fallen upon Sullivan, raking his troops with rounds of cannon fire, then hounding them into the swamps and marshes, piling the bodies in heaps amid the putrid waters or pinioning them to trees with bayonets. "Dispatched the rebels . . . after we had surrounded them," wrote one British officer, leaving the fields "so noisome with the Stench of the dead Bodies" that they remained inaccessible for weeks to come.

Howe swept on to Stirling, engaged since four that morning in an artillery duel with a party of Scots Highlanders that had materialized on his right flank. Stirling had just gotten off a brisk cannonade when he heard firing above him and "found that General Howe with the main body of the army was between me and our lines." The Maryland and Delaware lines (the crack troops of the army) clung to a hillside, fighting off four times their number, while the other troops forded their way through British pickets to a marsh dividing their post from the heights encampment, plunged into and then swam a narrow river under a rain of British fire from above. Others were less fortunate. Soldiers in the right wing panicked, tried to fight their way through a wall of British soldiers, and were hacked to pieces in the woods. Both Stirling and Sullivan were prisoners, the former cornered in an orchard after four hours of valiant fighting, the latter taken in a cornfield, last seen by an awed subordinate heading into a double row of enemy soldiers, a pistol in each hand. Washington, on the parapet, was an anguished spectator to the panorama of destruction. All was over by late afternoon.

The wretched aftermath was worse. The soldiers huddled in their open trenches, drenched by a torrential rainfall, fatigued by unending watches, sleepless, dispirited, and ill. Nor were their flimsy barricades secure. The uncompleted redoubts were topped with brush, "affording no strong cover," said Washington grimly, "so that there was reason to believe they might be forced." Skirmishing continued through the downpour for the next two days. "The fire was very hot," wrote Colonel Moses Little, commander of the largest of the five beleaguered forts. "The enemy gave way, & our people recovered the gound. The firing ceased, and our people retired to the fort." Outside, Howe's troops were lining up in siege formation; on the twenty-eighth they broke ground barely 600 yards from one of the redoubts on the left. In a center fort, John Morin Scott peered out through a wall of water and saw a British cannon, on a hillock facing down into the middle of the lines. Behind them Admiral Howe's warships stood at the mouth of the East River, waiting for the wind to change. It was the classic siege position—artillery edging up to the trenches in the foreground while naval power cut off escape by sea. Thanks to a stiff northeast wind, blowing sheets of rain into the sails of Howe's armada, the second arm had not slipped into place. For Washington, the north wind was the breath of life.

Somehow, he held off panic through two days and nights. On the evening of the twenty-eighth, there was a secret meeting of the officers whose decision was unanimous and whose motion was kept a secret from the troops. At ten on the night of 29 August he began to draw his men off in acute precision from their places in the lines—a silent move of men in shadows, each line slipping into the place vacated by the one before, keeping up a false front to the watching British of a solid and undisturbed defense. At the ferry, the troops found a vast array of small craft—summoned in haste the day previous—lined up on the shore. All night the boats kept up their silent and incessant relays, bringing boatload after boatload to safety on Manhattan, as George kept his watch between the beach and trenches and the lines behind the row of soldiers thinned. About three there was a ghastly moment: a regiment had gone off early under mistaken orders, leaving a gaping hole in the front lines. George's reaction was short and violent: "Good God! . . . I am afraid you have ruined us." There was a brief flurry, and the regiment came back into the lines.

A few of the last troops were still in the trenches as a perilous light began to leak in from the east. Then a fog began to drift in from the river, covering both camps in a blanket that the rising sun turned only into a brighter and more incandescent haze. It began to lift, giving scant visibility, just as Washington stepped into the last boat to leave the shore. Two hours later the British swarmed into the empty trenches as Howe's ships, the wind having altered, sailed up the river's narrow sleeve. The arms had closed around an empty shell.

On the other shore the troops fell into Manhattan island, drenched, demoralized, and tired to the bone. "Extreme fatigue," George wrote John Hancock, "rendered me entirely unfit to take a pen in hand. Since Monday, we have scarce any of us been out of the lines . . . and for the 48 hours preceeding that, I had scarcely been off my horse, and had never closed my eyes." Kudos for his recovery were swallowed in a wave of bitterness and shock. "The retreat as a retreat must really be acknowledged a fine one," complained one New Yorker. "But why we were fortifying & preparing so long—with intention no doubt to keep it, and so suddenly be obliged nevertheless to evacuate it, is the rub." Other letters gave alarming symptoms of unraveling morale. ". . . vastly dispirited," wrote one soldier to a friend in Congress, "publickly say, but I believe without Reason, that they are sold . . . the Army is continually praying most ardently for the arrival of General Lee as their Guardian Angel. He is daily expected; his arrival will probably nerve their Spirits. . . . God knows what will be the event of this Campaign."

Unnerved, Washington struck back. "Every measure on our part is to be formed with some Apprehension that all our Troops will not do their duty," he wrote Hancock. "I confess, I have not found that readiness to defend even strong Posts." The city, he knew, was now untenable, and he was being forced into the position of risking a ruinous battle or staging a humiliating retreat. He was besieged by conflicting advice to hold, evacuate, or burn the city, and his confidence, never strong, began to crack. At last, after a three-week agony, he gave in to the "Wisdom of cooler moments and experienced Men" and began a pullback to the Heights of Harlem, a vast rock ridge that traversed Manhattan island east to west about three-quarters up the length of the island (or twenty miles from the city), a sheer drop of ninety feet above the plain below. It was the only thing to do, but the move tormented him, and his letters to Congress revealed the strain between "sense" on the one hand, and on the other, his growing concern for his slipping reputation and his aggressive will to fight. "Declining an engagement subjects a General to reproach," he wrote, ". . . but when the fate of America may be at stake . . . I cannot think it safe or wise."

His procrastination had already done its work. Sunday evening (16 September) was his date appointed to have the men and baggage safely transported to the heights. Sunday morning, he awoke to an immense barrage of cannon fire: warships blasting their way up both rivers, bombarded futilely from onshore batteries and the East River solid, shore to shore, with boats. Five thousand men (one-third of his army) were still at the Battery, with several hundred more strung out in the tiny forts along the shore. Panic reigned as they fought their way northward, through dense ground thick with underbrush and Indian paths choked with trees and tangled shrubs. Isolated incidents gave witness to their terror and distress. Henry Knox flung himself and two brigades into a mud fort without supplies or ammunition and determined to stay there or perish; he and his men were routed out (and led to safety) when Aaron Burr, then a young captain in the New York artillery, roared out his ultimatum: "If they remained, one half of them would be killed or wounded, and the other half hung, like dogs before night."

To the east, a terrified band of Connecticut militia fleeing a British landing at Kip's Bay, ran into and past an infuriated Washington, dodging the blows he dealt them with his riding crop. They vanished, leaving the dazed general standing alone within an hundred yards of the enemy, "so vexed at the infamous conduct of his troops," wrote Greene later, "that he sought death rather than life."

No lives were lost in the mad dash northward, but it had

197

been a close-run thing. At one point a troop of royal guardsmen had cut across a cow path (at modern Ninety-sixth Street) minutes after several hundred Americans had passed. That night Washington stationed three layers of his crack regiments between his camp and the enemy, to guard against a night attack. The wretched Greene, spending a sleepless night with his battalion in the buffer zone, was doubtless right in his insistence that a day's grace would have resulted in an orderly retreat. But the three weeks gone before had been Washington's responsibility, and the blame recoiled on his head.

Washington was safe for the moment behind his rock barricade, but beset more than ever with misgivings about his judgment and matériel. Not even the burning of New York on 18 September or a brisk rally the day previous in which Continentals beat off an advance guard of the British army could give more than a brief lift to his morale. The complaints that followed the retreat from Long Island appeared again: charges that he had given up too easily vied with objections that he had held on too long through pride. Part of the problem was his own devising—the false estimates of men and supplies that he had given out to mislead the British had caused Congress and his critics to expect more from him than a series of incessant and inglorious retreats. Political reasons prevented him from countering these charges in anything but private letters, and his bind began to eat into his nerves. He was gnawed at also by external problems. The makeshift army tended to fragment under pressure, desertions were frequent, and the inexperience of the officers showed badly in their inability to maintain morale or discipline in periods of inaction or fatigue. In the inactive month that followed, Washington sent a series of detailed letters to Congress, urging the correction of fundamental errors in the structure of the war. There must be a Continental Army, with equal payment and equal rules of discipline, rigidly enforced. Sufficient pay must be allotted to attract and train a corps of officers equipped for leadership; they were the backbone of the army, without which the rest was lost. More effective methods must be found to secure an adequate supply of equipment and of arms. Above all, the system of one-year enlistments must be scuttled; the present system consumed time and money and forced him to release men as soon as they had learned to function under fire, leaving him with a perennial crop of rookies with which to face the British guards. His pleas were restrained, but his anxiety showed in the repetition and the detailed insistence with which his case was made. He received no answers, and no change was made.

On 12 October the process of retreat resumed. Howe pushed naval passage through the northern end of Manhattan, forcing a dash into the mainland and a retreat through Westchester marked by intermittent skirmishes with the pursuing British, leaving trails of bloody hills and gutted farms. On 24 October they burned White Plains and got off behind a cloud of smoke to North Castle, embedded in the hills. Tiring of the pursuit, Howe headed south, leaving George the choice of following him to New Jersey or letting the middle states and Philadelphia fall without a blow. Washington's force was now down to 7,000, and he would have to leave a corps at Peekskill to guard the approaches to the upper Hudson, which the British might use to split rebel states in two. He could also look forward to 1 January, when the enlistment of his army would expire, and he could not delude himself that his record since April offered much inducement to enlist. As he contemplated his options, he slipped into a new morass of despair.

He was by now fighting a two-pronged struggle, for control over his wayward army and, more desperately, over himself. The debacles of the summer had been devastating to his fragile sense of esteem and security; whatever defenses he had built up in Boston were crumbling under the impress of events. He was capable of violent tirades against his soldiers: "a parcel of ------ . . . but it is best to say nothing more about them," he burst out to John Augustine, and there were doubtless other things he did not trust himself to write. Greene and others never forgot the sight of Washington flaying his troops with pistols on the day of the retreat up Manhattan island in a transport of mindless fury or the after-

199

math, when he stared, drained, into the faces of the advancing British, all but courting capture, in the tremors of complete exhaustion or the submerged desire to end his conflicts in the finality of absolute defeat. The scene was frightening—both in the glimpse it gave of the rage that lay beneath the stoic surface that he showed to all but intimates and as an indication of how thin the line of his control had worn.

He never again lost his grip in quite that manner, but his private letters showed a plunge into despair. The dominant note was a sense of intense pressure from his nerves, the things expected of him, and his frustration at the hands of his matériel. He compained that he was being blamed for failings that he could neither correct nor properly explain. He wrote his brother Samuel:

> Matters in this Quarter have by no means worn that favorable aspect you have been taught to believe . . . the Pompous Acct. of the Marches, and Counter Marches, of the Militia, tho' true in so far as relates to the Expense, is false in regard to the Service, for you could not get them to stay in Camp, or Fight when they were there . . . at no time since General Howe's arrival . . . has my force been equal to his; and yet people at a distance . . . have conceived that they were scarcely a mouthful for us.

His nerves were ravaged by the pull between his instincts and the curbs that he was forced to put upon them. The anguish showed in a dreadful letter to his cousin Lund:

> If I were to put the bitterest curse to an enemy this side of the grave, I should put him in my stead with my feelings; yet I do not know what plan of conduct to pursue. I see the impossibility of serving with reputation . . . and yet I am told that if I quit the service inevitable ruin will follow from the distraction that will ensue. In confidence, I tell you that I was never in such an unhappy, divided state since I was born . . . to lose all comfort and happiness on the one hand, whilst being persuaded that under such a system of management as has been adopted, I cannot have the least chance for reputation nor those allowances made which the nature of the case requires; and to be told, on the other, that if I leave the ser-

vice, all will be lost, is at the same time that I am bereft of every peaceful moment, distressing to a degree.

He ended with a plea that was pathetically in character: "If I fail, it may not be amiss that these circumstances be known, and declaration made in credit to the justice of my character."

"Divided" is the key word to this dilemma, for he was divided to the core—riven between nerve and caution, wish and substance, duty and the desire to break free. By late September the pressures on him had become so terrible that he talked openly of a desire to resign. ("I am told . . . that if I quit . . . inevitable ruin will follow from the distraction that will ensue.") Whom he spoke to (and who "told" him) is not mentioned, but it is likely it was Reed or Greene. He told Reed at one point that he wished he had enlisted as a common soldier or had gone to live in a wigwam in the west. The words suggest a need for release that is almost frightening to sense. In later years he would compare his service as the tenure of a "slave," implying not only work but enforced toil, a lack of choice or scope for action, and stifling and unendurable constraint. His words would suggest the cramp he put on his own instincts and how wretchedly he felt himself confined—by the defects of management in the army and in Congress and by the scanty nature and erratic conduct of his troops.

Meanwhile, his conflicts showed themselves in a paralysis of will. Pulled between expectations and realities, lacking in confidence, he tended to defer to others and to prolong decisions until they created real and present dangers for his troops. Perhaps his lack of military background was at least partially responsible. He was barely into his second year as general, and battlefield decisions that might have later appeared commonplace seemed to him singular and strange. But they did have the power to immobilize him in difficult situations, and this, not his rages, was the most dangerous result of his despair.

Indecision was to torture him again. Forts Lee and Washington guarded the approaches to the lower Hudson like two stone portals, the latter on the northwest shore of Manhattan island, the former facing it from the Palisades. Each was stocked with arms and cannon and held upwards of 2,000 men. He knew they were untenable; but the directions of Congress were ambiguous, and Greene insisted that they could be held. As usual, he delayed too long. On the morning of 16 November he and Greene, with two other officers, rowed over from the Jersey shore for yet another consultation on what should be done. Emerging on the shore, they got the first sight of British and Hessian forces converging on the fortress from the rear. Returning to the boat, they moored a short distance out into the water, where, half an hour later, they were anguished witnesses to the reduction of the fort. Greene was in torment. "I am mad, vexed, sick and sorry," he wrote, ". . . a most terrible event, its consequences are to be justly dreaded. Pray, what is said?"

What was "said" was unflattering and soon trebled in volume and in force. Two days later Howe's troops crossed the Hudson, scaled the Palisades, and took Fort Lee in twenty minutes, with yet another cache of arms and soldiers, the former to bombard the rebels, the later to languish miserably in prison ships, floating sewers anchored off New York Harbor, hideous dens of malnutrition and disease. The losses were disastrous in terms both tactical and human and, save for the debacle on Long Island, the most crippling blows yet of the war. They appeared to cap a siege of error and futility, and the source this time was clear.

George made anguished efforts to explain away the loss. "This Post . . . was held contrary to my wishes," he wrote John Augustine, "but being determined on by a full Council of General Officers, and having a resolution of Congress strongly expressive of their desires . . . I did not care to give an absolute order of withdrawing . . . till I could get round and see. . . ." Reed afterward said that he had never seen Washington as tortured or irresolute as then. Two years later, in a letter to Reed on unrelated matters, Washington suddenly digressed into an impromptu discussion of Fort Washington that revealed his scars as both immediate and deep:

I found General Greene . . . decidedly opposed to it; and when I found other opinions coincident with his, when the wishes of Congress . . . which were delivered in such forcible terms to me recurred . . . when I consid-ered that our policy led us to waste the campaign . . . caused that warfare in my mind, and hesitation, which ended in the loss of that garrison, and . . . filled me with the greater regret.

He ended on a note that was the key to everything and reflected his feelings about the events of the entire year: "Why I have run into such a lengthy discussion of this point, at this time, I am at a loss myself to tell. I meant to touch it *en passant*, but one idea succeeded another, till it would seem that I had been preparing my defense for a regular charge."

One way alone remained to redeem the season and rescue what remained of his prestige: to beat the British into New Jersey and get between Philadelphia and the advancing troops. This action turned into another rout. Harried relentlessly by Cornwallis and his *"magic lights,"* the Americans were all but driven through the Jerseys, evacuating post after post in haste and duress, leaving a string of British cantonments behind. At Brunswick they were nearly captured by the British advance guard; at Newark their rear guard left the city just as the first of the British troops entered from the other end. With failure came the expected breakdown in morale. "The British troops have gone into the Jersies only to receive the submission of the entire country," wrote one wretched soldier. "People join them almost in captain's companies to take the oath." No one was joining Washington's army, which had melted to 3,500 men in late November and was shrinking from desertions every day. The weather turned wretched, deluging the army in freezing hail, sinking spirits, and delaying transportation as wheels and wagons sank in seas of mud. On 8 December, George crossed the Delaware into Pennsylvania, bringing with him all the boats that he could manage and hacking the rest to pieces, leaving a splintered debris to confront Cornwallis on the Jersey shore. "We have prevented them from crossing," George wrote Lund Washington, "but how long we shall be able to do it, God only knows. . . . If everything else fails, will wait till the 1st of January, when there will be no other men to oppose them but Militia . . . your imagination can scarce extend to a situation more distressing than mine." Congress, anticipating failure, had fled to Annapolis on 17 December. Cornwallis remained for the moment on the far bank of the Delaware, waiting for the ice to form. "I see nothing to oppose him in a fortnight hence," George wrote John Augustine on 15 December, "as the Time of all the Troops . . . will expire in less than that time . . . *if every nerve is not strained to recruit the new Army . . . I think the game is pretty near up.*"

Into this grim picture came another form of danger, the product of his troubles since the beginning of the summer and of his torrential downhill slide. Charles Lee, the eccentric "genius," had just returned from a successful defense of Charleston, where southern troops had survived assault from British warships in a fierce ten-hour bombardment of 28 June. In absentia, Lee had become the custodian of the lost hopes of the army, the "Guardian Angel," whose presence would heal all. Benjamin Rush was among the men in Congress who had sent Lee ecstatic letters, contrasting his accomplishments with Washington's New York misfortunes, and the ensuing litany of loss. What else for the Guardian Angel than to try to spread his wings? Washington, miserably fighting his way through the Jerseys, found himself besieged on the internal quarter by rumblings of disaffection and intrigue.

His first inkling of trouble came in mid-November, when he had sent a series of repeated pleas to Lee—stationed with William Heath at Peekskill in the Hudson Valley—to bring his troops south to Washington's relief. Lee resisted, tried then to take *Heath's* troops, and departed at last (after insistent orders) with his own detachments, leaving Heath in due possession of his Hudson garrison and the conviction, delicately conveyed to Washington, that Lee was either traitorous or mad. On the road at last, Lee made slow and erratic progress, countering George's appeals for immediate succor with debate, diversion, and quixotic proposals that ran di-

204

rectly counter to the information that had been given him since the beginning of the month. "I am certainly shocked to hear that your force is so inadequate to the necessity of your situation." he wrote George ingenuously on 8 December, "as I had been taught to think you had been adequately reinforced." He did not believe the British posed a threat to Philadelphia; he had been told Cornwallis was heading west. "It will be difficult, I am afraid, to join you," he wrote at last to Washington, ". . . cannot I do you more service by attacking their rear?"

The real spine behind his stalling tactics came out in private letters he had written to friends in Congress and the army, scourging Washington and directing flattering attention to himself. To Rush he confessed himself "amazed" at the loss of the Forts Lee and Washington, adding, "I foresaw, predicted, all that has happened. . . . Let these few lines be thrown into the fire, and in your conversation, only acquit me of any share." To Gates, already George's rival, he had written on December 12: "*entre nous*, a certain great man is most damnably deficient—He has thrown me into a situation where I have my choice of difficulties—If I stay in this Province I risk myself and Army, and if I do not stay the Province is lost."

Lee had wrung a letter from Reed in the miserable aftermath of Fort Washington, thick with references to Lee's judgment and experience, and the commander's indecisive mind. Lee replied in an effusive answer, thanking him for his "obliging" letter, deploring "that fatal indecision . . . which in war is a much greater disqualification than stupidity," and ending with an insulting paragraph concerning his own plans: "I shall then fly to you; for to confess a truth, I really think our Chief will do better with me than without."

The letter reached camp when Reed had gone on an errand to Burlington and was opened by Washington instead. The result was a brief letter from Washington to Reed:

> The enclosed was put into my hands by an express from White Plains. Having no idea of it being a private letter . . . I opened it, as I had done all other letters to you . . . . This, as it is the truth, must be my excuse for seeing the contents of a letter, which neither inclination

nor intention would have prompted me to. I thank you for the trouble and fatigue you have undergone in your journey to Burlington. . . . My respects to Mrs. Reed.

What bothered him was less the criticism than the suggestion of intrigue. "I was hurt," he wrote Reed later, "not because I thought my judgment wronged . . . but because the sentiments were not communicated immediately to myself." Why had not Reed come to him with his critique? "Withholding that advice from me, and censuring my conduct to another, was such an argument of disingenuity, that I was not a little mortified at it."

Lee himself brought the affair to a bizarre conclusion, being captured by a British raiding party on the night of 15 December, four miles from his own army, in a tavern outside Basking Ridge. The circumstances were (and still are) curious, but Baron Ludwig von Closen who arrived with the French two years later was sufficiently intrigued by the odd story to visit the scene of the incident and leave for history his own account. Lee, he insisted, had repaired to the tavern with a guard of five soldiers *since he was rather smitten with the lady of the house.* Alas, the lady's cousin, irate (or jealous), had sent a message to a Colonel William Harcourt, on patrol with the British army, on Lee's trail and some miles away. Harcourt, Closen continued, "arrived like a bomb with 12 of his finest men at 4 o'clock in the morning," broke in the door, and seized Lee in his nightshirt as his aides dived through a window and escaped. "Harcourt," observed Closen, "had always been noted for these thrusts with partisans and rapid movements . . . poor General Lee."

Lee's capture did not mitigate the pressures from without. British cantonments were still strung out in a line through New Jersey; Cornwallis was still on the bank of the Delaware; Washington's army was ready to dissolve. About 20 December (elaborating perhaps on past discussions), George received this note from Joseph Reed: "Would it not be possible . . . to make a diversion, or something more at Trenton. . . . If we could possess ourselves again of New Jersey . . . the effect would be greater than if we had never

206

left." Washington answered on 23 December: "Christmas-day, at night, one hour before day, is the time fixed . . . for Heaven's sake keep this to yourself, as the discovery of it may prove fatal to us, our numbers being less than I had any conception of; but necessity, dire necessity, will, nay must, justify an attempt." On Christmas Eve, Rush visited Washington and found him much depressed, talking endlessly, lamenting "the ragged and dissolving state of his army" in pitiable terms. As he talked, Rush noted, he scribbled absently on small scraps of paper, which he crumpled and scattered on the floor. On his way out, Rush picked one piece of paper and unfolded it outside. On it was what was to be the Trenton password: "Victory or Death."

Christmas Day it had begun to snow. At eight the men began the trek from their encampment to the ferry, walking head-on into a northeast wind that pressed them backward with each footstep and whipped a rain of hail about their heads. Some in the parade were shoeless, and icy slush seeped into the rags that they had tied around their feet. There was a cruel delay of two hours at the river as the barges, heavy with men and cannon, were impeded by blocks of floating ice. On the Jersey shore, the column split in two—one to follow Sullivan along the inland pathway, the other to take the river road with Washington and Greene. The march resumed in total silence, cannon veering crazily on the icy surface, the torches of the field artillery cutting vivid flashes in the night. There was one ghastly moment as Washington's horse slipped on the icy embankment, hooves flailing wildly, then righted itself as his unruffled rider grabbed its mane. About four a messenger arrived with news from Sullivan:* hail had soaked his guns and powder; not one small arm was fit for use. Washington's answer was to the point: "Tell General Sullivan to use the bayonet. I am determined to take Trenton."

Shortly after daylight they reached the first line of Hessian pickets, stationed about half a mile out of town. As the first gun opened, there was a noise like a resounding echo—Sullivan's cannon, bombarding in the west. Washington's

*Sullivan—and Stirling—were exchanged.

face, an aide noted, lit instantly—his pincer plan had worked. Pushing the terrified guards before them, they poured into Trenton from both sides of the town, clearing the streets with volleys of cannon, hounding the survivors through a maze of side streets and alleys, routing them with bayonets from the houses in which they had lodged. At this point a Hessian colonel, Andreas Wiederhold (who had been swept in with the advance guard by Greene), went in search of the commander, Commander Johannes Rall. Rall, having observed Christmas too exuberantly, surfaced only after repeated shoutings and then appeared "quite dazed." The groggy colonel seemed distracted as Wiederhold gasped out his story: " . . . the enemy were strong in numbers . . . not only above the town, but on both sides of it, so that he might take the matter seriously, and not consider it a bagatelle." Rall, however, "tottered back and forth without knowing what he was doing" and lost the last few moments that he had. With the rest, they staggered out into an orchard, to find the field ringed round by the Americans and cannon peering out of every path. "The poor fellows," wrote Knox (who commanded the artillery), "did not relish the prospect of forcing, and were obliged to surrender on the spot." The Americans took 1,200 men and seven cannons; Rall, a bullet in his lung, was carried back to die in Trenton Church. Seven months of defeat, retreat, and indecision had been capped and climaxed by a stroke of perfect movement, compact, incisive, sudden, and direct; the prospect of imminent disaster had freed the duty-ridden Washington to act within his nature and brought his first real triumph of the war.

Sadly, the victory had a bitter edge. Another detachment that was to cross above them and seize Bordentown was held up at the Delaware by excessive ice, and half the Trenton garrison escaped. With the rest, the Americans left empty Trenton in the afternoon, the patriots intrigued by their strange quarry, with their odd tongue, light complexion with a bluish tinge to it, and "hair cued as tight to the head as possible, sticking straight back like the handle of an iron skillet" from their skulls. This crossing, if chilling, was more diverting than the first. As ice floes clinging to the barges' keels began to sweep them downstream, the oarsmen "pounded the boats, and, stamping with their feet, beckoned to the prisoners to do the same . . . they all set to jumping at once, with their cues flying up and down."

They had come back to a peril nearly as deadly as before. Cornwallis was barreling through New Jersey with six regiments, and American enlistments were still up on New Year's day. At this point, Congress, in a sudden fit of sense (or panic) bestowed on Washington some of the powers for which he had been pleading (and which, if he had been backed for a full government, would have been formidable indeed). For six months he was to be allowed to raise sixteen batallions of infantry, light horse, artillery, and engineers; impress necessities from the countryside if he could not otherwise secure them; and arrest and detain all local citizens who impeded the Continental cause. Considering the temper of the countryside and his real abilities to compel obedience, his "powers" were less awesome than they seemed. His response, however, was in character: "Instead of thinking myself freed from all *civil* obligations, I shall constantly bear in mind, that as the sword was the last resort for the preservation of our liberties, so it ought to be the first thing laid aside." His first move was the use of the morale built at Trenton—and the pledge of a $10 bonus—to enlist his army for another year. The pledge was without the permission—or the knowledge—of the treasury, but necessity must rule. Glory, pelf, and dramatic pleas worked their combined magic, and he had his army for another year.

He nearly had it only for the next three days. On 2 January he crossed back into Trenton, camping in an exposed position with a wood to one side but otherwise hemmed in by two waters: a creek above them (facing upper Jersey) and the Delaware below. By the afternoon of 3 January, Cornwallis was a mile outside the city, trying to force a passage through the creek. A fierce barrage from cannon stationed on a hill on the south shore held him off till after sundown, and he determined to defer attack. He camped for the night on the north shore, planning to hit Washington at daylight. But at daybreak Washington was no longer there.

"Around two in the morning," wrote Charles Stedman, Cornwallis' aide-de-camp, "he retreated with profound silence, leaving his fires burning, his pickets advanced . . . quitting the main road, he took a large circuit through Allentown, and proceeded to Prince Town, which he intended to surprise." At sunrise Hugh Mercer, in the van of the Americans, met Colonel Charles Mawhood, coming down with three brigades to Cornwallis' aid. Startled, Mawhood took them at first for British troops. Recovering, he opened a cannonade on the outnumbered Americans, trapped them in an orchard between a ravine and their cannon, leveled them with fresh blasts of artillery, and waded in with bayonets. Trapped and frightened, the advance began to fall back to the rear. "I . . . heard Gen. Mercer command in a tone of distress, 'retreat!'" said one survivor. "He was mortally wounded, and died soon after. . . . I looked about for the main body of the army, which I could not discover. . . . At this moment, Washington appeared."

Glancing once at the bloodied terrain, George plunged through the melee to within thirty yards of the advancing British and disappeared in a burst of fire and a gigantic cloud of smoke. There was an ensuing moment of dead silence as the cloud obscured everything, and aides stood frozen in unutterable dread. It blew off a minute later, revealing George, possessed as ever, sitting calmly on his big white horse.

"Advance!" and the army plunged after him into the British center, driving them through the fields into the red brick buildings of the Princeton campus, where they holed up in schoolrooms, firing from class and chapel windows until blasted out by barrages of artillery or chased out at the point of bayonets. Knox's cannon, cleverly placed around the schoolyard, did incessant mischief; a cannonball fired by Alexander Hamilton caromed into the chapel and brought down a portrait of George II. Perpetrators of the early orchard massacre received a dreadful vengeance; convinced the foe had used their bayonets with excessive severity, Americans closed in on the survivors and slaughtered nearly sixty on the spot. Five hundred were taken in killed, wounded, or prisoners; the rest fled to Brunswick in chaotic state. Washington had lost fewer than fifty men, but the toll of officers was especially severe: John Haslet, whose Delaware Line was the cream of the army, and Hugh Mercer, who died three days later of his wounds. He had been brought off the orchard bleeding profusely, with multiple wounds and three deep stabs from a bayonet.

About two in the afternoon Cornwallis pulled up at Princeton "in a most infernal sweat—running, puffing, and blowing, and swearing at being so outwitted," in Knox's perennially cheerful prose. If so, the "cursing" doubtless renewed in freshets, for Washington once more had gone. He was now at Somerset Courthouse, from which a British garrison of 1,300 had gone to meet Cornwallis barely three hours before. Manic as ever in the flush of action, Washington wanted to push on to Brunswick and the British treasure chest—a coup which could have crippled the British disastrously—but his troops, "without either rest, rum or provisions for two days and nights," had collapsed about him to a man. Two days later he pulled into winter quarters at Morristown in north-central Jersey, safe behind a ridge of mountains, to carry on incessant guerrilla warfare, harassing British parties out of New York and Amboy, wearing down morale and numbers in a prolonged war of attrition and of nerves. The long British cantonments had been rolled back to the two points of Amboy and Brunswick, both near New York and sea power, the one on the banks of the Raritan, the other on a promontory at its mouth. Henry Knox was ecstatic: "The enemy were within nineteen miles of Philadelphia, they are now sixty . . . we have driven them from the whole of west Jersey. The panic is still kept up." Charles Stedman, objective even in catastrophe, traced the coup to Washington's use of surprise and timing to unbalance a much larger army and his disposal of small forces for the maximum effect. "By such judicious movements," he wrote in his *History*, "did Washington not only save Philadelphia and Pennsylvania, but recovered the greater part of the Jerseys, in defiance of an army infinitely superior to his, in discipline, resources and numbers." George had reached Morristown on 6 January, the traditional end to the Christmas season of beginnings and new birth. For the Americans, it had been closer to a resurrection—a literal revival from the dead.

What was to be made of General Washington, after a year and a half in command? He and his army were the

211

beneficiaries and victims of his nerves. He was superb in crisis, his mind cool, his energies unflagging, his decisions split-second and invariably correct. When tensions slackened, his judgments flagged, beset by hesitations and self-doubt. Then the "indecisive mind" was sadly true.

Unhappily, his triumphs had a cutting edge. Congress and the country, misunderstanding both his army and his troubles, took a view of his capacities that was sadly out of line—not knowing that his victories, surprise strikes at detached cantonments, carefully picked and executed, were the limits of his strength. He had whipped the British twice. Why could he not dispatch them in open battle in the next campaign? High expectation and low resource were to plunge him into a year of trouble and the most trying episode of his career.

XII

Storm

His slackness and remissness are so conspicuous that a general languor must ensue . . . a cry begins to be raised for a Gates, a Conway . . . a Lee.
—Philadelphia diarist, 1777

The new campaign began on a grim portent—the arrival of a second front. Burgoyne, the playwright-general, had gone home on leave over the winter season and sold Germain on an ingenious plot. In his bravura fashion, it starred himself and was designed to end the war in one dramatic stroke. He would invade New York from Canada, seize the Hudson at its north extremity, isolate the American army from its supply line, and cut the rebel states in two. Howe in New York would either march up the Hudson to join him or wait at the southern end of the river to pick off the starving regiments at will. Either way, the coup would be complete.

"General Swagger" disappeared into the northern wilderness on 8 May with 8,000 German and British regulars and a massive train of baggage and artillery and was hovering above Ticonderoga by the end of June. Astonishingly, that garrison, which had been inexplicably weakened, was evacuated on the night of 5 July—a stunning loss that shattered the Americans and sent the British into spasms of delight. London went into wild rejoicing; at Kensington, the

213

king burst into the queen's chambers crying, "I have beat them! Beat all the Americans!" in a euphoric show of addled glee. In America the results were devastating, recoiling with venom on the nominal command. Charges flew that Schuyler and his associates were bribed. "Paid for their treason," reported Thacher, "in *silver balls*." Schuyler, who had made himself vastly unpopular with the New England regiments, was swept out of the command, and Gates swept in, in a wave of fury and partisan fervor that bore traces of a superbly orchestrated coup. For Washington it was a loss of multiple consequence. Schuyler was a friend and ally, and Gates in power could be counted as a threat. More, he had to transfer some of his prized troops and officers to help Gates against Burgoyne—a crippling loss of his senior officers and a pitiful depletion of his stores. George, facing Howe across the Hudson, mired in enforced inaction, was forced to brood on a growing list of problems and a mounting sense of pressure and constraint.

George had spent a wretched winter, waiting for the Howes to budge from their New York station and resisting efforts to lure him from his mountain passes into battle on the open plain. He did not dare move until he knew where they were going, and he did not yet thrust his army in set battle against blooded troops. As the months wore on into midyear, the inaction was beginning to irritate his army, and he was beginning to feel the flick of hostile criticism, chiding him for the waiting posture that troubled no one more than himself. On 18 June, when he had given up all hope of action, Howe loaded arms, troops, and horses aboard his brother's transports and disappeared off Sandy Hook—to vanish for seven weeks, incommunicado even to his own home office, leaving Germain to gnash his teeth in London over his perversity and the Americans to wear out supplies, nerves, and patience in incessant marches on the Jersey plains. Reports that Howe was headed up the Hudson brought them dashing north—only to backtrack and head south again when Howe was spotted off the Capes of Delaware on 24 July. Three days later he had disappeared again. "Since when," George reported from the Delaware, "nothing

214

having been heard of them, we remain here in a very Irksome State of Suspense." Suspicions grew that Howe was headed for Charleston for either a campaign or a feint. Still, George dared not follow him. "After we had made a considerable progress," he explained to Congress, "he might easily reimbark his Troops, and turn his arms against Philadelphia . . . without our being in a Condition to give the least aid."

George had just decided once and for all to march back to the Hudson when Howe appeared on 31 August in the Chesapeake, disembarked his cannon and his queasy army, and began the sixty-mile trek to Philadelphia by land. American expectations remained overblown. "How [sic] will make but a pitiful figure," John Adams wrote his wife in Quincy. "General Washington, with a very numerous Army, is between Wilmington and the Head of Elk." In reality, George's situation was far worse. He had been weakened by detachments to the northern army. There was little comfort in the hostile middle country, and he was beginning to suffer from an ominous breakdown in supplies. At times, fully one-fourth of his army was in the hospital for want of shoe leather, and the sudden defection of Thomas Mifflin, his quartermaster general, without warning or replacement, had left him in the lurch. Lafayette, joining the army outside Philadelphia in August found them "a strange spectacle . . . almost naked . . . ill armed, and still worse clothed." This was the force with which George was to encounter Howe. On 11 September the armies were to come face to face at last.

The Brandywine is a shallow creek that winds its way in pools and rivulets through southern Pennsylvania and the upper portion of the Chesapeake called the Head of Elk. Forests and farms surround the water, guarding its shores with steep wooded hills. The forces met on either side, Howe on the south bank with Cornwallis and a troop of Hessians under General Wilhelm Knyphausen; Washington on the north, his main army massed at a center crossing under Greene and Anthony Wayne with 5,000 others under Sullivan five miles upcountry to the right. At 8 A.M. there was a tremendous roar as Knyphausen opened fire, hurling 5,000

Hessians into Wayne in a seesaw battle loud with the bombardment of eleven cannon on each side of the crossing and marked by intense hand-to-hand combat at the creek. Until two in the afternoon the battle continued even, the Americans aided by a friendly terrain that let them fire down into the faces of the British and by the clever placement of their guns. George, at the center ford, remained uneasy, anxious about Sullivan and the continuing absence of Howe. The Hessians were less than half the British complement. Where had the others gone?

Through the morning George had sent anxious messages and at eleven received the news he feared. Howe, with the bulk of the British army, was bearing down on Sullivan near the upper ford. George ordered Sullivan to cross the creek and fall on the left wing of the enemy and pulled Greene out of the center to march to his support. He himself was about to leave with Greene when a second message stopped him short. Sullivan wrote that a second spy saw nothing of the enemy, and prior information had been wrong. George recalled his orders, pulled back Greene, and the cannonade went on. But he remained uneasy and at two in the afternoon received a frantic note—Howe had been spotted raising a cloud of dust four miles back into the country, barreling down on Sullivan with eighteen cannon and 10,000 men.

Nothing was left but a frantic effort at a save. Greene began a mad dash northward as Howe hurled himself at Sullivan, still in the process of forming on a hill. Greene arrived an hour later as Sullivan was being driven from the hill for the fifth time, the summit disputed muzzle to muzzle, the slopes of the hill bloody and spotted with the dead. Clinging to the road and to a ridge above it, Greene beat off successive waves of British and Hessians for more than two hours, letting Sullivan's troops come off between his columns, retreating himself under heavy fire as night fell. From the middle ford came a tremendous clatter: as Howe attacked Sullivan, the Hessians hit Wayne with new fury, flinging reserves of men into his decimated ranks. The cannonade began anew, shattering the valley with fresh clamors, ending only after sunset when the Hessians swarmed across the creek under a

216

smoke cover and took the station vacated by Greene. Wayne joined Greene and Sullivan in the retreat to Chester, Washington among the last of them being seen within 200 yards of the enemy, almost within range of their guns. They all reached Chester about midnight, knocked into some order at a bridge by Wayne and Lafayette, the new recruit, now standing white and solemn, blood from a calf wound dripping in his boot. Washington again tried to put the best face on matters, blaming addled intelligence for the defeat. But the error had put the capital in danger, tarnished his luster, and brought a dire drop in his prestige.

Everything that followed bore the imprint of mischance. A promising attempt to attack a British detachment on 16 September was wiped out in a torrential rainstorm, known thereafter as the Battle of the Clouds. Four days later Wayne's brigade, sent out on a scouting mission, was all but destroyed at Paoli in a midnight massacre—three batallions of British dragoons fell upon the sleeping Continentals and cut them to pieces in the light of their campfires, leaving the field strewn with the dead and mutilated and the campsite sodden with their blood.

After that a doomed effort to keep the British on the far side of the shallow Schuylkill ended in predictable failure, Howe drew the Americans off to their right twelve miles, doubled back and crossed at an unguarded station in the night. Congress had left on 18 September in a wild midnight scramble, one congressman clinging bareback to his horse's mane, to pass through Lancaster on 21 September and settle for the duration at the inland town of York. Howe entered Philadelphia on September 26.

More than ever, George had to redeem his name. On 3 October, Howe moved out with two-thirds of his army into Germantown, a settlement ten miles out of the captured capital, a thin line of ten houses fronting a rolling prospect of orchards, farms, and fields. At three in the morning of 4 October, Washington's troops were on the march. His plan was intricate and perhaps too delicately devised. Wayne and Sullivan (with George himself) were to hit the British center; Greene, coming roundabout by a side road, was to attack the left; two columns of militia on the right and the far left were to close the wings. At daybreak the edge of the American advance plowed into the British pickets, driving them through their camp into an orchard hemmed with stone fences and thick with trees. There the British rallied and began a brisk hand-to-hand battle—when the American center rolled over them, pushing them back through three miles of fields and orchards in a deepening fog that absorbed the smoke of battle into an increasingly impenetrable mist. Wayne was in a rage over the Paoli massacre, and his pursuit had an added edge. Howe, roused by the sound of fire, peered out from his headquarters to see his light infantry flying toward him in droves. He was roaring at them to form and face the enemy ("It's only a scouting party!" he is said to have shouted) as three columns of Americans roared over the hill facing him, fronted by three cannon, and shot off a blast that hit the tree that he was standing under, burying the general in a cascade of leaves. Ecstatic, the Continentals rolled through the British columns, scattering all before them in the mad confusion of retreat. Victory appeared assured.

Two miles beyond Germantown stood a stone mansion, solid, square, and all but impenetrable, built by Judge Benjamin Chew. Flying back, an ingenious colonel of the British 40th dashed into the fortress with his regiment, blocked the doors and began spraying the Americans from the upper windows with a fierce barrage of shot. Knox wheeled up a line of guns and began an earsplitting cannonade; no impression was made on the stone walls of the mansion, but the doors and windowsills were splintered, and the inner walls still bear the scars. Efforts to force entry were unavailing; an aide of Sullivan's was killed by a shot from the cellar while trying to set fire to a window as John Laurens led another party in a futile effort to push in the door. James Wilkinson, an aide to Gates, saw the house weeks later, still in deplorable condition, the inner rooms pocked and shattered, the front doors splintered and shot through from more than forty balls.

The early mist had turned into a blanket fog, black and sooty, lighted only by a sudden flare of white or orange as yet another gun went off. In the diminished vision, the clamor at

218

the Chew house appeared to some of the advanced parties as a burst of British fire in their rear. Wayne, a mile past, thought Sullivan in danger and, wheeling around, turned back in that direction, training his guns on the noise behind. (Unknown to him, the move isolated the Ninth Virginians, who had pushed ahead into an orchard and now found themselves surrounded by the British on three sides.) Greene appeared, an hour late, confused by the fog and the roundabout pathways; the sound of his shots began new panic, and some of his detachments began firing on Wayne. The scene became chaotic as the troops, confused and all but sightless, spent their bullets on each other or in random shots into the mist. "The fog," wrote Washington, "represented their friends to them for a reinforcement of the Enemy, as we attacked in different quarters . . . and were about closing the wings." Smoke, condensing in the heavy fog, wrote another officer, "increased the fear in some to think themselves surrounded, which, like an electrical shock, attacked some thousands, who fled in confusion without the appearance of an enemy." Officers who tried to rally them were swept aside. Stumbling and sightless, they went pouring back over the ground that they had taken, tripping upon bodies and debris. All was over before 10 A.M.

The aftermath of the odd battle was grisly and bizarre. Many bodies had been lost in the fog-bound marshes and were recovered only after days of prolonged search. The American list of casualties, at first low, climbed in three days past the 1,000 mark as repeated forays brought in added dead. Nor were the British spared. "They say more than 200 Waggons came in loaded with their wounded," Washington reported, "the Hospital, at Philadelphia, and several large meeting houses are filled." Nothing could appease the anguish at the loss of a triumph they had come so close to holding in their hands. "Howe for a long time could not persuade himself that we had run from victory," wrote Anthony Wayne, who had some trouble believing it himself. Washington tried to put a good face on the matter, but in a private letter to John Augustine, the bitterness came out. "The anxiety you have been under, on Acct. of this Army, I can easily conceive, would to God there had been less cause for it, or that our situation at present was such as to promise much. . . . In a word, it was a bloody day; would to Heaven I could add, that it had been a more fortunate one for us."

At this grim moment he had news of mixed import. Burgoyne, driven farther and farther from his base in hostile, densely wooded country, crippled by disease and desertions, hemmed in by droves of militia from New England and upper New York State and crushed in two battles—12 September and 7 October—had surrendered to Gates near Saratoga on 17 October. Rumor had it that success in the last two ventures had been due less to Gates than to Benedict Arnold, who, sidelined by Gates after weeks of an intense, ongoing battle, had crashed back into the middle of action, led the Americans in three fierce charges that broke the back of enemy resistance and was removed, still shouting violently, only after a cannonball had shattered his right leg. One week later Burgoyne appeared at Gates' headquarters to present his sword to that general—and adjourn to his tent for a ceremonial dinner of boiled mutton and watered rum, served on wood planks placed over two barrels and presented on a service consisting in its entirety of two glasses and four plates. Burgoyne surrendered 6 generals, 300 officers, and 6,000 men. Till Yorktown it was the biggest capture of a British army and, till Yorktown, the most stunning of the war.

Washington celebrated with a *feu de joie,* but something less than a full heart. For some time he had considered Gates a rival, and the triumph contrasted too acutely with his own ill luck. Finely tuned to nuances of power, he sensed a shift in balance, a diminution of his own authority and a subtle measure of rebuke. Some of this surfaced in his address to the army the morning after he had received the news: "This is the Grand American Army, and of course great things are expected of it. . . . What shame and disgrace will attend us, if we suffer ourselves in every instance to be outdone?" Was he speaking of the armies or of Gates and himself? Great things were expected of him and of these he had accomplished none. "Outdone," "shame," "dishonor" were doubtless the words he turned upon himself. In York, rumor had it that "when General Washington received the account of Burgoyne's defeat, he stood silent for some time."

One hope remained of making the British position in Philadelphia untenable and forcing them from the city at an early date. Three forts stood at the entrance to the Delaware, training guns on river shipping, bolstered by cheveaux-de-frise, iron spikes protruding from the riverbed, to rip the hulls of ships that floated by. On 22 October, Howe began assaults upon the forts. Washington did not reinforce them sufficiently to hazard battle because, as Greene and Laurens had it, he declined to risk the army, or, as Henry Lee explained it, reinforcements from Gates at Albany failed to arrive on time. On 15 and 20 November the British took Forts Mifflin and Mercer, access up the Delaware, and title to a prolonged and unchallenged stay. The clamor grew, and even the loyal Wayne joined in the rising chorus of distress: "It was a saying of one of the first generals, that whenever he intended to do nothing he always called a Council of War. . . . I wish I had not been a witness of more than one instance of the truth of this observation during this campaign." George longed to end the season with a new attack, but Howe was securely lodged behind a row of redoubts, and an anguished canvass of his general officers produced a consistently negative response. "Hazardous & must end in Ruin," answered Sullivan. ". . . if you fail, the people who are now so fond of censuring will change their clamor . . . and censure you." On 18 December he pulled into winter quarters at Valley Forge, a high plateau northeast of the city, under a growing cloud of censure and constraint. Defeat and frustration had already eaten into the army's confidence. The political effects of failure were about to show their faces.

Political York fell upon Washington and his supporters in a medley of rumor and of rage. Word went around the capital that the general was "weak." "His slackness and remissness are so conspicuous," penned one diarist, "that a general languor must ensue. . . . A cry begins to be raised for a Gates, a Conway, a De Kalb, a Lee." (Thomas Conway was the braggart and adventurer from Ireland via the French army, who had endeared himself to a faction in Congress by

221

informing them—falsely—that his say-so could make or break French interest in the fortunes of the United States. He, like Gates, was close to Rush and Thomas Mifflin, whose defection had left George in the lurch at Brandywine. Conway and Washington appear to have detested each other upon sight.) Rush had made a medical inspection of Washington's camp in October and turned his report into an acidulous attack on Washington, his assistants, and his aides. Once back, he embarked on a correspondence, all intense and much anonymous, whose unvarying subject was the decline of the army under George Washington and its projected resurrection once in different hands. "The Northern Army has shown us what Americans are capable of doing with a GENERAL at their head," he wrote in a note (unsigned) to Patrick Henry. "A Gates, a Lee, or a Conway would in a few weeks render them an irresistible body of men." He accused Washington of nuturing Caesarian ambitions, and told John Adams this anecdote of Gates: "I told him a few days ago that if I thought he *alone* was able to save this country, I should vote for his being banished. 'Yes,' he said, with a spirit truly republican, 'you would do better to have my throat cut.'" To Gates himself, he wrote a letter that sounded strongly like an invitation to a coup. "We have had a noble army melted down by ill-judged marches, which disgrace their authors. . . . How different from your conduct and your fortune! . . . this army will be totally lost, unless you come down and collect the virtuous band who wish to fight under your banner . . . . Congress must send for you. I have a thousand things to tell."

George had no knowledge of these machinations, but by late autumn he had collected enough of his own portents to sense the broad delineations of a plot. Gates had refused to inform him of Burgoyne's surrender and then wrote a note so insolent that it had been the talk of Congress for weeks. Alexander Hamilton, sent north to collect troops for the southern theaters, relayed accounts of delay and insubordination, plus outspoken warnings: "General Gates has won the entire confidence of the Eastern States . . . he might use it, if he pleased, to discredit the measure. . . . " At length, Hamilton detached a lesser number and sent them

south with a "In confidence I will tell you . . . I do not believe you would have had a man if the whole could have been
held at Albany with any decency."

Congress threw extravagant promotions to Gates' allies,
jumping Conway from brigadier to major general and Gates'
aide, James Wilkinson, from colonel to brigadier. Gates was
made president of the new Board of War a supervisory body
(independent of Washington's command and coequal to it).
Numbered among its members were Mifflin, Wilkinson (as
secretary) and Conway who was also made inspector general,
a post of great power, held by Baron von Steuben later in the
year. By now Washington was receiving from diverse sources
reports of factions aiming at his overthrow by indirect and
subtle means. "They dare not appear openly as your enemies," wrote James Craik, who had seen Rush at York, "but
. . . will throw such obstacles and other difficulties in your
way, as to force you to resign." Washington at this point may
have remembered Mifflin's defection in the summer, which
led him to enter Brandywine and Germantown with the
army short of everything and one-fourth of his forces sidelined for the want of shoes. He likely connected Lee's performance in 1776 with Hamilton's reports of Gates. Doubtless,
he thought also of Gates' finesse in cutting Arnold out of
credit for Burgoyne's surrender and of his adroit dislodging
of Philip Schuyler from the command in the north. Thus far,
however, the plot remained elusive in nature, textured so
finely that he could not move against it without appearing
himself divisive, oversensitive, or mad. What was his escape?

The answer came in a letter Conway had written to
Gates. Ironically, it was Gates' aide, James Wilkinson, who
supplied the leverage, and Wilkinson's *Memoirs* to which we
are indebted for details. Wilkinson was still at Albany when
Gates received the missive, a detailed exposition of Washington's errors at Brandywine, which Gates pored over, handed
around his official family, and went so far upon several occasions to read to his assembled officers himself. Wilkinson put
no number on these public readings, but they appear to have
been sufficiently frequent for Wilkinson to have committed
parts of them to memory by the time that he was sent (19 October) to carry the good news of Burgoyne's surrender

223

south. En route to York he had stopped at Reading for a long chat with Mifflin (at which Washington's flaws were once more lovingly dissected) and then, a storm beginning, a dinner with Stirling and his aides, which "the rain continuing without intermission" appeared to have gone on for days. Confined (and inebriate), the warriors indulged in reminiscence, Wilkinson favoring his hosts with Gates' comments on the northern battles, while "his lordship fought over the battle of Long Island in detail." Somewhere in the course of the assorted ramblings, Wilkinson appears to have repeated a part of Conway's letter, which he seemed to have been too drunk to remember and Stirling too drunk to hear. But one of Stirling's aides did hear, and remember, and in the morning told a sobered Stirling, who passed it on to George.

Washington's response—a note to Conway—was typically incisive and concise:

> Sir:
> A Letter which I received last Night, contained the following paragraph:
> "In a Letter from Genl. Conway to Genl. Gates, he says: 'Heaven had been determined to save your Country, or a weak General and bad Counsellors would have ruined it.'"
> I am Sir Yr. Hble Servt.
> GEORGE WASHINGTON.

The secret plot exploded into daylight in a cacophony of fireworks and noise. There was a scene between Conway and Washington, a confrontation of brass and iron, in which (said Gates) Conway "acknowledged his letter . . . and . . . said much harder things to his face." "*An éclairissement,*" wrote Gates to Conway, "in which you acted with all the dignity of a virtuous soldier . . . pray let me know which paragraph was copied off." Mifflin also consoled Conway and sent Gates a scolding letter, praising his sentiments but chiding him for indiscretions which might bring trouble to some of his best friends. Wilkinson (whose part had not yet been uncovered) returned to Albany to find Gates in near hysterics, insisting that Hamilton in his late and angry visit had rifled his papers when he had stepped out of the room. A bizarre correspondence developed between Gates and Washington, the former rambling and obsequious, the latter masking an explosive ire in lengthy letters of a coldly acid tone. Gates shifted remarkably in the course of the dialogue, insisting first his papers had been "stealingly copied," then (when the contents had been revealed to him) that they had been forged. George controlled himself with an exquisite discipline (he feared the public impact of a semiwar between the first and second generals), showing his contempt for Gates mainly in the detailed precision with which he unraveled and exposed the successive skeins of apologia, always changing, with which Gates assailed him almost week by week. It was Conway on whom he dumped the burden of his wrath. If his concern was so immense, George queried, why had he not brought his comments to George in the course of the campaign season instead of delivering them weeks afterward to Gates? George wrote to Gates later:

> It is greatly to be lamented that this adept in Military science did not employ his abilities in the progress of the campaign. The United States have lost much from that unreasonable diffidence, which prevented his embracing the numerous opportunities he had in Council, of displaying those rich treasures of knowledge and experience he has since so freely laid open to you.

A wealth of venom was in his final words:

> Willing as I am to ascribe to all his pretensions, and to believe that his remarks on the operations of the Campaign were very judicious, and that he has sagely descanted on many things that might have been done, I cannot help being a little skeptical as to his ability to have found out the means of accomplishing them. . . . These Minutiae, I suspect, he did not think worth his attention, particularly, as they might not be within the compass of *his* *views.*

Conway himself had resigned as inspector general and gone back to a York now churning with political debate. The officers at camp had protested *en masse* against his presence,

and the open hatred of the younger members—Laurens, Lafayette, and Hamilton—had made his life too miserable to
bear. "I met with a reception from your Excellency such as I
never met with before from any general during the course of
thirty years in a very respectable army," he wrote indignantly
to Washington. " . . . I remain in a state of inaction until
such time as your Excellency will think fit to employ
me . . . since you cannot bear the sight of me. . . . I am
ready to go wherever Congress thinks proper, and even to
France."

Intrigue continued in the makeshift capital at an unabat-
ed pace. *Thoughts of a Freeman,* an anonymous tract of forty-
five attacks on Washington, achieved wide, if erratic, circula-
tion. Henry Laurens, president of Congress, found one edi-
tion dropped upon his stairs. John Fitzgerald, an aide of
Washington's, saw a copy of the Conway letter that had made
the rounds of Congress and was appalled. "Though the
paragraph quoted by Colonel Wilkinson was not set down
verbatim," he wrote back to Washington in horror, " . . . in
substance, it contained that, and ten times more." Congress
remained distracted, caught between the two wings of the
army, and hung up on the unresolved matter of Conway's estate. "The kind of correspondence he carried on with General G---- was not known at the time of his promotion," a New
Jersey congressman wrote Stirling. "I cannot say what Congress will do."

George, at the center, was the most restrained of all. He
could not explain himself without revealing the pitiable
weakness of his army and inviting enemy attack. "My enemies take an ungenerous advantage of me," he wrote Henry
Laurens. "They know the delicacy of my situation, and that
motives of policy deprive me of the defence I might otherwise make. . . . I cannot combat their insinuations, however injurious, without disclosing secrets, it is of the utmost
moment to conceal." "Cruel" and "ungenerous" were other
words he used (in private letters) to describe his tormentors
and in deference to the unique constructions of his bind. It
was cruel indeed that he should be blamed for the inaction
that was itself a torture and the cause of which—chaotic man-

226

agement—he had repeatedly held up to Congress for the two and one-half years of his command. Cruel, too, that the condition of impotence should repeat itself, that he should be as powerless to attack his tormentors as he had been in the first place to attack the enemy, and for the same reasons of state—fear of exposing a weakness in the army that might prove fatal to its life. No circumstances could have been more tortuous or more diabolically designed. Doubtless, it fed his sense of fetters upon fetters, of unendurable constraint. It was in this context that he called himself a "slave."

The impasse dissolved presently, though not through any move of his. Gates, Conway, and their followers had devised a scheme for an "irruption" into Canada, in a move to divert attention from their flounderings, stun Congress with a colossal victory, and remove Lafayette from Washington, to whom he had become attached. The marquis was ordered to Albany to join Conway in command of the campaign. He resisted—"I am sure I will become very ridiculous and laughed at"—but Washington dissuaded him, and his letters en route to his commander give a cogent story of the demise of the cabal. On 9 February the marquis sent his first letter back to camp: "I go on very slowly, sometimes drenched by rain, sometimes covered by snow, and not entertaining many handsome thoughts. . . . Lake Champlain is too cold for producing the least bit of laurel, and if I am not starved I shall be as proud as if I had gained three battles." The nonappearance of an informant, scheduled to meet him in a tavern in Albany, set off another torrent of complaint: "I fancy he will be with Mr. Conway sooner than he has told me; they will perhaps conquer Canada before my arrival, and I expect to meet them at the governor's house in Quebec."

Ten days later things had got worse. The informant never surfaced. The troops were surly, and supplies were scarce. And every general in the area—including Schuyler and Arnold—had told him point-blank an invasion of Canada was suicidal nonsense and must be suspended at once: "I have consulted everybody, and everybody answers me, that it would be madness to undertake this operation. I have been

227

deceived by the Board of War . . . the want of men, clothes, money, and the want of time, deprives me of all hope."

Lafayette's opinion was shared by others, as revealed in a letter to Hamilton from George Clinton of New York:

> I need not ask you who contrived and planned the Northern Expedition. I have seen the Marquis's Instructions. They are a Curiosity indeed. They suppose the Enemy are to be pannic Struck & fly on the Approach of our Army. Our Army . . . were to take the advantage of this, pursue them & take . . . Montreal. . . . What a pitty we had not Men sufficient to have carried this all into Execution, and that those we had were not cloathed or paid.

The Canadian venture was the deathblow to the conspiracy; "Gates, a Lee or a Conway" was never to have the opportunity of making the army an "irresistible" body of men. The northern fiasco had shown all concerned too graphically the character that war under their direction would assume. As befitted its nature, the death throes of the cabal were suitably bizarre. Gates fell out with Wilkinson, who challenged him to a duel outside Reading Church. Gates met him, not with pistols but with open arms. There was a tearful reconciliation as aide and general walked around the church for half an hour, parting in a glow of understanding that lasted until Wilkinson returned to Valley Forge. There Washington, in a carefully orchestrated session, confronted him with the Gates-Conway correspondence, whereupon the solid front dissolved. " . . . seemed a good deal surprised at G-----ss. Letters," George wrote Stirling later, "and was not at all sparing in his abuse of him and C----y." Wilkinson went back to his tent in a savage humor, and resigned a few days later from the Board of War.

Conway returned in a rage from his Canadian debacle and threw in his commission to Congress. "The unaccountable way of boxing me about is not the usage which I ought to expect as an officer," he complained to Gates. No one was more surprised than he was when Congress voted to let him do just that. "I had no thoughts of resigning," he wrote Gates plaintively. "Perhaps Washington could use me in the next

228

campaign." Washington could not, and Conway sent Gates another letter: "I will volunteer . . . to serve with you." Instead, Gates sent him off to Congress, with a note urging that his status be clarified and that he be "honorably employed, or respectfully dismissed." There Conway entered a series of quarrels, culminating in a duel on 4 July 1778 in which he took a bullet in his chest. On what he believed his deathbed, Conway wrote a letter to Washington, begging forgiveness for "having done, written, or said any thing disagreeable" in the course of his American career. Recovering from his wound and his contrition, he returned to France.

Through much of the winter, Gates had been making frantic efforts to disengage himself, explaining himself to Washington as a hapless victim of machinations and appearances and putting the maximum distance between Conway and himself:

> As to the gentleman [he wrote to George in April] I have no personal connexion with him. . . . NOR HAVE I WRITTEN TO HIM, save to certify what I know to be the contents of the letter. . . . I solemnly declare that I am of no faction; and if any of my letters taken aggregatedly or by paragraphs convey any meaning, which in any construction is offensive to your excellency, that was by no means the intention of this writer. . . . After this, I cannot believe that your excellency will suffer your suspicions or the prejudices of others to induce you to spend another moment upon this subject.

Gates was thereafter shipped to Peekskill (a command under Washington's jurisdiction) and thence to Boston, out of the main line of combat and out of harm's way. The Board of War (and Mifflin) were permitted to fade into obscurity; Rush discovered that his military appointment had been allowed to lapse. When Charles Lee was exchanged in April, 1778, and returned to the army, he found few of his old allies in evidence, and those with distinctly lowered heads.

George's reaction had been politic and generous; he had embraced Lee like a brother and even held a chilly hand out to the loathed and still-distrusted Gates. To Landon Carter, he revealed his inner feelings: "Three men, who wanted to aggrandize themselves . . . finding no support . . . slunk back, disavowed the measure, and professed themselves my warmest admirers." But to Gouverneur Morris, his friend in Congress who had tried to calm him, he showed his vulnerability and an unrelieved measure of alarm: *"You say all will yet be well;* I wish it heartily, but am much mistaken, if there are not some secret and retrograde Springs. . . . "

Too much had happened to make him secure in power or to let him regard his continued dominance as less a burden than a prize.

There was another matter of internal danger that proved impervious to machinations, skill, or politesse. Hideously ill-supplied throughout the fall and winter, the army at Valley Forge had slid into a morass of suffering that no amount of pleas to Congress could ease. "Our troops: *Heu Miseros!* The skeleton of an army presented itself to our eyes in a naked starving condition, out of health, out of spirits," wrote Gouveneur Morris to John Jay after a visit to Valley Forge with a committee of Congress in early 1778. "For some days past there has been little less than a famine in the camp," George wrote Governor Clinton on 16 February, "a part of the army has been a week, without any kind of flesh." Étienne du Ponceau, a volunteer from the French army, recalled seeing soldiers poke their heads out of their doorways to murmur, "No bread, no soldier." Another Frenchman was astonished to see officers walking about in what he took to be hospital gowns and bed sheets and discovered to his horror that they were. "What then is to become of the Army this Winter?" Washington wrote Congress, "and . . . what is to become of us in the Spring? . . . Since the month of July, we have had no assistance from the Quarter Master Genl. . . . Soap, vinegar, and other Articles . . . we see none of nor have I seen since the battle of Brandywine; the first indeed we now have little occasion of, few men having more than one shirt."

The deprivations took their toll of morale and action: mutinies were narrowly averted on several occasions, foraging expeditions took men away from harassments of the enemy, and one foray against a British scouting party had to be

230

abruptly canceled when the men turned up short of provisions and of shoes. Complaints of inaction in these circumstances drove Washington to new heights of rage:

> We find Gentlemen, without knowing whether the Army was really going into Winter Quarters . . . reprobating the measure as much as if they thought Men were made of Stocks and Stones, and equally insensible of frost and Snow. . . . I can assure these Gentlemen that it is a much easier and less distressing thing to draw remonstrances in a comfortable room by a good fire side than to occupy a cold, bleak hill, and sleep under frost and snow, without clothes or blankets. However, although they seem to have little feeling for the naked and distressed soldiers, I feel superabundantly for them, and from my soul, I pity those miseries, which it is neither in my power to relieve or prevent.

The one bright spot in the dismal winter was the arrival of yet another foreign volunteer. Frederick William Augustus Henry Ferdinand, Baron von Steuben—not, as he claimed, a past lieutenant general in the Prussian army but a veteran of many years of European service and a master of discipline and drill. His size, manner, and guttural accent (his English was restricted to expressive curses) made an immediate impression, and in short order the sight of the baron putting lines of bedraggled Continental soldiers and French volunteers through their paces became a commonplace occurrence in the camp. "Believe me, my dear Baron," Steuben wrote his friend, the Prussian ambassador to France, " . . . the task I had to perform was not an easy one. My good republicans wanted everything in the English style; our great and good allies everything according to the French *mode;* and when I presented a plate of *sauerkraut* dressed in the Prussian style, they all wanted to throw it out of the window." Nonetheless, he persevered in his profane performance, "proving by *Goddams* that my cookery was the best.".

By the end of March he had made astounding progress, introducing a regular step into the army and teaching ten or twelve batallions to maneuver with the precision of a single corps. Steuben was so impressed that he threw a ball for the

231

officers, "on condition that none should be admitted that had on a whole pair of breeches . . . torn clothes were an indispensable requisite for admission, and in this the guests were very sure not to fail." The tattered guests clubbed their rations of tough steak and old potatoes, finishing the feast with hickory nuts and Salamanders, a rum concoction set on fire and consumed. "Such a set of ragged, and at the same time, merry fellows," said Steuben's aide, with vast affection. "The Baron loved to speak of that dinner, and of his *sans culottes.*"

For the "sans culottes," enduring winter in their threadbare garments, such moments of levity were seldom, and their persistent sufferings could not be laughed away. Worse than the deprivations was the sense they were induced artificially. Congress lacked the power to compel the country to sell the army its necessities and the capacity to make an equitable distribution of the few goods it had managed to procure. Anthony Wayne ordered cloth in November to furnish his regiments, but by April it had not arrived. The officers found reviewing their ragged troops an almost unendurable experience and became the anguished conduits for incessant pleas for food and clothing that they were unable to reject or to relieve. For Washington, it was yet another instance in which he was called on to exert personal influence to avert the disastrous consequences of the gross deficiencies within the state. "No man, in my opinion, ever had his measures more impeded than I have, from every department of the army," he complained to Henry Laurens, who could do no more than agree. It did not speak well for the future in the event of a prolonged war.

Domestic woes were suddenly diminished by the clamor of events abroad. France, having fed the colonies arms and money since the beginning of the insurrection, decided at last to take a formal role. Washington's resilience and the surrender of Burgoyne had roused the fears of French diplomats that British disquiet would produce concessions leading to an Anglo-Saxon rapprochement. "*Aut nunc aut nunquam* [Now or never]," wrote the Count de Vergennes, the French foreign minister, to Armand de Montmorin, the

French ambassador to Spain. "Events have surprised us, they have marched more rapidly than we could have expected . . . there is no more time to be lost." To the reluctant Spanish, Vergennes emphasized the dangers of a reunited British empire to the Bourbon crowns. "The interests for separating the English colonies from their mother country, and preventing them from ever being reidentified in any manner whatsoever, is so important, that even if it had to be purchased at the price of a somewhat disadvantageous war, if the two Crowns brought about that separation . . . they should not regret that war, whatever the issue may be." To Spain, fearful of a rising western empire, he added a soothing note: "France has no wish to see them play the world power," adding that internal dissensions would keep the Americans weak and malleable for years to come. France gave the United States another loan and sent ten warships under the Vice Admiral Charles Hector, Count d'Estaing, to blockade the British in Philadelphia in July. The formal treaty of alliance was signed on 18 February at Versailles.

Vergennes' suspicions had been nothing if not correct. Less than two weeks after the secret treaty, the North administration did a volte-face in Parliament, "ventured on taking the very opposite part to all they had been doing," reported Horace Walpole, informing their stunned listeners they must abandon all thoughts of conquest and "stoop to beg peace with America *at any rate.*" In the uproar, North announced he would "treat with Congress, with anybody," and tossed out an astounding plan for confederation or virtual autonomy under the crown. A crew of startled Whigs, including Burke and Charles James Fox (the plump young rising star of the opposition), were swept into unaccustomed agreement with the administration, but, as Walpole noted, "the latter threw a bomb." Fox challenged North to announce to Parliament that accord between France and America already had been signed. "If so, said he, the Administration is beaten by ten whole days . . . the whole House must concur with the propositions, though probably now they would have no effect."

The convulsion brought a spate of further efforts at rap-

233

prochement, each more bizarre and ineffective than the last. Franklin at Passy had a series of approaches, one from a "Charles de Weissenstein" (whom he believed to be the king himself), who communicated through letters sequestered in odd places and offered to placate the American leaders through gifts of cash and titles which Franklin, in a rage, refused. A Sir John Dalrymple made a suggestion to Parliament: "Might not the Ministers . . . or the King himself write a private letter to Washington . . . desiring him to make terms for America fair and just . . . and that the terms for himself should be the dukedom that was given to Monk?" Charles Monk was the rebel who was bought off by a title from an uprising in 1670 against Charles II. The offer was not made.

What did develop was the Carlyle Commission, a group of three delegates—the Earl of Carlyle, William Eden, and George Johnstone, onetime governor of Pennsylvania—sent to "treat" with Congress in 1779. The trio arrived, unfortunately, in May, shortly after news reached the states of the French treaty and shortly before the expected arrival of D'Estaing. Their approaches to Congress were not well received. Undeterred, they made other offers, some less formally, one through a Mrs. Ferguson (the wife of an exiled British sympathizer) to her old friend Joseph Reed. As Reed recounted later, she invited him to dinner, "talked much on the subject of her private troubles, imperceptibly slid into that of the British Commissioners," and concluded by assuring Reed that if he would assist in the promotion of reunion, "I might have £10,000 sterling, and any office in the colonies in his Majesty's gift." Reed went straight to Washington, debated over making the story public, and then went to Congress, telling everything except the lady's name.

Other offers, it developed, had been made to Robert Morris and several other men. They served only to enrage Washington and to turn the face of the colonies implacably away. As Henry Laurens noted after the commissioners had returned to Britain: "If all the fine things now offered had been tendered some time ago . . . there is no doubt but that the people of America would joyfully have embraced the

234

proposition, but now what answer can be given but that which was returned to the foolish Virgins?—'the door is shut.'"

France's entry as a naval power had already brought a change. The threat of blockade had made Philadelphia untenable and forced a British pullback to New York. Howe's departure was assured in any case—he was tired and dispirited, and his policy of orthodox warfare and slow movements had been only intermittently successful against Washington's tactics of evasion, feints, and sudden flash attacks. His officers gave him a gala sendoff on 18 May, the general and aides sailing downriver to the piazza of the Wharton mansion, decked in marine and medieval motifs, for a night of feasting, fireworks, and tournaments, in which junior officers, decked in plumes and "armor," had at each other incessantly with lances, firearms, and swords. ("Concluded about Seven the next morning," wrote one reveler, who added that the fireworks, which began about ten in the evening, had gone largely unnoticed, since heads by then had gotten "fat.") It was Sir Henry Clinton, called down from Manhattan, who had the unhappy job of supervising the evacuation and sweeping up the debris. On 16 June the British left the city, trailing an immense load of luggage (much of it from Tory expatriates), for the forty-mile trek on low-lying coast roads to the embarkation point at Sandy Hook. "Amazing," wrote one Tory of the spectacle. "The wagons only, in the line of march, extended 12 miles in length." George, sprung at last from Valley Forge, trailed him, watching hungrily, his mind divided between harassment and attack. A British escape would mean another stalemate and a less-than-pleasant obligation to the French. Open battle remained risky. Which way would he jump?

Clinton's train crawled northward through the sweltering flatlands, halted frequently by stopped wells, demolished bridges, and roads blocked by felled trees—a tempting target for the following Americans, made all the more so, by memories of the autumn's failures and the winter's burden of intrigue. The canny Greene wrote George what he had himself suspected: that his army owed the cause a victory, and that this might be his moment to oblige.

Others demurred, and the way north was broken by extensive quarrels, terminating in a four-hour session at Hopewell Township on 24 June on the virtues of cautious harassment against head-on attack, Lee insisting upon stalling tactics as Wayne fumed in a corner and Hamilton, taking notes of the proceedings, ground his teeth in rage. At first, Lee, with the brigadiers behind him, appeared to have won over George. Beset by doubts and still uncertain, Washington detached a corps of 1,500 to harass Clinton's lines. But he was still unhappy, and pleas from Lafayette, Green, and Hamilton helped change his mind. He sent Wayne with an added 1,000 to join the party, the whole to be formed into an advanced body under the command of Lafayette. There was an understanding that if the advance attacked under favorable conditions, the full army would come to its support. To Lafayette, he sent the longed-for message: "You will attack them as occasion may require by detachment, and if a proper opening should be given . . . with the whole force of your command."

Trouble started the next day. Lee wrote George a letter, strange even by his standards, that infused strategy with questions of precedence and intrigue. He had first rejected command of the advanced body, he told Washington, thinking it mistaken and too trivial to suit his elevated state. Further considerations, however, had served to change his mind. Ceding command to Lafayette would have an odd appearance. Could he command the advanced corps after all? He chose, however, to end the appeal on a distinctly addled note: "So far personally; but to speak as an officer, I do not think that this detachment ought to march at all."

Caught in these crosscurrents, George arrived at a solution that added new complications to the whole. He could not withdraw the command from Lafayette, he explained to Lee, without wounding the feelings of the marquis; therefore, some accommodation had to be reached. Lee was to head toward Lafayette with two more detachments from the main army and, upon juncture, take command from him.

236

March toward the Marquis with Scott's and Varnum's brigades [George wrote to Lee in his instructions]. Give him notice that you are advancing . . . and . . . are to have command of the whole . . . but, as he may have formed some enterprise . . . you will give him every assistance and countenance in your power. This, as I observed before, is not quite the same thing, but may possibly answer, in some degree, the views of both.

Joined at last, the advance moved closer to the British on the day and evening of the 27th, sending back intermittent reports on progress through the night. About five in the morning of the 28th, word came to the main army that the advance was edging up on the rear of the British and was ready in an hour's time to strike. The army left its baggage and began a quick march to the front. George had just stopped near Monmouth Courthouse (on the near side of a ravine between himself and Clinton's army) to order Greene to fall on the right wing of the British when a fifer appeared from the direction of the battle, almost incoherent with fatigue and terror, to gasp out that the advanced corps had broken suddenly and was in full flight back through the ravine. George (according to his aide Robert Harrison, who was beside him), appeared "surprised, and rather exasperated . . . threatened the man, if he mentioned a thing of this sort, he would have him whipped." He had scarcely finished when they were overwhelmed by two brigades sweeping toward them "in great disorder . . . and so distressed with fatigue they could barely stand." Shouting that he was going to investigate, Harrison plunged head-on into the retreating troops, weaving his horse in and out of the erratic columns, struggling to hear—and shout—information above the tumult of the mob. "By God!" cried one colonel as Harrison pushed past him, "they are flying from a shadow!" Another shouted, desperate and "agitated," that "he had no place assigned to go where the troops were to halt." Farther back, he found "General Maxwell . . . as much at a loss as any other officer . . . he had received no orders upon the occasion . . . and was totally in the dark." At the very rear he discovered Wayne and Scott together, "no otherwise concerned than at the retreat itself, and told me it was impossible to tell the cause." They stood together some minutes discussing the mystery, when a flying wedge of British grenadiers dashed out of the woods at them, sending the aide and generals flying back after the rest.

George, at the south side of the ravine, was in the center of a melee of retreating soldiers, milling in intense confusion or dropping by the roadsides from the heat. Tench Tilghman, at his side, heard him shout questions at the officers, one of whom, a Colonel Shreve, "answered in a very significant manner, smiling, that he did not know, but that he had retreated by order, he did not say whose." Another, a Major Howell, "expressed himself with great warmth at the troops coming off; and said he had never seen the like." Joseph Plumb Martin, sitting under a tree near a defile, saw Washington cross the road near him "in a great passion . . . I heard him ask one of our officers 'by whose orders the troops were retreating,' and being answered, 'by General Lee's.' He said something, but he was too far off for me to hear it distinctly. Those who were nearer to him said that his words were, 'd---n him.'"

Lee himself was now borne up on the last wave of retreating troops. Washington (according to Tilghman) "rode up to him with some degree of astonishment, and asked him, what was the meaning of this? General Lee answered, 'Sir . . . sir. . . .'" Tilghman took it "that he did not hear the question," and Washington asked it again. Lee took some time in answering, replying finally with a story about bad intelligence, disobedience, and insubordination of his underofficers (meaning, as it turned out later, Wayne). "He said that, besides, the thing was against his own opinion. General Washington answered, whatever his own opinion might have been, he expected his orders would have been obeyed, and then rode on to the rear of his retreating troops." Harrison tore up, hot and breathless, to gasp out the news that the British army was behind him and would be upon them in fifteen minutes' time. Martin saw George standing, facing the advancing enemy, remote and thoughtful on his English charger, while the shot from the British artillery tore up the ground about his feet. Then, as Harrison

238

recalled it, he "looked about and said that it appeared to be an advantageous place to give the enemy the first check." Two Connecticut brigades were posted under Wayne against a fence near an orchard to take the first thrust of the grenadiers, while artillery on a hill above them fired over their heads into the British force. Behind this line, he made a quick deployment: Greene on the right with Knox's guns behind him; Stirling on the left; the center massed in the orchard to back up Wayne, now being pushed by weight of numbers from his position at the fence into the rear. Clinton had changed his line of march the night before, and it was the cream of the army—grenadiers and light infantry—that now plowed into Wayne.

A ferocious artillery duel began in the orchard; Martin saw a shot from a small cannon shatter the thighbone of a captain and slice off the heel of a private standing in his rear. The temperature had reached 98 in the orchard, the soldiers dropping from heat as often as from bullets, crawling off to collapse in the shelter of the shade trees or drink with their hands from cold spring water, from which upwards of 100 died. Washington was everywhere, bringing order out of chaos, riding unconcerned through a barrage of bullets that buzzed like hail around his head. His bay charger was shot under him. Calmly he called for another and remounted on the field. Laurens and Hamilton also lost horses, Hamilton's dumping him painfully, then rolling over on his arm. Martin, still in the orchard, recorded another instance of battlefield aplomb. "Molly Pitcher" (Mary Hayes), the wife of a captain of artillery, had followed her husband onto the field of battle and took up her post beside him, stoking cannon as the flares fell all around. One shot from the British cannon tore through her petticoat, ripping off the lower portion of her skirt. The awestruck Martin bore due witness to her nonchalance: "Looking at it with apparent unconcern, she observed that it was lucky it did not pass a little higher, for in that case it might have carried away something else."

The American lines had solidified in their positions, Steuben's training making the vital difference, as they formed under fire for the first time in the war. Clinton hurled himself at Stirling, north of the road, and was flung back in a fierce struggle, then moved south to hit the American right. Greene forestalled him, cannonading from a line of artillery mounted on a hillside, driving him back to the edge of the ravine. There was a respite of about an hour while the exhausted troops gasped along the roadsides. Then, reinforcements arriving, Clinton threw the grenadiers at Wayne, back at his old post in the orchard, now strewn with bodies and damp with blood. Wayne waited till the bayonets had come within forty paces, then leveled a blast of musket fire that dropped them almost to a man, the leader falling at the feet of the Americans, who dragged the body and the colors off. "They returned, and were again repulsed," wrote John Laurens, "they finally retreated over the strong pass where . . . General Washington had first rallied the troops. We advanced in force . . . remained looking at each other, with the defile between us, till dark."

Clinton withdrew to the ridge first occupied by Lee, "so overpowered with fatigue that I could press the affair no further," both his flanks anchored by thick woods and morasses, approachable only at the center by a narrow causeway through a swamp. Washington, in a state of manic energy, had lined up two brigades on each side and rolled up a line of artillery to plunge through the center when it became too dark to see. The day's heat clung to the steaming orchard, strewn alike with the wounded, the exhausted, and the dead. Still plotting movements, George dropped at last beside Lafayette under an oak tree, planning to hit Clinton at the first light of dawn. But the British stole off about two in the morning, and by daylight they were gone.

The wrath of the army descended on Lee. "Unnecessary, disorderly, and shameful" was the best that Washington could say about his conduct, and his lesser officers were more bitingly irate. "Mr. Clinton's whole flying army would have fallen into our hands, but for a defect of abilities or good will in the commanding officer of our advanced corps," wrote John Laurens. "His precipitate retreat spread a baneful influence everywhere." Hamilton was more incensed: "I cannot persuade myself to be in good humor with success so far inferior to what we in all probability should have had, had not the finest opportunity America ever possessed been fooled away by a man, in whom she had placed a large share of the most ill-judged confidence . . . this man is either a driveller in the business of soldiership, or something much worse." Wayne and Scott sent Washington a formal letter charging Lee with gross misconduct on three counts: disobeying Washington's orders to attack Clinton; pulling back from a favorable position for unexplained reasons; and exposing thereby their advanced parties who might have been left to face the brunt of Clinton's army by themselves. Implicit in their wording was the sense that Lee had acted either from distraction or a callous disregard: "General Wayne . . . sent Major Fishbourne to General Lee, requesting that the troops might return to support him. . . . Major Fishbourne returned, and said that General Lee gave no answer, than that he would see General Wayne himself, which he never did." Wayne and Scott sent again for assistance, but "this request met with the same fate as the last." "Our retreat from the Court-House was not occasioned by the want of numbers, position, or wishes of both officers and men," they said in summation, ". . . no plan of attack was ever communicated to us, or notice of a retreat, until it had taken place in our rear."

Lee meanwhile had written Washington a letter of his own (misdated 1 July), complaining both of the "singular expressions" with which Washington met him on the field at Monmouth and the growing conviction in the army that he was responsible for turning a potential triumph into an inconclusive draw. "Neither yourself, nor those about your person could . . . be in the least judges of the merits or demerits of our manoeuvres," he insisted. "To speak with a becoming pride, I can assert that to these manoeuvres the success of the day was entirely owing. . . . I have a right to demand some reparation for the injury committed, and unless I can obtain it, I must . . . retire from a service at the head of which is placed a man capable of offering such injuries." Washington's answer, correct and frigid, left no doubt about the form the accounting would assume. "I am not conscious of having made any very singular expressions at the time of meeting you. . . . What I recollect to have said was dictated by duty, and warranted by the occasion. As soon as circumstance will permit, you shall have an opportunity of justifying yourself to the army, to Congress, to America, and to the world."

Lee's court-martial began on 3 July, moving from one campsite to another as the army resumed its progress, reaching a point northwest of New York City (where Clinton had limped in the week after Monmouth) on 17 July. Witness after witness for the army described Lee's actions in terms of incoherence, misdirection, and the utter lack of a coordinated mind. Steuben mentioned great disorder, Maxwell that Lee did not know on which wing his brigade was posted, Hamilton that he heard no orders given to cover the retreat. A brief delay on 6 July produced new rancor—an irascible letter from Lee to the New Jersey *Gazette,* accusing Washington of character assassination and claiming credit for all successes on the field. "Savors of insanity, or flows from worse sources," was Wayne's comment on the letter, which added to the conviction in the army that Lee was either intriguing or deranged. The court was angrier than ever when it reconvened in Paramus on 13 July, with Lee examining John Laurens on the stand.

"Were you ever in an action before?" Lee asked the youthful aide.

"I have been in several actions," Laurens answered. "I do not call that an action, as there was no action previous to the retreat."

On 19 July (at Peekskill) Lee began his summation for himself. It consisted almost in its entirety of criticisms of all others in the field. Wayne, he complained, was intemperate and insubordinate, Hamilton "flustered and in a sort of frenzy of valour," while Washington's criticisms had taken him completely by surprise. "I confess," he said, "I was disconcerted, astonished, and confounded by the words and manner with which his Excellency accosted me . . . so novel and unexpected from a man, whose discretion and decorum I had from the first of our acquaintance stood in admiration of, that I was for some time incapable of making a coherent

242

answer to questions so abrupt." They had, Lee said, been more astonishing, in view of his own conception of his contributions to the day. "I really thought the troops entitled to the highest honor; and that I myself, instead of the thundering charges brought against me, had meritted some degree of applause."

On 13 August, Lee was found guilty of all counts against him: insubordination, disobedience of orders, and failure to attack. The results were passed on to Congress, which dallied over them for five months longer, finally upholding them (and terminating Lee's commission) on December 5. The passions generated did not end with this; Lee was called out by a succession of Washington's adherents (including Wayne and Hamilton) and was finally wounded in a duel with John Laurens on December 24. Nor were the diehards in Congress appeased. "This sentence has not diminished my veneration," Benjamin Rush wrote his wife after the final verdict. "I shall always view him as the *first* general in America." "Conway, Mifflin, and Lee were sacrificed to the excessive influence and popularity of *one man*," he later wrote another sympathizer. "For my part, I wish to see something like the ostracism of the Athenians introduced among us . . . republics should be illuminated by *constellations* of great men."

Lee himself continued to write violent letters edging further into fantasy and rage. One of these (oddly addressed to Washington's friend Robert Morris) can stand as his final judgment on the case:

> In the words of my Lord Chatham, have we not a gracious prince on the throne? Is he not still the same? I trust he is, but there is something rotten betwixt him and his people . . . not content with robbing me . . . a most hellish plot has been formed (and I may say at least not discouraged by headquarters) to destroy forever my reputation. . . . I never retreated but by his positive order, who invidiously sent me out of the field when the victory was assured. Such is my recompense for having sacrificed myself, my connections, and perhaps my whole fortune, for twice having extricated this man and his whole army out of perdition, and now having given him the only victo-

243

ry he ever tasted . . . by all that is sacred, General Washington had scarcely any more to do in it than to strip the dead.

Lee dropped out of sight into obscurity, nursing his wounds of pride and body as he rattled between Philadelphia and his lodgings in Virginia, accompanied mainly by the enlarged and ever-present pack of dogs, whose company he more than ever had reason to prefer to humankind. Now and then he fired off other letters, exercises in besotted petulance that occasioned little more than saddened curiosity. Opinion in the army varied from the belief that he had been seduced to treason during his captivity to the prevalent idea that he was mad. George himself ranged between irritation and detached pity, prompted by the knowledge that he no longer was a present danger and softened by the suspicion that Lee was not properly responsible and therefore an unseemly target for attack. "The motives which actuated this gentleman," Washington wrote in 1779 after yet another of Lee's eruptions into newsprint, "can better be accounted for by himself than by me."

Opinion spread thereafter in the army that the man who had been for three years second-in-command of all its actions had been for much of that time impaired in his judgments and possibly deranged. If Lee was not overtly hysterical on the battlefield, his wandering demeanor suggested a species of internal collapse and estrangement from reality which, if less dramatic, was not less real. His last years, full of sulks and peevish quarrels, added to the impression of accelerating disease. He died in Philadelphia in 1782, surrounded by atrocious squalor, attended (as always) by his dogs. The provisions of his will indicated the bizarre quality that had colored and at last controlled his life. In it, he requested that he be buried not less than one mile distant from any Baptist or Presbyterian meeting house, since "I have kept so much bad company while living, I do not wish to continue it when dead."

XIII

Desperation

The history of the war is a history of false hopes and temporary expedients. . . . I see nothing before us but accumulating distress.—WASHINGTON to two correspondents, September, 1780

The grand entente, that was to win the war in one season, was off to a disappointing start. D'Estaing, who planned to trap Clinton at the mouth of New York Harbor, arrived a week too late to catch him and then was deterred by shallow water from passing the bar at Sandy Hook. For two weeks his fleet stood outside the harbor in a mute display of impotent splendor, as D'Estaing (as John Laurens wrote Washington) "laments the insipid part he is playing . . . and sighed at not being Engaged." To become engaged, he sailed to Newport, to meet an American force under Sullivan, Greene, and Lafayette, and join a land-and-sea action to trap the British garrison of 6,000 in its island fort. George's letters from his camp just north of New York City began to take an anxious note. A coup of this dimension would cripple the war effort of the empire, force a partial withdrawal from the continent, and perhaps end the war before the spring.

He was still waiting when reports from Newport began to take disturbing turns. Lafayette fought with Sullivan over his troop dispositions, since "by it, the French battalions wd land under cover of American fire, and play a humiliating

245

secondary part." D'Estaing and Sullivan had trouble coordinating plans for their attack. Sullivan, caught short by the late arrival of his militia, wrote to delay the invasion, but D'Estaing had made his arrangements and entered the harbor, plowing through a barrage of British cannon fire on 8 September. Exposed to fire from his decks, the British pulled their troops from the north side of the island, whereupon Sullivan "took the hardy resolution of availing himself of this move, and threw his whole army across." The French were enraged. "Convinced their troops injured by our landing first," John Laurens wrote to his father, "and talked like women disputing precedence in a country dance." The next day British Admiral Thomas Graves arrived from Manhattan, with eighteen ships of the line. D'Estaing sailed out to meet him—and into a violent storm, that blew the fleets apart without touching, sending a battered Graves back to New York Harbor, and D'Estaing to limp to Newport eight days later, his flagship dismasted and rudderless and his other ships in similarly wretched shape. Two days later he sailed for Boston, in spite of the appeals of Greene and Sullivan and the tearful pleas of Lafayette. Demoralized by this measure, the American militia decamped on the hurry, dwindling in days from 9,000 to between 4,000 and 5,000. Sullivan, stranded on Newport, was left to hack his way back to safety through a wall of British fire, which he did in a six-hour battle on 26 August. "Vexacious and truly mortifying," wrote Greene to Washington. "The garrison was so important, and the reduction so certain, that I cannot with patience think of the event."

The failure at Newport soon appeared the minor prelude to the rupture of the treasured and long-sought entente. Sullivan vented his fury in a violent attack on D'Estaing. ". . . issued something like a censure in general orders," Greene wrote Washington. "Indeed, it was an absolute censure. It opened the mouth of the army in very clamourous strains." Letters descended on George from every quarter, breathing fire and distress. "I must confess that I do most cordially resent the conduct of the Count," complained Sullivan, adding, "to combat all these misfortunes . . . requires a degree of temper and persevering fortitude, which I can never boast of, and which few possess." Lafayette on his part was equally irate. "Would you believe," he wrote to Washington, "that forgetting any national obligation, forgetting what they were owing to that same fleet . . . the people turned made their departure . . . wishing them all the evils in the world. . . . You cannot have any idea of the horrors which were to be heard on that occasion. . . . I am upon a more warlike footing . . . than when I came near the British lines."

Appalled at the impending collapse of the alliance, George dashed in to set things back to rights. Letters, alternately stiff and soothing, went out to Sullivan and Lafayette. On the French defection, his attitude was brutally direct: "Prudence dictates that we should put the best face upon the matter," he wrote one bemused correspondent, and, to another, "I intend to ascribe it to necessity, from the damage suffered in the late storm." About internal rancors, his feelings were the same. "It is of the greatest importance that the soldiers and the people should know nothing . . . or, if it has reached them, that ways may be used to stop its progress, and prevent its effects." He begged Greene to use his influence to soothe the French through Lafayette. "He will . . . take any advice coming from you in a friendly light, and, if he can be pacified, the other French gentlemen will of course be satisfied, as they look to him as their head." It was to Greene also that he concluded with this note: "You can conceive my meaning better than I can express it, and therefore fully depend upon your exerting yourself to heal all."

The chastised principals worked to mend the shattered fragments of accord. Sullivan apologized to D'Estaing; Lafayette (now pacified) worked to smother reverberations at Versailles. In Boston (whence the fleet had gone) the French were courted assiduously, Hancock doing heroic duty as a host, keeping his doors open and his wine uncorked in a show of bonhomie as politic as it was desperately contrived. D'Estaing for his part played the perfect guest, receiving each overture with exaggerated gratitude and accepting a portrait of Washington on board his flagship with such enthusiasm that he was barely dissuaded from firing off twenty-one guns. Even a riot, in which French sailors were mauled

247

badly by a Boston mob, was defused by an adroit statement from Greene: "The late affray . . . has been found to originate from a parcel of soldiers belonging to the Convention troops."* "If this is not strictly true," confessed John Laurens, "it is a story which policy wd. encourage," adding that the French "seemed satisfied," perhaps because they had been ordered to appear so by D'Estaing. D'Estaing left in November with the alliance still intact and a tenuous promise to return to the North Atlantic in the summer of the next year—a full-scale move against the British would have to wait, if ever, until then.

George, facing Clinton in the lower Hudson Valley, was back at square one, shaken by the Newport venture and heartsick over his third failure to bag a British army in as many months. Politic as he appeared in his public utterance, his real feelings emerged in a private letter to John Augustine: "An unfortunate storm, and some measures taken in consequence . . . blasted, in one moment, the fairest hopes that ever were conceived." It was the distress that he experienced, but did not dare otherwise express. Neither his face-off with Clinton nor his relations with his French cohorts were likely to be immediately relieved. Frustration, strain, and tenterhook diplomacy vis-à-vis his allies were to be his portion for the next two years.

Internal weakness replaced foreign intrigue as the focus of anxiety and stress. Merchants bought vast stores of cloth, grain, and metals, selling them back to the government at inflated prices, bringing the army to the edge of desperation while amassing golden hoards of profit for themselves. Congress could not control the vast corruption; in fact, it sometimes engaged in it itself. Samuel Chase, member from Maryland, cornered the grain market in 1779, bringing upon himself the wrath of Alexander Hamilton—"Infamous in itself, repugnant to your station, and ruinous to your country"—but not, alas, of his state legislature, which acquitted him in a notoriously rigged vote. George visited Philadelphia on 22 December and found an entrenched cadre of

---

*British troops captured with Burgoyne at Saratoga and detained at Boston as prisoners of war.

the nouveau riche, corrupt and dazzling, entertaining themselves and distracting Congress with a daily round of liquid entertainments that began about midday and continued to the small hours of the night. Benedict Arnold, now military governor, seemed a symbol of the fall of morale and esprit. The hero of Saratoga was living above his head at the peak of society, courting the daughter of a rich merchant of questionable loyalties and sliding fast into a morass of intrigue. Charges that he fattened his purse by renting out army wagons for private transport would lead to his court-martial in the spring.

George moved shaken through the round of revels, a grim and prescient specter at the feast:

> Your money is now sinking 5 p. Ct. a day in this City [he wrote Benjamin Harrison], and yet, an assembly, a concert, a Dinner, or Supper (that will cost three or four hundred pounds) will not only take Men from acting in but even thinking of this business, while a great part of the Officers . . . from absolute necessity, are quitting the Service, and the more virtuous few . . . sinking by sure dgrees into beggary and want.

Appeals to fight inflation, raise taxes, control speculators ("I would to God that one of the most atrocious of each State was hung in Gibbets") went for nothing with a Congress that was day by day ceding power after power to the states. "All the business is now *attempted,* for it is not done, by a timid kind of recommendation from Congress to the States," he complained bitterly, calling the resulting structure "a many headed Monster, a heterogenious Mass, that never will or can, come to the same point." Later that winter there was a mutiny in the New Jersey Line, contained only when the state Assembly rushed in a new supply of clothes. George dutifully scolded the soldiers, but his heart was not in it, and he saved his biting censure for Congress and the states. He commented acidly:

> It is lamentable that the measure should have been delayed, 'Till it became in a manner extorted. The causes of discontent are too great and too general, and the ties

that bind the officers to the service are too feeble to admit of rigor. . . . The patience of men, animated by a sense of duty and honour will support them to a certain point, beyond which it will not go.

Running through everything was his despair at the disarray of the civil structure and its lack of power to control events. All his woes—finance, the unstructured nature of the army, his endless troubles with supply and discipline— seemed to wind back to this sore. Who was to sink money, cage the "harpies," harness the resources of the continent, and control and regulate the whole? Not the states, jealous and consumed in local issues, or Congress, enervated to begin with and now cutting its own sinews by the day. Ideas of human nature as a force demanding discipline, of equity as a plant to be preserved through power, and of central power as the agency of justice were to grow and flower in this period and be with him for the remainder of his life.

None of this was a proper basis for a new campaign. Late in spring he was writing Congress, "I am much mistaken if the resolve of Congress hath not an eye to something beyond our abilities: they . . . are not . . . sufficiently acquainted with the state and strength of our army, or of our resources, and how they are to be drawn out. The powers *may* be beneficial, but do not let Congress *deceive* themselves by false expectations founded on a superficial view." Enlistments trickled in in disturbingly low numbers, and Indian raids along the Mohawk Valley had become so terrible that he was forced to detach 5,000 men under Sullivan to end the reign of terror in the North. His letters to Congress became increasingly grim. "I am exceedingly mortified that the circumstances of the Army with respect to numbers, oblige me to a mere defensive plan, and will not suffer me to pursue such measures as the public good may seem to require, and the public expectation to demand." To Joseph Reed he wrote sarcastically, "You may form a pretty good judgment of my prospect of a brilliant campaign, and the figure I shall cut in it, when I inform you, that excepting about 400 Recruits from the State of Massachusetts Bay (a portion of which . . . are children, hired at abt. 1500 dollars each for nine months service) I have had no reinforcement to this Army since last Campaign." And to Congress, again, pathetically: "I hope it will be remembered that the Army has been diminished by the expiration of the term of Service . . . that a considerable part . . . is detached upon the Western expedition, and that scarcely a single man has taken the field from any of the States." His one bold move of the summer was an isolated attack on a detached cantonment—Stony Point, at the west bank of King's Ferry, seized by Clinton in June, 1779, and won back by Wayne on 17 July in a midnight strike with unloaded muskets and the bayonet, an exquisite set piece of military execution and the one highlight of a depressing year. Otherwise, he was held fast in lassitude, hobbled by his lack of arms and men. To Horatio Gates, who wrote a letter urging a "glorious" attack on New York island, he sent a bitter and acid-toned response:

> With respect to my plans, the only offensive ones I could have in contemplation independent on contingencies has been explained to you. I mean the Western expedition. Our defensive ones must depend upon the movements of the enemy. I imagined you had too just an idea of the comparative state of their strength and ours to make a particular explanation on this head unnecessary. But the opinion you express . . . of the glorious opportunity of making an attack upon New York, shows that you must either greatly overrate our force or undervalue that of the enemy . . . the force remaining at New York . . . by the lowest computation, was not less than 9,000 serviceable men. . . . You will judge from this state of facts whether the opportunity for attacking New York was a very glorious one or not.

His only hope remained D'Estaing. The count had told him he might sail to the northern coastline when the hurricane season made action impossible in the West Indies in the late summer and the early fall. The drawbacks were the uncertainty of D'Estaing's intentions, George's inability to exert pressure on him, and the humiliating prospect that his forces might be too low and ragged to tempt the French into an attack against New York. On 16 September he met the Duke de la Luzerne at West Point for a humiliating interview, in which he was forced to admit that he could not guarantee an army of sufficient stature to secure a definite commitment from D'Estaing. Reluctantly, he was forced to accede to the French alternative: an attack on the British forces in Georgia and the Carolinas, which had recently captured Savannah and begun to edge into the lower South. He had also made a damaging impression. Elbridge Gerry would inform him later that the French had warned in a disquieting manner against a further repetition of delays.

The best he could come away with was a promise that D'Estaing would aid in the assault on Savannah and then, if possible, head north. Straining at the leash as ever, George made heroic efforts to call out the militia and sent the Marquis and Hamilton to Long Island to wait for the first signs of D'Estaing:

> I . . . am now to authorize you [he wrote them on 12 October] to engage the whole force . . . in such an enterprize against the enemy's shipping as the Count and you may agree to undertake. In a word, I will aid him, in every plan of operations against the enemy at New-York, or Rhode Island, in the most effectual manner that our strength and resources will admit. He has nothing more to do, therefore, than to propose his own plan.

But D'Estaing failed to appear or even write to him, and his letters took on a tone of desperation as the autumn days wore on. He wrote Lafayette on 20 October:

> We have been in hourly expectation for the last 15 days of seeing Count D'Estaing off Sandy-Hook. We have not heard a Syllable . . . since the 8th of Sept; these Accts. mentioned that the Count intended to make his attack the next day. Under these circumstances, you may easily form an idea of our impatience and anxiety. We are making every preparation in our power for an extensive and perfect co-operation with the fleet (if it comes.)

"Awkward and expensive," he wrote Henry Laurens of his situation, and exploded in a tortured letter to John Parke Custis on 10 November:

252

> We have waited so long in anxious expectation of the
> French fleet at the Hook, without hearing anything from
> it, that we begin to fear that some great convulsion of the
> earth has caused a chasm between this and that state . . .
> why, if nothing is done . . . are we not informed of it?
> . . . There seems to be the strangest fatality, and the
> most unaccountable silence . . . that can be conceived.

A day later he wrote to Du Portail and Hamilton, "I do not expect myself, that he will arrive in this Quarter, or if he should, that the enterprize which was proposed could now be prosecuted. It is too late to begin." On 14 November he wrote again to Laurens, asking the permission of Congress to disband the militia, which had been idling three months at vast expense. Two days later he learned the reason for the silence and the long delay—D'Estaing had been mauled mercilessly off Savannah in a fierce naval battle on 9 October and was limping back to France in disarray. "Good God!" wrote the Count de Grasse, who had sailed with him. "It would have been necessary to have seen it to believe it, and, in not saying the half, we would have been thought to exaggerate. . . . But nothing is so true, and I would not wish to repeat the experience for a million of revenue. The navy suffered a long time the fruits of that campaign."

Washington's official comment on the end of his hopes was expressed simply in a letter to George Clinton on 16 November: "I am now to inform you that the idea of a cooperation with His Excellency the Count D'Estaing in this quarter is intirely at an end."

Washington drew his army into Morristown on 21 December, down to his winter complement of 7,000 soldiers and desperately short of rations and matériel. His weakness was so great as to prevent even the notion of a move against the British fortress on Manhattan when Clinton withdrew 5,000 men for a land-and-sea attack on Charleston on 31 December. Bitter cold created intense suffering, burying the camp in successive snow-storms and coating the Hudson with a six-inch crust of ice. The wretched soldiers stayed close to their fires, huddling in groups of four and five for warmth. One night gale winds ripped apart a marquee under which

253

five soldiers had been sleeping; before cold woke them, they were all but buried under snow. Storms also blocked the roadways, reducing the supply of rations to a trickle and then to nothing at all. "The snow is now from four to six feet deep, which so obstructs the roads as to prevent our receiving a supply of provisions," wrote Thacher, "We are frequently for six or eight days entirely destitute of meat, and then as long without bread."

Deprivation led to wholesale plundering, necessitating gruesome punishments which the reluctant officers felt obligated to perform. Offenders could suffer the "wooden horse," a rail they were forced to straddle with weights tied to their feet; the "gauntlet," a track lined with men wielding scourges and blocked at intervals with bayonets to keep them from running through too fast; or the lash, a whip contrived of tiny knotted cords that cut the skin at every stroke. In extreme cases, offenders were whipped daily, the lash cutting the scar tissue of the day previous, preventing healing and making the pain excruciatingly intense. The men endured this last, wrote Thacher, by placing a bullet between their teeth, "on which they chew . . . till it is made quite flat."

Washington's pleas for relief from Congress fell on barren ground. Nathanael Greene, his reluctant quartermaster general, sent terrible reports from Philadelphia of the collapse of credit and of contracts for food, clothes, and tents for the army canceled in mid-progress as Congress ran out of cash. Recruits returning at the end of winter found the army at low ebb. "Week after week without meat, without clothing, and paid in filthy rags," wrote one saddened soldier, "I despise my countrymen. I wish I could say I was not born in America. I once gloried in it, but now I am ashamed."

Bad news from the Carolinas added to the travail of the spring. Charleston fell to Clinton 12 May 1780, ceding 5,500 Continental soldiers, countless stores and ammunition, and unchallenged entrée to the lower South. William Moultrie, one of the defenders, recalled the dying moments of the siege: "Fire . . . incessant the whole night . . . shells . . . like meteors crossing each other and bursting . . . It appeared as if the stars were tumbling down." The next day the royal fusilliers, Hessian grenadiers, and artillery took

254

possession of the city, planting the British colors on the gates. Determined to treat the Americans as rebels, not an army, they forced them to file out with colors cased, denied the small ceremonies usually accorded the survivors of a siege. In a final gesture of insult the militia were released. "They are allowed to go home and plow the ground," wrote one British officer. "There they can *only* be useful."

Cornwallis headed into the interior two days later in his career of subjugation, hounding rebels, harrying guerrillas, and leaving a trail of desolation through the state. On 29 May the Tory Legion of Banastre "Bloody" Tarleton cornered a band of Virginia militia at the Waxhaws near the border of North Carolina and dispatched them in a scene of memorable atrocity, killing 113 after capitulation, and leaving 150 others hideously mangled on the field. A camp surgeon watched in horror as the legionnaires hacked their way through the heaps of bodies, tossing the corpses aside on bayonet points to stab the living underneath. Dead and wounded alike were cut and slashed about the face. "For fifteen minutes after every man was prostrate, they went over the ground, plunging their bayonets into every one that exhibited any signs of life." In the flush of terror, it appeared all hope was dead. Resistance crumbled as the British swept through the state. "The people at that time were not much accustomed to arms," wrote one provincial colonel, "& finding no troops to support them, Submitted when they saw the King's troops in possession of the back country. Posts were established at Augusta, Ninety-Six, Camden, Cheraw Hill & Georgetown. The Conquest of the Province was complete." To Washington, confined as he was in the northern sector, the opening of a second front was very nearly disastrous, necessitating the departure of Gates with 1,200 precious Continentals to stem the tide of blood. His scrawny army was cut ever closer to the bone.

At this moment news arrived that gave his sunken spirits a brief and tantalizing life. Lafayette had gone home in 1779 to plead the cause of the Americans and, with his accustomed ardor, had dropped a bomb upon Vergennes: "I am thoroughly convinced . . . that it is highly important for us to send a body of troops to America. If the United States should

255

object . . . I think it is our duty to remove the objections, and even to suggest reasons for it." At length, Vergennes agreed to an initial shipment of 8,000 from six of France's oldest regiments, with an escort of nine warships commanded by Admiral de Ternay, under the baton of one of France's premier lieutenant generals, Jean Baptiste Donatien de Vimeur, Viscount de Rochambeau. Rochambeau's credentials sounded reassuring (experience on European battlefields since the age of sixteen) as did the names of the French regiments, Bourbonnais, Soissionais, Royal Deux-Ponts, Saintonge. European regulars—to the Americans, it seemed a step from quicksand onto rock. Lafayette reached Boston at the end of April, bringing the good news first to Washington, then to Philadelphia, Congress, and the French envoy to the capital, the Chevalier de la Luzerne. His scenario was simplicity itself: Ternay would cancel out the British navy, while the allied force converged upon New York. The war might be over before fall.

Sadly, nothing happened as foreseen. Half the transports failed to arrive at the embarkation point in France. Rochambeau waited till mid-April, then loaded half his troops on the available vessels, then was delayed until 2 May by contrary winds inside the roads of Brest. He sailed at last into Newport Harbor on 12 July—directly ahead of two fleets of British warships, which the next day sealed the harbor in an iron ring. "M. de Ternay's vessels have been blockaded the whole time," Lafayette wrote sadly to a friend in Paris, "and the English have nineteen vessels there." Still, hope remained that the second shift of French men and warships might break through the blockade. Unless detained by an absolute catastrophe, Lafayette told his Parisian correspondent. the second division would arrive quite soon.

Delay meanwhile wreaked havoc with the Americans, who had (again) called out the militia at astronomical expense.

I am reduced to the painful alternative either of dismissing a part of the militia [Washington wrote Congress on 20 August] or let them come forward to starve. . . . If we adopt the first, we shall probably not be able to get them out again . . . and to let them come on without the means of assistance would be absurd. . . . It is impossible for us to form any calculation of what we are to expect, and consequently to concert any plans.

On 25 August he had a letter from Rochambeau. The second division, blockaded in Brest by a British squadron, could not break out until the end of summer, making it October at the earliest before it could arrive. George dismissed the militia—for the third year running—and gave up all hopes about New York. Inured to disappointment, he made no direct comments, but he doubtless would have been in sad agreement with the bitter charge of Axel von Fersen, an aide to Rochambeau: "vegetating at the very door of the enemy, in a most disastrous state of idleness and uncertainty . . . inactive, and shamefully so."

"Shameful" was the word for the next news from the South. On 16 August, Gates had met Cornwallis outside Camden, South Carolina, in a masterpiece of mismanagement that surpassed the expectations of his foes. He faced the first charge of the British troops with green militia, who, at the sight of bayonets, threw down their arms and fled, leaving a large void between the ranks of regulars, through which the British horses came pouring, circling around to strike against their flanks. The Maryland and Delaware lines stood firm against repeated onslaughts, until the infantry, charging at once with fixed bayonets, shattered them beyond repair. Gates compounded the disaster with a mad dash to Hillsborough, perhaps (as he claimed) to find a post at which to rally, but giving rise to extended rumors that he, like his militia, fled from fear. "One hundred and eighty miles in three days and a half," marveled Hamilton in caustic wonder. "It does admirable credit to the activity of a man at his time of life."

To Washington, disaster made the disgrace of an old rival lose a good deal of its charm. The southern militia was scattered, the Continental lines were decimated, and the South, to the Virginia border, was open to British attack. "If they push their success in that quarter," he wrote grimly, "there is no saying where their career may end." (Cornwallis was already nursing plans—shared by Germain, but not by Clinton—of moving his force into Virginia, and making that the major theater of the war.) The end result, for Washington, was to push him closer to the wall. Since the southern country was too wild and too sparsely settled to sustain militia, he must detach more troops from his own thin resources or cede all states below the Pennsylvania line. The tenuous connection between means and necessity was again becoming perilously thin.

Anxiety was coming from another area. Rochambeau was pressing him for an interview that he was desperately anxious to avoid. Pitifully short of men and wherewithal, shaken by the debacle at Camden, he could approach the French on no other grounds than supplication, a situation which he shrank from, for reasons of both policy and pride. With Alexander Hamilton, there was a series of discussions on methods of extracting French pity without inviting French contempt, which, for all the exercise of their joint imaginations, came up with nothing at all. The meeting itself, held in Hartford, Connecticut, on 17–20 September, was anticlimax, save for the chance for the generals to compare disappointments, and take each other's measure face to face. For the rest, there was only a muted sharing of speculation and regrets. "Nothing conclusive," George reported to a friend on 4 October. "We could only combine possible plans on the supposition of possible events, and engage mutually to do everything in our powers against the next campaign." Against the tableaux of three years' futility, "suppositions" must have had a bitter ring. "The history of the war is a history of false hopes and temporary expedients," he wrote one correspondent; and, to another, "I see nothing before us but accumulating distress."

His forecast was more accurate than even he had guessed. En route back from Hartford he made a sudden decision to look in on West Point, the mid-Hudson fortress that controlled the access to the northern part of the river and whose control had passed to the crippled Arnold in the summer of the year. With Lafayette, he crossed the Hudson on the morning of 24 September, to find the guns dismantled and the fort in disarray. Perplexed and more than slightly anxious, he recrossed the river and headed for the estate on the east bank occupied by Arnold and his wife. In the court he saw Alexander Hamilton (who had gone on before him), white and speechless, with a sheaf of papers in his hand. Washington read them, and then turned to Lafayette. Arnold had gone to the British and had nearly taken West Point.

The defection had been brewing twenty months, in an atmosphere of grievance and of greed. Arnold had suffered over Gates' rebuffs at Saratoga and at the long refusal of Congress, on political grounds, to raise his rank to major general, since the quota for his state was filled. Joshua Hett Smith, a resident of Stony Point, whom the American generals had used for frequent errands, told courts later that Arnold had complained to him of being "heartily tired," "ill-used" by Congress in "not sufficiently ESTIMATING HIS SERVICES," slapping his crippled leg, and asking vociferously, "Where can I seek for compensation for such damages as I have sustained?"

At first, he sought compensation in dazzle, with his large house (Mount Pleasant, a stone mansion in Philadelphia where Howe had held court) and his small bride, a Tory beauty who had socialized extensively with the British in their occupation and seemed to have preferred them greatly to their gauche successors with their lack of cash and politesse. Philadelphians could see the pair dash about the city in a liveried carriage, mixing with the new elite of speculator society, throwing huge entertainments in their majestic mansion, and running up majestic debts. Arnold made an effort to eke out his army salary with a scheme to rent out army wagons for a private hauling business, but Congress rewarded his enterprise with a court-martial and a reprimand, leaving his pride wounded and his debts as grievous as before. Brooding now over insults to his purse and ego, he appeared to reach the answer to them both. Sometime in the spring of

259

1779, Sir Henry Clinton began to receive the first of a series of subtle intimations that a ranking American general was ready to change sides. Arnold's court-martial cast a cloud on his potential value, but on his acquittal this shadow slipped away. "Information was given me that he would most certainly . . . be employed again," Clinton wrote to Germain later, "with an offer of surrendering himself under every possible advantage to His Majesty's Arms."

The first connection was made between Peggy Arnold and her good friend from the British occupation, Clinton's adjutant general, the plausible and dashing John André. Initially, they masked details of ammunition, stores, and troop movements through coded gossip about mutual acquaintances and shopping lists of "Articles for Mrs. Moore." Arnold himself later graduated to ciphered expositions of his own. Although he was to protest vehemently that his defection was actuated by political motives, his correspondence reveals a different note: "As Life and every thing is at Stake, I will expect some Certainty. My property here Secure and a revenue equivalent to the risk and service. . . . Inform me what I may expect."

About the "service," André dropped a suggestion in June, 1780, a year after the correspondence had begun. "I should stile a partial blow the taking possession of a considerable Seaport and defeating the troops assigned to the defense of the province so as to be able to make a progress through it. . . . Could you obtain a Command in Carolina? The rest you must understand."

"Carolina" went successively to Gates and Greene, but in July, 1780, "Mr. Moore" was given command of West Point and its dependent forts. He had something worth selling, and negotiations reached a frantic pace. In the space of four days—11–15 July—Arnold sent no less than four letters to the British, all on the themes of financial security and risk. He made his final offer on 15 July:

> . . . S. Henry secure to me my property, valued at
> ten thousand pounds Sterling, to be paid to me or my
> Heirs in case of Loss . . .—pounds per annum to be se-

cured to me for Life. . . . If I point out a plan of cooperation by which S.H. shall possess himself of West Point . . . twenty pounds Sterling I think will be a cheap purchase for an object of so much importance.

Arnold kept pressing for an interview, and Clinton reluctantly agreed. On the night of 21 September, Smith rowed from Stony Point to the British warship *Vulture* anchored in midriver, beguiled by a story from Arnold that he was to receive a Tory civilian bearing "intelligence" and bring him back to Arnold on the shore. Aboard ship, however, Smith was confronted with John André, in the full dress of a British officer, his martial outfit in contrast with his deferential manner and pink cheeks. With André wrapped in a cloak (and the oars muffled in sheepskin) Smith rowed him to a cove on the west bank of the river; Arnold limped out of the shadows, and the two held a ghostly converse until dawn. As André was about to return to the *Vulture*, fire from rebel shore guns drove the ship downriver, necessitating a return to New York through a no-man's-land of partisans between King's Ferry and the safely Tory country of the Bronx. Arnold brought the uneasy André back to Smith's house where he stayed all day while Arnold plotted; Smith at one point saw him peer through an upstairs window at the *Vulture*, with a sigh of infinite regret. Somewhere in the course of the day, Arnold gave André a pass made out to one "John Anderson" and talked him, reluctantly, into changing his uniform for civilian clothes.

At twilight Smith and André emerged, the latter now attired in Smith's dark jacket, high boots, and round and slightly tarnished beaver hat. Boatsmen at King's Ferry recalled their odd demeanor, André wrapped in his cloak and utterly silent, Smith almost hysterically jovial, chattering maniacally as the small boat crossed the water to the eastern shore. In the inn in Westchester where they spent the night, André's anxieties increased. Smith recalled that he tossed restlessly, called for his horse at the first sign of daylight, and appeared in the morning haggard and distraught. Smith took him some miles further and set him on the White Plains

261

road. About nine André was stopped near Tarrytown by three rebel partisans, who, made suspicious by his rattled manner, searched him and at last discovered papers hidden in his boots. He was taken to the nearest army post at North Castle where an addled colonel took the pass to be a forgery and sent it, with André, up to Arnold at West Point. He also sent a note to Washington, enclosing the papers found on André, which included detailed drawings of West Point and its defenses, in Arnold's hand.

André had just departed under guard when Benjamin Tallmadge, Washington's head of the secret service, arrived. Tallmadge was stunned when the colonel spilled his story and, after extensive arguments, succeeded in having André recalled. The letter, however, went forward, reaching Arnold at his headquarters the next morning—24 September—as he sat at breakfast with a party of his own and Washington's aides. There was a bizarre moment as he read the ruin of his expectations under Alexander Hamilton's unsuspecting eyes. Excusing himself, Arnold left the table, ducked out a window at the side of the house, and ran to his barge in the river, where he was rowed downstream to the *Vulture,* anchored now in Tappan Bay. (On arrival, he turned over his oarsmen as prisoners; Clinton, less merciless, pardoned them the next day.) The papers sent to Washington missed him en route back from Hartford and reached Arnold's headquarters later in the day. It was these that he took from Hamilton's hands.

Nothing was left the stunned Americans but to guard against attack. Aides sent on a mad dash to Croton in an effort to catch Arnold arrived far too late. Posts up and down the river received urgent messages to arm. The Pennsylvania Line, routed out of bed at three in the morning, reached West Point in early morning, having covered fifteen miles in four hours; Wayne reinforced all approaches to the fort at Stony Point. Events on the human level proceeded with variety and pace. Washington and his embarrassed aides climbed the stairs to Arnold's bedroom for a confrontation with his wife; Peggy Arnold threw a bravura scene, clutching her child and sobbing hysterically, letting her negligee fall open

262

to reveal distracting areas of skin. ("An amiable woman, frantic with distress for the loss of a husband she loved tenderly," the susceptible Hamilton wrote to Elizabeth Schuyler, his fiancée and future wife. "It was the most affecting scene I ever was witness to.") Embarrassed, stricken (and besotted), the Americans released her to join her husband in New York. En route she showed a new side of her personality to Theodosia Prevost, the widow of a British officer (and soon to marry Aaron Burr), at whose house Peggy and her escort stayed. In company, the scenes continued; alone, the hysterics stopped. Peggy told her hostess she was "heartily sick of the theatrics she was exhibiting . . . that she was corresponding with the British commander—that she was disgusted with the American cause . . . and that, through great persuasion and unceasing perseverance, she had ultimately brought the general into an agreement to surrender West Point."

Smith had been apprehended and dragged to headquarters before an impromptu court of Washington, his officers, and aides. There, in a state close to terror, he admitted that he had acted from faith in Arnold, whose rank and reputation had led him mesmerized into a succession of bizarre and sense-defying schemes. At North Castle, Tallmadge had become increasingly suspicious of André, watching his parade ground manner as he paced about his cell. "As soon as I saw Anderson," Tallmadge wrote later, "I became impressed with the belief that he had been *bred to arms.*" He mentioned this to his subordinate and requested him to notice his gait, "especially when he turned on his heel to retrace his course across the room." Tallmadge's musings were terminated about three in the afternoon when André requested pen and paper and wrote a letter to Washington, revealing his name, his rank in the British army, and his part in and his knowledge of the plot. The time of subterfuge was at an end.

Stricken, the army convened at Tappan, on 27 September, André lodged in the basement of a tavern while deliberations went on painfully next door. A court of fourteen officers, headed by an unhappy Greene, sat in a nearby church to hear evidence from assorted witnesses and pass a final judg-

263

ment on his fate. Their situation was exquisitely tormenting—instead of Arnold upon whom to vent their fury, they had the engaging and pathetically dignified André. His letter to Washington had been an effort to salvage his honor, apologizing not for his service to his army, but for the meanness of the circumstance involved. *"Against my stipulation, my intention, and without my knowledge beforehand,* I was conducted within one of your posts . . . *betrayed* . . . into the vile condition of an enemy in disguise." His demeanor in prison (he spent his time sketching) and his unfailing courtesy shook his captors; the impressionable Hamilton came distraught from his sessions with him, and even the seasoned Tallmadge was overwhelmed. "I foresee my fate," André told Hamilton, asked for pen and paper to write a last note to Clinton, and, for the first time, burst into tears. In New York, Clinton was ill with anguish and remorse. "Poor André throws a damp on all," he wrote to his two maiden sisters, "upon me greater than I can describe . . . should he suffer, you will easily believe it will be impossible for me to continue to serve . . . even if they keep him prisoner it will be horrid to live. . . . Good God, what a *coup manqué*."

A desperate mission sent by Clinton to Tappan to bargain for André was fruitless; the Americans would trade him for no one but Arnold, and the British would not give Arnold up. Reluctantly, George insisted that the rules of war be followed strictly, being necessary to bolster the existence of the rebel state. On 29 September the verdict was handed down "that Major André, Adjutant-General of the British Army, ought to be considered as a spy from the enemy, and that, agreeably to the law and usage of nations . . . ought to suffer death."

André took the news with predictable composure and greeted his wretched executioners with admirable cheer. "Affectingly awful," was Thacher's description as André made his way to the gallows at noon on 2 October, between the lines of strained and silent men. There was one ghastly moment as he caught sight of the gibbet. He had made a request to die by firing squad—a soldier's death, not a spy's—and had not been told it had been reluctantly denied. There was a dreadful stumble; then the words "It will be but a momentary pang." On the gallows, he was still true to form, taking the noose from the hangman and fixing it himself around his neck. The wagon lurched out suddenly, giving him a "most tremendous swing," sending the corpse flying in a great arc, then rocking gently, then, in moments, dangling horribly still.

The execution sent shock waves through both armies, leaving devastation on all sides. "When I saw him swinging under the gibbet, it seemed for a time as if I could not support it," wrote Tallmadge later, "all the spectators seemed to be overwhelmed . . . and many were suffused in tears." The British in New York wore black armbands for weeks. "A murderer & a Jesuit" was the best Clinton could say of Washington. "W. has committed premeditated murder. He must answer for the dreadful consequences. . . . Make peace with Spain & give me 10,000 men more . . . you may as well expect to see fire and water in peace together as your humble sert. in with these *miscreants.*"

The one participant immune from suffering was the precipitator of it all. For it was Arnold's insistence that André change out of his uniform that altered his status irrevocably from prisoner of war to spy. Nonetheless, Arnold sent this note to Clinton less than two weeks after André's death:

> In a conference which I had with Major André, He was so fully Convinced of the reasonableness of my proposal for being allowed Ten thousand pounds Sterling for my Services . . . that he assured me . . . tho he was Commissioned to promise me only Six thousand . . . He would use his influence and recommend it to Your Excellency . . . and from his State of the matter he informed me, He had no doubt Your Excellency would accede. . . .
>
> You will not think my Claim unreasonable, when you consider the Sacrifices I have made.

The affair knocked the wind out of the army at a time when it had little energy to lose. A direct result was the immediate cessation of all intelligence from New York—Arnold had passed Clinton the names of all of Washington's informants, and Clinton had the spies confined. Longer-range effects persisted, emanating from three things: André's

265

death, Arnold's treachery, and the increasing knowledge of how close their call had been. "Had it succeeded, all agree it would have ended the rebellion," Clinton wrote. "I prepared for a movement up the North River. . . . Mr. Washington must have instantly retired from King's Bridge, and the French troops upon Long Island would have consequently fallen into our hands."

Just how thin a thread the army hung on became apparent in the course of the inquiries begun after the arrest of André and continuing in some cases into spring. Especially chilling was the testimony of one John Pawling (or Paulding), the head of the patrol that had picked up "John Anderson" near Tarrytown the morning of 23 September. André, in neutral territory, had taken the patrol for loyalists and greeted them accordingly. Caught out, he stumbled, then tried to bribe them with a pocket watch. "I told him to dismount," said Pawling, ". . . he said, 'My God, I must do anything to get along,'" laughed awkwardly, and pulled out Arnold's pass. Now irrevocably suspicious, they began to search his clothes. "I told him to pull off his boots," said Pawling, ". . . I felt the papers in his stocking . . . I looked on the back of the papers . . . and I said to the young fellows who was with me, 'This is a spy.'"

The counsel queried him on one important point.

Q. When pulling out his pass from General Arnold, what was the reason you did not let him go?
A. Because he said before he was a British officer. *Had he pulled out General Arnold's pass first, I should have let him go.*

Shock waves from the trial persisted through the winter, causing new fissures in the army's shaken base. Greene had just reached West Point to take command there when he was shipped off, within hours, to pick up Gates' pieces in the southern theater. His letters for months afterward were a dreadful medley of deprivation and despair. Arnold himself, now a British brigadier, was ravaging Virginia (George's home country), spreading terror and alarm through the

266

province in an orgy of inverted rage. The new year of 1781 dawned with mutinies in the Pennsylvania, then the New Jersey lines. Quick action stemmed the damage, but the Pennsylvania Line—Wayne's pride— was shattered, and two ringleaders were shot.

One month later came another "mutiny": a spat between Washington and Hamilton flared into a bitter quarrel, Hamilton resigned in a flurry of letters to his friends (and Washington's) so petulant, irrational, and potentially destructive to his own ambitions as to suggest strongly that he had suffered a lapse of judgment from prolonged and unremitting strain. Both fatigue and Arnold figured in his outburst—he was sick at heart at his constant job of suppressing disorder among starving soldiers, and André's death had hit him hard. Very much like André (and in his position as aide to a commanding general), he might have seen the execution as some measure of betrayal, and he never forgave Washington for his refusal to allow André to be shot. Other things figured in the rupture: the orphaned Hamilton had a troubled background, and Washington was a special figure in his mental universe, the focus of his affection and his rage. For Washington too, it was a special deprivation: the loss of one of the "sons"—with Lafayette and Laurens—he had compulsively "adopted" to assuage the lack of his blood children and the wan nature of his ward. Taken with the other blows, it formed a disturbing pattern of endemic exhaustion in the army, of waning resources, and of fraying nerves. Habits of discipline were breaking under the strains imposed on them, and the bonds of concord were wearing perilously thin.

He faced the fact that this campaign might be his last. Vergennes read stiff lectures to John Laurens (sent to Versailles on a desperate errand to secure a $10,000,000 loan) before shipping him home at last with the money; a new admiral, Barras, to replace Ternay, who had died during the winter; and a promise that Admiral de Grasse (then in the West Indies) would appear on the North Atlantic coast to give a temporary naval superiority in the early fall. "At the close of this year, his Majesty will have given, or lent . . . the sum of twenty million," Vergennes wrote Lafayette. "If the war, as appears probable, is prolonged beyond the present campaign, I hope that we shall not be called on with similar demands. I forewarn you, that it will be quite impossible to satisfy them. France is by no means an inexhaustible mine."

Clinton was still in New York with a corps of 10,000 men. He had not, as George expected, drained his force to aid Cornwallis but had instead been reinforced. In the South, however, events had taken an unexpected turn. Perpetual risings, complained Cornwallis, had kept the Carolinas in a bloody turmoil, undoing his conquests in a series of guerrilla forays almost as soon as the last of his horse passed out of sight. He was tired of sniping, worn out by exhausting marches, and fatigued by Greene's tattered legions, who drew him ever northward, closer to climactic battles, and then vanished out of sight. Greene faced him at last near the Virginia border at Guilford Courthouse on 15 March in a chaotic daylong battle, Greene (true to his policy of victory through losing) pulling off the field at nightfall, leaving the woods scattered with the British dead. Everyone—Clinton especially—expected Cornwallis to follow Greene back south to secure the Carolinas, but the earl had another idea. "I am quite tired of marching about the country in quest of adventures," he wrote the astonished William Phillips, head of the British expeditionary forces in Virginia. "If we mean an offensive war . . . we must abandon New York, and bring our whole force into Virginia . . . if our plan is defensive . . . let us quit the Carolinas . . . and stick to our salt pork in New York."

Clinton, of course, envisioned a war based on the poles of New York and Charleston, with Virginia as a "diversion" in between. "His Lordship *disobeyed my orders, and acted contrary to his duty in doing so*," he wrote in his *Memoirs* later. ". . . I had every reason to be exceedingly hurt." On 10 April Cornwallis began his move to the Virginia border and on 19 May took command of the joint forces at Petersburg (Phillips having died of fever two days earlier), relieving Arnold, who, "rich as a nabob" from his compulsive plundering, returned to an infuriated Clinton in New York.

Cornwallis in Virginia, with no sea cover and the ocean

268

at his back—Rochambeau's ideas of allied action began to take a new and solid form.

The count took matters into his own hands. On 8 May the ship from France arrived at Boston, bringing Barras, the foreign loan, and suggestions from Versailles that Rochambeau use De Grasse in the autumn for an attack on Canada or Penobscot Bay. These aroused in him even less enthusiasm than Washington's insistence that they attack New York. "It became urgent that I should get out of my present embarrassing situation and do my best for the service of the two nations," he noted in his *Memoirs*. "My first step was to request an interview with General Washington, and he accordingly appointed to meet me at Wethersfield, near Hartford, on the 20th of May." Blooming in his mind was the conviction that the Chesapeake was the place for the junction of De Grasse and the allied armies and Cornwallis, whom he had last seen across a battlefield in Prussia in 1756, the proper bird to bag. Maneuvering his ally to this conclusion became the guiding object of his mind.

At Wethersfield (as expected), he found Washington more fixed than ever on New York. ". . . scarcely another object in view but an expedition against the island," he noted in his diary, adding that George considered a Virginia expedition a secondary object, for which there was "no necessity" to plan. Reason, argument, and veiled threats failed alike to move him, and the count at last realized he was confronting something beyond rationality in Washington's ironclad resolve. Normally flexible, George was in the grip of the obsession that could seize him in the wake of prolonged tension, such as his insistence on the Braddock road in his last campaign in 1758, when emotion backed up and blocked perspective, resulting in a ruinous distortion of his views. Rochambeau argued, then suddenly caved in. George thought he had won him around to his position, but an entry in the journal of Rochambeau's son, noting Washington's intransigence, suggests the true design: "It was therefore necessary to fool him, and to seem to adopt his plan, but to form others."

269

Making plans with Washington for an invasion of New York City, Rochambeau sent a ciphered letter to De Grasse, ostensibly a report on conditions, that stressed nonetheless three things: Clinton's strength on Manhattan Island, the failure of D'Estaing to enter New York Harbor, and the tempting weakness of the British position in the South. His conclusion (as recorded in his journal) gave De Grasse a gentle shove: "I then suggested, as my own opinion, the propriety of attempting an expedition to the Chesapeake."

At the same time Washington was writing to the French ambassador in Philadelphia, urging him to use his influence to bring De Grasse to Sandy Hook. "I assure you, that General Rochambeau's opinion and wishes concur with mine, and it is at his insistence principally that I make you this address."

Swords alight, in a rainbow parade contrasting brilliantly with the bedraggled Americans, the French joined the Americans at Dobbs Ferry on 16 June, presumably to plan for an attack on New York. George spent the next month hovering dangerously about the British outposts, reconnoitering within sight of enemy cannon and making manic forays that set the Frenchmen's teeth on edge—one, a dash at Fort Washington on 1 July, in which his advance guard was nearly captured; another, an expedition with a group of engineers to a small peninsula surrounded by British outposts, in which he and Rochambeau were nearly isolated and picked off. While the engineers gauged the width of the inlet, the generals dozed off beneath a hedge. Shortly, the sleepers were awakened by the whizzing sound of shells. "I hastened to call General Washington," Rochambeau recorded, "to remind him that he had forgotten the time of the tide." Dashing to the milldam, they discovered it had overflowed. Clutching their saddles, they were rowed to safety as aides, in a great spray of water, drove their horses to the other side. "This maneouvre," wrote Rochambeau, "which lasted nearly an hour, was fortunately for us, unseen."

Rochambeau was aware of the pressures upon Washington, which were driving him to try to force events. He wrote De Grasse on 11 June that the Americans were at the end of their resources, that George, despite efforts to conceal his

270

weakness, had no more than 6,000 men. George himself became depressed and "mortified" at the lack of progress of his troops. "No Militia are yet come in," he wrote in his diary on 10 July, "and other things drag on like a cart without wheels." Slowly, the maneuvers of the French commanders had begun to take effect. Rochambeau pressed him on 20 July for a plan to send on to De Grasse, and he was forced to admit for the first time that "I had neither Men, nor means adequate" to attack the fortresses of New York. On 23 July came another tightening of the knot—Barras had written him that he would not leave Newport for New York Harbor until De Grasse arrived, putting an end to his pleas for Barras to reach New York immediately "lest in the attempt any disaster should happen . . . ascribed to my obstinacy in urging a measure to which his own judgment was oppos'd."

He was coming to realize that French judgment had been "oppos'd" to New York from the beginning and that further obstinacy might recoil on him with irrecoverable effects. Rochambeau's scheme of watchful waiting was beginning to yield results.

Other elements of the French scenario were falling into place. Cornwallis, sullen and defensive, was moving northeast into the tidewater under a barrage of biting letters from New York. "Your lordship will, I hope, excuse me if I dissent from your opinion of the manner in which that army should be employed," Clinton wrote acidly. ". . . *take a defensive station in any healthy situation you choose.*" Clinton's idea was to establish a naval station to harass American communications and provide cover for British naval action in Chesapeake Bay. Yorktown, he suggested, would secure their works at Old Point Comfort, which protected Hampton Roads.

Harassed by Clinton and hounded by a ragtag force of 1,000 Continentals under Lafayette, Wayne, and Steuben, Cornwallis moved through the middle country to the James and York, avoiding battle, save for accidental strikes: on 6 July, Wayne set a scouting party on what he took to be a small detachment of the British rear at at Greenspring in Virginia (near Jamestown), and was thunderstruck to see the British army hurl itself at him from the woods. Valiant as ever, he flung his force forward in a wild bayonet charge, then pulled

271

off in the ensuing tumult and fell back on Lafayette. *"Madness!"* wrote one dazed survivor. "Mad A------y, by G-d, I never heard of such a piece of work . . . eight hundred troops opposed to five or six thousand veterans, upon their own ground. . . ." Undeterred, Cornwallis pulled into Yorktown in late July, to erect his "naval station" on the high bluff facing down into the York River, one mile from the river's mouth. For Cornwallis—and for Clinton—it was an unwilling compromise, a grudging draw between the two nether poles of offensive and withdrawal. For Rochambeau, at Dobbs Ferry with an unnerved and unnerving Washington, it was the answer to his prayers.

For Washington, it was the end of his. De Grasse informed him, via Rochambeau, that he would reach the Chesapeake in mid-September with 12,000 francs for the army and 3,000 soldiers under the Marquis de Saint-Simon. Even the sense of action held the nugget of regret. "I feel myself unhappy," he wrote in his Circular to the States on 12 August, "in being obliged to inform you, that the Circumstances in which I find myself . . . have induced me to make an Alteration of the Main Object, which has hitherto been held in view." The very terms in which he wrote his proclamation— "unhappy . . . obliged . . . Circumstances in which I find myself"—ring of constraint and of suppressed desire, the forcible curtailment of the dream. The strength of that vision and its long pull on the minds of the Americans can be sensed long distance in the letters of Nathanael Greene: "The shell and shot . . . must make a terrible rattling . . . Methinks I hear the cannon roar."

There would be no rattling against the fortifications of New York. Yet the swift relief from the three years' tethering held a heady measure of release. For Washington, although reluctantly, the project held its own appeal—a stroke on his own doorstep, involving his favored tactics of deception, motion, camouflage, surprise. The longed-for ploy of land and naval forces was about to close around a British army—if not the army that he had foreseen. They would gull Clinton, skip New York, come up behind Cornwallis, and pin him between the army and the sea.

XIV

Denouement

I consider myself to have done only my duty.
—WASHINGTON to the president of Congress,
November, 1781

The secret coup involved two elements: deception and the prompt arrival of De Grasse. Failure of either could mean rescue or reinforcement for the camp at Yorktown and nullify the last chances at success. Clinton at New York was not alarmed when the combined armies made a mass crossing at King's Ferry on 20–25 August in a vast show of guns and color, the dun-colored tatters of the bedraggled Americans massing for the first time with the starched array of France. Nor did he think it exceptional when the allies passed on to Sandy Hook, camping as if for months' duration, constructing vast brick ovens huge enough to feed an army through a siege. The ruse, though elaborate, was camouflage. The ovens were—and remained—empty, and by 28 August the troops were gone.

Nothing, or no one, could move fast enough. "I am almost all impatience and anxiety," Washington wrote Lafayette on 2 September, and, later, to the outgoing governor of Virginia: "Circumstances pressing upon me . . . and Time slipping from me too fast." On 2 September the American army passed through Philadelphia in a cloud of dust two miles long, followed next day by the French, "with a complete band of music, which operates like enchantment," and the added harmony of battle dress. George, however, remained uneasy, as he confessed to Lafayette: ". . . distressed beyond expression to know what is become of the Count de Grasse, and for fear the British Fleet, by occupying the Chesapeake . . . should frustrate all our flattering prospects. . . . I am also not a little anxious for the Count de Barras, who was to have sailed from Rhode Island on the 23d . . . and of whom I have heard nothing since." Incurably restless, he headed for the Chesapeake on 4 September, leaving Rochambeau and the Marquis de Chastellux to a leisured tour of the local battlefields, including a visit to Germantown, where they stared for some time at the Chew mansion, still pocked with cannon, the shattered windows and the splintered door. En route to the Head of Elk, however, George had a message that stopped him in his tracks. The French, returning by water to Chester, saw him at the dock, waving his hat, with an expression of the utmost ecstasy: De Grasse had arrived in the Chesapeake, with 3,000 soldiers and twenty-eight ships of the line.

"Nothing now gives me impatience," he wrote Du Portail on 7 September, "but the two things you mention, not hearing from the Count de Barras . . . and [the] resolution for the departure of the fleet." There was a brief, idyllic interlude at Mount Vernon with Rochambeau and Chastellux, then (14 September) the ride to Williamsburg to join Lafayette, Wayne, Steuben, Governor Nelson with 3,000 militia, and the 3,000 French under Saint-Simon—all stunned, as Lafayette (out of sickbed, and faint with malaria) flew at his hero, "hugged him as close as it was possible, and absolutely kissed him from ear to ear." The next day came the message that was the answer to his prayers: De Grasse had met Graves on 5 September and driven him, broken, to New York, while Barras, under cover of the tumult, slipped into the Chesapeake with his vast load of cannon and eight sail of the line. Three days later George met De Grasse on his giant flagship *Ville de Paris,* Knox in hysterics as the huge admiral cried out, *"Mon cher petit général!"* flung himself at an astonished Washington, and kissed him on both cheeks. The conference was to have resolved the crucial point—that De Grasse would

274

stay past his deadline of 15 October to the safe conclusion of the siege. Two days later the impulsive admiral threw a scare into them all. Having heard that a British fleet under Admiral Robert Digby was on his way down, he determined to set out to meet him, and sail as soon as the wind permitted for New York. Horrified pleas from Washington, Rochambeau, and Lafayette dissuaded him, and the blockade remained intact. At five in the morning of 28 September the allied lines moved out from Williamsburg and, by five that evening, were before the walls of York.

Siege warfare brought the war an altered tempo—scarcity replaced by plenty, improvisation by formality, skirmishing by step-by-step procedures laid down in the seventeenth century by the French military strategist Claude Vauban. Successive lines of trenches, dug parallel to the walls of the besieged city and filled with heavy cannon, moved inexorably closer to the lines. The first days of October saw the beginning of the *danse macabre*. Intensive scouting determined the placing of the first parallel and construction of the primitive batteries to shelter the workers at their task. Throughout the British shelled them with a rain of fire, shots arcing from their barricades to burst inside the allied ranks. The bombardment was incessant; on 2 October an allied soldier counted 352 shot. Alexander Scammell, one of Washington's favorite junior officers, was carried in dying from a bullet wound; James Thacher watched in horror as a cannonball took off three men. George himself displayed an eerie composure that added to his growing legend of sangfroid: he and Du Portail, with a covering party, were walking within 300 yards of the British cannon when a shot whizzed past them, causing all to dive for cover—except Washington, who, calm as ever, continued peering through his glass. Thacher recalled another incident in which a shell landed at the feet of Washington and the camp chaplain, burrowing into the earth beside them and spraying both with a shower of sand.

Mr. Evans, much agitated, shook his hat at Washington, and said, "See here, General."

275

"Mr. Evans," replied his excellency, with his usual composure, "you had better carry that home and show it to your wife and children."

On the night of 5 October the lines were drawn for the first parallell, workmen laying strips of pine wood end to end over the lines marked out by engineers; Washington once more caused consternation by appearing alone and unguarded within forty rods of the British guns. The next night—6 October—entrenchment began. George himself wielded the first pickax, "that it might be said," wrote one soldier, "that General Washington, with his own hands, first broke ground at the siege." There was a sweep of shadows and a crunching noise as 2,000 shovels broke into the sandy ground. By dawn the British found themselves encircled by a wide arc of trenches two miles long, encompassing four redoubts and a flying trench, facing their own advanced redoubt by the river, and trained to fire on their warships in the bay. ". . . under their noses!" exulted an American as the first British shots rang out, sailing above the heads of the allied workers, now safely under cover in their lines. At noon the allied armies filed into their trenches in a grand array of drums and color, the Americans on the right arm of the angle, the French, their standards flying, on the left. The British garrison had already been showing signs of accelerating distress; an outpost on Gloucester Point, a promontory across the York River, had been mopped up by an allied action on 3 October. Now carcasses of dead horses came floating by the hundreds downstream—slaughtered by the York garrison, which could no longer keep them in feed. Slaves, ill with smallpox, were turned out into the allied lines in a grisly scheme to infect and devastate the camp. Instead, the plan proved fruitless—Washington had inoculated his army in the winter of 1780–81—and the wretched slaves wandered off to die hideously in the woods beyond the allied trenches or the sandy washes of the swamps. Past the corpses—human and animal—came the endless stream of wagons, bringing dismantled cannon from Barras' ships. Night and day the work continued, soldiers, in rotating shifts of eight hours each, fixing the heavy guns inside the lines. "Extremely severe," wrote Dr. Thacher of his duty on 8 October. "Our regiment labors in the trenches every other day and night, where I find it difficult to avoid suffering by the cold. . . . We erected a battery last night in front of our first parallel without annoyance from the enemy. Two or three of our batteries [are] now prepared to open on the town. . . ."

At three in the afternoon of 9 October Washington put a flare to a huge cannon on the far right of the lines. There was a blast, silence, then a furious discharge, splintering the embrasures beneath the British cannon, driving the ships in the river close to the Gloucester shoreline, arcing over the barricades into the town beyond. The first shot was audible as it rattled through the houses. Rumor said it crashed into the British headquarters, burned over a table at which a large party of officers were lunching, landed in a tremendous crash of glass and china, and killed or wounded the soldier at the head. Terrified British soldiers pitched their tents inside their trenches as the inhabitants fled to the river, hiding in the hillsides in the rocks and caves.

The remnants of the British cannon exploded in a violent response. A ball whizzed past the nose of an American soldier and dropped him instantly, his skin intact and spotless, but "his skull shattered all in pieces, and the blood flowing from his nose and mouth." French and American soldiers in the trenches watched the dreadful passage of the shells ascending slowly in great parabolic movements, arcing over the barricades to the center of the city, "raising clouds of dust and rubbish . . . blowing the unfortunate wretches . . . more than twenty feet in the air." Other times the shells themselves were seen, whirling and burrowing great tunnels in the earth, then exploding in a vile cascade of sand and bodies, bricks, and mangled limbs. On the night of 10 October shots from the French batteries set fire to the *Charon,* a forty-four-gun ship at anchor in the York River, igniting it instantly in a golden web of light. Dr. Thacher wrote:

> A torrent of fire which, spreading with vivid brightness among the combustible rigging and running with amazing rapidity to the tops of the several masts . . . while all around was thunder and lightening from our nu-

277

merous cannon and mortars . . . in the darkness of the night, presented one of the most sublime and magnificent spectacles. . . . Some of our shells, overreaching the town, are seen to fall into the river, and bursting, throw up columns of water, like the spouting of the monsters of the deep.

Daily, new cannon had been added to the allied trenches, joining their fire to the deafening barrage. On 11 October they had begun the second parallel, a line of trenches halfway between the first lines and the British barricades, barely 300 yards from their big guns. A sheet of fire from smaller ammunition poured out from the British trenches, mainly from two redoubts, nine and ten, advanced almost to the allied outworks, guarded by moats and abatis and bristling with guns. "The entire night was an immense roar of bursting shell," wrote one American, and George himself confessed to "a more galling Fire . . . much annoyance, and . . . a considerable loss."

For the first time, allied casualties reached a disturbing pitch. A Frenchman saw a gunner, his foot carried away by a bullet, lament only "not to have had time . . . to discharge the cannon I had pointed" and die in a pool of blood. It was decided to end the carnage in a single stroke. Just before eight in the evening of 14 October twin teams of French and Americans crouched before the redoubts, waiting for their signal of three bright rockets in the eastern sky. Their muskets were empty; they were to use the bayonet. At eight the flares exploded, and they plunged into their redoubts, the Americans shoving aside the miners who were hacking down the defenses and tearing at the half-axed abatis with their hands. Under a shower of grenades they dashed across the trenches, stumbling past and tripping into the craters their own bombs had made. Hamilton hopped on the shoulders of a taller soldier and tumbled over into the fortress; the rest followed, blades flashing, backing the defenders to the walls. Eight were killed and thirty wounded in the sudden sortie, a staggeringly low amount. Lafayette sent a taunting message to his brother-in-law, the Viscount Viomenil: he was in *his* redoubt; what had happened to the French? The viscount shot back that he would be in in five minutes—and he was. The French had waited for their miners to ax down the abatis, which had cost them twenty minutes and as many men. Then *"Vive le Roi!"* and they piled through, into a blast of shells and musket fire, slashing at the gunners with their bayonets. Twenty-seven were killed and 109 wounded; one soldier nearly lost his sight and hearing when grains of sand were hurled into his face. Through the assault, British fire played incessantly on all parts of the allied lines, breaking around the conspicuous figures of Washington, General Benjamin Lincoln, and Knox. Dr. Thacher caught an exchange between George and one of his aides: "Colonel Cobb . . . said to his excellency, 'Sir, you are too much exposed here. Had you not better step back?' 'Colonel Cobb,' replied his excellency, 'if you are afraid, you have liberty to step back.'"

The bloodied redoubts were absorbed into the second parallel and outfitted with heavy guns. "Not less than one hundred pieces of heavy ordnance have been in continual operation during the last twenty-four hours," wrote Dr. Thacher on 16 October. "The whole peninsula trembles under the incesant thunderings of our infernal machines." That night the British made a brief, doomed effort to spike some of the allied cannon; they were beaten off, and the barrage resumed. In Yorktown the damage was hideous: fierce bombarding had reduced the ambuscades to ruins, with stockades, platforms, guns, and gun carriages pounded together into an earth-and-metal mass. Houses stood honeycombed and tottering; books and furniture were crushed in the wreckage or strewn in pieces in the streets. Cornwallis had left his headquarters, now a trembling mass of shattered woodwork, and repaired to a grotto in the yard. French and American soldiers, visiting the town days later, found a nightmare scene of ruin as they picked their way among debris and rubble, skirting the frequent shards of rotting flesh. Fragments of decaying bodies were a common sight among the bricks and broken glass. "Carcasses of men and horses," wrote a French chaplain, "half covered with dirt, whose moldering limbs, while they poisoned the air, struck dread and terror to the soul."

On the night of 17 October, Cornwallis played a wild

card—a sea escape to Gloucester on the north shore of the York River, followed by a mad dash north. He had embarked most of his garrison when a storm blew up, driving his boats far down the river and making it impossible to retrieve the troops on board. Morning came with his troops divided and his remaining boats employed in bringing back his men. At daylight the allied batteries opened up their deafening barrage. "We at that time could not fire a single gun," Cornwallis wrote to Clinton later. "One eight inch, and little more than one hundred cohorn shells remained." The allied cannon continued their thundering attack. Mercifully, a British drummer appeared on the trenches about 10 A.M.

There was a two-day interval in which terms of capitulation were worked out. Washington was adamant that the British repay the insult handed out in Charleston, when the American garrison was forced into a disgraceful exit from its lines. There was a brief exchange between Major John Ross, the British agent, and George's deputy, John Laurens:

> That gentleman observed, "This is a harsh article."
> "Which article?" said Colonel Laurens.
> "That the troops shall march out with colors cased, and drums beating a British march."

Laurens agreed that they were "harsh" and brought up the terms of Charleston. "But," said Ross, "My Lord Cornwallis did not command at Charleston." Laurens' answer was an echo of Washington, from his reception of Howe in 1776 to the dreadful hanging of André. "There, sir, you extort another declaration. It is not the individual that is considered here. It is the nation."

At two in the afternoon of 19 October the British emerged from their shattered barricades, marching between unending lines of French and Americans, the former spruce in brilliant uniforms, the latter ramrod stiff in rags. The British appeared grim and sullen, "much in liquor," said one American, and, another, "like boys who had been whipped at school." Echoes resounded of an old unpleasantness: Cornwallis sent his second, Brigadier General Charles O'Hara, to hand his sword to the allies, claiming he was indisposed. The British approached the surrender field with their eyes fixed firmly on the French alignment; O'Hara made a movement to present his sword to Rochambeau. Rochambeau forestalled him with a motion to his aide, Mathieu Dumas, who had escorted the vanquished generals to the spot:

> M. de Rochambeau . . . made me a sign, pointing to General Washington who was opposite to him . . . .
> "You are mistaken," said I to General O'Hara. "The commander-in-chief of our army is on the right."

Washington passed O'Hara to *his* second, Benjamin Lincoln, who had been humiliated at Charleston, and the sword at last changed hands. One by one, the British regiments moved into a circle formed by French hussars and dropped their muskets in a growing heap of wood and steel. Then they walked back into ruined Yorktown in the golden autumn light.

News of the blow reached London on 25 November, Germain bringing word to North at Downing Street shortly after noon. He "took it as a ball in the breast," exclaiming wildly, "'Oh God! It is all over!' repeated many times, under emotions of the deepest consternation and distress." North hung on (to his dismay and the king's insistence) through four months of Whig fury, brought down at last on an irresistible tide that took Germain and Sandwich with him in mid-March. "Swepped," said George III pitiably of his Cabinet as he was forced to accept (27 March 1782) a coalition of Shelbourne and Rockingham, fat with his old enemies, Grafton, Conway, Camden, and Burke, and his newest tormentor, Charles James Fox. Distracted, the king sketched out the rough draft of an abdication speech—"his Majesty . . . with much sorrow finds he can be of no further utility to his native country which drives him to the painful step of quitting it forever"—and for a time the royal yacht was seen moored in the Thames near Kensington, fully rigged and set for flight. Sir Guy Carleton, governor-general of Canada, was called to Manhattan to replace Clinton and preside over the eventual evacuation of the troops. A motion brought in the Commons had passed by nineteen votes on 27 February to authorize the king to seek peace with the Americans and finish the offensive war. Britain's war against its onetime colonies was all but at an end.

George was the hero, the man of the hour, the focus of attention, the cynosure of all eyes. "It is his merit which has defended the liberty of America," wrote the Frenchman Claud Blanchard, "and if she enjoys it . . . it is to him alone that she will be indebted for it." Among the merits were the odd blend of ice and fire, tenacity and flair. There were the headlong dashes into enemy fire, the unconcerned and almost ostentatious strolls through shells and bullets, the flash attacks on enemy cantonments, always sudden, always unexpected, always from the bottom of the pit. Balancing these were the gray hours—the months and years within the harness that revealed another pole of character: nerves tamed into staying power by his relentless sense of duty and an enormous effort of the will. Through the rest ran mutability, an adaptability to men and circumstance, using illusions to his own advantage, cajoling his men with soothing motions, confounding the enemy with distraction and surprise. Somewhere in the blend of fire, rock, and mercury lay the dimensions of the hero, who had given insurrection its legitimacy and sustained a random army on his will. Journals of French soldiers, entranced by their first view of the "republican hero" (and influenced no doubt by memories of their own fat king), give invaluable glimpses of Washington at his moments of despair and triumph, at this climactic juncture of his life.

Some things were the same: the blue eyes, now slightly hollow in their sockets, but active and lively, the straight features; pale and pockmarked skin; the brown hair, graying slightly, lightly powdered, and pulled back into a queue. He was still "majestick," tall enough to tower over almost all contemporaries, moving with grace, speed, and an awesome power, striding about a cantonment, taking his horses (which he schooled himself) full speed over fences or, in a rare moment of leisure, picking up a weight his aides had been shot-putting and hurling it twice the length that it had gone before. There was the reserve, with its elements of danger and a brooding sorrow. Fersen noted a "sadness" in his features, and others remarked his soldiers feared his silence more than the wooden horse. "Permits himself a restrictive gaiety," wrote Luzerne of his leisure moments, suggesting by his adjective a constant self-surveillance and an unbroken habit of control. He still liked to keep men at arm's length.

Yet the reserve could crack or melt disarmingly in intimate company or with his aides. French officers give engaging pictures of the nightly sessions after dinner, from nine to eleven, around tables cluttered with bottles, cheese, and dishes of small green hickory nuts, half cracked with a hammer, where, through interminable toasts with Madeira, beer, and grum (an odious mixture of rum and water), the general, his face softened by "the most gracious and amiable smile," sat among the emptied glasses and the growing heap of nutshells, chatting familiarly and gaily with his aides. Once one George Bennet, a Tory captured within continental waters on Long Island Sound, was brought to Washington's headquarters in Newburgh. He found himself invited to wine and then dinner, placed at the left hand of Martha Washington, chatty as ever in her plain woolen outfit, while George, in a blue coat and unruffled linen, carried on an amiable banter with his staff. True to his Virginian breeding. George's camp, wherever he moved it, bore less the air of a court or spit-and-polish military establishment than of a large and unpretentious country house. "His conversation," wrote Luzerne, "is as simple as his habits and his appearance. He makes no pretensions, and does the honors of his house with dignity, but without pompousness or flattery . . . he sometimes throws and catches a ball for whole hours with his aides." "Affable," "gentle," "mild" are adjectives that appear over and over in the accounts of French visitors. "He is masculine looking, without his features being less gentle," wrote Luzerne, on their first meeting. "He received us with a noble, modest, and gentle urbanity and with that graciousness which seems to be the basis of his character. . . . I have never seen anyone who was more naturally and spontaneously polite."

"Proportion," "harmony," and "balance" are other

words that recur in the French descriptions and accounts, suggesting not only a basic symmetry of face and body, but the gentling of an inherently savage and powerful physical presence through inner discipline and will. Mathieu Dumas noted the perfect harmony of his countenance; Chastellux, the "idea of a perfect whole . . . well made and exactly proportioned, his physiognomy mild and agreeable, but such as to render it impossible to speak particularly of any of his features, so that in quitting him, you have only the recollection of a fine face."

Doubtless, this sense of bridled power was the key to his final triumph—the exercise of authority, stemming not from office (for his legitimacy was doubtful and his system chaotic and improvised), but grounded in magnetism and personal appeal. "General in a republic," wrote Chastellux, "he has not the imposing stateliness of a maréchal of France, who gives *the order*; a hero in a republic, he excites another sort of respect, which seems to spring from the sole idea, that the safety of each individual is attached to his person"—an assessment echoed almost to the syllable by his colleague the Count de Ségur: ". . . he inspired rather than commanded respect, and in the eyes of all the men around him, one could read their real affection and whole-hearted confidence in a chief upon whom they seemed to rely entirely for their security."

"Balance" was at once the key to his hold over people and the most mysterious portion of the whole. It is hard to reconcile Chastellux's descriptions of harmony and moderation in a man consumed by ambition, capable of rages, eaten by self-doubt—unless that balance takes its power from the tension of conflicting forces, the forced harmony of violent extremes. Evidence exists, from men who knew him at all stages of his life in public, of both his temper and his uncertainty and the pains he went to to gain "habitual ascendancy" over them both. Enough remained of both to give elusive strain to the character he had so laboriously constructed; "the most illustrious . . . in our century," wrote Axel von Fersen, "not to say unique."

Some things had not changed: the diffidence and the habitual aversion to applause. Victory found him subdued, contained, and, on the matter of his role in the triumph, all but mute. "Accordingly done" was the most that he could say of his accomplishment, and his private letters showed the habits of fatigue and anxiety that had worn deep grooves into his brain. "My greatest fear," he wrote to Greene in Carolina, "is that Congress, viewing this stroke in too important a point of Light, may think our Work too nearly closed, and- . . . fall into a State of Languor and Relaxation . . . if unhappily we sink into that fatal Mistake, no part of the Blame shall be mine." In his progress north, dotted with receptions from ecstatic state assemblies, he channeled thanks to his officers and allies and read his puzzled audiences stern lectures on the continued need for more exertion by the states. "It had better not have happened," he wrote Robert Hanson Harrison, "if it should be the means of relaxation, and sink us into supineness and security," as if he had never known what "relaxation" meant. As for his own contribution, he remained characteristically subdued. "I consider myself to have done only my duty," he told Thomas McKean, the retiring president of Congress. To the Executive Council of Pennsylvania he added this note, implicit in his life and character: "My Services I consider as my Country's due."

One more "service" remained to him before he could quit his task. By April, 1782, reports had trickled into his camp (now at Newburgh in the Hudson Valley) that Congress might discharge the army without pay. Appalled, he deluged Congress with a flood of threats and urgings, while holding down the army with one hand. "Much soured," he wrote of the mood of the disgruntled soldiers, warning that fear might lead the officers to dangerous designs. One such—a letter in May from an addled colonel urging him to set up a military dictatorship—drew a horrified response: "You could not have found a person to whom your schemes are more disagreeable . . . banish these thoughts from your Mind, and never communicate, from yourself or anyone else, a sentiment of the like nature." Still, Congress balked, and he wrote more urgent letters as the year wore ominously on. "It really appears, from the conduct of the States, that they do not conceive it necessary for the Army to receive any thing but hard knocks; to give them pay is a matter which has long been out of the question," he wrote to James McHenry, and he sent an unsettling message to the secretary of war: "I cannot help apprehending that a train of Evils will follow, of a very serious and distressing Nature . . . while in the field, I think it may be kept from breaking out into Acts of Outrage, but when we retire into Winter Quarters . . . I cannot be at ease."

Homesick and miserable, he spent the winter in "dreary" Newburgh, watching his sullen army and mourning the death of John Laurens, killed in a skirmish in the Carolinas in the fall. In February came some dreadful news: an impost that would have allowed Congress to pay soldiers had been defeated by the states. Washington was desolate, and his friends in Congress schemed in desperation to use the threat of army terror to pressure "weak minds" in council to a speedy granting of due funds: Hamilton had already written Washington that he might have to hold down the army and had gone before a committee of Congress to tell its startled members that the officers were about to oust Washington for a wild general to lead them in a coup d'état. Before they got much further, trouble erupted from another source. Three anonymous petitions (later traced to one John Armstrong, a former aide-de-camp to Gates) made the rounds of Newburgh, calling for "deeds of outrage and violence," from mass desertions to a march on Congress with bayonets. For three days the camp teetered on the edge of violence, caught between loyalty and rage. Rebellion appeared imminent. Which way would they fall?

George moved quickly to halt the downward plunge. At noon on 15 March he met his troops head-on in a tense and crowded meeting at the Temple Hall. There was an appeal to law and patience, to the verdict of history, to shared suffering and his fights on their behalf. Near the end he produced a letter from a friend in Congress, "made a short pause; took out his spectacles, and begged the indulgence of his audience . . . observing at the same time that he had grown gray in their service, and found himself growing blind."

"The meeting," George wrote the president of Congress, "terminated in a manner, which I had reason to expect." "I said, or meant to say," he later wrote a shaken Hamilton, "the army was a dangerous engine to work with, as it might be made to cut both ways."

No one knew better how keen that edge could be.

Thirty-three days later (19 April) news of the peace settlement was read to the army from the steps of Temple Hall. The troops were dismissed through the disgraceful expedient of indefinite "furloughs" (to evade payment of full settlements) and sent off with promissory notes in lieu of cash. Oddly, there was only one outbreak of violence: troops from Lancaster marched on Philadelphia on 19 July, surrounded the State House where Congress was sitting, driving that body to Princeton—and then Annapolis—before being dispersed themselves. For the rest, they left quietly. "Some . . . went home the same day their fetters were knocked off," wrote Joseph Plumb Martin, himself unfettered on 11 June. "Others stayed and got their final settlement certificated; which they sold to procure decent clothing and money sufficient to enable them to pass with decency through the country, and to appear something like themselves . . . among their friends."

For Washington—still commander—there was an interminable stretch of waiting as the last scenes ran their course. He made a trip through the Mohawk Valley to Crown Point in August, followed by a two-month stay in Princeton, clearing up the remainder of his paperwork. "Genl. Carleton sent me word that . . . in November he should evacuate," he wrote to Rochambeau in irritation, "but we have already experienced so many disappointments, that I shall scarcely believe they *are going,* until they are without *Sandy Hook.*" It was not until 25 November that he entered New York City, as the last of the British transports disappeared through the Narrows, the grim condition of the battered city, barricaded, and still gutted from the fire, in bizarre contrast with the show of state and panoply and the dazzling fireworks at Bowling Green. At noon on 4 December at Fraunces' Tavern, he had a farewell dinner with his officers. "Such a scene of sorrow and weeping I had never before witnessed," wrote Benjamin Tallmadge, "and hope I may never be called upon to witness

287

again." Typically, Washington made no mention of the episode or of the fetes before it—the first ripples of a wave of adulation that was about to overwhelm him and whose implications (it was to become apparent later) he was beginning to regard with dread. Not a word of the crowds that had begun to surround him everywhere, that filled the streets as he walked to the Whitehall ferry, that massed about the landing as his barge pushed off into the bay. The "approbation" he had always longed for had assumed a malign aspect, a remorseless public expectation that would become more and more a burden and, in some respects, a threat. Like his ambition, his success was taking on a dual nature that would plague and pull him for the remainder of his life.

That he *was* a hero was a fact impossible to shake. People mobbed him, jammed the streets, ran to see his carriage, pushed to touch his hand. His progress south was a succession of parades and hysteria; wild celebrations marked his passage through Brunswick, Princeton, and Trenton; he entered Philadelphia on 8 December to the roar of cannon and the riotous cacophony of bells.

Wilmington and Baltimore feted him with feasts and dancing; at Annapolis on 22 December he was dined by Congress in a "din of a most extraordinary nature, and most delightful influence . . . every man seemed to be in heaven, or so absorbed . . . not a soul got drunk, though there was wine in plenty, and the usual number of thirteen toasts." Following that there was a ball in the State House, where "he danced every set . . . that the ladies might have the pleasure of dancing with him, or, as it has since been handsomely expressed, *get a touch of him*"—a phrase suggesting both the pull of power and his transmutation into an almost-legendary state. At noon the next day he resigned his commission, surrendering the temporal part of his power. But his legend went with him into retirement, making his renunciation of influence a matter of mere form.

What, now, of his world beyond the war? Since Yorktown, his speeches and his letters had rung with one persistent note: that peace "will put period not only to my Military Service, but also to my public life." Much of this was genuine, reflecting desperate fatigue and enervation, and a craving

288

for (as he told Benjamin Harrison) "that relaxation and repose which is *absolutely necessary* for me." But there was another reason (admitted later), reflecting an anxiety that had begun already to prey upon his mind: a belief that statements of his intention to retire completely—repeated often, recorded in Congress, and printed in all the gazettes and papers—would be an insurmountable safeguard and barrier against any schemes (or temptations) to bring him back to public life. His words were strong and no doubt truthful in some part. But his sense of a need to guard against the future revealed an inner tension and a nascent struggle in his mind.

There were other symptoms of his odd duality. In the same months he was making his declarations of retirement he was reading stiff lectures to army and to state assemblies, pressing his *idées fixes* of power, union, and central governments able to pervade and overrule the states. His circular letter to the states on the disbanding of the army in July was a lengthy *political* document, astonishing and radical in its prescriptions, looking *beyond* Congress to a blueprint of his own: ". . . there should be lodged somewhere a supreme power to regulate and govern the general concerns of the confederated republic . . . whatever measures have a tendency to dissolve the union, or contribute to violate or lessen the sovereign authority, ought to be considered as hostile to the liberty and independency of America." His private letters also ring with his concerns and anxieties: until a firm union ruled the federation, it was no better than a "rope of sand."

What should happen, in "retirement," if the rope of sand should break? He was now a presence, impressive in exerting or withholding power, potent in action, never more threatening than when in repose. There was no escaping his new role at the center, even if that had fully been his wish. His conflicting statements in his last years in the army shadowed the beginnings of another struggle, and his retirement was to begin his private war.

PART FOUR:

These
United
States
1784-1799

XV

Prelude

I greatly apprehend that my Countrymen will expect too much from me. . . .—WASHINGTON to Edward Rutledge, 5 May 1789

George was home, for his second retirement, the soldier sunk once more in the country gentleman, determined, as he wrote Chastellux, to view life "in the calm light of mild philosophy . . . with that serenity of mind, which the Soldier in his pursuit of Glory, and the Statesman of Fame, have not time to enjoy." That serenity itself remained elusive was revealed in a letter of 20 February 1784 to Henry Knox:

> I am just beginning to experience that ease, and freedom from public cares, which, however desirable, takes some time to realize . . . it was not till lately that I could get the better of my usual custom of ruminating as soon as I awaked . . . and of my surprise, after having resolved many things in mind, to find that I was no longer a public Man.

Was surprise the major part of his experience, or was he clinging to some portion of the past? The evidence of the six years following reveals a mind divided and perplexed.

All was far from tranquil on the domestic front. There

293

were his shadow brothers, erratic and unsettling: Charles, entering the fourth of his five marriages, and Samuel, ever-lastingly in debt. There was his half-mad mother, living by herself in Fredericksburg, complaining chronically and pla-guing him with her financial woes. She had written him one letter in his term as commander, to complain about an over-seer on a holding for which George paid the bills. "She says she can get nothing from him," George wrote John Augus-tine. "It is pretty evident . . . that I get nothing from thence, while I have the annual rent of between eighty and an hundred pounds to pay." A more conscious act of vicious-ness was her appeal in 1780 to the state legislature of Virgin-ia for a pension, on the grounds that she was living in great poverty, owing to her children's neglect. The request was quashed on an appeal from Washington, but the general had little peace. "I learn," he wrote John Augustine, "that she is, upon all occasions and in all companies, complaining of the hardness of the times, of her wants and difficulties . . . if not in direct terms, at least by strong innuendoes . . . which not only make *her* appear in an unfavorable point of view, but *those also* connected with her. . . . I wish you to rep-resent to her in delicate terms, the impropriety of her complaints, and the *acceptance* of favors, even when they are voluntarily offered," adding in a tacit confession of her madness, "It will not do to touch upon this subject in a letter to her, therefore I have avoided it." That the humiliation lasted was suggested by a reference to "some things which have given, and still continue to give me pain." She could have found no more consummate piece of malice or a more exquisite vengeance on her son. On his return her response was to badger him for money—not a word about his travail in the war. Lack of parental attention is often the source of unending insecurity and persistent questioning of worth. One wonders if his endless search for approbation had its roots herein.

There was Martha, the bargain bride, married years be-fore in his first retirement as part of his accommodation to a disappointing life. What was her role in his broad horizons now that his life had widened out? She was the one person he had written to daily in the press of his official business (though these letters have now been destroyed). She joined him each year in winter quarters, adding a grace note of affability and a homely touch of warmth. At every stop she had become a chatelaine of the encampment; soldiers at Valley Forge recalled her going the rounds of the dreadful hospitals with soups and potions, a heavy shawl about her rounded figure, her woolen dresses fastened with a thorn. "A short, thick woman," recalled one veteran, "very pleasant and kind. She used to visit the hospitals, was kindhearted, and had a motherly care." Another Martha (Mrs. Theodorick Bland) gave another picture of the Washingtons *à deux* when she lived in Morristown ("a very clever little village") in the winter of 1777–78, visiting them every day between tea and dinner and sending her in-laws by letter a picture of domestic bliss. "His worthy lady," she reported happily, "seems to be in perfect felicity, while she is by the side of her 'Old Man.' "

How perfect was this felicity for Martha and for her "Old Man"? Reports and stories from this period leave no doubt that the social graces of the commander had matured under power and acclaim. "Our noble and agreeable commander," enthused Mrs. Bland to her sister-in-law, "commands both sexes, one by his excellent skill in military matters, the other by his ability, politeness, and attention" —especially at soirees and riding parties, when "he throws off the hero, and takes on the agreeable chatty companion. He can be downright impudent sometimes, such impudence, Fanny, as you and I like." Another glimpse of the "impudent" general came from a Major Shaw, in attendance at winter quarters outside Philadelphia in 1779. At Mrs. Biddle's soirée, Shaw reported, a Mrs. Olney had told an attentive Washington that "if he did not let go her hand, she would tear out his eyes, or the hair from his head; and that though he was a general, he was but a man." Shaw was later driven to complain himself at the excessive revelry, kept up till 2 A.M. for three nights running, with George himself a prime offender, dancing upwards of three hours with dark-eyed Kitty Greene. Though fatigued, Shaw retained his humor and perspective. "Upon the whole," he added later, "we had a pretty little frisk."

What of the commander, who, after all, was "but a

man"? Stories flourished in the hothouse of notoriety, spawning scandal by the yard. He was reported to have fathered Alexander Hamilton in his visit to Barbados in 1751 with his dying brother Lawrence; Hamilton was born in the West Indies and out of wedlock, but not, alas, till 1755. He was rumored to have sired Eliza Jumel, queen of the New York demimonde. (Eliza later claimed to have been the only woman in the world to have slept with both Washington and Napoleon and her career thereafter showed a penchant for both statesmen and bizarre intrigue. She claimed an affaire with Alexander Hamilton, married Aaron Burr in 1836, when that disgraced roué was seventy-seven, and divorced him three years later on charges of adultery, with Alexander Hamilton, Jr., representing her in court.) George was also rumored to favor intrigues with the wives of his officers, sparked perhaps by his rapport with Kitty Greene and perhaps by the sensuous tenor of a letter to Lafayette in 1779 on a proposed introduction by the latter to his young marquise:

> Tell her that I have a heart susceptible of the tenderest passion, and that it is already so strongly impressed that she must be cautious of putting love's torch to it, as you must be in fanning the flame. But here again, methinks, I hear you say, I am not apprehensive of danger. My wife is young, you are old, and the Atlantic is between you. All this is true, but know, my good friend, that no distance can keep *anxious* lovers long asunder, and that the wonders of former ages may be revived in this. But alas! Will you not remark that amidst all the wonders . . . no instance can be produced where a young woman from *real inclination* has preferred an old man. This is so much against me, that I shall not be able, *I fear*, to contest the prize with you.

Susceptibility, passions, torches, flames—what can be made of this, in conjunction with his other constant references to similar incendiary themes? Some years later he would write a letter to his stepgranddaughter, cautioning her on the impact of amatory instincts, of "inflammable matter" and "passions . . . more easily raised than allayed." And it was at this time that he wrote (24 December 1784) this letter to the

Reverend William Gordon about the marital adventures of a friend:

> I am glad to hear that my old acquaintance Colo. Ward is yet under the influence of vigorous passions. I will not ascribe the intrepidity of his late enterprise to a mere *flash* of desires, because in the course of his military career, he would have learned to distinguish between false alarms and a serious movement. Charity therefore induces me to suppose that like a prudent general, he had reviewed his *strength,* his arms, and ammunition before he got involved in an action. But, if these have been neglected, and he has been precipitated into the measure, let me advise him to make the first *onset* . . . with vigor, that the impression may be deep, if it cannot be lasting, or frequently renewed.

How did Martha, plump and cozy, fit into this scene? A French officer at Morristown observed that George "admires pretty women . . . notices their gowns and how their hair is dressed. He does it quite openly, and before his wife, who does not seem to mind at all." Did her composure stem from assurance or from realism, from her trust in a limited arrangement entered knowingly and carefully maintained? Sometime between Washington's death in 1799 and her own two years later, Martha Washington fed into a fireplace at Mount Vernon all but two of his immense store of letters to her, sending up in smoke and ash the subtle interstices of their lives. The coarser evidence remaining suggests a warm alliance, the surviving letters showing, if not the passion revealed to Sally Fairfax, a reservoir of affection and at least a limited rapport. "Patsy" (as he called her) may have stood for the home side of his nature, hidden by her wish as well as his decision from history's intruding eye. As she proved, Martha Washington concurred with at least one instinct of her second husband: that personal arrangements were matters that the world "has no business" to know.

A distinct drop in feminine appreciation would be one of the penalties of retirement as George moved once more into the shelter of his counterlife and pulled the routine of the plantation around him like a shell. Whatever its shortcomings, it stood for safe harbor, the antithesis to his other world of storm and danger, expectation, tension, and fatigue. Mount Vernon, with its calm round of settled patterns, was the ideal balance to war and diplomacy and their intense, unsettling demands. Was it more than that? In his first paragraph of his first inaugural, George referred to it with mixed feelings and much passion as "my asylum . . . my retreat." The words themselves contain an interplay of meanings, suggesting both comfort and constraint; green trees and sweet rivers, but also exile and incarceration, a place of almost shameful hiding, a refuge for the ailing or unfit. Within two years of the day he resigned his commission, he was complaining of headaches and oppressive feelings, symptoms of internal tension and debate. The next six years were to be a fever chart of his emotional struggles, played out against a background of national disintegration and decline.

Ripples had begun to stir the surface before the signing of the peace. In March 1783, Alexander Hamilton had written him a pleading letter, begging him to use his influence to urge the drifting states to coalesce. George's answer was a study in evasion and ambiguous response:

> All my private letters have teemed with these sentiments . . . but how far any further essay by me might be productive of the wished for end, or appear to arrogate more than belongs to me, depends so much upon popular opinion . . . that it is not easy to decide . . . the prejudices of the majority, make address and management necessary to give weight to opinions which are to combat the doctrines of those various classes of men.

Who in the country had more influence over public opinion, and who had more address? Several days later, a letter to Lafayette defined his diverse pulls:

> The honor, power and true interest of this Country must be measured by a Continental scale . . . to form a Constitution, that will give consistency, stability and dignity to the Union, and sufficient powers to the great Coun-

cil . . . is a duty which will be incumbent upon every man . . . and will meet with my aid as far as it can be rendered in the private walks of life.

Private walks and duty—how far could they coincide? At first, he made valiant efforts to disengage himself, immersing himself in plantation matters, promoting western land development, making a new trip to the Ohio Valley in 1785. Yet the greater world intruded constantly, drawing infuriated outbursts as the states foundered in chaos and disunion and congressional vigor sank to an appalling low. "Shameful . . . truly Shocking," he wrote to one friend after a dismal congressional showing, and to another, his fears that "[we must] molder into dust and become contemptible" unless a firm hand took the helm. To another friend, who voiced fears of autocracy, he sent a caustic response: "I have no fears arising from this source. . . . But I have many, and powerful ones . . . from half-starved, limping government, that appears to be always moving upon crutches, and tottering at every step." To James Madison, his pale young neighbor whom he had lately adopted as a friend and confidant, he sent a bitter letter: "We are either a united people, or we are not. If the former . . . let us . . . act as a nation, which have national objects to promote, and a national character to support. If we are not, let us no longer act a farce." To Lafayette, he wrote, 10 May 1786, a letter that held a form of hope: "the people, not always seeing and frequently misled, must often feel before they can act right . . . the discerning part . . . have long since seen the necessity of giving adequate powers to Congress . . . and the ignorant and designing must yield to it ere long."

How long, however, before matters righted of themselves? Shay's Rebellion, in September, 1786, sent a shudder through the state. Farmers in western Massachusetts, maddened by inflation and chaotic finance, advanced on Boston armed with guns and pitchforks, crossing the state without opposition until dispersed at last outside the city by terrified state guards. Discerning people were frightened on two counts—that administration had deteriorated to the point of making people desperate and that officials had remained

299

helpless before riot for so long. Civic leaders, George among them, had a horrified response. "Good God!" he wrote to Henry Knox of the disturbances. "Who, besides a Tory, could have foreseen, or a Briton predicted them? . . . even at this moment . . . it seems to me like the vision of a dream . . . if the powers are inadequate, amend or alter them, but do not let us sink into the lowest state of humiliation . . . and become a by-word in all the earth." To Henry Lee, he sent another outburst: "To be more exposed in the eyes of the world, and more contemptible than we are already, is hardly possible," and met Lee's suggestion that he use his influence with an acidulous response: "You talk, my good Sir, of employing Influence. . . . I know not where that Influence is to be found. . . . Influence is no government. Let us have one by which our lives, liberties, and properties will be secured, or let us know the worst at once."

Yet he was capable of writing, at almost the same time, an astounding letter to George William Fairfax in England about the "tranquillity and rural amusements" that his ex-neighbor had found. "I am getting into the latter as fast as I can, being determined to make the remainder of my life easy. Let the world or the affairs of it go as they may."

What could budge him from his web of conflict and the ambiguities in which he seemed enmeshed? In 1786, in the middle of his struggles, came a canny letter from John Jay: "It is in contemplation to take measures for a general Convention. . . . I am fervent in my wishes, that it may comport with the Line of Life you have marked out for yourself to favor your Country with your Counsels on such an important and *signal* occasion. I suggest this only as a Hint."

"*Signal*" occasion—a phrase meant to rouse him, without awakening his fears. Did anyone believe that once he had been pulled again into the government, it could be a one-shot thing? Not Jay, not his good friend Alexander Hamilton, and certainly not George himself, whose subsequent answers showed evasiveness and dread. His first reply held a guarded sentence: "I scarcely know what opinion to entertain." Jay, doubtless backed by Hamilton, followed with a cataclysmic picture drawn to feed into his fears: anarchy, lead-

300

ing to riot, followed by a cry among the propertied for repression and a crown. Could this warning draw the sleeping lion from his lair? George again backed off, in an answer of extraordinary complexity. He began on a note of acquiescent horror, displaced responsibility from himself to others—"Would to God that wise measures may be taken in time to avert the consequences we have but too much reason to apprehend"—and ended on a note of absolute retreat: "It is not my business to embark again upon the sea of troubles. Nor could it be expected that my sentiments and opinions would have much weight on the minds of my countrymen."

"Not my business" . . . "troubled seas." Yet his younger friends had jumped headlong into the currents, and the tides were about to draw him in. A meeting at Annapolis in September, 1786, to discuss trade agreements had shamefully drawn representation from only five of fourteen states. But of the members rattling around the city, Hamilton and Madison had thrown a bomb: a convention to revise the makeshift government, to be held in Philadelphia the first week in May.

As expected, George's name topped the list of delegates submitted to the Virginia legislature, bringing new anxieties and a barrage of pressure from his friends. "Should this matter be pressed," he wrote one on 26 December, "what had I best to do? You as an indifferent person . . . can determine upon better ground and fuller evidence than myself." He asked if the states were truly serious or if this attempt, like others, was about to fizzle out. If so, "there is an end of Federal Government," the states would return home "mortified," their delegates disgraced. "A disagreeable situation for any one of them," he concluded, "but more particularly so for a person in my situation. If no further applications are made . . . of course I do not attend." Here was a sign of yet another terror—if he were involved in an abortive measure, his reputation, raised so painfully, would topple to the ground. To Henry Knox, he sent a chilling letter: "*In confidence,* I inform you that it is not, at this time, my purpose to attend." To Governor Edmund Randolph he expressed yet another cause of his diffidence: "It will, I fear, have a tendency to sweep me back into the tide of public affairs."

Hunting for excuses, he came upon a new diversion: he had turned down an invitation to appear at Philadelphia at a convention of the Order of the Cincinnati (an organization of officers of the Revolutionary War); his appearance there at yet a new convention would be improper, and "disrespectful to a worthy set of men." Yet the same month he wrote again to Knox: nonattendance might be read as a flight from duty; what ought he to do? "Inform me confidentially what the public expectation is . . . that is, whether I will, or ought to be there? . . . My final determination cannot be delayed beyond the time for your reply."

Domestic troubles intruded upon public conflicts to add new strains to his conjecturings and cloud his mind with images of loss. In April he had buried John Augustine, "A Brother who was the intimate companion of my youth, and the friend of my ripened age." Less anguishing but more complex was the problem of his mother, now ill with cancer, whose present wasting and approaching death doubtless raised mixed feelings of contrition and relief. The pressures told, George complaining in late April of being "so much afflicted with a Rheumatic complaint . . . as to be under the necessity of carrying my arm in a sling for the past ten days." Was the ailment purely physical or the manifestation of internal stress? A year later he was to make a confession to Alexander Hamilton that explained much of the torment of his life: "I will not suppress the acknowledgement . . . that I have always felt a kind of gloom upon my mind, as often as I have been taught to expect I might, and perhaps ere long be called to make a decision."

Late in March he was still wavering, writing, "I do not conceive that I can with any consistent conduct, attend." On 9 April, however, he sent Edmund Randolph an all but apologetic acceptance of his fate: "My consent is given contrary to my judgment, because the act will . . . be considered as inconsistent with my public declaration . . . not only in the files of Congress, but . . . almost all the Gazettes and Magazines." His tone throughout remained defensive, as if absolving himself from complicity in his ultimate decision or defending himself against some self-invented charge. To Robert Morris he sent a long account of his inner turmoil, ending, "I assure you . . . it was not until after a long struggle I could obtain my own consent." It was from Morris' house in Philadelphia that he wrote on 6 June to Lafayette

> You will be surprised, my dear marquis, to receive a letter from me at this place . . . more so, when you hear that I am again brought, contrary to my public declaration . . . on a public theatre. Such is the vicissitude of human affairs, and such is the frailty of human nature, that no man . . . can well answer for the resolutions he enters into. The pressure of the public voice was so loud, I could not resist the call.

George was duly present as the convention opened on 25 May in Independence Hall, snapped up at once (doubtless to his horror) for the presiding seat. True to form, he thanked the members, declared himself inadequate to the demands of the office, begged forgiveness for his anticipated errors, and sat down. These were the last words of any content he was to utter on the convention floor. For four months, until the convention adjourned in mid-September, he sat in all but total silence as the scaffolding went up for the strong government he yearned for and he felt the noose being measured for his neck. What else was he to make of the debates on the "executive officer," as it was funneled down from the tripartite, or shared, executive to the focus of a single man? More astonishing than anything was the contrast between his official silence and the inner rage within his letters to his friends. "Weak at home and disregarded abroad is our present condition, and contemptible enough it is," he wrote to a friend in Virginia. And to Thomas Jefferson, then American envoy to Paris, he sent this explosion on 30 May: "The situation of the General Government (if it can be called a government) is shaken to the foundation, and liable to be overset by every blast . . . . In a word, it is at an end, and unless a remedy is soon applied, anarchy and confusion will inevitably ensue." Incessantly he railed against the opponents of central power, who tried to fetter the emerging government and had to be dragged along the path to union, step by painful step: "The men who oppose a strong and energet-

303

ic government, are, in my opinion, narrow-minded politicians, or under the influence of local views." His fury was intense and violent, fueled by the rage he had carried since the Revolution and infused by fears of the subtle menace of their antipower pleas. Yet he still would not speak out against them on the floor. When Alexander Hamilton left at the end of June, for reasons that remain mysterious, George sent him an odd letter on 10 July: "I almost despair of seeing a favorable issue to the proceedings . . . and do therefore repent having had any agency in the business. . . . I am sorry you went away. I wish you were back. The crisis is equally important and alarming, and no opposition . . . should discourage exertions till the final signature is offered." Why this rebuke to Hamilton on his defection when he was committing one nearly as baneful of his own? Was it his old fear of exposing his ignorance before a room of legal experts or a deeper dread of where the longed-for tide of government would lead? As he explained later, "While rivetted to the toils and perplexities inseparable from the Commission . . . I sought not to avoid trouble. . . . But to rip open again the disagreeable subjects that seemed to be closed forever . . . the sacrifice would be too great."

At home his inner war went on. Which would win—duty and power or retirement and ease? While raging in private against the enemies to ratification, he nonetheless sent the Constitution off to his own state legislature with nothing better than a lukewarm endorsement, and a sentence near the end: "I accompany it with no observations; your own Judgments will at once discover the good."

There was a reason for this renewed retreat. He had barely unpacked from Philadelphia when Gouverneur Morris had sent him an explicit and not unexpected note:

> Should the idea prevail that you would not accept of the Presidency, it should prove fatal in many parts. . . .
> Of all men, you are the best fitted to fill that office. Your cool steady temper is *indespensably necessary* to give firm and manly tone to the new Government. . . . You *must*, I repeat *must*, mount the seat.

Washington's reaction was to pull into his shell again, the old syndrome of external silence covering commotion at the core. In June, 1788, as the country was buzzing with news of his coming accession, he sent an office seeker this astounding note: "I was not a little concerned at an application for employment under a Government which does not yet exist, and with the Administration of which . . . it is *much more* than possible I may never be concerned."

Anguished mail flew back and forth between George and his associates and among the associates themselves, the latter pressing their necessity, the former staging an increasingly besieged and weakening retreat. Even so, it was not until 3 October, at the close of a protracted and emotional exchange with Alexander Hamilton, that he was driven to accept his fate: "It would be . . . with a fixed and sole determination of lending whatever assistance might be in my power . . . in hopes that at a convenient and an early period, my services might be dispensed with, and that I might be permitted once more to retire—to pass an unclouded evening, after the stormy day of life."

What had caused the paralyzing stress? In a sense, the presidency he had half eluded was the ordained apex of his life—the dream of status gained and service rendered, brought from England with the early Washingtons and honed to an exquisite finish at that enchanted castle of his childhood, Belvoir. Undimmed by time and distance, the voices still retained their ancient magic: Lord Fairfax, Sally, and the colonel; Plutarch and Addison, *Cato,* with its themes of duty and ambition, commingling in the honorable life: "My life is grafted on the fate of Rome." While he lived, the wholly private life would be intolerable, an amalgamation of irresponsibility and shame. He was shaped, by birth and breeding, for a public man.

Yet this heritage had left the legacy that made his destiny so hard to take. Behind the conquering hero stood the odd man out, the half brother from the lower level of the family looking up in adoration, first at Lawrence and young Augustine, then at the dazzling Fairfax clan. Commander as he was, he had spent the first half of his existence measuring

305

himself against his betters, finding himself wanting, struggling to solidify a position of whose viability he was constantly in doubt. In his mind's eye he was the outsider, existing on sufferance, acting under the scrutiny of a critical universe, examining his imperfect credentials for their flaws. Each advance in worldly terms had brought a contradictory reaction: the outlet for his monumental energies and the chance to have his insufficiencies revealed, imparting ambivalence to all his actions and making it impossible for him to exist in tranquillity in a state of either trial or of peace.

Like his appointment to the army, the presidency held a special dread: the chance to exhibit his deficiencies on the truly global scale. To Henry Knox, he compared his emotions to those of a criminal being taken to the gallows, and to another friend, as bowing to necessity, with a heart burdened with distress. When the messenger arrived at last on 14 April with the news of his unanimous election by the electoral college, he returned an astonishing response: "I wish . . . there may not be reason for regretting the choice." In Baltimore three days later, en route to his inauguration in New York, he spoke again of his incompetence. At his inauguration at New York on 30 April he spoke of himself as "inheriting inferior endowments from nature" and begged his electors, in case of catastrophe, to take the blame for it upon themselves. Sometime in the month he had also composed a paper (never delivered) for possible presentation to Congress that was little short of a complete apology—for the Constitution, his career, and himself. On 5 May he sent a letter to his friend Edward Rutledge that was a definition of his fears:

> I greatly apprehend that my Countrymen will expect too much from me. I fear, if the issue of public measures should not correspond with their sanguine expectations, they will turn the extravagant (and I may say undue) praises . . . into equally extravagant (and I may hope undeserved) censures. So much is expected, so many untoward circumstances may intervene . . . that I feel an insuperable diffidence in my own abilities. . . . I shall stand in need of the countenance and aid of every friend.

What kind of man was this new President, chosen to stabilize the nation, who had given such a demonstration of the instabilities within himself? He still looked the hero, intimidating others with his presence, reassuring with his agile grace. John Adams, a man not given to compliments, sent a list in 1807 to Benjamin Rush (another nonadmirer) of Washington's "talents," topping his list of ten with four pertaining to his looks: "An handsome face. . . . An elegant form. . . . Graceful attitudes and movements. . . . A tall stature, like the Hebrew sovereign chosen because he was taller by the head than the other Jews." The dumpy Adams, later dumped, may have been reaching out for compensation, tracing Washington's greater success as an executive to reasons less damaging to his esteem. "I have made out ten talents without saying a word about reading, thinking, or writing," he added to Rush, "upon which subjects you have said all that need be said." Rush had been a leader in the movement to oust Washington in 1777, and what he had "said" of his abilities may be surmised. That the test of executive ability was the capacity to *adapt* knowledge to contingencies appears to have slipped both their minds.

George had a lack of formal scholarship, of political history, and of legal expertise. This was a defect. On the plus side were resource, diplomacy, and the odd balance of complementary traits—improvisation and tenacity, force and guile, the ability to see the greater picture and meticulous attention to detail. Of the last, there can be no doubt; Jefferson recounted later that George had seen and passed on every piece of business that went through the hands of his department heads.

> Generally, they were simply sent back after perusal; which signified his approbation. Sometimes he returned them with an informal note, suggesting an alteration or a query. If a doubt of any importance arose, he reserved it for conference . . . he was always in accurate possession of all facts and proceedings in every part of the Union . . . formed a central point for the different branches; preserved a unity of object and action among them; exercised that participation in the gestation of affairs which his

office made incumbent on him; and met himself the due responsibility for whatever was done.

What later happened in default of this is shown in Jefferson's next sentence: "During Mr. Adams' administration, his long and habitual absences . . . rendered this kind of communication impracticable, removed him from any share of the transaction . . . and parcelled out the government, in fact, among four independent heads." Washington, in charge of a chaotic army, had learned the hard way the virtues of command. No power would be "parcelled out" by him.

He was an aristocrat, very much of the supervising classes, looking down upon the lower orders with a mixture of obligation and distaste. Thus his affinity for the more high-toned of his contemporaries: Robert and Gouverneur Morris, Henry Laurens, John Jay, and Philip Schuyler of New York. To his credit, his definitions ran along the lines of attitude, making him able to admit people of the middle classes, like Greene and Knox, and even Alexander Hamilton, whose beginnings were so bizarre and scandal-ridden as to transcend mediocrity into high drama of their own. Like his friends, he drew his lines on the grounds of minds, not money, between those ruled by passions only and his class of "discerning men." To George William Fairfax, he had written: "The people must *feel* before they will *see*; consequently are brought slowly into measures of public utility." Hence, the intention to direct opinion, even if unpopular at first. As for tone, his public record had been a cry for power. What chance of his letting the controls won for the central government slip back to the states? To complaints about these powers, he had a definitive response: "I have never yet been able to discover the propriety of placing it absolutely out of the power of men to render the essential services, because a possibility remains of their doing ill."

Yet he was willing to give argument an open rein. In the disjointed notes of his unfinished address to Congress were these subtle and intriguing lines:

> Shall I . . . set up my judgment as the standard of perfection? . . . Shall I arrogantly pronounce that who-

ever differs from me, must discern the subject through a distorting medium, or be influenced by some nefarious design? The mind is so formed in different persons as to contemplate the same object in different points of view. Hence originates the difference in questions of the greatest import, both human and divine.

Later he wrote to Benjamin Harrison, who had split with him over the Constitution and the issue of central powers:

My friendship is not in the least lessened by the difference, which has taken place in our political sentiments. . . . Men's minds are as varient as their faces, and where the motives of their actions are pure, the operation of the former is no more to be imputed to them as a crime than the appearance of the latter; for both, being the work of nature, are equally unavoidable. Liberality and charity . . . ought to govern in all disputes.

Washington had the instinct for power, tempered by intrinsic tolerance—energy without repression, perhaps the perfect blend. In the end, he had come into office for one purpose: to infuse union on the makeshift structure and save the confederation from destruction and contempt. It would not be easy. He knew his enemies: the governors, the local interests, the "darling Sovereignties" of the states. All would fight the new arrangement he had come to power to enforce. He knew the country, vast and variant, torn on a thousand lines of class and interest, between the forces of the coast and the backcountry, the commercial and the landed interests, the rising tide of paper money, and the ghastly traffic of the slave. What he did not yet know of was the divisive nature of his aides. How was he to know that Madison and Hamilton, who had worked as one for the Constitution, had a double nature, that in Hamilton's passion for energy and Madison's for balance lay the potential of a deadly split? Or that Jefferson and Adams, soul mates in Europe in the 1780s as ambassadors to France and England, had a similar bank of discord in the variance between their natures, the one luminous, the other grim? Ideally, the setup was to balance differences of region and estate: Washington and Adams, Hamilton and Jefferson, sinking differences in a harmony of minds. In reality, it was to set up a clash of interests and principles that was nearly to blow the government apart.

President of the United States—the terms themselves seemed makeshift and fragile, vulnerable, with an unpleasantly transitory ring. It was Washington himself, "but a man," who was to endow them with reality—back again upon the sea of troubles, which seemed to have no borders and no end.

XVI

Division

*How unfortunate . . . that internal dissensions
should be harrowing and tearing our vitals
. . . without more charity . . . the fairest prospect
of happiness and prosperity that ever was presented.
to man, will be lost.*—WASHINGTON to Thomas
Jefferson, 23 August 1792

Washington's administration was obsessed with power: power and its limits, power and men. John Adams, his Vice President, who was not his friend, stayed on the outskirts of the
government, breaking with his own friend, Thomas Jefferson, over matters of ideals and of ambition, waging an intense war with Alexander Hamilton for possession of the
Federalist legacy, laced with venom and intense bitterness,
raging in turn at Hamilton's ancestry—"Bastard Bratt of a
Scots pedlar"—his rumored habits—"his fornications, his
incests, his adulteries"—and at last, tracing his ambitions to a
"super abundance of secretions, which he could not find
whores enough to draw off." Jefferson and Hamilton, in
State and Treasury, would indulge in a historic feud. Madison, in a position of great power as speaker of the House,
would split with Washington and Hamilton, both friends of
years' standing, and move into alliance with Jefferson in the
seeds of formal opposition to the state. Jefferson would
break with all but Madison, as the softer quality of his visions

311

clashed against their grimmer natures and the dissimulations he was driven into by the shyness of his character raised suspicions of connivance and intrigue. John Jay and Gouverneur Morris, in the Supreme Court and the increasingly besieged French capital, remained in a remoter orbit, intimates of Washington and Hamilton, once among their few (and cherished) supporters in the wartime Congress, now personal friends and moral allies, repositories of affection and of trust. In time, they would move closer to their patrons, forming a knot of Federalist power, filling the gaps among advisers that opened as the others dropped away.

George himself would move through the dissolving picture, first above and then among the partisans, changing imperceptibly and unwillingly from hopeful moderator to unhappy participant and then into the center of discord. Through his terms he fought the tendency, confessing sadly at the end to Jefferson, "I was not a party man myself." Fearing the concentric forces at work within the federation, he had hoped at first to hold himself above the struggles, preserving his presence as the symbol of union to which all parties could repair. In some measure, he was to succeed. Countering this were his dread of internal chaos and his desire to weld the states together along the lines that had obsessed him since his term as a beleaguered general in the ghastly tumult of the war. Unwillingly, his sense of power was to make him partisan and propel him to the center of the storm.

Hamilton and Madison were the first to fly asunder, splitting over differences of power that had been hitherto obscured. Haunted by his experience with wartime chaos, fearing another slide into disunion, Hamilton evolved a series of related plans to bind the states together and the moneyed classes to the Union with hoops of gold and steel: the Assumption Plan (1790) to combine the debts of the states and pay them off through the central government; the plan (1791) for the Bank of the United States; and his scheme (1792) for federal assistance to domestic industries, all designed to weave financial interest into the scheme of union and knit the states into an economic web. He had hoped that his old friend would back him, but Madison had been disturbed by the shift in power from the landed to the commer-

312

cial interests, shocked at the scabrous hordes that clogged the streets to deal in stock transactions, and frightened above all by a threat to the balance of the Constitution in the accretion of power in both the central government and the executive branch. "A dangerous accumulation," he insisted, "a disproportion of power," or, as he was to write much later in what was probably the true explanation of his motives, "Departures from the fair and true construction of the instrument have always given me pain." Though he chipped in in June, 1790, to end a paralyzing congressional deadlock over the Assumption Bill, he became increasingly distressed at Hamilton's programs, seeing his old friend eventually not only as the patron of "usury, knavery, and folly," but as the instigator of an evil trend. "If Congress can do whatever in their *discretion* can be *done by money*," he wrote in answer to one of Hamilton's arguments, "the Government is no longer a limited one, possessing enumerated power, but an indefinite one," subverting the sanctioned limits of the Constitution and opening an endless vista of aggression and expanse. But an inventive government, bold and fluid, cleverly weaving greed and "interest" in the service of the commonwealth, had been the dream of Washington and Hamilton since their days together in the revolutionary army, and the conflict was to split the government in two.

Madison's resistance had begun the opposition to the administration, but Madison, withdrawn, delicate, and happiest as a thinker or political technician, was not to be the leader of his cause. This was Thomas Jefferson, already feuding with John Adams and, like Madison, growing alarmed and restive at the mercantile and centrist trend. He had been alarmed by a series of essays written in Adams' first year of his term as Vice President that seemed to tilt in the direction of a crown. Adams was not close to Washington or Hamilton, did not share their passion for innovative government, and was (as he confessed later) suspicious of commerce, financial politics, and banks. But he had a stronger authoritarian streak than either, a deep love of order, and a strong sense of the value of form and ceremony to keep the masses in control. In 1790 he had published a series of articles that examined the hereditary principle as a stabilizing force. He had written:

313

An illustrious descent attracts the attention of mankind . . . it is a name and a race that a nation has been interested in, and is in the habit of respecting. Benevolence,
sympathy, congratulations, have been so long associated
to these names in the minds of the people that they are become national habits . . . a youth, a child of this extrac-
tion . . . attracts the eyes and ears of all companies long
before it is known or inquired whether he is a wise man or
a fool.

Jefferson, hot from a long stay at the obese court of the
Bourbons, was appalled. In 1791, when Thomas Paine wrote
a virulent defense of the French Revolution, Jefferson sent it
on to a printer with a reference to "the political heresies that
have sprung up among us," which, when printed (contrary to
Jefferson's expectations) raised a storm. "The Question
everywhere," Adams wrote him angrily, "was, what Heresies
are intended by the Secretary of State? The answer
was . . . the Vice President's notions of a limited monarchy,
an hereditary Government, of Kings and Lords," which "op-
erated as a Hue and Cry to all my Enemies . . . to hunt me
down like a Hare." Adams stayed out of the resulting furor;
but his son, John Quincy, commenced a violent attack on
Jefferson, and Madison's commiserations showed the rival
camps into which both sides were splitting and the widening
cracks within the state. "Mr. Adams can least of all complain," Madison insisted, referring to a previous book that
Adams had published. "Under a mock defense of the Republican Constitutions of his Country, he has attacked them with
all the force he possessed." Jefferson apologized to the distracted Adams, but could not resist a parting dig. Near the
end of a long and exceedingly ambiguous letter, he added:
"Mr. Paine's principles . . . were the principles of the citizens of the U.S." In an embarrassed explanation to Washington he hit the same defensive chord, maintaining, "I have for
Mr. Adams a cordial esteem, even since his apostasy to hereditary monarchy and nobility . . . though we differ, we
differ as friends should do." Was it upon John Quincy, greatly gifted, who Jefferson suspected Adams of wishing the national gratitude to descend? The double rupture between

314

two sets of friends, now narrowly linked only through Washington's influence, was a storm warning of divisions over power and policy, complicated by ambition, and poisoned by suspicions of betrayal and intrigue.

Adams had a son who would follow him into high office and, finally, into the presidency itself. But it was not Adams who became the final focus of Jefferson's anxiety and rage. This was Alexander Hamilton, who had no prior place in Jefferson's affections, who had infinitely more power, and whose indiscretions fed as much into his fears. In Hamilton's suggestion to the Constitutional Convention that the President and members of the Senate hold life offices, Jefferson thought he saw the outlines of subversive intent, and in Hamilton's financial program, he thought he saw the means: a corrupt squadron of bought legislators, purchased through stock favors, ready to vote the way into an English system at the first summons of their master's voice. "Hamilton was not only a Monarchist, but for a monarchy bottomed on corruption," Jefferson wrote in his *Anas,* a journal of gossip and memoranda he had begun keeping in New York in 1790, "for an hereditary king, with a House of Lords, and Commons corrupted to his will." Fearful of Hamilton's power (and his long rapport with Washington) he wrote detailed letters to the President, calling Hamilton a colossus fat on corruption, engrossing all of the executive departments, and diverting the people from wholesome pursuits of an agricultural persuasion into immoral and debilitating flings with funds.

Shy and diffident, he drew back from head-on conflict, working instead through channels both politic and indirect. Assured of a backing from the southern states (whose economic structure had turned them against the administration), he made a tour of the Northeast with Madison in late 1791, organizing opposition on the state and local levels, consorting with Hamilton's New York rivals (who were to become Jefferson's vice presidents), the virulent Governor Clinton and the corrupt and glittering Burr. In October, Philip Freneau, a translating clerk in Jefferson's office in the State Department, surfaced as the owner and editor of the

315

National Gazette (an answer to the pro-Federalist *Gazette of the United States*), which deluged Hamilton and his measures in a torrent of abuse.

Hamilton, who saw his schemes as the cement of union without which liberty would falter, could find no point in Jefferson's onslaughts except an ambitious desire to supplant him in Washington's confidence and, eventually, to supplant Washington himself. To his friends, Hamilton denounced plans to change the republican system as "absurd . . . *criminal* and *visionary*," insisting that his repeated talk of the frailties of the elective system stemmed from concern for its future, rather than from preference for another form. Stung to the quick by the attacks on his motives, as well as on his policies, he began a savage rebuttal in the *Gazette of the United States,* branding Jefferson as "arbitrary, persecuting, intolerant and despotic," hiding behind a guise of bucolic purity as he plotted the subversion of the state. His rage at Jefferson, resentment of his tactics, and his fear of their potential power surfaced in a remarkable article in that paper on 20 September, in which he attacked Jefferson as an "intriguing incendiary . . . the aspiring turbulent character," a "concealed voluptuary" lusting not for flesh, but power, "Caesar *coyely refusing* the proferred diadem . . . *rejecting* the trapping, but tenaciously grasping the substance of imperial dominion." It is indicative of their joint suspicions that Jefferson had already turned the Caesar image upon Hamilton, noting in his *Anas* in 1790 that Hamilton had once insisted in his presence that Julius Caesar was the greatest man who ever lived. To Jefferson, shy and unmartial, Hamilton's ebullient candor and his reputation for battlefield bravado must have combined to give this a metallic and unpleasant ring. It was doubtless with the same edge of muted horror that Jefferson told Washington of a conversation in Philadelphia in which Philip Schuyler was reputed to have favored the installation of an hereditary line of rule. For if Schuyler did say this, whom could he have meant but Alexander Hamilton, who was like a child to the heirless Washington and whose many children had Schuyler blood?

Washington at first had appeared stunned by the explosion, his passion for union and for energy in government running head-on into his old distaste for censure and his new terror of a sundering of bonds. To Madison (whose friendship he still tried to cling to) he described his situation as scarcely tolerable and his temper, that old sign of constraint and anxiety, began to flare again. Adams wrote that Jefferson had seen him fling the *Aurora* (a Republican journal) across the room with a "damn" of the author, and he indulged privately in violent tirades against Freneau. And to a friend in Virginia, who had been growling about the centrist trends in government, he sent a letter that presaged a major theme: that opposition journals maliciously distorted the intent of his programs, representing union as despotic power to stir the people's fears. "If they tell the truth, it is not the whole truth . . . whereas . . . if both sides were exhibited it might . . . assume a different form in the opinion of just and candid men who are disposed to measure matters on a Continental Scale."

His rage was complicated with his dread of secession and his feelings for Jefferson himself. He had despised Gates and Lee among his critics in the Revolution, and many of the enemies of the Constitution were local politicians, small and mean, venal men of tiny vision, defending small enclaves of power against absorption in the whole. Jefferson was different—an immensely gifted man from the highest levels of Virginian society, with a supple intellect (if without Washington's clarity or Hamilton's intensity), nourished by extensive travel, of great tensile quality and of enormous diversity and scope. Tall and gangling, sandy-haired with hazel eyes and a pale, freckled skin stretched over his bony features, he had a social manner of enchanting diffidence, and his scholarship and contact with the great minds of Europe doubtless caused Washington some awe. (There is some evidence that compelling emotional factors held an underlying pull on Jefferson—as they did on Hamilton—producing a bond of complex facets and tremendous strength. Jefferson's own father, like George, a giant, a woodsman, a surveyor and mapmaker, had died when his adoring child was fourteen.) Secession hovered through his presidency, the dark shadow of union,

317

alive in the novelty of the federation, the diversity of interests, and the fragile nature of the bonds. Emotion and interest dictated that he retain Jefferson (agreeing to disagree, if necessary) as the soldering of the Union went on.

He made brave efforts to mend shattered bonds. When Jefferson, in February, 1792, gave his first indication of his wish to leave the government, George talked him out of it with the plea that the shock would shake the government and another argument that was more finesse than fact: that State, Jefferson's province, was a more important department than was the Treasury, which dealt only in finance—a specious case, since Hamilton's ideas on what to do with finance were defining the scope of executive power and the limits of constitutional law. Jefferson stayed; but the tensions mounted, and in July, George tried a harsher tack. In the most direct language that he was ever to use with Jefferson, he told him that his suspicions of Hamilton (George did not name names) had gone far beyond justice or reality and that his fears of counterrevolution had been overdrawn. (There might be *"desires,"* George told Jefferson, but there were no *"designs."*) Cleverly, he turned Jefferson's fears of monarchy around. Attacking Freneau for assailing the government, he warned that disunion would lead to anarchy, which would bring on a clamor for a crown. Then came a shattering remark. He told Jefferson that "He considered those papers as attacking him directly, for he must be a fool indeed, to swallow the little sugar plums here and there thrown out to him. That in condemning the administrations of the government, they condemned him, for if they thought they were measures pursued contrary to his sentiments, they must conceive him too careless to attend to them, or too stupid to understand."

Properly doubtful of the success of this effort, George tried a new approach. One month later in the space of three days, he wrote three nearly identical letters to Hamilton, Jefferson, and Edmund Randolph, his attorney general (who often voted with Jefferson), making grim references to "internal dissensions . . . harrowing and tearing our vitals," warning that the continued strife would shred the govern-

318

ment, and the "fairest prospect of happiness and prosperity . . . be lost." His tone throughout was conciliatory, as if to coax conciliation from the three. His gentle tone, however, only inspired the irate parties to spill their troubles into what appeared to be his sympathetic ears. Hamilton sent a violently agitated letter in which he accused Jefferson of systematic efforts to destroy him, motivated by malice, jealous of his powers, and his personal rapport with George. Jefferson, he wrote, had attacked him from his first days in office, had formed and led a party in Congress to destroy him, had subsidized the *National Gazette* "to render me . . . as odious as possible," and had assailed, not only his measures, but his morals, in a vicious whispering campaign. While the slurs remained personal, he insisted, he had held both his tongue and pen. But when they threatened to lap into the precious binding of the union, "I considered it as a duty to endeavour to resist the torrents and . . . draw aside the veil."

Jefferson, for his part, savaged Hamilton for his attacks on *him*, defended Freneau as a man of genius, and accused Hamilton again of scheming to shift the process of succession from an electoral system to one in which power was transmitted through "the loins of fools and knaves, passing from the debaucheries of the table to those of the bed." He concluded with an attack on Hamilton's character, cloaked in a defense of his own:

> Though little known to the people of America, I believe, that as far as I am known, it is not as an enemy to the Republic, nor an intriguer against it, nor a waster of its revenue, nor prostitutor of it to the purposes of corruption. . . . I will not suffer my retirement to be clouded by the slanders of a man whose history, from the moment at which history can stoop to notice him, is a tissue of machinations against the liberty of the country which has not only received and given him bread, but heaped its honors on his head.

That there could be no accommodation became painfully evident in a meeting between George and Jefferson in the early morning of 1 October 1792 at Mount Vernon as the two Virginians were preparing to leave for Philadelphia for

319

the fall. Jefferson recorded the conversation with what must have been a sinking heart. George told him that there were not ten men of reputation in the country who had ever thought of monarchy; that interest could not be overlooked in the foundation of government; that some intermingling of the public and private interest was inevitable and, if well managed, not undesirable; that it could not be eliminated unless men of all interests were excluded from Congress; that Hamilton had saved the nation's economy; and that he himself had no intention of rerouting the directions he had allowed the nation's policy to take.* (Later he would tell Jefferson that if any Americans sought a monarchy, it was proof of their insanity, as the republican spirit was too entrenched to be moved.) That Jefferson himself remained obdurate was evident in a plaintive letter from Washington shortly after their return:

> I did not require evidence of the extracts which you enclosed me, to convince me of your attachment to the Constitution. . . . I regret, deeply regret, the difference in opinion which have divided you and another principal officer. . . . I have a great, a sincere esteem for you both, and ardently wish that some line could be marked out by which both of you could walk.

But there was no line wide enough, and tensions grew, breeding doubts about his own capacities and a recurring desire to retreat. Madison found him one day in an intense depression, brooding over his imagined insufficiencies and talking darkly of retiring in March. "He said," noted Madison, "that he could not believe or conceive himself necessary to the successful administration of the Government; that . . . he had from the beginning found himself deficient in many of the essential qualifications, owing to his inexperience"; that he was the indirect object of the attacks aimed at Hamilton; that he would prefer "to go to his farm,

---

*It is worth noting in this context that Jefferson's tactics in using the ambitions of men he detested in building the political machine later won, and kept him in, the presidency were not at all unlike the policy of using greed to build up the finances of the country, which Hamilton instigated and Washington condoned.

320

take his spade in his hand, and work for his bread" than endure the office one term more. Was he rehearsing arguments, inviting reassurance, or simply putting up a finger to the wind? It was his habit to indulge in all three possibilities, as well as, under pressure, to disparage his abilities and denigrate himself. He was strained by his dual role as partisan and mediator, wearied by his role as linch pin, and apprehensive that the blasts aimed now at Hamilton would devolve in time on him. He may also have used Madison as a conduit to Jefferson and the opposition, hoping to frighten them into some measure of accord. Stunned, Madison rushed in with soothing noises, claiming that the disputes were an argument for his remaining, and mingling assurance with grim verbal pictures of the fragile Union shattering under the beleaguered leadership of Adams, Jefferson, or Jay.

Jefferson himself, one of the men proposed by Madison, faced the prospect of Washington's retirement with horror, sending George a tortured letter that balanced his dependency with his resentment and his growing rage. "This is the event at which I tremble," he wrote to Washington, insisting that his presence alone tied the South to the Union and prevented a violent rupture of the states. "The confidence of the whole Union is centered on you. Your presence is more than an answer to violence and secession. North and South will hang together if they have you to hang on; and if the first correction . . . should fail in its effect, your presence will give time for trying others, not inconsistent with the union and peace of the States." The "correction" was the first biennial election of the House of Representatives, which Jefferson hoped would form a make-weight to the Federalist temper of the Senate and the executive branch—a tribute to Washington, coupled with an underplayed rebuke.

Hamilton, for his part, feared the alteration on which Jefferson had hung his hopes. He wrote Washington in a panic that an Opposition Congress without his restraining hand would unravel the union to its confederation status and sink it in weakness and disgrace. As for George himself, "it had been better, as regards your character, that you had never consented . . . than . . . to leave the business unfinished, and in danger of being undone."

321

It was Edmund Randolph, however, who sent the most compelling note of all: "Should a civil war arise, you cannot stay at home. And how much easier . . . to disperse the factions . . . than to subdue them, after they shall appear in arms?"

There was no answer to this last appeal. On 4 March 1793 he duly took his second oath of office and delivered (if that was the word for it) an inaugural message barely two sentences in length:

> I am again called upon by the voice of my country to execute the functions of the Chief Magistrate. . . . This oath I am about to take . . . if it shall be found during my Administration of the Government I have in any instance violated willingly or knowingly the injunctions thereof, I may . . . be subject to the upbraidings of all.

His mood was conveyed in a note in a letter earlier that year to Henry Lee: "To say I feel pleasure in the prospect of commencing another tour of duty would be a departure from the truth."

Conditions in the Cabinet continued to carom downhill. Less than one month after the completion of this small, grim ceremony, an attempted reconciliation with Jefferson met with a decided rebuff. "I told him that my concurrence was of much less importance than he seemed to imagine," Jefferson recorded, informed him again that a coalition was impossible, that the South was on the point of insurrection over the financial programs, and launched into another attack on Hamilton's "corrupt squadron" and monarchical designs. Washington apparently listened with resignation, for, as Jefferson noted, "On this subject he made no reply." The tensions between the two were nearing the point of acute discomfort, yet they remained in an embrace of necessity, Jefferson dreading the implications of an outright break with Washington, George fearing the loss of his prime channel to the South. Their increasingly strained interchanges were pored over by the Republicans* with intense anxiety, as re-

*As the opposition had begun to call themselves.

322

vealed in a letter to Jefferson from Madison and James Monroe:

> It appeared to both of us that a real anxiety was marked to retain you in office; that over and above other motives it was felt that your presence and implied sanction might be a necessary shield against certain criticisms from certain quarters; and that the departure of the only councillor possessing the confidence of the Republicans would be a signal for new and perhaps very disagreeable attacks . . . whilst this end is pursued, it would be wise to make as few concessions as possible . . . in a word, we think you ought to make the most of the value we perceive to be placed on your participation in the Executive councils.

But few concessions were coming to Jefferson from the President, and his despair was growing more acute. Though he protested his innocence to Washington's face—"I told him . . . I kept myself aloof from all cabal and correspondence . . . and saw and spoke with as few as I could"—he had formed a program to dismantle the financial system, strip the Treasury of part of its administrative powers, and drive Hamilton from the Cabinet on the grounds of fiscal improprieties through a series of congressional attacks. Late in 1792 a lead had seemed to open to the latter end: a jailed embezzler had sent word to Republican congressmen—Monroe among them—that evidence in his possession could convict Hamilton of fraud. Further investigation, however, dispelled the matter, as Hamilton's later embarrassed confession made clear: "The charge against me is a connection with one James Reynolds for purposes of improper pecuniary speculation," Hamilton wrote. "My real crime is an amorous connection with his wife . . . with his privity and connivance . . . with the design to extort money from me."

The story was an odd tale of entrapment and vulnerability that shed strange light, if not on Hamilton's political infamy, then on a perverse streak within his character wherein this most ambitious of all creatures appeared periodically to invite ruin and disgrace. A Maria Reynolds had arrived at his

323

office in the summer of 1791, pleading desertion and poverty and begging the assistance of a loan. There appeared to have been an implicit sexual undertone to the encounter, which following events confirmed. Bringing funds to her rooming house that evening, he was shown upstairs to a bedroom, wherein, as he recounted, ". . . conversation ensued, from which it was quickly apparent that other than pecuniary consolation would be acceptable." Consolation continued through the summer, Betsy Hamilton being conveniently out of town. James Reynolds, however, was not. Discovery followed, then blackmail (whether planned or fortuitous has never been determined), Reynolds draining Hamilton of something more than $1,000 before allowing him to disengage himself sometime in early spring. (To his credit, Hamilton tapped neither public funds nor those of his immensely rich father-in-law to subsidize the payments for his lapse.) It was the autumn after when Reynolds, jailed at last, appealed to Hamilton for assistance and, rejected, turned then to Monroe. Dismissed by the congressmen as silly and not criminal, the affair rested until it reappeared in a political pamphlet four years later in its original guise—that Hamilton had used Reynolds in a scheme to defraud the Treasury and had betrayed the public trust.

More peculiar than the incident was Hamilton's treatment of the affair. Rather than let a trace of doubt cloud his public record, he released a pamphlet of his own, a confession of extraordinary length and candor, in which he paid protracted attention to his gullibility, and to what he referred to as "my vanity," in preferring to believe, after many months and countless shakedowns, that Mrs. Reynolds really cared for him. "There is nothing worse in the affair than an irregular and indelicate amour," he ended. "For this, I bow to the just censure which it merits. I have paid pretty severely for the folly, and can never recollect it without disgust."

Why did Hamilton leap into an encounter so rich in the potential for entrapment, and why, discovered, did he choose not only to confess but to dissect his error in such exquisite and self-flagellating detail, inviting public scorn, the contempt of his patrons, on whom he was still dependent, and the estrangement of his wife and children, to whom, despite his wanderings, he remained devotedly attached? Men of the most profound ambition sometimes have a counterdrive to self-destruction, a courting of a real or a symbolic death. Why did the young lieutenant colonel parade his troops on top of the barricades at Yorktown in full view of the British cannon—a bravura gesture, but a suicidal one, that stunned all those who watched? Why did he, dependent on Washington's favor, start a quarrel with his patron, insult him to his face and through intermediaries, and then send infuriated and potentially explosive letters to men who were Washington's friends as well as his? And why, in 1804, did he goad a rival—a man of notorious mental imbalance and violent temper—into a duel; ignore all opportunities to extricate himself; and go, determined to be shot at, but not to fire, to his fatal interview with Aaron Burr?

Partial failure did not deflect the opposition's rage. In March, 1793, Jefferson fed a list of fifteen charges to a friendly congressman, accusing Hamilton of speculation, corruption (again), and misappropriation of the foreign debt. Hamilton had juggled funds to pay off domestic debts with foreign moneys, but this was the extent of his infamy and he was readily absolved. In a bitter note, Jefferson laid the result to a Congress dominated by Hamilton's creatures, "bank directors . . . stock jobbers . . . blind devotees," and persons too "good humored" to vote for guilt. Determined now to retire from a government dominated by his enemies, he relieved his tensions in letters both vehement and grieved. To Madison, he described himself as:

> Worn down with labors from morning to night, and from day to day; knowing them as fruitless to others as they are vexatious to myself, committed singly and in desperate and eternal contest against a host who are systematically undermining the public liberty . . . the rare hours of relaxation sacrificed to the company of persons of the same intentions, of whose hatred I am conscious even in those moments of conviviality when the heart most wishes to open itself . . . giving every thing I love . . .

for every thing I hate . . . without a single gratifica-
tion . . . in present employment or in future wish.

Hamilton at the same time was writing to *his* friends in
the same dark temper, seeing himself also as a defendant under siege. To Jay, he wrote of his "burden and perplexity,"
quarrels that distracted him from the business of his office,
and "intrigues to stab me in the dark." To a distant friend, he
wrote a painful letter:

> Every friend I see, from a place I love, is a cordial to
> me—and I stand in need of something of that kind now
> and then. The triumphs of vice are no new things under
> the sun . . . hypocrisy and Treachery will continue to be
> the most successful commodities in the political Market. It
> seems to be the destined lot of Nations to mistake their
> foes for their friends, and flatterers for their faithful ser-
> vants.

Running beneath this was a mood of anxiety at the split between himself and the mass of his countrymen that would
lead him to describe himself as exotic and alien and sink him
in a deepening despair. "To see the character of the government . . . so sported with," he wrote his friend, the Federalist senator Rufus King years later, "puts my heart to torture. Am I then more of an American than those who drew
their first breath on American ground? Or what is it that thus
torments me at a circumstance so calmly viewed by almost everybody else? Am I a fool—a romantic Quixot—or is there a
constitutional defect in the American mind?"

Adams, too, remained an exile, estranged now from
Jefferson, jealous of Washington's preference for Jay and
Hamilton, suspicious alike of Jefferson's ingenuous modesty
and Hamilton's audacious dash. Odd man out among all parties, he felt his lack of notice deeply—"to be wholly overlooked and to know it are intolerable"—and his resentment
surfaced in a series of essays written in his first year in office
when the limits of his influence had become indisputably evident to all: "A regard to the sentiments of mankind concerning him every man feels within himself; and if he has reflected and tried experiments, he has found, that no exertion of

326

his reason . . . can wholly divest him of it. In proportion to our affection for the notice of others is our aversion to their neglect." What neglect had come to Adams, overlooked in presidential councils, and what experiments had been tried and failed? Again, in an ostensible discussion of the effects of poverty, he limned his inner picture of himself:

> The poor man's conscience is clear, yet he is ashamed. His character is irreproachable, yet he is neglected and despised. He feels himself out of the sight of others, groping in the dark. . . . Mankind takes no notice of him. He rambles and wanders unheeded. . . . He is not disapproved, censured, or reproached, *he is only not seen.*

What was *"seen"* too clearly were the ravaging dissensions in the state. "I am solicitous for your fame, & yet cannot applaud your system," Henry Lee had written Hamilton in a series of anguished letters, deploring the cut of policy across affection and the growing notes of rancor and discord. "Why cannot men differ in politics . . . and yet hold highly established regards?" Lee and Hamilton could, and did, remain friends through a series of intense debates on policy, but the young old-soldiers were among a few. The string of broken friendships was long and dreadful, compounding differences of theory with rankling undertones of betrayal and distrust. Hamilton's and Madison's, Adams' and Jefferson's were among the friendships that lay shattered—along with George's with George Mason, whom he referred to in a letter to Hamilton as "my neighbor and my quondam friend." Subtleties of power had broken the united front. The brilliant generation that had made the Revolution had come together against the strident threat of rampant power, sounding defiance in a single note, immense and solid, sending its clamor to the corners of the earth. But it had slipped up on the minor levels, disintegrating into a jangle of discordant noises, a shattering cacophony of sound. It had taken all of Washington's immense reserve of force and guile to impose the illusion of external union upon this unruly choir, in which even his own voice was assuming a slightly strident tone. And the worst had not yet come.

Since 1789 tremors of the French upheaval had cast their shadows on domestic politics, throwing new fuel on local fires, the bloody backdrop to domestic war. Suddenly, all changed, becoming at once more violent and more globally intense, threatening to pitch the United States from its careful neutrality into the conflicts of the European scene. By the beginning of 1793 Louis XVI had been beheaded, Gouverneur Morris was sending home appalling reports of the September Massacres, "Citizen" Genêt, first ambassador of the French Republic, was en route to the United States with 300 blank commissions to enlist Americans in the French service, and revolutionary France and Britain were at war.

XVII

Whirlwinds and
Meteors

*. . . political evils, which, in all ages, have grown
out of such a state of things as naturally produce
whirlwinds and meteors. . . .*—JOHN JAY to
Washington, 4 December 1795

Predictably, Jefferson's response to the French convulsion
was ecstatic, seeming as it did a second shot at revolution, re-
deeming what had gone wrong in his own. "Rather than it
should have failed, I should have seen half the earth devastated," he wrote in January, 1793. "Were there left but an
Adam and an Eve in every country, and left free, it would be
better than as it is now." George, dreading foreign conflict,
was considerably less sanguine; he was disturbed by the reports of French atrocities and concerned lest domestic sym-
pathies for the new republic might involve America in war.
To forestall the letter, he issued on 16 April 1793 a Proclamation of Neutrality, forbidding Americans to involve themselves in the interests of foreign powers, under penalty of
law. Republicans erupted in a rage. George, they claimed,
had shown indifference to the cause of liberty, and had arro-
gated powers to the executive belonging to the legislative
branch. "A most unfortunate error," wrote the unhappy
Madison. "If France triumphs, the ill-fated Proclamation will
be a millstone, which would sink any other character, and
will force a struggle even on his own." Was it "ill-fated" or a

329

necessary stroke? Excessive power and "indifference" to liberty—George would face a struggle with them both.

He quickly learned what he was up against. Genêt had docked at Charleston, ominously distant, to a clamorous welcome: mobs jammed the quayside to toss cheers and flowers; civic leaders feted him at jovial and wine-soaked dinners, loud with toasts to "France and Liberty" and the singing of the "Marseillaise." Striking up a quick rapport with the besotted governor, Genêt talked him into a massive arming of Sullivan's Island (the promontory guarding the approach to the island city) and into commissioning 200 Americans to arm their vessels as privateers. Ruddy, small, and bustling, Genêt made his way up the inland route to Philadelphia, feted at every town and city, leaving behind a spoor of pro-French Democratic Societies (modeled on the clubs that had spurred the French Revolution) and a string of harbors stocked with captured British ships. At Philadelphia he was disingenuous before a stony Washington—"We wish you to do nothing," Jefferson quoted him to Madison, "but what is for your own good." Within days, however, he had reverted to his old activities, dragging the coastal waters for British trawlers and bringing a hail of protests from the British embassy upon governmental heads. When crossed, Genêt became insolent, talking of appeals to the people and of taking his case to Congress over Washington's head. On 8 June he told Jefferson that he would respect Washington's judgments *"Till the Representatives shall have confirmed or rejected them"* and then informed George himself that he had usurped the powers belonging to the legislature and that he should have convened Congress in the spring. George tried to keep the lid on his explosive temper, but sometimes even he gave way. In his *Anas,* a shaken Jefferson gave a stunned account of an explosion in the Cabinet over a cartoon in Freneau's paper showing "King" George being taken to the guillotine:

> He . . . ran on much on the personal abuse which had been bestowed on him; defied any man on earth to produce one single act of his since he had been in the government, which was not done on the purest motives; that

he had never repented but once the having slipped the moment of resigning his office, and that was every moment since; that *by God* he had rather be in the grave than in his present situation; that he had rather be on his farm than to be made *Emperor of the World;* and yet that they were charging him with wanting to be a King.

(There was, Jefferson added, "some difficulty" in returning to the subject of the day.) To George, it was a return to the old terrors—his will against external pressures—that had dogged him in the dark days of the war. It was here again (in an anguished letter to Richard Henry Lee) that he once more called himself a slave.

This was not the measure of Genêt. On 5 July he called on Jefferson with a plan for using American territories (along with some Americans) in a scheme to detach Britain's colonial possessions in the new world from their parent state. Reading "very rapidly," he spun a list of his requests: passes for agents to travel to Louisiana and Canada and encourage the inhabitants to insurrection; money for two generals from Kentucky to take New Orleans and establish Louisiana as an independent state, connected in commerce with America and France. Jefferson was meanwhile calling Genêt "calamitous" and writing tortured letters to his friends:

> Hot headed, all imagination, no judgment, passionate, disrespectful, & even indecent towards the P. . . . He renders my situation immensely difficult. He does me justice personally, and, giving him time to vent himself & then cool, I am on a footing to advise him freely . . . he respects it, but then he breaks out again on the very first occasion, as to show that he is incapable of correcting himself. To complete our misfortune, we have no channel of our own through which we can correct the irritating representations he may make.

Jefferson had not begun to reach the limits of his troubles with Genêt. On 6 July—with Washington at Mount Vernon, attending a dying nephew—privateers had seized the British merchant vessel *Little Sarah,* hauled it up the Schuylkill within view of Philadelphia, rechristened it the *Petit De-*

mocrat, and stocked it out in martial fittings with fourteen iron cannon and a crew of 120 men. Appalled, the governor sent a messenger to the French minister, who returned with a grim report: Genêt refused to disarm the vessel, threatened an appeal from the President to the people, mentioned the expected arrival of three French battleships, and warned that an effort to retake the *Sarah* would be repelled in blood. The governor dispatched a troop from the state militia to face the *Sarah* from the shoreline and sent pleas for advice to the truncated Cabinet, meeting without Washington and itself on the point of war. Jefferson had gone to see Genêt, who refused to promise anything, saying merely that the ship would not be ready to sail before the coming Wednesday, when George was expected to return. A violent fight broke out inside the Cabinet, Jefferson claiming Genet's word was a positive assurance, Knox* and Hamilton insisting a battery be built at Mud Island, to fire on the *Sarah* if it attempted to depart. Jefferson dissented, calling the move too serious to be undertaken by the Cabinet, but in the *Anas* his real reasoning emerged: "I would not gratify the combination of Kings with the spectacle of the two only republics on earth destroying each other for two cannon . . . nor . . . add this country to that combination, turn the scale of contest, and let it be from our hands that the hopes of man received the last stab."

George returned on 11 July to find the ship at Chester, the Cabinet at loggerheads, and affairs in status quo. The same day he sent a letter to Jefferson revealing both his growing irritation and his rising rage at France:

> After I read the Papers put into my hands by you, requiring "instant attention," and before a messenger could reach your office, you had left town. . . . Is the Minister of the French Republic to set the Acts of this Government at defiance *with impunity?* . . . What must the World think of such conduct, and of the Governmt. of the U. States in submitting to it? . . . Circumstances press for decisions, and as you have had time to consider them (upon me they have come unexpectedly) I wish to know

*Secretary of war in the first Washington Cabinet.

332

your opinion . . . before tomorrow, for the Vessel may
by then be gone.

Whatever the opinion was, it arrived too late; early on the
morning of the 12th the ship slipped out from Chester and
was gone. Its conduct in succeeding days—firing on more
British merchant vessels—remained a humiliation and goad-
ing sore. George was silent, but Jefferson's *Anas* of 12 July
holds this comment on his mood: "It appears to me the President had wished the Little Sarah had been stopped by military coercion, that is, by firing on her. . . . I do not believe
he would have ordered it himself had he been here, though
he would be glad if we did."

Washington's reaction was to hold a three-day meeting
of his cabinet, in the end forcing Jefferson to write a stiff letter to Gouverneur Morris, detailing Genêt's atrocities and
asking him to press for his recall. Genêt's reaction was to
leave for New York in a fury, breathing threats of military
reprisals and warning Washington that he had 1,500 seamen
at his command. Knox found him there in early September,
writing irate letters to his political adherents and leaking
parts of his diplomatic correspondence to the press. His succeeding conduct veered close to the bizarre. At his direction
a French consul in Boston seized a privateer from the mar-
shal who had detained it, using guns taken from a French fri-
gate; a week later he repeated his performance in New York.
George was about to pack him off summarily when another
revolution in French politics tumbled the ruling faction to
the ground. Genêt, as a member of the disgraced party and
the symbol of a failed foreign policy, was summoned home
by the new rulers, no doubt to the guillotine. Genêt flung
himself on Washington's mercy, asked for and received asylum, and subsided, with a docility foreign to his prior character, into domesticity with a daughter of Governor Clinton of
New York, living a blameless, apolitical existence until he
died quietly in 1836. It is difficult to imagine which of the local parties drew the deepest sighs of relief at this denoue-
ment, ending as it did with a domestic whimper instead of a
martial bang.

Doubtless, the strain had much to do with the retirement of Thomas Jefferson in January, 1794, after a year which he described later as unceasing torture, torn as he had been between anger at Genêt's aggressions and his own conviction that his country had taken a decidedly wrong turn. Washington let him go reluctantly, for he treasured his experience and cherished the credit that he held with France. The constant tension between them, compounded of respect battling a barely veiled hostility, was something he had come to cherish less. That the connection between them had suffered an irreparable erosion is suggested in a growing list of short words and long silences—Jefferson got no written tribute from the President when he left office; Hamilton, when he left one year later, was to receive not only one, but two. Domestic concord, all but shattered by internal politics, had now been torn beyond repair.

Other signs of violence, sharp and brutal, were further to split the government in two. Genêt's commotion had barely ended when Britain, on its own volition, seemed about to push the country into war. There was an old complaint: British posts on the Canadian border had not been evacuated as promised after the peace treaty, remaining nests for warfare from which hostile Indians could constantly descend. There was a new one: the Cabinet orders of 8 June and 6 November, authorizing the forced seizure of neutral vessels carrying supplies to France. Republicans exploded, and Federalists received a stream of anguished complaints from aggrieved merchants, staunch supporters of the government but forced by suffering into cries for vigorous response. Madison, stubborn, small, and indefatigable, flung measure after measure into the House for a trade war with Britain, overridden in the Senate but pushing the country ever closer into war. "One firebrand is scarcely quenched before another is thrown in," Adams wrote in agitation to his wife. "If the sound part of the community is not uncommonly active . . . we shall be drawn off our neutral ground." Complaints from Thomas Pinckney, the American ambassador to London, received no response. Then, in March, a Boston Federalist, writing to a senator, dropped a suggestion in the

334

pot: "The sufferers here think that a special deputation
. . . wou'd be more efficacious than making the representation through a common medium. . . . Such a temper cannot be expected to continue for any length of time."

Both the embassy and the ambassador—George's (and Hamilton's) good friend, John Jay—sent the opposition into a rage: what was the purport of this Anglophile, but to sell both France and freedom to the crown? Incensed Republicans exchanged anguished letters, of which this note to Madison from Jefferson sets the prevailing tone: "A more degrading mission could not have been proposed: and why is Pinckney to be recalled: for it is impossible he should remain there after such a testimony that he is not confided in. . . . I suppose they think he is not thorough fraud enough."

George himself packed Jay off with wishes for an accommodation, laced with potshots at his critics back at home. "No man more ardently wished you *complete* success," he wrote to Jay that autumn. " . . . I shall endeavour to keep things in *status quo* until your negotiation assumes a more decisive form, which I hope will soon be the case, as there are many hot-heads and impetuous spirits among us, who with difficulty, can be kept within bounds."

Before Jay's return, however, hot-heads were to light new fires and raise tensions to the breaking point at home.

Distillers in the backcountry of the western states had fretted under the excise tax on whiskey since Hamilton had imposed it as part of his program to fund the government in 1791. In July, 1794, fueled perhaps by the climate of respectable sedition, they attempted to "repeal" the tax by force. After a series of pleas for accomodation and amnesty had been met with added violence, George, with Hamilton and Henry Lee, led a massive army of 15,000 across the Alleghenies in late autumn to quell the first internal threat to the regime. The Whiskey Rebellion ended rapidly, with small commotion and no blood (the two convicted "traitors" were pardoned by Washington the next year), but the precedent had sent a tremor through the state—for the Federalists, the sight of armed force against legitimate authority; for the Republicans, the sight of the government in arms. To

335

George, the linkage appeared inescapable: French pressures had worked on domestic insurgencies to bring the system to its knees. On 16 November, he took advantage of his annual address to Congress to unleash a violent tirade, tracing the rebellion to local incendiaries and dropping the onus at the opposition's door. Republicans were staggered at this outburst of presidential rage. Madison wrote of plots to demolish the Republicans by connecting them all to sedition; Jefferson sent a hysterical letter from Monticello saying he expected civil war. This was still the climate when Jay's Treaty arrived from London on 25 March, 1795, bringing with it Britain's agreement to vacate the northern posts the year after, some harsh restrictions on American trading privileges, and the opening of parts of the British colonial possessions to American commerce, a province hitherto sacrosanct. Politically, it replaced France with Britain as most favored nation, secured to Britain a plentiful flow of material to fuel its war effort, and cut forever the chances of the United States to act as trading ally and silent partner to the French. It also ruled out the chances of war between the United States and Britain, which had loomed before this as a present threat. Jay himself had known from the beginning that peace with Britain would bring war at home. "I carried with me a fixed opinion that *no treaty whatever* with Great Britain could escape a partial, but violent opposition," he wrote George later, adding grimly in another letter a resigned reference to "political evils, which, in all ages, have grown out of such a state of things as naturally produce whirlwinds and meteors."

Whirlwinds and meteors were about to descend on the United States.

The Republicans fell upon the treaty in a cascade of incandescent rage. "The ruinous bargain," wrote Madison, while Jefferson, more emotional, was likewise more extreme in his remarks: "an execrable thing . . . an infamous act . . . nothing more than a treaty of alliance between England and the Anglomen of this country, against the Legislature and people of the United States." James Monroe, Jefferson's pale and pop-eyed protégé who had replaced Morris as ambassador to France, sent a transatlantic contribution to the brawl: "If this treaty had parted us from France, the views of Engld. wd. have been completely answered, and believe me, there were some moments when I had the most disquieting apprehensions on that point." After the Senate passed the treaty in late June, the seaports erupted in a rage. Mobs in Boston, Charleston, and Philadelphia burned copies of the treaty (crying, "Take it, and kick it to the Devil!"), demonstrated before the offices of British consulates, desecrated buildings, burned the British flag. City streets and country roadways were illuminated the length of the Republic with burning effigies of Jay. In New York, in a debate at City Hall, Hamilton, speaking for the treaty, was bombarded with a stream of brickbats, stones, and ripe tomatoes and at length was hit upon the forehead with a rock. Tradition has him saying, "If you use such knock-down agruments, I must retire," as he retreated, bleeding, from the scene. ("It was observed," a Boston Federalist wrote to Rufus King, "that your Jacobins were prudent to endeavour to knock out Hamilton's brains, to reduce him to an equality with themselves.") Suspicions rose among the stunned officials that the wave of protests might cause the British to cancel the treaty on their own. "The country rising into flame," Oliver Wolcott* wrote the wounded Hamilton, "their Minister's house insulted by a Mob—their flag dragged through the Streets as in Charleston & burnt before the doors of their Consul . . . can they believe that we desire peace?" Almost as distressing as the threat of British rancor was the note running through the correspondence of the Republicans—that the riot over the treaty made it the ideal issue with which to break the protective cloak that George had flung around the Federalists and to turn the government around. "This is an act which speaks for itself, and in which not he alone is compromitted," Monroe wrote Madison from Paris, speaking at once of Jay, his treaty, and his clique. "If he [Washington] rejects it . . . the publick opinion will afterwards perhaps be pronounced with still greater decision . . . This will form a basis upon which our republican system and connection with

*Secretary of the treasury after Hamilton resigned.

France may not only rest with safety, but hereafter . . . be greatly improved." What was George to do in this crisis, the most staggering of his political career? Political riot or war against the British Empire—his finesse would now be tested to the full.

Washington was at Mount Vernon for the summer, removed in body from the storms and chaos but in mind vulnerable and disturbed. With the treaty approved by the Senate, the issue devolved on him alone. "My opinion is the same now as it was," he wrote Edmund Randolph on 22 July, "namely, not favorable to it, but that it is better to ratify it in the manner the Senate had advised . . . than to suffer matters to remain as they are," adding, "If the Treaty is ratified, the partisans of the French (or rather of war and confusion) will excite them to hostile measures . . . if not, there is no foreseeing *all* the consequences which may follow, as respects G.B." His real fears centered on the riots and the uses they might be put to by the French. "It is the Interest of the French," he wrote to Alexander Hamilton, "to avail themselves of such a spirit, to keep *us* and *G. Britain* at variance, and they will . . . accordingly do it. . . . I predict much embarrassment to the government therefrom." Two weeks later he had ratified, sadly aware of what form the repercussions were likely to assume. "I am . . . preparing my mind for the obloquy which disappointment and malice are collecting to heap upon my character," he wrote Edmund Randolph, at the time unmindful of the fact that the slippery Randolph was soon to be the most energetic heaper of them all. To Henry Knox one month later he explained his choice: the treaty was the path of duty to which popularity must yield. This was his high tone, the note of statesmanship, the voice of *Cato* and Belvoir. On the lower scale, he vented his annoyance in caustic jabs at the French party, "working like bees to distill their poison" and beguiling the electorate with "diabolical" untruths. When the riots tapered off about December, he wrote to Jay himself, hopeful about the chance for ultimate accordance but ending on a bitter note: "The dregs, however, will always remain, and the slightest motion will stir them up."

By December he had added evidence of the prevalence of "dregs" among his countrymen and, worse, of where they might be found. In late August, Edmund Randolph, his official connection to foreign governments and the last Republican to have his official confidence, had been discovered in a secret correspondence with the French ambassador Fauchet.

The letters themselves had come to his attention in a manner almost fittingly bizarre. Sent on a French packet from Fauchet to his government, the pouch that they were concealed in was flung overboard in a battle with a British warship and was retrieved by a British sailor from the waves. Sent at once to Whitehall, they were shipped back across the Atlantic to the British minister, who read them happily to Oliver Wolcott over a convivial bottle of wine. Apparently, the letters implicated Randolph in an effort to beg money for the Whiskey Rebels from the French. Hauled before a stony quorum of Washington and his department heads, Randolph told a story that the summer previous he had heard of a plot to ruin him politically by some New York Federalists and begged Fauchet (as Wolcott told Hamilton) to finance an inquiry into the nature of the "scheme." Later there was another story, changing the story into a plot to ruin France. "The whole is idle nonsense," continued Wolcott, "& Fauchet's attempt by a posterior act to invalidate the evidence of a confidential letter will not succeed." Nonetheless, George was now left with the problem of securing another secretary, all the worse since Randolph had been the last sop thrown to the opposition and had shown from the beginning a compulsion to explain himself in print. "It is not difficult to perceive what turn *he* and his friends will give the act," Washington wrote grimly, "that his friendship for the French nation, and his opposition to a compleat ratification have been the cause."

An article in the gazettes on 26 September was a grim presage, accusing Washington of bias and of denying Randolph access to official papers with which to clear himself. "You are at liberty to publish, without reserve, *any* and *every* private and confidential letter I ever wrote you," George replied in a frigid fury, adding, "to whom, and for what purpose you mean to apply the following words . . . 'I have been the mediated victim of party spirit' will be found in your defense, without which I shall never understand them. I cannot conceive that they were aimed at me." The *Defense,* which surfaced in November, was a volume of partisan and personal abuse, "intending to *shew,*" George wrote Hamilton, "that my *final* decision [on the treaty] . . . was the result of party-advice." Regarding it at first as dangerous, he sent a letter to Hamilton on 22 December, seeming to urge him to a counterattack. "What do you think of it, and what notice should be taken? . . . You are as fully acquainted with my sentiments relative to the warring powers of F. & E: and have heard as strong sentiments from me, with respect to each, as ever he did. . . . But if you have seen his performance, I shall leave you to judge of it, without any comments of mine." Hamilton, for once the more moderate, counseled temperate advice: "It does not surprise me. I consider it as amounting to an admission of guilt . . . and I am persuaded this will be the universal opinion. His sentiments against you are viewed by all whom I have seen as base."

Hamilton was right, and the *Defense* fizzled, finding small support among Republicans; but the episode left George more convinced than ever of the devious nature of French diplomacy and the underhanded tactics of the left. "Political suicide" was his term for any further efforts at amalgamation in his Cabinet; balance was a casualty of war. "They will receive none but tories hereafter into any department of the government," wrote Jefferson sadly, and Madison was equally distraught. "Through what official interstice," he queried plaintively, "can a ray of republican truth now penetrate to the President?" As it happened, the President's interest in "republican truth" had descended to an all-time low. Bipartisan politics had been wiped out by the Randolph debacle and would never be revived.

Another casualty was the Cabinet itself. An extensive and humiliating hunt among the Federalists turned up nothing, and George was forced at last to settle for the revised lineup of Wolcott at Treasury, James McHenry at War, and Timothy Pickering, Randolph's undersecretary, at State—a distinctly third-rate trio, whose main qualifications were their slavish devotion to their Federalist masters and their abject dependence on their advice. Washington and Hamilton suspected all three (correctly) of fanaticism or ineptitude, Hamilton warning Washington against Pickering—"something warm and angular in his temper . . . will require much a moderating eye"—and Wolcott against himself—"If I have a fear . . . it is lest the *strength* of your feelings . . . should prevent that pliancy to circumstances which is sometimes indispensable. I beg you only to watch yourself upon this score." About McHenry, whom they had come to love as an aide-de-camp in the Revolution, both men were forced to admit shortly after he took office that their old friend was in waters way above his head. "I early discovered," George wrote Hamilton later, "that his talents were unequal to the great exertions of deep resources. In truth, they were not to be expected . . . it was a Hobson's choice."

Hamilton thought he had the answer to this precipitate decline. "He would not accept," he wrote to Washington after Rufus King had refused to fill the seat of the ousted Randolph, extrapolating on conclusions drawn from his own painful past:

> Circumstances of the moment conspire with the disgust which a virtuous and independent mind feels at placing itself *en but* to the foul and venomous shafts of calumny, which are constantly shot by an odious confederation against virtue . . . a first rate character is not attainable. A second rate must be taken with good dispositions and barely decent qualifications. . . . 'Tis a sad omen.

In reality, it was George and Hamilton together who were the unwitting architects of the Cabinet's decline. They had never lost the symbiotic relationship begun in the Revolution, and Washington continued to consult him frequently and, less frequently, John Jay. For George, it was less the dependence that his enemies had claimed than of his working method: "I am anxious, always," he had written to Hamilton, "to compare the opinions of those I confide in with one another; and those again (without being bound by them) with my own, that I may extract all the good I can." He continued to extract the good from Hamilton during crises after Hamilton's retirement, sometimes with embarrassing results—consulting him extensively on the amendments to

Jay's Treaty and preferring his opinions to those of his restructured Cabinet *en masse.* On 14 July 1795 he had written a letter to Hamilton that included this astounding paragraph: "I have told Mr. Randolph that your sentiments do not agree with those which I have received from the Officers of Government, and have desired him to reverse them." One can imagine the emotions of the unhappy Randolph on being notified that the decisions of the Cabinet were to be overridden by the opinions of a private lawyer in New York. It was an astonishing note to send an officer and one whose consequences should have been foreseen. What chance, in these conditions, of attracting others than idolators or fools? "The offices are once more full," Adams wrote his wife on 8 February 1796. "But how differently filled than when Jefferson, Hamilton, Jay, &c. were here!" Adams, in his turn, was to suffer greatly from the inheritance of a Cabinet trained to take their lead directly from these stars. The selection of Pickering had been a humiliating spectacle, a process of barrel scraping, and in Pickering himself—narrow and fanatical—George had come close to the bottom indeed. The Cabinet itself slid still further from its old heights of creative power to a purely instrumental agency, acting out decisions made above, shadowed by the incessant letters passing on the mail routes between Philadelphia and Mount Vernon and New York. (Wolcott for some time had been writing to Hamilton for advice on how to administer his department almost day to day.) Hamilton, in retirement, retained his de facto position as prime minister, dropping even the essential business of his law practice to send extensive documents to Washington by mail. The precedent was to prove contagious. Later, when he and George were both retired, they were to come very close to running the government themselves.

One last-ditch ploy remained to the Republicans: to cut out the Jay Treaty in the House. Though the treaty had passed both the President and Senate, the Republicans now insisted, House members had the right to pass on any measure whose provisions affected the interests of their constituents or themselves. "On the precedent now to be set," Jefferson wrote Monroe on 26 March 1796, "will depend the future construction of our Constitution, and whether the powers of legislation shall be transferred from the President, Senate, and House . . . to the President, Senate, and Piamingo, or any other . . . Indian chief." To Madison, he added in an astounding footnote: "I see no harm in rendering their [the House's] sanction necessary, and not much harm in annihilating the whole treaty-making power, except for making peace." The first step in the planned campaign was to demand correspondence relating to the treaty from the executive branch. On 25 March, John Adams sent an apprehensive letter to his wife: "The House . . . have applied for the papers, and the President has their request under consideration. He is not at all pleased with this." Robert Livingston had made the "request" on 2 March before a packed session of the House. Washington was to hand over Jay's instructions and all correspondence and documents relating to the treaty, except such as affected negotiations ongoing at the time. Madison relayed the succeeding sequence in a shaken letter to Monroe: "Every eye was then turned to the President. The prevailing belief was, that he would send a part, if not the whole, of the papers called for. . . . You will find by his Message . . . that he not only ran into the extreme of an absolute refusal, but assigned reasons even worse than the refusal itself."

The answer, sent on 30 March, was cuttingly abrupt:

> The power of making treaties is exclusively vested in the President, by and with the advice and consent of the Senate . . . it is perfectly clear to my understanding that the assent of the House . . . is not necessary to the validity of a treaty . . . a just regard to the constitution and to the duty of my office . . . forbids a compliance with your request.

A bitter passage showed his fury at what he considered the insidious veiling of a partisan attack: "In this construction . . . every House of Representatives has heretofore acquiesced; and until the present time, not a doubt or suspicion has appeared."

"The absolute refusal was as unexpected as the tone and tenor of the message are improper and indelicate," Madison wrote to Jefferson; yet from political sense or lingering affection, he would not turn on George himself. Who had composed the diatribe? Jay and Hamilton, to save themselves at Washington's expense. "There is little doubt in my mind that the message came from N.Y., when it was seen that an experiment was to be made, to the hazard of the Pres., to save the faction from the Reps. of the people," he told Jefferson, adding, "The effect of this reprehensible measure . . . is not likely to correspond with the calculation of its authors" as there was strength enough to Congress to withstand even this assault. To preserve the solid front among the opposition, he cautioned, it was necessary to avoid an open war with George.

He was right about the venom but wrong about its spring. There was one author, and that was Washington himself. He had written to Hamilton for suggestions, but Hamilton's letter had arrived too late to be incorporated into his message, reaching him on the morning the address was to be read. As expected, the papers matched each other almost point for point. "Finding the draft I had prepared embraced most, if not all, the principles which were detailed in the paper," he explained to Hamilton, "I sent in the answer wch. was ready," preserving Hamilton's immensely detailed version for reference if he was challenged upon legal grounds. To Hamilton, he revealed his rage at Congress and the step-by-step workings of his mind:

> From the very first moment, and from the fullest conviction of my own mind, I had resolved to *resist the principle* wch. was evidently to be established by the call . . . and only deliberated on the manner in which this could be done. . . . to furnish *all* the Papers would be highly improper; and . . . a *partial* delivery . . . would leave the door open for much calumny . . . as it might, and I have no doubt, would be said, that all such as were essential to the purposes of the House, were withheld.

The question now was whether the House would vote the money to carry the provisions of the treaty into effect. Refusal might mean a constitutional stalemate of staggering proportions and a plunge into a European war. Britain was

344

reported growling; the British chargé d'affaires had given notice that the northern posts would not be evacuated until the treaty was in force. Other signs were equally disquieting: at a diplomatic reception in London, George III was reported to have stalked past Thomas Pinckney in a rage. The Republicans, calling themselves the "virtuous majority," continued railing at the treaty in the House. "I see nothing better than a crisis working up," commented the gloomy Adams, "which is to determine whether the constitution is to be brought to its end this year."

A majority of twenty had voted for the call for the papers that was the first test of strength. That was two-thirds of the House. Madison's letters began hopefully but soon showed a deepening decline. To James Monroe he had written on 18 April: "I trust, without being sure, that the House will be firm." On 23 April, in a note to Jefferson, his mood had changed: "The majority has melted, by changes and absence, to 8 or 9 votes. Whether these will continue firm, is more than I can decide."

Debate, emotional on both sides of the issue, climaxed near the ending of the month. On 28 April, Fisher Ames of Massachusetts, choking with asthma and barely able to stand, dragged himself before a packed assembly to detail in graphic images the plight of New England if the treaty failed—the Indian raids pouring down from the unvacated British fortresses, the rain of blood and fire on the land. John Adams was among those who sat rapt in the galleries, some stunned, others trying to check tears. "My God! How great he is!" murmured a judge who sat next to him; and even the opposition appeared moved. "Some of the jackasses," Adams wrote his wife later, "attempted to smile, but . . . 'grinned horribly ghastly smiles' . . . like Foulon's son-in-law when they made him kiss his Father's dead and bleeding head."

On 1 May the question came before the House. The first vote divided 49 to 49. On the second, the treaty carried, 50 against 48. "The progress of this business throughout has been to me the most worrying and vexacious that I ever encountered," a distracted Madison wrote to Jefferson that day. " . . . the more so as the cause lay in the unsteadiness, the follies, the perversities, and the defections among our friends." Later, surveying the scope of the debacle, he gave this assessment of the cause:

> The name of the President and the alarm of war have had a greater effect than were apprehended. . . . A crisis, which ought to ahve been arranged as to fortify the Republican cause, has left it in a very crippled condition; from which its recovery will be the more difficult . . . as the elections . . . where the prospects were favorable, have taken a wrong turn.

The fury of the Republicans descended on George. For he was the one man in the country who could have pulled the treaty through. The mood of the country was summed up in an answer to a query from Alexander Hamilton by a North Carolinian friend: "That a man should oppose the treaty they could account for and bear . . . but it was inconceivable to them that any man without improper motives, a bad heart, or a most perverted judgment, should speak with disrespect of the old man." Madison complained on 9 May to Jefferson, "The people have been made everywhere to believe that the object of the H. of Reps in resisting the Treaty was war; and have thence listened to the summons, 'to follow where Washington leads.'" Jefferson' himself had written concurrently, "Such is the popularity of the President that the people will support him in whatever he will do, without appealing to their own reason, or any thing but their own feelings toward him." To Jefferson, tormented and ambivalent, Washington seemed more than ever the "colossus," the patron of error and oppression, whose gigantic shadow canceled out his sun. "Curse on his virtues, they have undone his country," he burst out in one tormented sentence, dreaming of the time when Washington's retirement would leave him an open field. In an astounding letter to Philip Mazzei, an Italian friend, he drew a feverish picture of an electorate hemmed in on all sides by a hostile government, ending on a violently accusatory note: "It would give you a fever were I to name to you the apostates who have gone over to these heresies . . . men who were Samsons in the field and Solomons

346

in the council . . . who have had their heads shorn by the harlot England." Another portion held a stubbornly combative edge: "We are likely to preserve the liberty we have obtained only by unremitting labors . . . but we shall persevere."

The form this perseverance was about to take was foreshadowed in a letter to Madison from Monroe: "I earnestly hope that Mr. Jefferson will be elected . . . every thing will most probably be right here from that moment."

Washington, for his part, was in a sustained fury at the assaults on his powers, his policies, and himself. Where he had till lately tried to play the honest broker, he had now come to believe with Hamilton in the implacable duplicity of the opposition side, talking now, as he did, of "the pretensions of that Party to . . . the patriotic zeal and watchfulness, on which they endeavour to build their own consequence, at the expense of others, who have different views from them." He hinted to an old acquaintance that the assault on the treaty had endangered both peace and the presidential office for partisan and noxious ends. "With respect to the motives wch. have not only brought the Constitution to the brink of a precipice, but the peace, happiness, and prosperity of the Country into imminent danger, I shall say nothing. Charity tells us they ought to be good, but suspicions say they must be bad." Charity did not keep him from making harsher statements to his closer friends. To Hamilton, he complained that every act of his was "misrepresented . . . to make it appear odious," and to Gouverneur Morris he wrote grimly of a "morbid tumor, always working," spreading poisons through the body of the state. His mood was not improved by a tense exchange of letters with Jefferson, who had been reported to him by Henry Lee from Virginia as having denounced him consistently throughout the state. There was an uneasy exchange between the two reluctant enemies, Jefferson anxious and blaming Lee for everything, Washington reproachful and remote. Yet at the end, even to this man he had begun to suspect as at least a partial enemy, he could not prevent a *cri de coeur*:

Until within the last year or two ago, I had no conception that parties would, or even could, go the lengths I have been witness to . . . that, while I was using my utmost exertions to establish a national character of our own . . . I should be accused of being the enemy of one Nation, and subject to the influence of another . . . that every act of my administration would be tortured, and given the grossest and most insidious misrepresentations . . . in such exaggerated terms, as could scarcely be applied to a Nero; a notorious defaulter; or even to a common pickpocket. But enough of this. . . . "

He was determined to step down at last. "I regret exceedingly that I did not publish my valedictory address the day after the Adjournment of Congress . . . " he wrote to Hamilton on 26 June. "It would by having preceded any unfavorable change in our foreign relations . . . render my retreat less difficult and embarrasing. And it might have prevented the remarks which more than probably will follow . . . that I delayed it long enough to see, that the current was turned against me, before I declared my intention to decline." Even his retirement was to be shadowed by the venom that had entered every phase of public life. Four years before, he had sketched out notes for his Farewell Address, showing the drafts for comment and revision to Hamilton, Madison, and Jay. That was when Madison was still his friend. Now, writing his address a second time (this time with Jay and Hamilton), he resisted Hamilton's suggestions that he delete a certain paragraph—on the grounds that Madison had seen it and would be more inclined to believe that his sentiments were real. Madison and his friends would realize that he had always wanted to retire and that he had no intentions to intrude the powers of the executive beyond its lawful bounds. "And besides," he concluded bitterly, "it may contribute to blunt, if it does not turn aside, some of the shafts which it may be presumed will be aimed at my annunciation of this event; among which, conviction of fallen popularity, and despair at being reelected, will be levelled at me."

* * *

348

John Adams was the "neutral" candidate, Federalist, but outside the ruling circle, between the poles of Jefferson on one side and on the other of Hamilton and Jay. He was sought by both sides as the buffer against the encroachments of the other, although Hamilton, preferring Charles Pinckney, had begun a flurry on his behalf—an action that would further chill the cool waters between himself and Adams and cause endless trouble in the years ahead. Jefferson's wooing of Adams, touched with something of their former friendship, had begun early in 1796. "It is to be considered," he had written Madison, "whether it would not be on the whole for the public good to come to an understanding with him as to his future elections. He is perhaps the only barrier against Hamilton's getting in." To another Republican he wrote later, "There is reason to believe that he is detached from Hamilton, & there is a possibility he may swerve from his politics in a great or less degree." "Detached" was a cool word for the estrangement between the man who had hoped to appear as the legitimate second to Washington and the "Creole bastard" who had edged him out. Yet Hamilton, too, preferred Adams as the lesser evil: "Every thing must give way to the great object of excluding Jefferson. . . . We have every thing to fear if this man comes in." The budding strains of the succeeding era were presaged in a letter from Hamilton to Rufus King on 15 February 1797 after the ill-tempered election had taken place: "Mr. Adams is President, Mr. Jefferson is Vice-President. Our Jacobins say they are well pleased, and that the *lion* and the *lamb* are to lie down together. . . . Skeptics like me quietly look forward to the event, willing to hope, but not prepared to believe."

At the time this mattered less to Washington than the fact that he was getting out at last. On 4 March he turned the office over to John Adams with genuine, if temporary, relief, serene and smiling, cooly courteous to Thomas Jefferson, whom he was seeing for the first time since his resignation and for the last time in his life. Yet the rancor smoldered, as his actions of his last years would reveal. Hence the tone of this note to Gouverneur Morris, who had begged him to accept another term: "By a firm adherence . . . to the neutral policy . . . I have brought on myself a torrent of abuse in the factious papers . . . and from the enmity of the discontented of all descriptions therein."

His last term had truly been a time of war. The tensions that had simmered underground in his first term, affecting individuals merely, had broken out in the second into riot and violence, challenging him with ballots and with guns. Yet he had stood his ground among them, fighting first for domestic power and then for nonengagement, "to be on friendly terms with, but independent of, all the nations of the earth." What was this, but his primal obligation, the continuation of his commitment and the fulfillment of his trust? "We are an Independent Nation, and act for ourselves. . . . We will not be dictated to by any Nation under Heaven . . . if we are to be told by a foreign Power . . . what we *shall do* and what we *shall not do,* we have Independence yet to seek."

XVIII

The Bottom of the Hill

I was no more at liberty than a man in prison, chained to the floor, and bound hand and foot.—JOHN ADAMS to Benjamin Rush, 13 October 1812

Washington's third, and last, retirement was the most strife-torn of his life. For John Adams, his successor, it meant office without the cachet of influence, which increased his native insecurities and created a state of unremitting stress. For George, shorn of office but with influence, it meant a partial shedding of the mask. The false front of the Roman states-man, cool arbiter of civil discord, dropped from a nature ba-sically violent, obsessed with honor, and complicated now by the neccessity to share stage center for the first time in twen-ty-seven years. Almost certainly on the subconscious level, his mind slipped back to his last experience with shared authori-ty—the French and Indian War, with its British troops and hostile governors, marked for him by a frantic reach for power, incessant squabbles over rank and honor, and fierce, contentious quarrels with his chiefs. Office, duty, and the fear of failure had acted as restraints on him, bridling his pride and violence and keeping his aggressions, somewhat muffled, under wraps. The loosened reins freed once more his native fires, in a twilight return to his first nature, before his life ran out.

* * *

His shaky standoff with the opposition had shattered in conditions heavy with betrayal and intrigue. James Monroe, his last ambassador to Paris, dismissed after extended quarrels in the final months of his administration, laced into him in an extended pamphlet, *A View of the Conduct of the Executive of the United States,* a prolonged, petulant, and vituperous discharge of grievances, charging Washington with treachery, "British" measures, and dereliction to the cause of liberty and France. Jefferson was enchanted—"Monroe's book is considered as masterly by all those who are not opposed in principle, and it is deemed unanswerable," he wrote Madison—George was less amused. *His* copy, annotated with answers as long as the original document, is now in the library at Harvard, crisscrossed with addendum in his best sarcastic style, venom leaking out of every line. Quiet loathing pervaded his note to Pickering: "Colo. Monroe passed through Alexandria last week, but did not honor me with a call. If what he has promised the public does him no more credit than what he has given to it . . . his friends must be apprehensive of a recoil." The *View,* for all its faults, was in the open. Worse was to come.

The humorless Monroe had never been an intimate or a semiequal, and the attack brought irritation but no pain. The break with Jefferson was something else. There was the Mazzei letter, printed in 1797, in a tortured mistranslation from the Italian version, with its odious references to corruption, monarchy, and Samsons shorn. This time Jefferson did not attempt to extricate himself. "It would be impossible for me to explain," he wrote James Madison, "without bringing on a personal difference between General Washington and myself, which nothing before the publication of this letter has ever done. It would embroil me with all those with whom his character is still popular . . . that is `. . . nine-tenths of the people of the United States." George said nothing, but it added to an accretion of distrust, almost unwillingly collected and refined. Then, in October, 1797, he received a letter from one "John Langhorne," dumping abuse on his detractors in the opposition and seeming to invite a virulent response. George answered with a tempered letter, which would have appeared to bring both incident and correspondence to a close. But John Nicholas, a neighbor and an ultra-Federalist, was present at the post office to see the answer claimed and taken, not by "Langhorne," but by Peter Carr, "a favorite nephew of your *very sincere friend* Mr. Jefferson, raised and educated directly by him from a child, and . . . entertaining sentiments, I do assure you . . . very different indeed towards *you* from those contained." Jefferson himself had no part in the bizarre entrapment; but the link appeared to cap a skein of intrigue and hidden malice, and George's response suggested the impression that previous events had made. To Nicholas, he sent an enraged letter: "Nothing short of the Evidence which you have adduced . . . could have shaken my belief in the friendship, which I had conceived, was possessed for me, by *the person* to whom you allude," adding with some bitterness, "It is not at all surprising . . . that the correspondence should have ended when it did, for the penetration of *that man* would have perceived at the first glance of the answer that nothing was to be drawn from that mode of attack." Through his lines runs a sense of complete betrayal at the hands of a man whose opposition he had tried to shelter and whose regard he had tried through dreadful discipline to keep. To his death, his comments on *"that man"* were to be filled with rancor, and his outbursts at the opposition laced with special rage.

For Jefferson, the rupture brought a torment of an intense and anguished sort. That he had suffered greatly from his need to battle Washington was revealed early, both in his own confessions and in his displaced and troubled methods of attacks—loyalty intermixed with malice, malice compounded with remorse. That he eventually found it impossible to live with is revealed in the correspondence of his later years. It was to Martin Van Buren, a rising politician of the next generation (who was to become President himself in 1837), that he wrote an extraordinary letter on 27 June 1824, two years before his own death at the age of eighty-six, that showed in dazzling clarity both his talents for self-expiation and the special burden of his need. Ill feeling between himself and Washington became the entire fault of intermediaries, "prone to antipathies, boiling with party passions, and under the dominion of those readily welcoming fancies for facts." The Mazzei letter, which he had readily admitted in 1797 came too close to truth for comfort, had become by 1824 "an unqualified falsehood . . . infamously false," with allusions to an "interpolated paragraph" (never mentioned in 1797) and references to a "misrepresentation of a single word, which entirely perverted its meaning, and made it a pliant and fertile text." The cessation of contact between himself and Washington after 4 March 1797 is sloughed off in a labored explanation:

> But one session of Congress intervened between that and his death . . . in my passage to and from which, as it happened to be not convenient to call him, I never had another opportunity; and as to the cessation of correspondence . . . no particular circumstance occurred for epistolary communication, and both of us were too much oppressed with letter writing, to trouble the other with a letter about nothing.

So much for his troubles with Washington. His troubles with Washington's policies were explained away by making George the dupe of a designing party which beguiled him into erroneous measures "not imputed to him, but to the councellors around him," without his knowledge and against his will. "General Washington," he went on to Van Buren, "after the retirement of his first cabinet . . . had no opportunity of hearing both sides of any question. His measures, consequently, took more the hue of the party in whose hands he was. . . . He lived too short a time after, and too much withdrawn from information, to correct the views into which he had been deluded; and the continuing assiduities of the party drew him into the vortex of their intemperate career." This of the man whose judgment Jefferson had described as "perfect" and of whose absolute control of his own government he had often taken note. Yet how else to justify the final break-off and the dissensions that had taken place? Especially poignant is this wishful explanation at the end of a long letter containing a judicious and almost loving account of Washington's character, written in 1814 to Dr. Walter Jones:

354

After I retired . . . great and malignant pains were taken by our federal monarchists, and not entirely without effect, to make him view me as a theorist holding French principles . . . which would lead infallibly to licentious-ness and anarchy. . . . And to these he listened the more easily, from my known disapprobation of the British treaty. I never saw him afterwards, or these malignant insinuations should have been dissipated before his just judgment, as mists before the sun.

Less misty was the fact that the relationship was doomed to founder, George being especially sensitive to the sort of subterranean and indirect maneuvers that Jefferson's dilemma had forced him to pursue. The intrigues of Gates and Lee in the Revolution had sensitized him to the threat of hidden enemies, and intimations of subversion ever after could throw him into a rage. Jefferson's subtle forays had embittered him more than anything, and the end of his angry letter to John Nicholas showed the depth and level of the wound:

Attempts to injure those who are supposed to stand well in the estimation of the People, and are stumbling-blocks in their way . . . is one of the means by which the Government is to be assailed, and the Constitution destroyed. . . . The conduct of this Party is systemized, and everything that is opposed to its execution, will be sacrificed, without hesitation or remorse.

His last faint ties to the opposition had broken with a painful snap. His tense relations with his own successor were about to undergo extensive strain.

Adams and Washington had worked uneasily in tandem, distant and suspicious of each other, separated by a gulf of frigid courtesy, to Adams' discomfort and by George's outright wish. "Mr. Adams," wrote Jefferson of Washington, ". . . whom he certainly did not love." Now the President, Adams moved uncertainly in the footprints of the hero-soldier, dwarfed in his immense shadow and always

355

slightly in the shade. Squat and edgy, with a tendency to fidget in public, he lacked the dignity that George had always been able to put over, and his round figure, with its large head with tufts of white hair protruding, made him appear less the Roman hero than a figure of mild fun. Adams knew—and sometimes acknowledged—the extent of his eclipse: that the heart of the party still clung to George in his retirement, while Hamilton, the changeling and the dark successor, exercised his magic from New York. Adams' Cabinet, passed on intact from Washington, regarded him as a contemptible usurper, serving him with disdain and on sufferance, while taking direction and venting grievances in extended letters to Mount Vernon and New York. "He spoke of his *masters,* as he called his heads of department, as acting above his control, and often against his wishes," Jefferson wrote to Benjamin Rush of Adams, and to Adams himself of "the Pickerings, the Wolcotts, the Tracys, the Sedgwicks* . . . then your secret, as they are now your open enemies . . . with whom we supposed you in a state of duress." (Defying him, Pickering, McHenry and Wolcott made a conspicuous appearance at Washington's birthnight ball on 22 February 1798—a sore point with the Adams family and which the Adamses did not attend.) Adams knew this but did not dare move against them, considering the group a bequest from his idolized predecessor, whose arrangements he did not dare disturb. George himself continued to correspond with the department heads (though not with Adams), receiving complaints and information, discharging consolation and advice. High on the list of exchanged grievances were complaints about the French, who had broken relations after ratification of the Jay Treaty and were currently treating the three-man delegation sent over by Adams with contempt. Then, in the spring of 1798, negotiations with the Directory collapsed, bringing the chance of war with a European power, the threat of invasion from French possessions in the West Indies, and the need for the unmartial and marginally popular President to raise and man an army and unite the country behind it and himself.

*Federalist Senator and friend of Hamilton.

356

To the besotted Cabinet, there was one choice for the hand to lift the rusted sword. "The storm thickens, and . . . our vessel will soon require its ancient pilot," McHenry wrote Washington in ecstasies. "May we flatter ourselves . . . you will accept the command of all our armies? . . . you alone can unite all hearts and hands." Even in advance of this, Hamilton had bombarded his old patron with a rain of anxious letters begging him to step back into the field. George at first threw up token resistance to this fourth irruption into public life. "The Opposers of Government would denounce it at once as a restless Act, evinsive of my discontent in retirement," he warned McHenry, "and that my love for it was all a sham." Yet at the same time he was outlining in suspicious detail the exact conditions under which he would accept command. He must appoint the highest-ranking officers, especially his General Staff. All brigadiers must meet with his approval. And the old rule from the Revolution, that rank in a new army must depend on prior status, must be scuttled once for all. "Under the rose" he wrote McHenry, "I do not . . . conceive that a desireable set could be formed from the old Generals," citing age and sickness, lack of talents, and political attachments to the French. To McHenry, he repeated what would emerge as his obsession: that his reputation rested on this endeavor and that to save it he must have complete control. "If a judicious choice is not made of the principal officers . . . it can never be rectified. . . . The character . . . of the Army would be lost in the Superstructure; the reputation of the Commander in Chief would sink in it, and the Country be involved in inextricable expense." To Hamilton, a mere lieutenant colonel at the close of the Revolution, he had written in early April: "I should like, previously, to know who would be my coadjutators, and whether you would be disposed to take an active part."

It was not until 22 June that Adams essayed his first awkward letter, at once vague and obsequious, filled with almost embarrassing self-abnegation and inexplicit pleas for the use of George's "name." What passed through the mind of the President as he realized he must crawl back under the stifling wing of his predecessor is unrecorded at the time, though he

357

later wrote to Benjamin Rush that he was "mortified" at the need to borrow George's glory to prop up his regime. Washington's answer was properly cautious, save for his veiled insistence on one point: "There is one thing . . . on which I can give a decided opinion . . . that the greatest circumspection be used in appointing the General Staff . . . so many limbs, or parts of the Commander . . . on whom he *must* depend."

George was already weighing the merits of his prospective officers when McHenry arrived at Mount Vernon on 11 July, bearing yet another vague and abject letter from the President and his commission as Commander in Chief of the armies raised in the service of the United States. How much power did he really have? George later, with the vehemence born of absolute assurance, insisted violently that his compliance rested on his powers to control the staff. "It was the ground on which I *accepted* and *retained* the commission," he later wrote to Adams in a fury, "and . . . the authority on which I proceeded to the arrangement that was presented to you by the Secretary of War." So insistent was he that he had urged McHenry to return to Philadelphia for an absolute confirmation of his rights. McHenry refused, insisting that the powers were inclusionary and that to have raised questions would have insulted Adams' good faith. What would have happened if Adams had been presented with this ultimatum from the start? Harsh though it was, it might have cleared the air. As it was, boundaries of influence remained uncharted, and president, commander, and major generals slid together into a morass of intrigue.

Jealousies, confusion, and cross-purposes plagued the "arrangement" from the start. Three men were to be raised to major general, the first of these to serve as George's aide and surrogate and representative (until action) in the field. Hamilton was his inevitable first choice for alter ego, but he was junior in rank to many officers, including his two rival claimants, Charles Cotesworth Pinckney and Henry Knox. Knox was unthinkable, obese, and ailing, his limited capacities dimmed by age. Pinckney, however, the round-cheeked and deceptively baby-faced soldier-diplomat, now en route

358

home from the abortive French mission, was able, gifted, and possessed of an immense skein of connections in the Carolinas, from which exposed and vulnerable area the projected French invasion was expected to ensue. For days, George swung between Pinckney and Hamilton, besieged by hysterical letters from Pickering on Hamilton's behalf, torn between a desire to work with his confidant and a fear that a slight to Pinckney would bring vast defections in the South. "Being senior to Colonel Hamilton, he would not, I am morally certain, accept a junior appointment," George wrote an overheated Pickering. "Disgust would follow, and its influence would spread. . . . Under this view . . . I think it would be impolitic, and might be dangerous, to sow the seeds of discontent." At the same time, he assured Hamilton he would remain his de facto second, regardless of the formal line. "My wish to put you first, and my fear of losing him, are not a little embarrassing," he wrote Hamilton, adding of Pinckney in another letter: "I confess . . . my prime motive in gratifying him is that he might come forward with all his force." It was not until 18 July that he sent back his list to Adams, in descending order of their seniority and ascending order of his own convenience, of Hamilton, Pinckney, and Knox. What Adams felt is unrecorded, but his later actions indicate that he was stunned. What the generals themselves felt was another matter and brought about a storm.

Old friends but ambitious claimants, the nominees fell headlong into a tangle of intrigue. Knox sent Washington a wounded letter in which he called their twenty years of friendship a "delusion" and threatened to return a refusal to the secretary of war. "I should have been previously consulted on an arrangement, in which my feelings and happiness have been so much wounded." he wrote plaintively, "or . . . I should not have been dragged forth to public view at all." A stricken Hamilton (Washington had sent him Knox's letter) wrote to Pickering in intense agitation—he would not hurt Knox or Washington, but Knox *and* Pinckney set above him would drop him to third place and set a precedent where a countless line of senior officers could supersede him, which was too degrading to his pride. Where he had sent Washington endless letters in mid-July advancing his

359

own claim to preference, he now appeared to tack about. He told George he would agree "cheerfully" to any arrangement he might make. George might, however, be mistaken in the opinion of Pinckney's intransigence he seemed to have locked into his mind. If approached with tact, Pinckney might agree to third rank in the line of precedence, in which case all problems would be solved.

Pinckney himself, in mid-Atlantic through most of the furor, docked at New York in late summer and had barely been off the boat ten minutes before flustered aides dashed up to tell him he had landed in the middle of a squall. His first impression was that his compatriots had gone insane. He declared himself delighted to be junior to Hamilton—"I rejoiced in his appointment, and would with pleasure serve under him"—and even, if need be, to Knox, although the obstinacy of the latter had somewhat changed his mind. Because of this, he indicated he would not repeat an offer made to Washington to let Knox take his place. Yet if George himself in his capacity should revise the order to arrive at that conclusion, he would neither leave the service nor complain.

Nor was this the end of George's troubles. With his generals immersed in emotional crosscurrents, he was heading to a break with Adams in his mind, making the army more than ever the focal point among contending factions, the symbol of power lost, regained, or held. As his later letters were to show in dreadful clarity, a train of incidents had built a cloud of anger and suspicion in his mind: recruitments lagged, information had been slow in reaching him, and Adams had not exchanged a word with him since the letter accompanying his commission, which had been dated 7 July. Four brigadiers had been appointed, to his "disgust" and without his knowledge; so had an adjutant general whom he detested, although he had warned Adams that this officer in particular must have the "*entire* confidence" of the commander in chief. McHenry, in the War Department, was a willing but an addled conduit. Hamilton had arrived at the army base in Trenton to find things in chaos and the usually pliant McHenry oddly resistant to his efforts to set matters right. "I had thought that he would have been glad . . . to

360

make me useful to him," Hamilton wrote plaintively to Washington, "but the idea has thus far been very partially embraced." What else, but for the pair to use each other to channel direction of the army into their own hands? "I will endeavour to impress him with the propriety of requiring your assistance," George wrote back to Hamilton, adding hopefully, "by bringing you thus in contact a thousand other matters will fall in." Hamilton returned the favor in a letter to McHenry himself: "It will be agreeable to the Commander-in-Chief to receive frequent communications from you . . . have a full statement made out of what is further doing, and send it to him." How could the two, used to command in war and politics, shed their ingrained habits now? Their view was summed up admirably in this passage in a letter to Hamilton from George: "Delicacy, if matters become serious, must yield to expediency. The stake we play for is too great to be trifled with . . . write me as often as you can."

To what more was the President expected to yield? In early August he had told McHenry that "in his opinion Colonel Hamilton was not entitled to stand so high, and that he did not know the merits, which gave General Pinckney preference to Knox." A stunned McHenry reminded him that this was Washington's preference and showed him a letter on the subject that George had written to Hamilton and Hamilton had given to him. Adams appeared pacified and was only prevented from sending in the nomination by Pickering's announcement that the Senate had adjourned. The day after, however, some thing or other had caused a very great change in his mind. He now said that he could not think of placing Hamilton before Knox. An intense scene followed, in which Adams appeared to back off. "He finally agreed to follow your arrangement," McHenry later wrote to Washington, "upon my admitting that any of the parties if dissatisfied . . . might have their claim discussed and settled by a board of officers, or the commander-in-chief—A few days after . . . the President suddenly left Philadelphia, without apprising either Mr. Pickering or me."

It was at Quincy, far from the Cabinet (and Washington)

and close to Knox and Abigail, that Adams sent, on 14 August, the note that set McHenry on his ears:

> General Knox is legally entitled to rank next to General Washington, and no other arrangement will give satisfaction . . . the consequence of this is that Pinckney will rank before Hamilton. If it be consented that the rank will be Knox, Pinckney, and Hamilton, you may call the latter two into immediate service . . . any other plan will occasion great delay.

McHenry answered in a frantic letter 22 August, warning of "disagreeable consequences," reminding him that the arrangement had come directly from Washington who had made acceptance of his designations the condition of his command. He suggested to Adams that he write to Knox, asking that his acceptance be conditional, pending new adjustments to be worked out by George. He also told the other members of the Cabinet, one of whom, Pickering, wrote to Hamilton in a rage:

> The original letter from General Washington to you, McHenry now informs us, was by him shown to the President, notwithstanding which you have seen where you would have been placed. McHenry said also that General Washington made your appointment to be the *sine qua non* of his accepting the chief command. The weight of this fact seems to have escaped the President's recollection, or he would not have desired that General Knox should take the rank of you.

Adams answered McHenry on 29 August. He had not passed on McHenry's suggestions to Knox (public or private) as "neither contain sentiments that I can approve." On the rank of the generals, he remained unmoved. Prior rank must govern present status; Knox must lead the list. In a sentence of startling transparency, he made a mock pretense of obeying Washington and then slipped the reason for his fears: "I made the nominations according to the list presented to me by General Washington, in hopes that the rank might be settled among them . . . believing at the time . . . that the

362

nomination and appointment would give Hamilton no rank at all."

On the subject of Washington he was cuttingly succinct:

> I said, and say now, that if I could resign to him the office of President, I would do it instantly . . . but I never said I would hold the office . . . while he should exercise it . . . There has been too much intrigue in this business with General Washington and me, and if I shall ultimately be the dupe of it, I am much mistaken in myself.

Hamilton's first response was moderation, pending an appeal to George. "In the last resort, I shall be inclined to have much deference for his wishes" he wrote to Pickering of Washington, but a week of brooding changed his mind. "My mind is unalterably made up," he wrote McHenry on 9 September. "I shall certainly not hold the commission on the plan proposed, and only wait an official communication to say so." McHenry's answer offered sympathy and the outlines of a plan: "I cannot blame you for your determination. Mr. Pickering, Mr. Wolcott, and Mr. Stoddert have agreed to make a dutiful representation to the President. You will not, of course, hear from me . . . till the result is known." Wolcott wrote Hamilton on 19 September: "Measures have been taken to bring all right, if the thing be at all practicable. . . . I request you to *say nothing* and *do nothing* until you hear from me." The "measures" were to dump the entire correspondence between Adams and McHenry into the lap of Washington, complete with the damaging comments upon Hamilton and the devastating remarks about himself. On 24 September came a terse note to Hamilton from George.

> I have seen the correspondence between the President of the United States and the Secretary of War . . . But as it was given in confidence . . . I had no ground on which I could proceed. I have therefore written for an official account of the President's determination, as the foundation of the representation I propose to offer him. . . . Until the result of this is known I hope you will suspend a final decision, and let matters remain in Statu quo.

It was on 25 September that he dropped his bomb—an extraordinary letter running eleven printed pages, venom dripping out of every line. Other grievances were mentioned, but his rage centered on three points: Adams' appointment of inferior officers was damaging the Army; Adams was engaging in a war of spite on Alexander Hamilton; and, in reversing the order of the major generals, he had welshed on his promise to Washington and delivered a personal insult to him. Why had Adams not bothered to ask his conditions before sending on the offer of command? "I would have told you . . . on what terms I would have consented . . . you would then have been enabled to decide, whether they were admissable or not. This opportunity was not afforded, *before* I was brought to public view. To declare them *afterwards,* was all I could do, and this I did, in explicit language, to the Secretary of War." Adams' ideas of rank were imbecilic; they would clog the upper levels of the army with aging incompetents, sink maturing talents near the bottom, and doom the venture to inevitable disgrace. "What then is to be done with General Dayton, who never ranked higher than Captain?" George inquired of an officer whom Adams had placed in a high post. "The principle will apply with equal force in that case as in the case of Hamilton and Knox." He himself had proceeded to appoint his direct subordinates, conscious of the stakes to the country and to his reputation and assured that his right to do so was the understood condition of command. And what had happened? "I will now respectfully ask, in what manner these stipulations on my part have been complied with? . . . You have been pleased to order the last to be first, and the first to be last." Would the President kindly inform him if he intended to appoint further officers without his concurrence and if the reversal of the major general would be allowed to stand?

Never mentioned, but implicit throughout, was the larger meaning of his words: Adams must give him his aides and his army, or he would force a battle to the end.

Washington's mood was violent; the cold disdain that he had shown to Adams transmuted into fire for his friends. To Pickering, he raged at the President's "departure in almost every other instance from what I considered a solemn com-

364

pact; and the *only* terms on which I would . . . hazard everything dear and valuable to me." To another correspondent, asking intervention with Adams on an army matter, he wrote acidly, "As I think I stand upon very precarious ground, in my relations to him, I am not overzealous in taking *unauthorized* steps, when those that I thought *were authorized,* are not likely to meet with much respect." To McHenry, he delimned the limits to which he was prepared to go: "You will be at no loss to perceive . . . what my determination is, if he perseveres in this Resolution," adding the (unheeded) warning: "Burn this as soon as it is perused, as I will do your answer, that neither the one, nor the other, may appear." Later he sent McHenry the first copy of his letter to Adams, with a chilling intimation of his plans: "The rough draught . . . I send for your perusal, but with the express desire, that the contents may not be divulged, unless the results should make it necessary for me to proceed to the final step. . . . If there is no disposition on his part to do this, the public must decide which of us is right and which is wrong."

On 9 October, Adams sent the beaten-down response: "I some time ago signed the three Commissions and dated them on the Same day, in hopes Similar to yours, that an amicable Adjustment . . . might take place among the Gentlemen themselves. But, if these hopes are disappointed, and Controversies should arise, they will of course be submitted to you as Commander in Chief."

Terse as ever in victory, George sent the letter to Hamilton, confirming the outcome of the coup: "General Knox is fully acquainted with my sentiments . . . and I hope no fresh difficulties will arise with General Pinckney. Let me advise you therefore to give, without delay, your *full* Aid to the Secretary of War." To McHenry, he sent another note, revealing yet another small concern:

> Enclosed is a copy of the President's letter to me, which I request may be, with this letter, burnt as soon as they are read. . . . Otherwise a knowledge that the contents of my letters to, and from him, are in the possession of others, may induce him to believe . . . that intrigues are carrying on, in which I am an Actor, than which, nothing is more foreign from my heart.

This was not the end to the skirmishing between the displaced administration, which still considered itself in power, and its uneasy and disputed heir. If Adams had lost the battle for the army, he still held control over the war. On 7 February 1799 Theodore Sedgwick, one of Hamilton's devoted cadre in the Senate, wrote his master a horrified letter recounting a conversation with the President the night before. Alone, the two men had been discussing the military situation when the President suddenly burst out, "If you must have an army, I will give it to you, but remember, it will make the government more unpopular than all their other acts." There followed a dissertation upon taxes, public burdens, and the army and its unutterable expense. Sedgwick listened on in mounting horror. "I cannot say I was astonished," he later wrote to Hamilton. "Astonishment is a sentiment which he has for some time lost the power to excite." Composing himself, the senator was interjecting some new plans for army organization when Adams dropped his bomb:

> He asked me, what additional authority it was supposed to give the commander-in-chief? I answered none; that all that was proposed was to give him a new title.
> "What," said he, "are you going to appoint him general over the President? I am not so blind but I have seen a combined effort among those who call themselves the friends of government, to annihilate the essential powers of the President. This, sir, (raising his voice) my understanding has perceived, and my heart felt."

Appalled, Sedgwick pressed him for incidents, to which Adams answered, "if I had not seen *it*, it was improper for him to go into detail. This," concluded Sedgwick in a concise statement of their views of the President, "shows we are afflicted with an evil for which . . . no complete remedy can be applied."

How complete was the evil they discovered on 18 February. Adams fired off a rocket that was to blast the army to a hollow shell. He sent to the Senate the nomination of William Vans Murray, American ambassador to the Netherlands, as minister plenipotentiary to Paris, along with a conciliatory message from the foreign minister of France. "Evidently

366

kept secret," wrote Jefferson, who had detested the war and the army, "from federalists of both houses, as appeared by their dismay." High Federalists were enraged. "I have neither time nor inclination to detail all the false and insidious declarations it contains," Sedgwick wrote Hamilton of the French mission. "Had the foulest heart and ablest head in the world been permitted to select the most embarrassing and ruinous measure, it would have been precisely the one which has been adopted. . . . This would be true was Mr. Murray the ablest negotiator in Christendom; but with all his virtues, he is feeble, unguarded, credulous, and unimpressive. I have not decided ultimately what I shall do." Murray's reputation, apparently, was what Adams had been counting on. In an acrimonious session with his Senate leaders, Adams insisted he would defend the powers of his office against external influence, then promised that if Murray were vetoed, he would propose a joint commission of three ambassadors, with two of the three empowered to act for them all. The three named were Murray, Chief Justice Oliver Ellsworth, and Patrick Henry (changed later to Governor William R. Davie of North Carolina when Henry afterward declined). This compromise was the arrangement that prevailed. "At a meeting of the federal members," Sedgwick wrote Hamilton, "it was agreed to reject the nomination. . . . This is everything which, under the circumstances, could be done."

Washington, like his followers, was stunned. "I was surprized at the *measure,* how much more so at the manner of it?" he wrote to Alexander Hamilton. "This business seems to have commenced in an evil hour . . . and I wish mischief may not tread in all its steps." Later he was appalled when Adams shipped the three off to France in November, in defiance of the Senate and the Cabinet, and stunned beyond measure when McHenry wrote him plaintively on 10 November that Adams had at last turned upon his Cabinet and was about to drop at least one of the three. "Stricken dumb," he described himself in his answer to McHenry, adding that the country was "moving by hasty strides to some awful crisis" and that "I have, for some time past, viewed the political concerns of the United States with an anxious and painful eye." Was it distrust of France, or Adams, or rage at the challenge to his own right to direct the country, after an undisputed reign of over twenty years? Through the lines ran both his distaste for Adams and the evidence of an underlying truth: that he had indeed regarded his Cabinet as Adams had in the beginning—as a bequest from the man who was and would always be *the* President and whose arrangements were not to be disturbed. As so often in his background, there was evidence of a hidden battle between reason and violence, diffidence and power, the wish to abide peaceably by the laws of the succession and the habit of power he had held unchallenged since 1775. Now he had an added reason to make Adams the special target of his rage. Like Jefferson, the President had told George one thing and done another. He had gone behind his back to make attacks upon him; George had been willfully deceived.

Adams, like Jefferson, however, had been forced into subversive tactics by a complex of emotions of his own—an immense need to escape the stifling influence of a gigantic figure for whom his feelings were a tangle of resentment, jealousy, loyalty, and awe. George's unique hold on the American people made open opposition dangerous, while his character, with its odd shoots of charm and its engaging diffidence, caught the escapees in snares of enervating guilt. For his natural rivals—and there were many—it created an untenable situation, to which subversion was the only answer and from which only men like Hamilton who could work only with and through him could be spared. For the rest, the dilemma had been drawn: they would always suffer agonies in their efforts to escape him, and he would always feel betrayed.

That was the end of the army, of the last effort of Washington's heirs to cling to power, and, as it developed, of the addled plans of Alexander Hamilton to join with Britain to drive France and Spain from the Americas, which he had nurtured in secret (no one knows how seriously) and of which he had never breathed a word. As Adams feared, their revenge was terrible. Hamilton, the ousted heir, turned on him with a savage attack that split the party down the middle and turned him out of office in 1801. George was not alive to witness this last humiliation, but Adams never doubted the role he would have played. "I believe he expected to be called in again," he wrote years later, "as he certainly would have been had he lived. . . . I was then convinced we must have him or Jefferson, and I thought him the least visionary of the two. Considering his connection with Hamilton, I am now not so clear I was right."

Adams never recovered from those months of agony that had made him face the truth he always feared—that as President he was still in shadow, that the heart of power lay with other men. Though he could never admit that he had brought George back to power (or the weakness that had forced him to it), he never ceased to rage at the agents of his humiliation, in letters whose outraged cadence showed the depth and rancor of his wound. Years after the affair was over, he was railing at Hamilton—"An insolent cox-comb . . . a bastard brat of a Scotch pedlar . . . in a deliri-um of ambition . . . blown up with vanity by the tories, had his eyes fixed on the highest station in America, and he hated every man, young or old, who stood in his way"—at the army—"Hamilton's project . . . appeared to me to be proper only for Bedlam"—and about the troubles he ran into in his attempts to tone it down—"I could not do it without quarrel-ling outright with my ministers, who Washington's appoint-ment had made my masters, and I gave it up." Other times, he fantasized about a loyal army (reeling off lists of George's enemies) and of the fate that would have met him if he had tried to bring it off:

> I ought to have said No to the appointment of Wash-ington and Hamilton and some others, and Yes to the ap-pointments of Burr, Muhlenberg, and some others. I ought to have appointed Lincoln and Gates and Knox and Clinton. . . . But if I had said Yes and No in this man-ner, the Senate would have contradicted me in every in-stance. . . . Washington would have been chosen Presi-dent at the next election . . . and Hamilton would have been appointed commander in chief.

It was on Washington that he vented the burden of his wrath:

> He felt weary [he explained to Rush] and longed for retirement, though he soon found solitude more fatiguing, more disgusting, and longed to return to public bustle again . . . my popularity was growing too splendid, and addressed to me from all quarters piqued his jealousy. The great eulogium, "First in war, first in peace, first in the affections of his country," was suspected by him and all his friends to be in some danger . . . . I believe he expected to be called in again . . . as he certainly would have been if he lived.

Scattered through this were the few rational statements that caught his torment clear: "I was no more at liberty than a man in prison, chained to the floor, and bound hand and foot. . . . Washington ought either to have never gone out of public life, or he ought never to have come in again."

Washington himself subsided into paperwork on the now-useless army, contenting himself with a running stream of sideswipes at Adams and the opposition to his friends. Why was the President at Quincy, when he sould be at the helm? "His absence," George wrote McHenry, "gives much discontent to the friends of government, while its enemies chuckle at it, and think it a favorable omen." As expected, calls deluged him from disgruntled Federalists (among them Gouverneur Morris and Governor Trumbull of Connecticut), urging him to run for President in 1800 and save them from the disaster that Adams had become. "Should you decline, no man will be chosen, whom you would wish to see in that high office," wrote Morris with his remorseless logic. "Is retirement in the strict sense of the word a possible thing? And is the half retirement, which you may attain to, more peaceful than a public life? . . . has it not the disadvantage of leaving you involved in measures which you can neither direct not control? . . . from envy and slander no retirement is safe but the grave."

George responded to these entreaties with acerbic nays—less, as it developed, from respect for Adams than from distaste for a grueling battle and fears that after two unanimous elections he might win by a narrow and contested vote. To Trumbull, he declined to stick his neck out for the dubious pleasure of uniting the Federalist vote. "Let me ask, what consolation, what satisfaction, what safety, should I find in support, which depends upon caprice? . . . The favorite today may have the curtain dropped on him tomorrow, while steadiness marks the conduct of the Antis, and whoever is not on *their* side must expect to be loaded with all the calumny that malice can invent." More, there was the problem of his reputation. "I should be charged with inconsistency, concealed ambition, dotage, and a thousand more etceteras." Further, the party was on the wrong track. "If principles, instead of men, are not the steady pursuit of the Federalists, their cause will soon be at an end."

Ignored or overlooked in this last sentence was the central fact of his political career: that men—*one* man—had carried principles that the mass of the people were ready to reject.

George, at the time of this projected fourth trajectory, was nearly sixty-eight years old. He was now the lone survivor of his family, the next to last, the scapegrace debtor Samuel, having died in August, 1799. "I was the *first,* am now the *last* of my father's children," he wrote his cousin, Burgess Ball. "When I shall be called upon to follow them, is known only to the giver of Life. When the summons comes I shall endeavour to obey it with good grace." Here is a note of fatalism, enlivened earlier by wit. In December, 1797, writing to her friend Eliza Powel in Philadelphia, Martha added a postscript from the general, asking to be told *"beforehand"* what rumor would say of his reputation if he should "go off in an Apopleptic, or any other fit." (". . . he thinks," added Martha, "all fits that end in death are worse than a love fit, a fit of laughter, and many other kinds which he could name.") Not that he intended to expire soon.

> Besides, as he had entered into an engagement with Mr. Morris, and several other gentlemen, not to quit the Theatre of *this* world before the year 1800, it may be *relied upon* that no breach of contract shall be laid him on that

account, unless dire necessity should bring it about. . . . In that case, he shall hope that they would do by him, as he would by them, excuse it. At present, there seems no danger of his giving them the slip, as neither his health, nor spirits, were ever in greater flow, notwithstanding, he adds, he is descending, and has almost reached, the bottom of the hill.

As it happened, he was to slip his contract by the edge of sixteen days.

On Thursday, 12 December 1799, George rode out as usual at ten in the morning for his daily circuit of his farms, heading this time into a spray of snow, hail and freezing rain, churned into swirls of icy pellets and whipped about him by a chilling wind. He returned about three in the afternoon, his cloak soaking, his neck wet and damp snow clinging to his hair. On Friday, noted his secretary, Tobias Lear (who was to take extensive notes of his final illness), he complained of a sore throat, "had a hoarseness, which increased in the evening; but he made light of it, as he would never take anything to carry off a cold, always observing, 'let it go as it came.'" Saturday morning he awoke between two and three, coughing violently, his throat raw and aching, barely able to speak. "He spoke but seldom, & with great difficulty," Lear wrote later, "in so low and broken a voice as at times hardly to be understood." Fearing chill, he refused to let his wife summon servants until it was almost dawn. Lear sent for Dr. Craik about seven in the morning and, returning, fed George a mixture of molasses, butter, and vinegar, which brought on convulsions and a near choking fit. Craik arrived about eleven, sent immediately for two consultants (who arrived in the afternoon between three and four), swathed the throat with a blister of cantharides, prepared a steam vapor of water and vinegar, and mixed a gargle of vinegar and tea. This potion had no more success than the first. "When he laid back his head to let it run down," Lear recounted, "it put him into great distress, and almost produced suffocation," catching on the constriction of congested tissue and running out of his mouth, mixed with phlegm. Another remedy, a

372

mixture of tartar and calomel, produced a copious discharge of the bowels, but no relief. There had been four bleedings, the first in the early morning, the last at four thirty, this taking thirty-two ounces with the blood now running thick and slow. On this last, there appeared to be a measure of dispute, Craik writing to the second doctor of the third consultant, Elisha Dick, "He was averse to bleeding the General, and I have often thought that if we had acted according to his suggestion . . . 'he needs all his strength—bleeding will diminish it' . . . our good friend might be alive."

His fatalism, always marked, astounded everyone, deferring to them with detached courtesy and planning his death with the cool precision that had run through his life. "He was fully impressed at the beginning of his complaint . . . that its conclusion would be mortal," wrote Craik and Dick in their report later, adding that he suffered treatment "rather as a duty" than from any sense of expectation or of hope. "During the short period of his illness," they added, "he economized his time . . . with the utmost serenity; and anticipated his approaching dissolution with every demonstration of that equanimity for which his whole life has been so singularly conspicuous." At four thirty, he whispered to Lear, who was sitting at his bedside, to ask Martha to bring him two copies of his will. She did; he looked at both, declared one useless, and asked her to burn it, which she did. To Lear, he then made one of the amazing statements of detached tranquillity that were to drop from him during the afternoon and night: "I find that I am going, my breath cannot continue long; I believed from the first attack it would be fatal . . . arrange and record my late military letters & papers—arrange my accounts & settle my books. . . . Let Mr. Rawlins finish recording my other letters, which he has begun." He then asked Lear if there was anything he had forgotten, as "he had but a very short time." Lear tried to assure him that he was not near his end. "He observed smiling, that he certainly was, and that it was the debt which we all must pay."

There were some signs of action. His restlessness continued through the evening in an endless quest for breath and ease. At eight in the morning and at five at night, he was lifted to a chair near the fire; but the exertion had been too terrible, and he was taken back. He continued restless, tossing frequently, murmuring to Lear who had helped to move him, "I am afraid I shall fatigue you too much." At six Craik, Dick, and Brown returned. "Dr. Craik asked him if he could sit up in in bed," Lear recorded. "He held out his hand to me & was raised up, when he said to the physicians, 'I feel myself going, you had better not take any more trouble about me; but let me go off quietly; I cannot last long.'" He subsided, and all retired, except Craik. He continued "uneasy and restless, but without complaining," asking Craik and Lear repeatedly for the time. "When I helped to move him at this time he did not speak," Lear wrote later. "The Doctor pressed his hand, but he could not utter a word."

At ten o'clock there was a change. He motioned, made several efforts, and then said to Lear, "I am just going. Have me decently buried, and do not let my body be put into the Vault in less than two days after I am dead."

He looked at Lear again.

"Do you understand me?"

"Yes, Sir," Lear replied.

"*'Tis well,*" he said.

These were his last words. Shortly before eleven his breathing eased. "He lay quietly," Lear wrote, "withdrew his hand from mine & felt his own pulse—I spoke to Dr. Craik who sat by the fire—he came to the bedside—the General's hand fell from his wrist. . . . Dr. Craik put his hand on his eyes and he expired without a struggle or a sigh."

Martha, at the foot of the bed, asked firmly, "Is he gone?"

Lear, speechless, raised his hand.

"'Tis well,' said she in a plain voice. 'All is over now. . . . I shall soon follow him.'"

The entombment was on 18 December. At noon, neighbors gathered at Mount Vernon, where the outsize coffin, containing the gigantic frame, rested in the portico, now draped in black. Services, scheduled for early afternoon, were delayed for the arrival of a party of militia and riflemen from Alexandria, who had requested to be present at the rites. Between three and four, minute guns sounded from a vessel in the river, and the procession formed. Members of the cavalry, infantry, and guard of Alexandria led the procession to the river's edge. Two servants led Washington's favorite horse down the gently sloping lawn. Six colonels bore the coffin, which held his cape and sword. Friends, "citizens," and members of the Masonic lodge of Alexandria followed in the rear. Martha, who did not join, watched from a window in the house.

At the river the military split into two lines of passage, and the mourners walked between them to the vault. There the rector of Christ Church of Alexandria read the simple service as the crash of gunshot from the river shook the quiet woods and fields. The mourners watched as the coffin was placed in the recesses of the vault. Then they turned and walked back up the hill.

This was the ending of the service, but the mere beginning of the shock. Sporadic tributes erupted spontaneously throughout the British Isles; French soldiers wore black armbands for an official mourning period of ten days. Later thousands mobbed the Temple of Mars in Paris for an hysterical eulogy to the "great father of liberty," sable draped on the walls and porticoes, the tricolor of the Revolution draped in black. Hamilton's desolation was predictable; less so the stunned outburst of John Adams to Congress—"I felt myself alone, bereft of my last brother"—when news reached the capital on the morning of 18 December. As strange in its own way was the reaction of Thomas Jefferson, who left Monticello on the way north from his winter recess on 21 December and by a route at once circuitous and leisurely did not arrive at Philadelphia until after the rash of tributes ended on 1 January—a reaction of both finesse and discomfort, as well as the act of a man as yet unable to come to terms with the dimensions of both his freedom and his loss.

The people, feeling loss and freedom of only the most frightening variety, expressed their sense of sudden devastation through measures at once poignant, dramatic, and bizarre. Philadelphia mourned on 26 December, in an immense and somber show of state—a grim parade of Congress, the judiciary, the Cabinet, and municipal officials, trailed by a vast train of the Cincinnati veterans and "citizens" in a nine-block walk through sodden weather from Congress Hall to the German Lutheran Church, where a mob of 4,000 sat in tears through a two-hour oration by Henry Lee. Prominent in the procession—and drawing sobs from the 10,000 who thronged the parade route—were a white stallion bearing Washington's saddle, holster, and pistols (with the boots dramatically reversed) and the immense black-draped and empty coffin borne by its six pallbearers as if it had contained the body of the hero, now eight days in its tomb—a last grasp at a "touch" of the commander, as well as an effort to fit the country into his quiet and too unmarked death. This was the "state" ceremony, but nothing surpassed the drama staged on 31 December by New York—a baroque parade marked in its passage around lower Wall Street by eight cannon captured from the British in 1776; the befeathered members of the Society of Saint Tammany, the leader bearing wampum bound in black ribbons; and thirteen "braves" carrying black-bordered state standards, and bearing black rosettes. Twenty-four maidens in white, strewing laurels preceded the bier—a monstrous edifice towering thirteen feet above the shoulders of the staggering soldiers, bearing a funeral urn of burnished gold above a series of ascending pedestals, brilliantly adorned with martial emblems, gold, blue, and scarlet against the velvet black. Nor was this the end of the mock ceremonies, mock entombments, mock parades. Baltimore mourned on 1 January; Boston on 8 January; Charleston on February 15. In all, about 300 cities, towns and villages in the United States. Military bases were put into mourning for a six-month period, ships ordered to dip their colors for three months, officers ordered into black. Official mourning had been declared to last to what would have been his sixty-eighth birthday, 22 February 1800. Again, on this dark anniversary, bells and cannon thundered, shops were shuttered, churches filled. It was not until the early winter dusk that the tributes ended, the parades of empty biers and caissons, the mobs thronging around empty caskets that contained nothing whatsoever but their hopes.

Afterward he subsided into myth and history, frozen for the ages in the heroic posture, blanched of both the iron and

376

the shadows, drained of the ambitions that drove him and the spells he cast on other men. The successive stages of his development—the driven boy, the striving soldier, the tormented general, the irate and skillful politician—vanished into the icon of the somber virtues, who was dragged reluctantly to power, exercised it without imagination, and dropped into retirement with no emotion but relief. Later comments did not help. Bonaparte, that extinct volcano, erupted briefly in his last exile to damn Washington with what was for him faint praise, setting George's wisdom and disinterestedness against his own rocketing and ruinous career, locking George forever in the grip of the dim virtues, on the side of tidy moderation as against dramatic dash. Jefferson made things no better in his own postmortems, written when he was an elder statesman and himself something of a pillar, doubtless well-meaning, yet entombing George still further in his marble coating, each word dropping like a block of lead. "Perhaps the strongest feature in his character was prudence," Jefferson wrote an aquaintance in a widely quoted letter in 1814, "never acting until every circumstance, every consideration, was maturely weighed." (Jefferson had not been through the war with the "prudent" Washington, had not seen him fidget his way through successive staff meetings, and had not seen his appalled aides barely restrain him from dashing his army to pieces against the British barricades in Boston in 1775 and Philadelphia in 1777–78. Nor had he known that the "prudence" was usually the result of a standoff between his aggression and his lack of confidence in himself.) Jefferson, Napoleon, and history appear to have missed the point. Prudence is nothing if it is not the rein on impulse; moderation is useless unless it involves the reconciliation of extremes. Their puppet could have functioned only in the most routine of circumstances; George spun stability from chaos out of forces and fires of his own. What were the things, on balance, that so neatly balanced out? New light must be thrown ontó his cracks and shadows before he is permitted to depart.

A shy hero is hard to come to terms with, much less a hero-general who begins each tour of duty with a public declaration of his defects, listing them with cool precision, and begging his listeners to remember, when disaster happens, that it was their fault and not his. This was in part a defensive action to deflect blame at the beginning, but in large part it rings true—the mark of the outsider, the déclassé half brother, on sufferance among his superiors, measuring himself against others better bred and better lettered, who have always had one leg up on him. At times, it was endearing—it took the edge off his ambition—and its political ramifications were immense. No man with this syndrome, so proclaimed and so insistent, could become a Caesar on the battlefield or make himself a king. It kept him in touch with his own humanity, an invaluable asset as general of a "free" army and as civil leader of free men. It also made it easy for him to disassociate himself from his offices; detesting ceremony, he would suffer it, sitting through loathsome civic functions, engaging in exasperating charades over titles with the Howes. (On the last, he made embarrassed explanations to the president of Congress—it was the status of the country that concerned him; he told them he did not care what anyone called *him*.) More in character was the note from Silas Deane to a relative through whose town George was to pass on his way to Cambridge in 1775, warning against undue shows of ceremony: "He is no lover of parade." In character also were the many plaints sent to friends who were urging him to speak out for the Constitution in the grim period following the war: he did not know on whom his opinions would have weight. On whom, indeed? Fancy a president who begins his first inaugural with a recital of his insufficiencies, including "inferior endowments," and warns his listeners of their folly in placing their country in his hands. Or who greets his nomination as general—a post he had not fought against too mightily—by bolting from the room.

His shyness makes it the more difficult to credit his aggression—and yet both of them were real. There is a streak of something close to a mad nature in a man whose instinctive reaction to near death is sheer exhilaration, who finds the whine of bullets "charming," and to whom the swirl of violence is a fine tonic that calms his nerves remarkably and

378

serves to clear his head. Later, as George II had predicted, the "charm" diminished—as applied to other men. George became prudent in his use of manpower and protective of his armies and took no pleasure in the waste of life. In the end, war itself became abominable. "My first wish," he wrote to David Humphreys, after he had left the army in 1785, "is to see this plague to mankind banished from off the earth." Yet the instinct continued, as applied to himself. His persistent train of actions in the long course of the war—the dashes into the heart of fire; the calm contemplations as bullets raked the earth about him (as if they worked some soothing magic); the casual strolls among the falling shells from British batteries—all point to something in his nature that found its deepest satisfaction in confrontation with extremes.

Later his aggression blazed in other forms—the fierce reaction to political opposition; the rage (in private letters) at the opponents of the Constitution; the tirades in the Cabinet that left the listeners limp. The vein of sarcasm that ran an acid river through his lifelong correspondence is his own best testimony to the conflicts within—a safety valve, a means of expressing venom while holding its objects at an arm's length distance, itself a conditioning of rage.

Candor was a virtue most esteemed by Washington, though only intermittently applied. Receptive enough to head-on criticism, he was outraged by the whispering campaign. Hence the fury at Gates and Conway; later at Edmund Randolph; last, at Jefferson himself. (Hence also the reason why Hamilton's confessions of his own spleen in the fracas of the 1790s went down better than Jefferson's insistence that *he* had done nothing at all.) As far as possible, George turned this code upon himself. (Under attack, he turned to sarcasm; an adversary was less likely to find himself the victim of backstage maneuverings than to have a vat of acid dumped upon his head.) In his earlier years he solicited criticism, asking to be told the worst. Part of this was self-defense—a public man must know how he looks to others—a preliminary to the avoidance of attack. (Later he would send detailed accounts of complaints against them to Hamilton and Gouverneur Morris, in the helpful spirit of camaraderie.) But beyond this calculation lay another level—the shy child, fearful of censure, conjuring critics, and determined at the start to know the worst. Thus the quest for candor, as the antidote to whisper—and, the sting of whisper when it struck. His complaint with Joseph Reed in 1776 was not that he had faulted Washington but that he had gone behind his back to Lee.

The candor had a reverse side, revealing the shadow master, conjurer of illusions, alive to the power of impressions as they flicked across the mind of other men. "Next to being strong, it is best to be thought so," he wrote to Patrick Henry and, to a member of Congress, "If the public believes it . . . it might as well be so." French soldiers paid awed tribute to his witchery with troops:

> It is uncertain how many men his army consists of [wrote Abbé Robin], this General has always found means to conceal the real number, even from those who compose it. Sometimes with a few troops he forms a spacious camp . . . at other times, with a great number, he contracts it to a narrow compass; then again, by detaching them insensibly, the whole camp is nothing more than the mere shadow and skeleton of an army, while the main body is transported to a distant part.

This quality did immense service to the army, saving it time and time over from dispersal or attack. Pertinent to this characteristic was an odd request to Congress for a travelling press to follow headquarters, with a clever man (the first press agent) to follow and spend his time writing the news George wished his countrymen to hear.

A sunny confidence in men and destiny was not among his traits. Many of his comments on human nature have a harsh, metallic temper, disturbing to notions of the benign (and brainless) *pater patria* or to modern concepts of the leader of a democratic state. Hence the grim notes on greed, self-interest, and shortsightedness, capped perhaps by this letter to John Jay: "Men will not adopt and carry into execution measures the best calculated for their own good, without the intervention of a coercive power." The "power" was to be strong government, run by people like himself. Did he believe that even this would be enough? "I do believe that General Washington had not a firm confidence in the durability of our government," Jefferson wrote to a friend after his own retirement. "He was naturally distrustful of men, and inclined to gloomy apprehensions," adding that a belief that democracy would at some time founder had influenced George to adopt receptions and other semiroyal ceremonies to ease the expected transition to a crown.

With this went a kindly eye to the temporal afflictions of mankind. Pride, ambition, flaws of judgment, the recoil of strained temperaments were accepted as the baggage of humanity, the necessary price of life. Washington had yet another safety valve—the eye that looked beyond action to the springs of motivation underneath. "However it may be the practise of the World," he wrote to Benjamin Tallmadge in 1782, "I have accustomed myself to judge of human Actions very differently, and to appreciate them by the manner in which they are conducted, more than by the event." This wise and kindly angle pardoned much. Some sins remained inadmissible: cowardice; dereliction of duty; failing to acknowledge the consequences of one's errors; welshing on one's friends. Beyond that, the commonplaces of morality took second place to charity and love. He took great vicarious pleasure in the rakish antics of Gouverneur Morris, went with Martha to pay calls on Robert Morris in his cell in debtors' prison, and sent Alexander Hamilton, in deep trouble in 1797 over his public confession of an adultery committed in 1791 with Maria Reynolds, a warm note of great affection (gallantly making no mention of his problem) with an immensely valuable wine cooler, sent to him from France by Lafayette.

"Disinterested" is another tag that has been hung on Washington, suggesting both inhuman virtue and immense subordination of the self. It is true that he shared with much of his generation the trick of character that welds ego to the larger purpose—that great tamer of ambition, without which it is always dangerous and otherwise could leave societies at the mercy either of insatiate adventurers or of talents too dim to raise their owners far above the crowd. This aside, how true does the image ring? George was President when his aides were Cabinet level, untouchable when they were vulnerable, fighting for succession and their lives. Was it character or circumstance that set Washington apart? He was contentious enough when up against a rival who could clip his wings. Alone and eminent, his anxieties focused on his fears of failure, rather than on outside attack.

Mutable as ever, his reactions changed against the shifting backgrounds of his life. The moderate interim of undisputed power (when he appeared at his most diffident) must be set against his conduct at the beginning and the end of his career in politics, when his status was disputed and his place seemed insecure. In the end, power, like so much in his life and character, must slip into the line of paradox—ardently fled from, ardently pursued.

The question remains—how much did he bring upon himself? He had set the machine in motion when he turned from his mother to his half brothers and the ever-wider rhythms of their world. "My inclinations are strongly bent to arms." For years, he hurled himself at power, clawed for preference, forced himself over and over on the attentions of the colony, the empire, the world. If he failed in his first young objective—to become an ornament of empire—he had set the stage for his wider glories, the pieces ready to fall, at the tipping of fate, into their place. If not the ultra in every department, he was in each succeeding crisis the one man with the combination of requisites to fill a special need—the political choice for the army; the inevitable choice for the state. There was no choice ever for the shy and driven half brother for whom fame and service, duty and ambition were inextricably interwoven and set into his bones and blood. His intermittent efforts at "retirement" (always with a hopeless sound about them) were recuperations, repair between exertions, the background for his efforts, and the necessary relief. In these swings of light and dark are the terrain of his interior, iron and mercury, ambition and diffidence, shadow and sun. Each element had its own place in his greatness, sharpening or softening some native metal, taming power, giving tolerance its bite. His passions, gigantic and troubling, were the bedrock of his genius, controlled to provide discipline, loosened to unleash the welding power that sustained and settled the nation he had helped to form. On these passions, now chained and now explosive, rested the United States.

Notes

Code	Title
Addison	Addison, Joseph, *18th Century Plays*, ed. Richard Quintana. New York: Modern Library, 1952.
AH, JCH	Hamilton, Alexander, *The Works of Alexander Hamilton*, ed. John Church Hamilton. New York: John H. Trow, 1850, 6 v.
AH, S	*The Papers of Alexander Hamilton*, ed. Harold Styrett and others. New York: Columbia University Press, 1961–73, 18 v.
Allen	*Narrative of Colonel Ethan Allen*, ed. Brooke Hindle. New York: Corinth Books, 1961.
André	*Major André's Journal*. New York: New York *Times* & Arno Press, 1963.
Beloff	Beloff, Max, ed., *The Debate on the American Revolution*. London: Adam & Charles Black, 1960.
Bernard	*The Barrington-Bernard Correspondence*, ed. Edward Channing and Archibald Cary Coolidge. Oxford: Oxford University Press, 1912.
Beverley	Beverley, Robert, *The History and Present State of Virginia*, ed. Louis B. Wright. Chapel Hill: University of North Carolina Press, 1947.
BF, B	*The Works of Benjamin Franklin*, ed. John Bigelow. New York: Putnam, 1904, 12 v.

BF, L *The Papers of Benjamin Franklin*, ed. Leonard. W. Larrabee and others. New Haven: Yale University Press, 1959–71.

Bonsal Bonsal, Stephen, *When the French Were Here*. Port Washington: Kennikat Press, 1968.

Bouquet *The Papers of Henri Bouquet*, ed. E. K. Stevens, Donald H. Kents and Autumn Leonard. Harrisburg: Pennsylvania Historical and Museum Commission, 1951.

Brodie Brodie, Fawn, *Thomas Jefferson, An Intimate History*. New York: Norton, 1974.

Brooke Brooke, John M., *The Chatham Administration*. Cambridge: Cambridge University Press, 1962.

Burke, B *Edmund Burke on the American Revolution*, ed. Elliot R. Barkan. New York: Harper Torchbooks, 1966.

Burke, S *The Correspondence of Edmund Burke*, ed. Lucy S. Sutherland. Chicago: University of Chicago Press, 1960, 5 v.

Burnett *Letters of the Members of the Continental Congress*, ed. Edmund C. Burnett. Washington: Carnegie Institution, 1921–36, 8 v.

Burr *Memoirs of Aaron Burr*, ed. Matthew L. Davis. New York: Harper & Brothers, 1836.

Byrd *A History of the Dividing Line and Other Tracts*, ed. T. H. Wynne. Richmond: 1866, 2 v.

Cappon *The Adams-Jefferson Letters*, ed. Lester Cappon. New York: Clarion Books, 1971.

Chinard *George Washington as the French Knew Him*, ed. Gilbert Chinard. Princeton: Princeton University Press, 1940.

Cleland Cleland, Hugh, *George Washington in the Ohio Valley*. Pittsburgh: University of Pittsburgh Press, 1962.

Clinton Clinton, Sir Henry, *The American Rebellion*, ed. William B. Willcox. New Haven: Yale University Press, 1954.

C & M *The Spirit of Seventy-Six*, ed. Henry Steele Commager & Richard B. Morris. Indianapolis and New York: Bobbs Merrill, 1958.

Conway Conway, Moncure, *Barons of the Potomack and the Rappahannock*. New York: the Grolier Club, 1892.

Crary *The Price of Loyalty*, ed. Catherine S. Crary. New York: McGraw-Hill, 1973.

Custis *Recollections and Private Memoirs of Washington*, George Washington Parke Custis. New York: Derby & Jackson, 1860.

Desmond, Desmond, Alice Curtis, *Martha Washington*. New York: Dodd Mead, 1944.

Dickerson	*Dickerson,* Oliver Morton, *Boston Under Military Rule.* Boston: Chapman & Grimes, 1936.
Dinwiddie	*The Official Records of Robert Dinwiddie,* ed. R. A. Brock. Richmond: Virginia Historical Society Collections, 1936.
Emerson	Emerson, Ralph Waldo. *Journals of Ralph Waldo Emerson,* ed. Edward Waldo Emerson and Waldo Emerson Forbes. Boston: Houghton Mifflin, 1912, v. 8.
F & I	Hamilton, Edward P., *The French & Indian War.* New York: Doubleday, 1962.
Fleming	Fleming, Thomas J., *Beat the Last Drum.* New York: St. Martin's, 1963.
Forbes	*The Writings of General John Forbes,* ed. Alfred Proctor James. Menasha: Collegiate Press, 1938.
Freeman	Freeman, Douglas Southall, *George Washington.* New York: Scribner's, 1948, v. 1–2.
Gage	*Correspondence of General Thomas Gage,* ed. Charles E. Carter. New Haven: Yale University Press, 1931–33, 2 v.
Gates	*Horatio Gates Correspondence.* New York: New-York Historical Society.
G III, Dobree	*Letters of King George III,* ed. Bonamy Dobree. London: Cassell & Co., 1935.
G III, Donne	*Correspondence of George III with Lord North,* ed. W. Bodham Donne. London: John Murray, 1867, 2 v.
G III, F	*The Correspondence of George III,* ed. Sir John Fortescue. London: Macmillan, 1927–28, 6 v.
Greene	Nathanael Greene Papers. Microfilm collection, New York Public Library.
GW, D	*The Diaries of George Washington,* ed. John C. Fitzpatrick. Boston: Houghton Mifflin, 1925, 4 v.
GW, F	*The Writings of George Washington,* ed. John C. Fitzpatrick. Washington, D.C.: Government Printing Office, 1933–34, 39 v.
GW, Ford	*The Writings of George Washington,* ed. Worthington C. Ford. New York: Putnam, 1889, 14 v.
GW, L	*Letters to Washington,* ed. Stanislaus Murray Hamilton. Boston: Houghton Mifflin, 1898, 5 v.
GW, R	*George Washington's Rules of Civility,* ed. Moncure D. Conway. New York: United Book Company, 1890.
GW, S	*The Writings of George Washington,* ed. Jared Sparks. Boston: Russell, Odroine and Metcalfe, 1834, 12 v.
Hamilton	Hamilton, Charles, *Braddock's Defeat.* Norman: the University of Oklahoma Press, 1959.
Hatch	Hatch, Alden, *The Byrds of Virginia.* New York: Holt Rinehart & Winston, 1969.

HSPM   *Historical Society of Pennsylvania Memoirs.* Phila-
            delphia: Lippincott, 1855.
JA, AB   *Diaries and Autobiography of John Adams,* ed. Lyman
            H. Butterfield. Cambridge: Harvard University
            Press, 1963, 4 v.
JA, AFC   *Adams Family Correspondence,* ed. Lyman H. But-
            terfield. Cambridge: Harvard University Press, 1963,
            2 v.
JA, CFA   *The Works of John Adams,* ed. Charles Francis Adams.
            Boston: Little Brown, 1851, 10 v.
JA, L   *Letters of John Adams, Addressed to His Wife,* ed.
            Charles Francis Adams. Boston: Little Brown, 1841, 2
            v.
JA, Peek   *The Political Writings of John Adams,* ed. George A.
            Peek, Jr. Indianapolis and New York: Bobbs Merrill,
            1954.
Jay   *The Correspondence and Public Papers of John Jay,* ed.
            Henry F. Livingston. New York: Putnam, 1891, 4 v.
JM   *The Writings of James Madison,* ed. Henry Gaillard.
            New York: Putnam, 1906, 3 v.
Jones   Jones, Hugh, *The Present State of Virginia,* ed. Richard
            L. Morton. Chapel Hill: University of North Carolina
            Press, 1956.
King   *The Life and Correspondence of Rufus King,* ed. Charles
            R. King. New York: Putnam, 1895, 6 v.
Knox   *Life and Correspondence of Henry Knox,* ed. F. S. Drake.
            Boston: S. G. Drake, 1873.
Lafayette   *Memoirs, Correspondence and Manuscripts of General La-
            fayette.* London: Saunders & Otley, 1839, 3 v.
Larrabee   Larrabee, Harold A., *Decision at the Chesapeake.* New
            York: Clarkson N. Potter, 1964.
Laurens   *The Army Correspondence of Colonel John Laurens.* New
            York: New York *Times* & Arno Press, 1965.
Lee   *The Lee Papers.* Collections of the New-York Histori-
            cal Society. New York: 1872–75, 3 v.
Marshall   *The Diary of Christopher Marshall,* ed. William Duane.
            New York: New York *Times* & Arno Press, 1969.
Martin   *The Adventures of a Revolutionary Soldier,* ed. George
            Scheer. New York: New York *Times* & Arno Press,
            1962.
Mason   *The Papers of George Mason,* ed. Robert A. Rutland.
            Chapel Hill: University of North Carolina Press,
            1970, 3 v.
McCardell   McCardell, Lee, *Ill-Starred General.* Pittsburgh: Uni-
            versity of Pittsburgh Press, 1958.
MHSC   Massachusetts Historical Society Collections, Boston.
Miller, AH Miller, John C., *Alexander Hamilton and the Growth of*

388

	the New Nation. New York: Harper Torchbooks, 1964.
Miller, T of F	Miller, John C., Triumph of Freedom. Boston: Atlantic-Little Brown, 1948.
Monroe	*The Writings of James Monroe,* ed. S. M. Hamilton. New York: Putnam, 1898, 4 v.
Moore	Moore, Frank, *The Diary of the American Revolution,* ed. John Anthony Scott. New York: Washington Square Press, 1965.
Morison	Morison, Samuel Eliot, *Sources and Documents Illustrating the American Revolution.* Oxford: Oxford University Press, 1965.
Morris	*The Life of Gouverneur Morris with Selections from His Correspondence,* ed. Jared Sparks. Boston: Gray & Bowen, 1832.
Mumby	Mumby, Frank A., *George III and the American Revolution.* London: Constable & Co., 1924.
Namier	Namier, Sir Louis, *Personalities and Powers.* New York: Harper Torchbooks, 1965.
Oliver	*Origins and Progress of the American Rebellion,* ed. Douglass Adair & John A. Schutz. Stanford: Stanford University Press, 1967.
O'Meara	O'Meara, Walter, *Guns at the Forks.* Englewood Cliffs: Prentice-Hall, 1965.
Palmer	Palmer, John MacAuley, *General von Steuben.* Port Washington: Kennikat Press, 1966.
Parkman	Parkman, Francis, *Montcalm and Wolfe.* New York: Collier Books, 1962.
PMHB	*Pennsylvania Magazine of History and Biography.*
Rankin	Rankin, Hugh F., *The American Revolution.* New York: Putnam, 1964.
Reed	*Life and Correspondence of Joseph Reed,* ed. William B. Reed. Philadelphia: Lindsay & Blakiston, 1847.
Robin	Robin, Abbe, *New Travels Through North America.* New York: New York *Times* & Arno Press, 1969.
Rochambeau	*Memoirs of the Marshal Count de Rochambeau.* New York: New York *Times* & Arno Press, 1971.
Rush	*The Letters of Benjamin Rush,* ed. Lyman H. Butterfield. Princeton: Princeton University Press, 1951.
S & A	*The Spur of Fame,* ed. John A. Schutz & Douglass Adair. Kingsport: Kingsport Press, 1966.
Schachner	Schachner, Nathan, *Alexander Hamilton.* New York: A. H. Barnes, 1961.
Serle	*The American Journal of Ambrose Serle.* San Marino: The Huntington Library, 1840.
Smith	Smith, Goldwin, *A History of England.* New York: Scribner's, 1969.

Smith, Narrative *Narrative of the Death of Major André.* New York: New York *Times* & Arno Press, 1971.

Smith, Trial *Trial of Joshua Hett Smith for Complicity in the Conspiracy of Benedict Arnold and Major André,* ed. H. B. Dawson. Morrisania, New York, 1866.

Spotswood *The Official Letters of Alexander Spotswood,* ed. R. A. Brock. Virginia Historical Society Collections, 1932.

S & R *Rebels and Redcoats,* ed. George F. Scheer and Hugh F. Rankin. New York: World, 1957.

Stedman Stedman, Charles, *History of the Late War in America.* New York: New York *Times* & Arno Press, 1965.

Stirling *The Life of William Alexander, Earl of Stirling, with Selections from his Correspondence,* ed. William Alexander Duer. New York: Wiley & Putnam, 1847.

Sullivan *The Sullivan Papers.* Concord, New Hampshire, Historical Society Publications, 1930–39.

Tallmadge *Memoirs of Colonel Benjamin Tallmadge.* New York: New York *Times* & Arno Press, 1967.

Thacher *Military Journal of the American Revolution.* New York: New York *Times* & Arno Press, 1967.

TJ, F *The Writings of Thomas Jefferson,* ed. Paul L. Ford. New York: Putnam, 1891, 4 v.

TJ, P *The Complete Jefferson,* ed. Saul K. Padover. New York: Duell Sloan and Pearce, 1943.

TJ, TJR *Memoirs, Correspondence and Private Papers of Thomas Jefferson,* ed. Thomas Jefferson Randolph. London: Colburn & Bentley, 1829, 4 v.

Tudor *Deacon Tudor's Diary,* ed. William Tudor. Boston: Wallace Spooner, 1896.

VD, BF Van Doren, Carl, *Benjamin Franklin.* New York: Viking, 1938.

VD, SH Van Doren, Carl, *The Secret History of the American Revolution.* New York: Viking, 1941.

Von Clausen *The Revolutionary Journal of Baron Ludwig von Clausen,* ed. Evelyn M. Ascomb. Chapel Hill: University of North Carolina Press, 1958.

Walpole, J *The Last Journals of Horace Walpole During the Reign of George III,* ed. A. Francis Steuart. London: Lane, 1910.

Walpole, L *The Letters of Horace Walpole,* ed. Mrs. Paget Toynbee. Oxford: Clarendon Press, 1904, 16 v.

Walpole, M *Memoirs and Portraits,* ed. Matthew Hodgart. New York: Macmillan, 1963.

Ward Ward, Christopher, *The War of the Revolution.* New York: Macmillan, 1962, 2 v.

Wayland Wayland, John W., *The Washingtons and Their Homes.* Staunton: McClure, 1944.

Wayne   Anthony Wayne Correspondence, New York Public
           Library.
Wheeler   *Voices of 1776*, ed. Richard Wheeler. New York: Cro-
           well, 1972.
Wilkinson Wilkinson, James, *Memoirs of My Own Time*. Phila-
           delphia: Abraham Small, 1816.

I

13, "The heavy, laden eyes," Emerson, p. 291.
15, "Any memoirs of my life," GW, F, v. 27, p. 371.
16, "common frequenter of Ale-houses," Freeman, v.1, p. 529.
17, "physick flowers," MHSC, p. 110.
18, "Hath a fine house, *Ibid.*
19, "People flock'd thither," Beverley, p. 289.
21, "I know of no others," Spotswood, v.2, p. 55
22, "His Maj'ty," *Ibid.*, p. 314.
22, "Brick houses," Beverley, p. 289.
23, "handsom, well-dress'd," Jones, p. 43.
24, "Being born to one of the amplest fortunes," Hatch, p. 175.
25, "Mr. Washington raises the ore," Byrd, pp. 72–73.

II

29, "No cornn in the cornn-house," Conway, p. 81
30, "When time has whitened my locks," Custis, p. 131.
30, "I have a brother," GW, F, v.1, p. 314.
30, "The arrival of a good deal of company," *Ibid.*, p. 109.
31, "*Imaginary* wants," GW, F, v. 26, pp. 43–44.
31, "Happiness depends," *Ibid.*, v.29, p. 162.
32, " 'George,' said his father," Weems, p. 12.
33, "In the spirit of a brother," *Ibid.*, p. 19.
34, "Go thy way," *Ibid.*, p.XIV.
34, "I have something to whisper," *Ibid.*, p. XV.
34, "You have a great deal of money," *Ibid.*, pp. XVIII–XIX.
35, "My neighbor," GW, L, v. 1, p. 277.
35, "Erudition in the Arts," GW, F, v. 35, p. 199.
36, "consciousness of a defective education," *Ibid.*, v. 28, p. 203.

36, "They are ringing," Smith, p. 432.
37, "not received the treatment," Freeman, v. 1, p. 69.
37, "I have no great opinion," Hatch, p. 168.
37, "The enemy killed of ours," Freeman, v. 1, p. 69.
37, "War is horrid in fact," Freeman, v. 1, p. 69.
38, "I hear Col. Gouge," Conway, p. 101.
38, "We have no great news," Conway, p. 163.
38, "A very handsom dwelling house," Wayland, p. 33.
39, "My father died," GW, F, v. 29, p. 36.
40, "a man of no very good breeding," Freeman, v. 1, p. 449.
40, "bounded by and within the heads," *Ibid.*, p. 450.

III

42, "At this crisis," GW, F, v. 30, p. 246.
43, "one youthful ebulition," Freeman, v. 1, p. 64.
43, "Wear not your Cloths," GW, Rules, p. 111.
43, "In the Presence of Others," *Ibid.*, p. 58.
45, "I should think our time," GW, F, v. 2, p. 293.
45, "A Roman soul," Addison, p. 13.
45, "Let not a torrent," *Ibid.*, pp. 20–21.
45, "this base, degenerate age," Addison, pp. 39–40.
46, "what pity it is," *Ibid.*, p. 48.
46, "valour soars above," *Ibid.*, p. 26.
46, "Bid him disband," *Ibid.*, p. 23.
46, "let us draw," *Ibid.*, p. 22.
47, "My life is grafted," *Ibid.*, p. 22.
48, "surveyors . . . valet de Chambre," Freeman, v. 1, p. 217.
48, "I have not yet seen," Conway, p. 238.
48, "I am afraid Mrs. Washington," *Ibid.*, pp. 239–40.
49, "I understand you are advised," Freeman, v. 1, pp. 198–99.
50, "We got our supper," GW, F, v. 1, ʾp. 9.
51, *Memorandum:* To Survey the Lands," *Ibid.*, p. 18.
52, "Amongst a parcel of Barbarians," *Ibid.*, p. 17.
53, "One thing, however," *Ibid.*, v. 30, pp. 246–47.
53, "While a courteous behavior," *Ibid.*, v. 35, pp. 295–96.
53, "Of the young and jouvenile," *Ibid.*, v. 26, p. 39.
53, "The more there are above you," *Ibid.*, v. 35, p. 282.
54, "I shou'd be glad," *Ibid.*, v. 1, p. 129.
55, "I hope your Cough," *Ibid.*, p. 13.
56, "happy news of my brother's," *Ibid.*, p. 18.
56, "situated very badly," *Ibid.*, v. 2, p. 365.

56, "I own no place can please me," GW, S, v. 2, p. 422.
56, "The Climate has not," *Ibid.*, p. 422.
56, "Though I was much mended," *Ibid.*, p. 423.
56, "I have now got to my last refuge," *Ibid.*, p. 423.
57, "The unhappy state," *Ibid.*
58, "Whereas we have received," Freeman, v. 1, p. 275.

IV

59, "They told me," GW, F, v. 1, p. 26.
60, "without censure," *Ibid.*, p. 35.
60, "In case any Attempts," Dinwiddie, v. 1, p. 59.
60, "My Orders to the Com'd'g Officer," *Ibid.*, p. 105.
62, "I have no complaint," *Ibid.*, pp. 172–73.
62, "There is some discontent," *Ibid.*, p. 171.
62, "I have not above," GW, F, v. 1, p. 46.
62, "freench armey," *Ibid.*, pp. 53–54.
62, "would have killed a cow," Cleland, p. 79.
63, "*I made them understand,*" *Ibid.*
63, "That very moment," GW, F, v. 1, p. 55.
63, "I have heard the bullets whistle," *Ibid.*, p. 70.
64, "If all are like," GW, Ford, v. 1, p. 94.
64, "I heartily congratulate," GW, L, v. 1, p. 2.
64, "Great Rejoycings," *Ibid.*, p. 8.
64, "As God has blessed," *Ibid.*, pp. 9–10.
64, "I hope the good Spirits," Dinwiddie, v. 1, p. 186.
64, "As Colo. Washington," *Ibid.*, p. 188.
64, "You cannot believe," *Ibid.*, p. 194.
65, "For want of proper instructions," GW, F, v. 1, p. 81.
65, "That the first Column," *Ibid.*, p. 83.
65, "I wish you had suspended," GW, L, v. 1, p. 13.
65, "It will yet require," *Ibid.*, p. 23.
65, "What a Tedious Suspense," *Ibid.*, p. 25.
66, "In a bad Hand," Cleland, p. 100.
67, "kick'd the fellow back side," *Ibid.*, p. 104.
68, "You will see," *Ibid.*, p. 152.
68, "The French have tied up," Walpole, L, v. 3, p. 254.
68, "On hearing of this letter," Walpole, M, p. 50.
68, "Washington not knowing Fr.," Dinwiddie, v. 1, p. 498.
68, "Washington and many such," Freeman, v. 1, pp. 423–24.
69, "I wish Washington," *Ibid.*, p. 415.
69, "They, finding where," GW, F, v. 1, p. 65.

70, "Our conduct is blamed," Cleland, p. 115.
70, "I have no doubt," GW, L, v. 1, p. 52.
71, "We should be," GW, F, v. 1, pp. 91–92.
71, "I sent You Orders," GW, L, v. 1, p. 31.
71, "What Men we can," GW, F, v. 1, p. 102.
71, "A gov'r is . . . much to be pitied," Dinwiddie, v. 1, p. 305.
71, "Such wrong-headed people," *Ibid.*, p. 300.
72, "I think the disparity," GW, F, v. 1, pp. 104–5.
72, "meet with my acquiescence," *Ibid.*, p. 106.
72, "Some new arrangement," *Ibid.*, v. 29, p. 49.
74, "It was to obey," *Ibid.*, v. 1, pp. 106–7.

V

76, "difficulties to which," *Ibid.*, v. 29, p. 41.
76, "as all the convoys," McCardell, p. 195.
77, "Before we parted," HSPM, v. 5, p. 417.
78, "I can very truly say," GW, F, v. 1, p. 115.
78, "To be plain," *Ibid.*, p. 107.
78, "I was invited to supper," McCardell, p. 158.
79, "I reckon the day," *Ibid.*, p. 164.
80, "I own I have my fears," O'Meara, p. 127.
80, "I have been greatly disappointed," McCardell, p. 171.
81, "The Duke," *Ibid.*, p. 268.
81, "He is extremely warm," *Ibid.*, pp. 169–70.
81, "If this method," BF, B, v. 1, p. 272.
82, "He smil'd at my ignorance," *Ibid.*
82, "I am hereby freed," GW, F, v. 1, p. 124.
82, "I saw myself a slave," Freeman, v. 2, p. 49.
83, "I see no prospect," GW, F, v. 1, p. 123.
83, "You will be informed," McCardell, p. 204.
84, "The General by frequent breaches," GW, F, v. 1, p. 133.
84, "We have a general," McCardell, p. 204.
84, "This day we marched," Hamilton, p. 17.
85, "What was looked on at home," Cleland, p. 131.
85, "I ac'd you," GW, F, v. 1, p. 142.
85, "I urg'd it," GW, F, v. 1, p. 143.
86, "with the most infinite delight," *Ibid.*, p. 144.
86, "This prospect was soon," *Ibid.*
86, "I have been now 6 days," *Ibid.*
86, "We hugged ourselves with joy," F & I, p. 155.
87, "much reduc'd and very weak," GW, F, v. 29, p. 42.

87, "Such was the confusion," Hamilton, p. 50.
88, "the wild Bears," GW, F, v. 1, p. 149.
88, "The Officers were," GW, L, v. 1, p. 71.
88, "The greatest part," O'Meara, pp. 146–47.
88, "Scandalous as the action was," Cleland, p. 148.
88, "They began to Ingage us," Hamilton, pp. 28–30.
88, "the unusual Hallooing," GW, F, v. 29, pp. 42–45.
89, "God put himself on our side," Cleland, p. 145.
91, "Who would have thought it?" BF, B, v. 1, p. 274.
91, "Thus died a man," GW, F, v. 29, p. 45.
91, "From our first," GW, L, v. 1, p. 73.
92, "good Opinion," *Ibid.*, p. 76.
92, "Who is Mr. Washington?" Bancroft, v. 2, pp. 423–24.
92, "so scandalous," GW, F, v. 1, p. 157.
92, "where the inhabitants," BF, B, v. 1, p. 274.
92, "Common sense would have prevailed," Dinwiddie, v. 2, p. 140.

VI

94, "Madam: If it is in my power," GW, F, v. 1, p. 159.
95, "Colonel of the Virginia Regiment," *Ibid.*, p. 175.
95, "Be not deceiv'd," *Ibid.*, p. 163.
95, "Nothing is to be seen," GW, L, v. 1. p. 103.
95, "No Officer," GW, F, v. 1, p. 164.
95, "You are to send," *Ibid.*, p. 178.
96, "Crowds of People," *Ibid.*, p. 206.
96, "3 drunken soldiers," *Ibid.*, p. 204.
97, "Desolation and murder," *Ibid.*, pp. 304–5.
98, "Appointment of an Aide-de-Camp," GW, L, v. 1, p. 216.
98, "If I expostulate," *Ibid.*, pp. 223–24.
99, "Indians are only match," GW, F, v. 1, p. 305.
99, "until an attempt is formed," *Ibid.*, p. 484.
100, "It will in some measure," GW, L, v. 1, pp. 375–76.
101, "You may call a Council," *Ibid.*, pp. 372–73.
101, "I hereby order you," Dinwiddie, v. 2, p. 553.
101, "If he leaves any of the stores," GW, L, v. 2, p. 19.
101, "To encourage them," GW, F, v. 1, p. 528.
102, "Whence it arises," *Ibid.*
102, "We are under no government," GW, F, v. 2, pp. 13–17.
103, "I cannot conceive," GW, L, v. 2, p. 45.
103, "I have been posted," GW, F, v. 2, p. 22.
103, "I am tired," *Ibid.*, v. 1, p. 514.

105, "Here is my son," Walpole, M, p. 74.

105, "We are no longer a nation," Parkman, p. 383.

105, "Indeed he shall be tried," Walpole, M, p. 62.

105, "marked for sacrifice," *Ibid.*, p. 67.

106, "The other two pacquets," BF, B, v. 1, p. 300.

107, "They are intended to relieve," GW, F, v. 1, p. 363.

107, "they not only cast," *Ibid.*, p. 240.

107, "If she is not immediately sent," *Ibid.*, p. 264.

107, "Any Soldier, who shall desert," O'Meara, p. 176.

108, "Your Honor will." GW, F, v. 2, p. 118.

108, "prone to censure," *Ibid.*, p. 13.

108, "I must assume the Freedom," *Ibid.*, v. 1, pp. 202–3.

109, "there was not an Indian," GW, L, v. 2, p. 82.

109, "Did I ever send," GW, F, v. 2, p. 172.

109, "My conduct to you," GW, L, v. 2, p. 204.

110, "I cannot agree," *Ibid.*, p. 216.

110, "While we pursue," GW, F, v. 2, p. 142.

110, "I do not know on whom, *Ibid.*, p. 154.

111, "We have not yet heard," GW, L, v. 2, p. 230.

111, "aske the favor," *Ibid.*, p. 159.

111, "For upwards of three Months past," *Ibid.*, p. 231.

VII

113, "the boundless power," Walpole, M, p. 86.

114, "No women follow the camp," Parkman, pp. 412–13.

115, "Pray, does not his *plan*," GW, F, v. 2, p. 165.

115, "be distinguished from the *common run*," GW, F, v. 2, p. 172.

115, "Major Carlyle mention'd," *Ibid.*, v. 1 pp. 130–31.

116, "I hope no exception," *Ibid.*, v. 2, p. 251.

116, "No sergeant or quarter master," Forbes, p. 17.

117, "An extream bad Collection," Cleland, p. 199.

117, "I am sorry you have met," Bouquet, p. 477.

117, "I am told," Cleland, p. 169.

117, "a gap which," Bouquet, p. 291.

118, "Colonel Washington writes me," Bouquet, pp. 277–78.

118, "All the letters I have," *Ibid.*, p. 179.

118, "The Virginia party," *Ibid.*, p. 252.

119, "The Virginians are making," GW, F, v. 2, p. 264, *fn.*

119, "A new system," Bouquet, p. 265.

119, "God knows what's intended," GW, F, v. 2, p. 249.

120, "I had an interview," Bouquet, p. 291.

120, "If Colo. Bouquet succeeds," GW, F, v. 2, p. 260.
120, "I said, and did, everything," *Ibid.*, p. 262.
120, "They have already work'd," *Ibid.*, p. 266.
120, "The General's Orders," GW, Ford, v. 2, pp. 75–76.
120, "By a very unguarded letter," Bouquet, p. 366.
121, "consult Colonel Washington," *Ibid.*, p. 478.
121, "d-ps or something worse," GW, F, v. 2, p. 277.
121, "If you are surpriz'd," *Ibid.*, p. 281.
121, "How is it to be accounted for?" *Ibid.*, p. 278.
121, "In all human probability," GW, Ford, v. 2, p. 84.
122, "every other thing answering," Bouquet, p. 343.
122, "numberless, damned petryfyd," O'Meara, p. 195.
122, "Send me as many men," *Ibid.*, p. 195.
122, "The Catawbas have left us," Bouquet, p. 180.
122, "Mr. Gordon the Engineer," Cleland, pp. 210–11.
122, "The immense confusion," Forbes, p. 186.
123, "to put an end," O'Meara, p. 199.
123, "I told them plainly," Bouquet, pp. 536–37.
123 , "sanguine and obstinate," GW, F, v. 2, p. 264, *fn.*
123, "to annoy the Enemy," *Ibid.*, p. 290.
123, "My heart is broke," Bouquet, p. 520.
124, "I cannot believe," Parkman, p. 454.
124, "62 killd," GW, F, v. 2, p. 292.
124, "A thousand men," Bouquet, p. 560.
125, "between two fires," GW, F, v. 29, pp. 47–48.
125, "After a Month's further Tryal," *Ibid.*, v. 2, p. 296.

VIII

126, "The world has no business," GW, F, v. 2, p. 287.
127, "you . . . to whom I stand," *Ibid.*, v. 1, p. 117.
127, "Charms even stranger," GW, L, v. 1, p. 39.
128, "deserve a corrispondence [*sic*]," GW, F, v. 1, p. 117.
128, "You express'd an Inclination," *Ibid.*, p. 137–38.
128, "for I have been greatly surprised," *Ibid.*, p. 147.
128, "You may thank my F'ds," *Ibid.*, p. 145.
128, "desirous . . . with loving Speed," GW, L, v. 1, p. 73.
129, "After thanking Heaven," *Ibid.*, p. 74.
129, "you know him," *Ibid.*, v. 2, p. 140.
129, "I think I should," GW, F, v. 2, p. 141.
130, "Sorry to give you," *Ibid.*, v. 37, p. 479.
130, "I have no person," *Ibid.*, v. 1, p. 502.

130, "you did one time partly promise," *Ibid.*, v. 1, p. 138.
131, "I hope he will return compos'd," GW, L, v. 1, p. 70.
131, "A Life that does Honour," *Ibid.*, v. 2, p. 38.
131, "I beg that you'll freely command me," *Ibid.*, v. 1, p. 250.
131, "He is more enamored," Desmond, p. 49.
131, "you will perhaps," GW, F, v. 2, p. 272.
132, "We have begun our march," *Ibid.*, p. 243.
132, "Yesterday I was honour'd," *Ibid.*, pp. 287–88.
133, "Do we still misunderstand," *Ibid.*, p. 292.
134, "Love may and ought to be," *Ibid.*, v. 34, p. 92.
134, "I have always considered marriage," *Ibid.*, v. 29, p. 103.
134, "I have just quit," *Ibid.*, v. 2, p. 322.
135, "It deprives our Enemies," Cleland, p. 225.
136, "I have heard the bullets whistle," GW, F, v. 1, p. 70.
136, "If all are like," GW, Ford, v. 1, p. 94.
136, "I wish for nothing more," GW, F, v. 1, p. 115.
136, "Desolation and murder," *Ibid.*, p. 340.
136, "The number of little paultry forts," *Ibid.*, p. 474.
136, "I exert every means," *Ibid.*, v. 2, p. 145.
136, "I do not know whom," *Ibid.*, p. 154.
136, "It is not to be wondered at," *Ibid.*, p. 17.
136, "We ought not to look back," *Ibid.*, v. 27, p. 308.
137, "I am now fixd," *Ibid.*, v. 2, p. 337.

IX

141, "not only from the world," GW, F, v. 27, p. 318.
141, "I have had much trouble," Conway, p. 81.
142, "am now tied by the Leg," GW, F, v. 2, p. 337.
142, "a propensity to the Sex," GW, L, v. 4, p. 427.
142, "I never did in my Life," *Ibid.*
142, "Farther than this," GW, F, v. 3, p. 44.
144, "I had never seen," Walpole, L, v. 4, p. 455.
144, "kind of unhappiness," Namier, p. 47.
144, "indolence, inattention," *Ibid.*, p. 49.
144, "As I have chosen," GIII, Dobree, p. 5
145, "Will seldom do wrong," Namier, p. 47.
145, "the ablest man of business," Walpole, M, p. 234.
147, "They were suppressed," Burke, B, p. 48.
148, "no Requisition has been made of me," Gage, v. 2, p. 334.
148, "if they relax," BF, L, v. 12, pp. 364–65.
148, "They are for taking," Mumby, p. 118.

148, "Modification was my constant," GIII, F, v. 1, p. 269.
148, "This hour is the most critical," *Ibid.*, p. 252.
149, "a little out of his head," BF, L, v. 14, p. 331.
149, "I felt attaching the name," Mumby, p. 120.
149, "I know not what struck me," Burke, S, v. 1, p. 237.
150, "If the act is not repealed," BF, B, v. 1, pp. 173–214.
150, "Pray see Lord Rockingham," GIII, F, v. 1, p. 220.
150, "engrosses the conversation," GW, F, v. 2, pp. 425–26.
151, "There is as yet," Mason, v. 1, pp. 68–69.
151, "He did not cultivate men," Brooke, v. 1, pp. 68–69.
151, "He made an administration," Burke, B, pp. 58–59.
152, "great abilities," Burke, S, v. 1, pp. 326–27.
152, "Dejection and flutter," Burke, S, v. 1, p. 332.
152, "The Earl of Chatham," Brooke, p. 93.
152, "seemed to create knowledge," Walpole, M, p. 173.
153, "I believe Your Lordship," Brooke, p. 95.
153, "no one in the Ministry," *Ibid.*, p. 94.
153, "Excessive on every occasion," *Ibid.*, p. 120.
154, "Absurdity itself," Burke, B, p. 5.
154, "The Commissioners have asked me," Bernard, pp. 148–49.
155, "His Majesty has thought it fit," Gage, v. 2, p. 173.
155, "Ready and ripe," Mumby, p. 196.
155, "You cannot act," Gage, v. 2, pp. 479–80.
156, "The town is now," Dickerson, pp. 2–3.
156, "Every thing now has," Gage, v. 1, p. 206.
156, "At a time when," GW, F, v. 2, p. 501.
157, "Gave himself up," Walpole, M, p. 224.
158, "The Administration," Brooke, p. 377.
158, "passed in the dotage," Burke, B, pp. 15–16.
158, "I am resolved," GIII, Dobree, p. 11.
158, "When I see," BF, B, v. 6, pp. 190–91.
159, "empty terrors and empty menaces," Burke, B, p. 37.
159, "His Majesty's present administration," Mumby, p. 251.
160, "I am clear," GIII, Donne, v. 1, p. 202.
160, "They tell you, Sir," Burke, B, p. 33.

X

162, "Thus has the winter," Mumby, p. 294.
162, "looked directly at Lord North," Miller, T of F, p. 25.
163, "made a Tea-pot of the Harbour," Oliver, p. 102.
163, "Notable and striking," JA, AB, v. 3, pp. 85–86.

163, "There is an ostrich egg," Mumby, p. 322.
163, "an Example of Terror," Burke, S, v. 3, p. 14.
163, "I have seen," GIII, F, v. 3, p. 59.
164, "This sort of unhappy Conflict," Burke, S, v. 3, p. 351.
164, "The torrent is still violent," BF, B, v. 6, p. 341.
164, "Be assured," Burke, S, v. 3, p. 532.
165, "I hope you will be firm," Gage, v. 2, p. 663.
165, "They talk of fixing," *Ibid.*, v. 1, p. 374.
165, "The Ministry may rely on it," GW, F, v. 3, p. 224.
166, "What reason is there to expect," *Ibid.*, p. 233.
166, "Speaks very modestly," Deane, v. 19, p. 27.
166, "The Congress will support," JA, AFC, v. 1, p. 160.
167, "Waste paper," JA, CFA, v. 10, p. 278.
167, "Either an effectual," JA, CFA, v. 9, pp. 641–42.
167, "The die is now cast," GIII, F, v. 3, p. 131.
167, "This most infamous Bill," Burke, S, v. 3, pp. 131–32.
168, "Long days make small sensation," Walpole, L, v. 9, p. 171.
168, "came down among," BF, B, v. 6, p. 424.
168, "was treated with as much contempt," *Ibid.*, p. 426.
168, "but all availed no more," *Ibid.*, v. 7, p. 33.
168, "He began at half-past three," Burke, v. 3, pp. 139–40.
169, "The more the better," Mumby, p. 382.
169, "geld all the males," VD, BF, p. 519.
169, "I think we have little hopes," Mason, v. 1, p. 214.
169, "It is reported in London," GW, L, v. 5, p. 127.
170, "I find it inserted," Mumby, p. 362.
170, "It is my full intention," GW, F, v. 3, p. 277.
171, "Had they gone out," Mumby, p. 385.
171, "You will March," *American Heritage,* June, 1965, p. 67.
171, "Isaac Muzzy, Jonathan Harrington," *Ibid.*, April, 1971, p. 98.
172, "All the hills," *Ibid.*, April, 1971, p. 101.
173, "Whoever looks upon them," S & R, p. 45.
173, "It appears that the general," *Ibid.*, pp. 49–50.
174, "Boston shut up," Tudor, pp. 52–53.
175, "Col. Washington," JA, AB, v. 3, p. 322.
175, "In the name of," Allen, p. 8.
176, "full of anxieties," JA, AB, v. 3, p. 318.
176, "If you don't concur," *Ibid.*, p. 318.
176, "I am determined," *Ibid.*, pp. 322–23.
176, "I hear that Congress," Walpole, L, v. 9, p. 225.
177, "Washington himself," Burke, S, v. 3, p. 187.
177, "A continued sheet of fire," S & R, pp. 62–63.
177, *"a moment that I never felt before,"* GIII, F, v. 3, p. 222.
178, "They kept up this fire," S & R, p. 56.
178, "walking away, slowly," Oliver, p. 126.
178, "A dear bought victory," S & R, p. 67.
178, "When I look to the consequences," GIII, F, v. 3, p. 223.
178, "The loss we have sustained," Gage, v. 2, pp. 686–87.

178, "All our prospects," Burke, S, v. 3, p. 160.
179, "I do not believe," Burnett, v. 1, p. 128.
179, "I hope the people of our province," JA, AFC, v. 1, p. 216.
179, "The partiality of Congress," GW, F, v. 3, p. 299.
180, "Lest some unlucky event," *Ibid.*, p. 292.
180, "on a wide ocean," *Ibid.*, p. 299.

XI

183, "Dirty and nasty," *Ibid.*, v. 3, p. 433.
183, "I expect . . . to render myself," *Ibid.*, p. 454.
184, "An odd genius," S & R, pp. 86–87.
186, "to confess my weakness," AH, S, v. 1, p. 4.
187, "No man perhaps," GW, F, v. 4, p. 450.
187, "I tremble at the prospect," Reed, v. 1, pp. 130–31.
187, "Which is mortifying," GW, F, v. 4, p. 319.
187, "Every means of distressing America," GIII, Donne, v. 1, p. 274.
188, "If we suffer," Walpole, J, v. 1, p. 515.
188, "Sheets of fire," Wheeler, p. 102.
189, "that fertility of genius," Stedman, v. 1, p. 167.
189, "During the forenoon," Thacher, p. 39.
189, "and the utmost horror and confusion," S & R, p. 166.
191, "I don't like your situation," Reed, v. 1, p. 202.
191, "the object worthy their attention," GW, F, v. 4, p. 395.
191, "Our whole force," *Ibid.*, v. 5, p. 166.
191, "something resembling," S & R, v. 166.
192, "We have Ships," GW, F, v. 5, p. 325.
192, "I have never entertained," *Ibid.*, v. 4, p. 321.
192, "When we reflect," Thacher, p. 46.
192, "Mr. Harrison said," *Ibid.*, p. 48.
193, "the arch-rebel Washington," Moore, p. 183.
193, "Sir, we have," C & M, pp. 426–27.
193, "implied everything," *Ibid.*
193, "as unexpected," Reed, v. 1, p. 215.
194, "Dispatched the rebels," C & M, p. 443.
194, "found that General Howe," GW, S, v. 4, p. 516.
195, "The fire was very hot," Ward, v. 1, pp. 231–32.
196, "Good God! . . . I am afraid," C & M, p. 447.
196, "Extreme fatigue," GW, F, v. 5, p. 506.
196, "The retreat as a retreat," Wayne MS.
196, "vastly disspirited," Jay, v. 1, p. 82.
196, "Every measure on our part," GW, F, v. 6, p. 28.

197, "Declining an engagement," *Ibid.*
197, "If they remained," Burr, p. 101.
197, "so vexed at the infamous conduct," Greene MS.
199, "a parcel of ------," GW, F, v. 6, p. 242.
200, "Matters in this Quarter," *Ibid.*, p. 169.
200, "If I were to put," *Ibid.*, p. 138.
201, "I am told," *Ibid.*
202, "I am mad, vexed, sick and sorry," Knox, p. 34.
202, "This Post . . . was held," GW, F, v. 6, pp. 244–45.
203, "I found General Greene," *Ibid.*, pp. 151–52.
203, "The British troops," C & M, p. 497.
203, "We have prevented them," GW, F, v. 6, p. 398.
204, "I see nothing to oppose him," *Ibid.*
205, "I am certainly shocked," Lee, v. 2, pp. 337–38.
205, "I foresaw, predicted," *Ibid.*, p. 288.
205, "*entre nous,*" *Ibid.*, p. 384.
205, "that fatal indecision," *Ibid.*, pp. 305–6.
205, "the enclosed was put," GW, F, v. 6, p. 313.
206, "I was hurt," Reed, v. 1, pp. 260–61.
206, "*since he was rather,*" Closen, p. 114.
206, "Would it not be possible," Reed, v. 1, p. 272.
207, "Christmasday, at night," *Ibid.*, p. 274.
207, "the ragged and dissolving state," S & R, p. 240.
207, "Tell General Sullivan," Rankin, p. 108.
208, "The enemy were strong," PMHB, v. 22, p. 466.
208, "The poor fellows," Knox, p. 37.
208, "hair cued as tight," C & M, p. 512.
209, "Instead of thinking myself freed," GW, F, v. 6, pp. 463–64.
209, "Around two in the morning," Stedman, v. 1, p. 236.
210, "I . . . heard Gen. Mercer," S & R, p. 248.
211, "in a most infernal sweat," Knox, p. 40.
211, "The enemy were," *Ibid.*
211, "By such judicious movements," Stedman, v. 1, p. 239.

XII

214, "I have beat them!" Walpole, J, v. 2, p. 131.
214, "Paid for their treason," Thacher, p. 86.
214, "Since when," GW, F, v. 9, p. 21.
215, "After we had made," *Ibid.*, p. 108.
215, "How [sic] will make," JA, AFC, v. 2, p. 332.
215, "a strange spectacle," Lafayette, v. 1, p. 19.
218, "Its only a scouting party," C & M, p. 626.

219, "The fog represented," GW, F, v. 9, p. 398.
219, "increased the fear," C & M, p. 630.
219, "They say more than 200 Waggons," GW, F, v. 9, p. 337.
219, "The Hospital," GW, F, v. 9, p. 398.
219, "Howe for a long time," Wayne MS.
219, "The anxiety you have been under," GW, F, v. 9, pp. 397–98.
220, "This is the Grand American Army," *Ibid.*, p. 378.
221, "when General Washington," Marshall, p. 137.
221, "It was a saying," Wayne MS.
221, "Hazardous, & must end in ruin," Sullivan, v. 13, p. 598.
221, "if you fail," *Ibid.*, p. 603.
221, "His slackness and remissness," Marshall, p. 159.
222, "The Northern Army has shown us," Rush, v. 1, p. 183.
222, "I told him," *Ibid.*, p. 191.
222, "We have had," GW, S, v. 5, pp. 484–85.
222, "General Gates has won," AH, S, v. 1, p. 354.
223, "In confidence I will tell you," *Ibid.*, p. 362.
223, "They dare not appear," GW, S, v. 5, pp. 493–95.
224, "The rain continuing," Wilkinson, p. 331.
224, "Sir: A Letter," GW, F, v. 10, p. 29.
224, "acknowledged his letter," Wilkinson, p. 331.
224, "An *éclaircissement*," GW, S, v. 5, p. 486.
225, "stealingly copied," *Ibid.*, p. 487.
225, "It is greatly to be lamented," GW, F, v. 10, pp. 440–41.
226, "I met with a reception," GW, S, v. 5, p. 503.
226, "I remain in a state of inaction," *Ibid.*, pp. 494–95.
226, "Though the paragraph quoted," *Ibid.*, p. 511.
226, "The kind of correspondence," Stirling, p. 192.
226, "My enemies," GW, F, v. 10, pp. 410–11.
227, "I am sure," Lafayette, v. 1, p. 159.
227, "I go on very slowly," Lafayette, v. 1, p. 153.
227, "I fancy he," *Ibid.*
227, "I have consulted everybody," *Ibid.*, pp. 155–56.
228, "I need not ask you," AH, S, v. 1, p. 436.
228, "seemed a good deal surprised," GW, F, v. 11, p. 125.
228, "The unaccountable way," Gates MS.
228, "I had no thoughts of resigning," *Ibid.*
229, "I will volunteer," *Ibid.*
229, "having, done, written," GW, S, v. 5, p. 512.
229, "As to the gentleman," *Ibid.*
229, "Three men," GW, F, v. 11, p. 306.
230, " *You say all will yet be well,*" *Ibid.*
230, "Our troops," Jay, v. 1, p. 174.
230, "For some days past," GW, F, v. 10, p. 469.
230, "No bread, no soldier," C & M, p. 648.
230, "What then is to become," GW, F, v. 10, pp. 193–94.
231, "We find Gentlemen," *Ibid.*, pp. 195–96.
231, "Believe me, my dear Baron," Palmer, p. 157.

232, "on condition than none," *Ibid.*, p. 149.
232, "Such a set," *Ibid.*
232, "No man, in my opinion," GW, F, v. 10, p. 194.
232, "*Aut nunc, aut nunquam,*" C & M, p. 682.
233, "ventured on taking," *Ibid.*, p. 694.
233, "If so, said he," *Ibid.*
234, "talked much on the subject," C & M, pp. 700–1.
234, "If all the fine things," *Ibid.*, pp. 697–98.
235, "Concluded about Seven," Crary, p. 317.
235, "Amazing. . . . The wagons only," Wheeler, pp. 301–2.
236, "You will attack," GW, F, v. 12, p. 117.
236, "So far personally," Lee, v. 2, p. 418.
237, "March toward the Marquis," GW, F, v. 12, p. 120.
237, "surprised, and rather exasperated," Lee, v. 3, pp. 72–74.
238, "answered in a very significant manner," Lee, v. 3, p. 81.
238, "in a great passion," Martin, p. 127.
238, "rode up to him," Lee, v. 3, p. 81.
239, "looked about and said," *Ibid.*, p. 75.
239, "Looking at it," Martin, pp. 132–33.
240, "They returned," Laurens, p. 198.
240, "so overpowered with fatigue," Lee, v. 2, p. 464.
240, "Unnecessary, disorderly, and shameful," GW, F, v. 13, p. 133.
240, "Mr. Clinton's whole flying army," Laurens, p. 200.
240, "I cannot persuade myself," Lee, v. 2, pp. 435–36.
241, "General Wayne," *Ibid.*, p. 439–40.
241, "singular expressions," *Ibid.*, pp. 435–36.
241, "I am not conscious," GW, F, v. 12, pp. 132–33.
242, "Savors of insanity," Wayne MS.
242, "Were you ever in an action?" Lee, v. 3, p. 56.
242, "I confess," *Ibid.*
243, "This sentence has not diminished," Rush, v. 1, p. 316.
243, "Conway, Mifflin," *Ibid.*, p. 220.
243, "In the words," Lee, v. 2, p. 457.
244, "The motives which," GW, F, v. 16, p. 8.
244, "I have kept," Miller, T of F, p. 327.

XIII

245, "laments the insipid part," Laurens, p. 208.
245, "by it, the French battalions," *Ibid.*, p. 218.
246, "took the hardy resolution," *Ibid.*, p. 220.

246, "Convinced their troops injured," *Ibid.*
246, "Vexacious and truly mortifying," Greene MS.
246, "Issued something like a censure," *Ibid.*
246, "I confess that I do most cordially," Sullivan, v. 14, p. 219.
246, "to combat all these misfortunes," *Ibid.*, p. 206.
247, "Would you believe," Lafayette, v. 1, p. 191.
247, "Prudence dictates," GW, F, v. 12, p. 367.
247, "I intend to ascribe it to necessity," *Ibid.*, p. 364.
247, "It is of the greatest importance," *Ibid.*, p. 387.
247, "He will . . . take any advice," *Ibid.*
248, "The late affray," S & R, p. 392.
248, "If this is not strictly true," Laurens, p. 228.
248, "An unfortunate storm," GW, F, v. 12, p. 488.
248, "Infamous in itself," AH, S, v. 1, p. 570.
249, "Your money is now sinking," GW, F, v. 13, pp. 467–68.
249, "I would to God," *Ibid.*, p. 383.
249, "All the business is now *attempted*," *Ibid.*, v. 19, pp. 131–32.
249, "It is lamentable," *Ibid.*, v. 15, pp. 43–44.
250, "I am much mistaken," *Ibid.*, p. 97.
250, "I am exceedingly mortified," *Ibid.*, v. 16, p. 9.
250, "You may form," *Ibid.*
251, "I hope it will be remembered," *Ibid.*, v. 15, p. 392.
251, "With respect to my plans," *Ibid.*, pp. 259–60.
252, "I . . . am now to authorize," *Ibid.*, v. 16, p. 483.
252, "Awkward and expensive," *Ibid.*, v. 17, p. 74.
253, "We have waited so long," *Ibid.*, p. 91.
253, "I do not expect," *Ibid.*, p. 93.
253, "Good God!" Larrabee, p. 86.
253, "I am now to inform you," GW, F, v. 17, p. 109.
254, "The snow is now," Thacher, p. 185.
254, "on which they chew," *Ibid.*, p. 186.
254, "Week after week," S & R, p. 432.
254, "Fire . . . incessant the whole night," *Ibid.*, p. 460.
255, "They are allowed," *Ibid.*, p. 463.
255, "For fifteen minutes," *Ibid.*
255, "The people at that time," Crary, p. 279.
255, "I am thoroughly convinced," GW, S, v. 7, p. 489.
256, "M. de Ternay's vessels," Lafayette, v. 1, p. 351.
256, "I am reduced," GW, F, v. 19, p. 403.
257, "vegetating at the very door," Bonsal, pp. 35–36.
257, "One hundred and eighty miles," AH, S, v. 2, p. 421.
257, "If they push their successes," GW, F, v. 20, p. 141.
258, "Nothing conclusive," *Ibid.*, p. 118.
258, "The history of the war," *Ibid.*
258, "I see nothing before us," GW, F, v. 20, p. 122.
259, "heartily tired," Smith, Narrative, p. 22.
260, "Information was given me," Clinton, p. 462.

260, "As Life and every thing," VD, SH, p. 442.

260, "Could you obtain," *Ibid.*, p. 446.

260, ". . . S. Henry secure," *Ibid.*, pp. 464–65.

263, "An amiable woman," AH, S, v. 2, p. 441.

263, "heartily sick," Burr, pp. 219–20.

263, "As soon as I saw Anderson," Tallmadge, p. 36.

264, "*Against my stipulation*," Clinton, p. 459.

264, "I forsee my fate," AH, S, v. 2, p. 466.

264, "Poor André," VD, SW, p. 479.

264, "that Major André," VD, SH, p. 487.

264, "Affectingly awful," Thacher, p. 227.

264, "It will be," *Ibid.*

265, "A most tremendous swing," *Ibid.*

265, "When I saw him swinging," Tallmadge, p. 38.

265, "A murderer & a Jesuit," SW, p. 481.

265, "In a conference which I had," *Ibid.*, pp. 480–81.

266, "Had it succeeded," Clinton, p. 463.

266, "I told him to dismount," Smith, Trial, pp. 43–46.

267, "At the close of this year," GW, S, v. 8, pp. 526–27.

268, "I am quite tired," S & R, p. 542.

268, "His Lordship *disobeyed*," Clinton, p. 301.

269, "It became urgent," Rochambeau, p. 44.

269, "scarcely another object," *Ibid.*, p. 45.

269, "It was therefore necessary," Fleming, p. 91.

270, "I then suggested," Rochambeau, p. 51.

270, "I assure you," GW, F, v. 22, p. 104.

270, "I hastened to call," Rochambeau, pp. 58–59.

271, "No Militia," GW, F, v. 22, p. 354.

271, "I had neither Men, nor means," GW, D, v. 2, p. 240.

271, "lest in the attempt," *Ibid.*

271, "Your Lordship will, I hope," Clinton, pp. 530–31.

272, "*Madness!*" S & R, p. 544.

272, "I feel myself unhappy," GW, F, v. 20, p. 26.

272, "The shell and shot," Knox, p. 96.

XIV

273, "I am almost all impatience," GW, F, v. 23, p. 71.

273, "Circumstances pressing," *Ibid.*, p. 112.

273, "with a complete band," *Ibid.*, p. 272.

274, "distressed beyond expression," GW, F, v. 23, p. 77.

274, "Nothing now gives me impatience," *Ibid.*, p. 101.

274, "hugged him as close," S & R, p. 549.
274, "*Mon cher petit général*," Larrabee, p. 261.
275, "Mr. Evans, much agitated," Thacher, p. 380.
276, "that it might be said," Martin, p. 232.
276, "Extremely severe," Thacher, p. 283.
277, "his skull shattered," Martin, p. 239.
277, "raising clouds of dust," Robin, p. 58.
277, "a torrent of fire," Thacher, p. 283.
278, "not to have had time," Robin, p. 59.
279, "Colonel Cobb said," Thacher, p. 285.
279, "Not less than one hundred," *Ibid.*, p. 286.
279, "Carcasses of men and horses," Robin, p. 65.
280, "We at that time," Clinton, pp. 585–86.
280, "That gentleman observed," S & R, p. 572.
280, "much in liquor," Larrabee, p. 269.
281, "like boys who had been whipped," S & R, p. 572.
281, "M. de Rochambeau," Rankin, p. 343.
281, "took it as a ball," *Ibid.*, p. 347.
281, "swepped," GIII, F, v. 5, p. 422.
281, "His Majesty . . . with much sorrow," GIII, F, v. 5, p. 425.
282, "It is his merit," Chinard, p. 69.
283, "Permits himself," *Ibid.*, p. 75.
283, "the most gracious and amiable smile," *Ibid.*, p. 65.
283, "His conversation," *Ibid.*, p. 75.
283, "He is masculine looking," *Ibid.*, pp. 74–75.
284, "idea of a perfect whole," *Ibid.*, pp. 62–63.
284, "General in a republic," *Ibid.*, p. 57.
284, ". . . he inspired," *Ibid.*, p. 37.
284, "the most illustrious," *Ibid.*, pp. 62–63.
285, "Accordingly done," GW, D, v. 2, p. 269.
285, "My greatest fear," GW, F, v. 23, p. 347.
285, "It had better not have happened," *Ibid.*, p. 352.
285, "I consider myself," *Ibid.*, p. 343.
285, "My Services," *Ibid.*, p. 362.
285, "You could not have found," *Ibid.*, v. 25, p. 273.
285, "It really appears," *Ibid.*, p. 269.
286, "I cannot help apprehending," *Ibid.*, p. 228.
286, "deeds of outrage and violence," S & R, p. 529.
286, "made a short pause," *Ibid.*, p. 531.
286, "The meeting terminated," GW, F, v. 26, p. 228.
287, "I said, or meant to say," *Ibid.*, p. 324.
287, "Some. . . went home," Martin, p. 281.
287, "Genl. Carleton sent me word," GW, F, v. 27, p. 191.
287, "Such a scene of sorrow and weeping," Tallmadge, p. 64.
288, "din of a most extraordinary nature," S & R, p. 585.
288, "he danced every set," *Ibid.*
288, "will put a period not only," GW, F, v. 23, p. 12.

289, "that relaxation and repose," *Ibid.*, v. 26, p. 488.
289, "there should be," *Ibid.*
289, "rope of sand," *Ibid.*, p. 359.

XV

293, "in the calm light," GW, F, v. 27, p. 314.
293, "I am just beginning," *Ibid.*, p. 340.
294, "She says she can get nothing," *Ibid.*, v. 26, p. 42.
294, "I learn that she is," *Ibid.*, p. 43.
294, "some things which have given," *Ibid.*
295, "a short, thick woman," *American Heritage*, April, 1958, p. 30.
295, "a very clever little village," S & R, p. 255.
295, "His worthy lady," S & R, pp. 255–56.
295, "Our noble and agreeable commander," *Ibid.*
295, "if he did not let go," *Ibid.*, p. 424.
296, "Tell her that," GW, F, v. 16, pp. 375–76.
296, "inflammable matter," *Ibid.*, v. 34, p. 91.
297, "I am glad to hear," *Ibid.*, v. 28, p. 115.
297, "admires pretty women," Miller, T of F, p. 491.
298, "All my private letters," GW, F, v. 26, pp. 276–77.
298, "the honor, power and true interest," *Ibid.*, p. 298.
299, "Shameful . . . truly Shocking," *Ibid.*, v. 28, p. 305.
299, "molder into dust," *Ibid.*, v. 27, p. 49.
299, "I have no fears," *Ibid.*, p. 306.
299, "We are either a united people," *Ibid.*, v. 29, p. 336.
299, "the people, not always seeing," *Ibid.*, v. 27, p. 306.
300, "Good God!" *Ibid.*, v. 30, p. 122.
300, "To be more exposed," *Ibid.*, p. 34.
300, "You talk, my good Sir," *Ibid.*
300, "tranquillity and rural amusements," *Ibid.*, v. 28, p. 468.
300, "It is in contemplation," Jay, v. 3, p. 187.
300, "I scarcely know," GW, F, v. 28, p. 431.
301, "Would to God," *Ibid.*, pp. 503–4.
301, "Should this matter," *Ibid.*, v. 29, p. 127.
301, "There is an end," *Ibid.*, p. 151.
301, "*In confidence,*" *Ibid.*
301, "It will, I fear," *Ibid.*, p. 187.
302, "disrespectful to a worthy set," *Ibid.*, p. 181.
302, "Inform me confidentially," *Ibid.*, p. 173.
302, "A Brother who was," *Ibid.*, p. 209.
302, "so much afflicted," *Ibid.*, pp. 208–9.

302, "I will not suppress," *Ibid.*, v. 30, p. 111.
302, "My consent is given," *Ibid.*, v. 29, p. 198.
303, "I assure you," *Ibid.*, p. 211.
303, "You will be surprised," *Ibid.*, p. 229.
303, "Weak at home," *Ibid.*, p. 238.
303, "The situation of the general Government," *Ibid.*, p. 224.
303, "The men who oppose," *Ibid.*, pp. 245–46.
304, "I almost despiar," *Ibid.*
304, "While rivetted to the toils," *Ibid.*, pp. 482–83.
304, "I accompany it," *Ibid.*, p. 278.
304, "Should the idea prevail," Morrison, p. 306.
305, "I was not," GW, F, v. 29, p. 509.
305, "It would be· . . . with," *Ibid.*, v. 30, p. 111.
306, "I wish . . . there may not be," *Ibid.*, p. 358.
306, "inheriting inferior endowments," *Ibid.*, p. 292.
306, "I greatly apprehend," *Ibid.*, v. 29, p. 509.
307, "An handome face," JA, S & A, pp. 197–98.
307, "Generally, they were," TJ, TJR, v. 3, pp. 493–94.
308, "The people must *feel*," GW, F, v. 28, p. 183.
308, "I have never yet," *Ibid.*, v. 30, p. 312.
308, "Shall I . . . set up my judgment," *Ibid.*, p. 299.
309, "My friendship," *Ibid.*, p. 223.
309, "darling Sovereignties," *Ibid.*, v. 29, p. 153.

XVI

311, "Bastard Bratt," JA, S & A, p. 48.
311, "his fornications," JA, S & A, p. 93.
311, "super abundance of secretions," Miller, AH, p. 523.
312, "I was not a party man," GW, F, v. 35, p. 119.
313, "A dangerous accumulation," JM, v. 1, p. 549.
313, "Departures from," JM, v. 3, p. 245.
313, "usury, knavery, and folly," *Ibid.*, v. 1, p. 552.
313, "If Congress can do," *Ibid.*, p. 546.
314, "An illustrious descent," JA, Peek, p. 180.
314, "the political heresies," Brodie, p. 261.
314, "The Question everywhere," Cappon, pp. 247–48.
314, "Mr. Adams can least of all," JM, v. 1, p. 536.
314, "Mr. Paine's principles," Cappon, p. 250.
314, "I have for Mr. Adams," TJ, F, v. 5, p. 329.
315, "Hamilton was not only," TJ, TJR, v. 4, pp. 460–61.
316, "absurd . . . *criminal* and *visionary*," AH, S, v. 11, p. 443.

316, "arbitrary, persecuting," *Ibid.*
316, "intriguing incendiary," *Ibid.*, v. 12, pp. 504–5.
317, "If they tell the truth," GW, F, v. 31, p. 51.
318, "*desires,*" TJ, TJR, v. 4, p. 478.
318, "He considered those papers," *Ibid.*, v. 4, p. 477.
318, "internal dissensions," GW, F, v. 32, p. 130.
319, "to render me," AH, S, v. 12, p. 348.
319, "the loins of fools and knaves," TJ, F, v. 6, pp. 107–8.
320, "I did not require," GW, F, v. 32, pp. 185–86.
320, "He said that he could not believe," JM, v. 1, pp. 556–57.
321, "This is the event," TJ, F, v. 6, p. 5.
321, "it had been better," AH, S, v. 12, p. 138.
322, "Should a civil war arise," GW, F, v. 32, p. 136, *fn.*
322, "I am again called upon," *Ibid.*, p. 374.
322, "To say I feel pleasure," *Ibid.*, p. 310.
322, "I told him that," TJ, TJR, v. 4, p. 488.
323, "It appeared to both of us," JM, v. 1, pp. 597–98.
323, "I told him," TJ, TJR, v. 4, p. 488.
323, "The charge against me," AH, S, v. 21, pp. 243–67.
324, "Conversation ensued," *Ibid.*
324, "There is nothing worse," *Ibid.*
325, "bank directors . . . stock jobbers," TJ, TJR, v. 4, p. 493.
325, "Worn down with labors," TJ, F, v. 6, pp. 290–91.
326, "burden and perplexity," AH, S , v. 13, p. 469.
326, "Every friend I see," *Ibid.*, pp. 469–70.
326, "To see the character," *Ibid.*, v. 18, p. 270.
326, "A regard to the sentiments," JA, Peek, pp. 177–83.
327, "I am solicitous," AH, S, v. 12, p. 353.
327, "my neighbor and my quondam friend," *Ibid.*, p. 129.

XVII

329, "Rather than it should have failed," TJ, F, v. 6, p. 154.
329, "A most unfortunate error," JM, v. 1, p. 584.
330, "We wish you to do nothing," TJ, F, v. 6, p. 260.
330, "*Till the Representatives,*" TJ, TJR, v. 3, p. 285.
330, "He . . . ran on much," *Ibid.*, v. 4, p. 503.
331, "Hot headed," TJ, F, v. 6, p. 339.
332, "I would not gratify," TJ, P, p. 1250.
332, "After I read," GW, F, v. 33, p. 4.
333, "It appears to me," TJ, P, p. 1252.
334, "One firebrand," JA, L, v. 2, p. 153.

335, "The sufferers here," King, v. 1, p. 552.
335, "A more degrading mission," TJ, F, v. 6, p. 504.
335, "No man more ardently," GW, F, v. 34, p. 16.
336, "I carried with me," Jay, v. 4, p. 186.
336, "political evils," *Ibid.*, p. 197.
336, "The ruinous bargain," JM, v. 2, p. 44.
336, "an execrable thing," TJ, F, v. 7, p. 40.
337, "If this treaty," Monroe, v. 2, p. 353.
337, "If you use," Schachner, p. 350.
337, "It was observed," King, v. 2, p. 20.
337, "The country rising," AH, S, v. 18, p. 531.
337, "This is an act," Monroe, v. 2, pp. 354–55.
338, "My opinion is the same," GW, F, v. 34, p. 244.
338, "It is the Interest," *Ibid.*, p. 263.
338, "I am . . . preparing my mind," GW, F, v. 34, p. 256.
338, "working like bees," GW, F, v. 34, p. 264.
338, "the dregs, however," *Ibid.*, p. 397.
339, "The whole is idle nonsense," AH, S, v. 19. p. 433.
339, "It is not difficult," GW, F, v. 34, p. 276.
339, "You are at liberty," *Ibid.*, p. 340.
340, "intending to *shew*," *Ibid.*, p. 347.
340, "What do you think," *Ibid.*, p. 404.
340, "It does not surprise me," AH, S, v. 19, p. 514.
340, "Political suicide," GW, F, v. 34, p. 315.
340, "They will receive," TJ, TJR, v. 3, p. 326.
340, "Through what official interstice," JM, v. 2, p. 80.
341, "something warm and angular," AH, JCH, v. 6, p. 163.
341, "If I have a fear," AH, S, v. 21, p. 22.
341, "I early discovered," GW, F, v. 36, p. 394.
341, "He would not accept," *Ibid.*, v. 19, p. 395.
341, "I am anxious," GW, F, v. 35, p. 103.
342, "I have told Mr. Randolph," *Ibid.*, v. 34, pp. 241–42.
342, "The offices are once more full," JA, L, v. 2, p. 195.
342, "On the precedent," TJ, TJR, v. 3, p. 330.
343, "I see no harm," *Ibid.*
343, "The House . . . have applied," JA, L, v. 2, p. 215.
343, "Every eye was then turned," JM, v. 2, pp. 96–97.
343, "The power of making treaties," GW, F, v. 35, pp. 3–5.
343, "The absolute refusal," JM, v. 2, p. 90.
344, "There is little doubt," *Ibid.*
344, "Finding the draft," GW, F, v. 35, p. 5.
344, "From the very first moment," *Ibid.*, pp. 6–7.
345, "I see nothing better," JA, L, v. 2, p. 219.
345, "I trust . . . the House," JM, v. 2, p. 92.
345, "The majority has melted," *Ibid.*, pp. 226–27.
345, "My God! How great he is!" JA, L, v. 2, pp. 226–27.
345, "Some of the jackasse," *Ibid.*

345, "The progress of this business," JM, v. 2, pp. 99–100.
346, "The name of the President," *Ibid.*, pp. 104–5.
346, "That a man," AH, S, v. 20, pp. 370–71.
346, "The people have," JM, v. 2, pp. 100–1.
346, "Such is the popularity," TJ, F, v. 7, p. 101.
346, "Curse on his virtues," TJ, TJR, v. 3, p. 334.
346, "It would give you a fever," *Ibid.*
347, "I earnestly hope," Monroe, v. 3, p. 25.
347, "The pretensions of that Party," GW, F, v. 35, p. 49.
347, "With respect to the motives," *Ibid.*, p. 30.
347, "misrepresented . . . to make it appear," *Ibid.*, p. 102.
347, "morbid tumor," *Ibid.*, v. 34, p. 483.
348, "Until within the last year," *Ibid.*, v. 35, p. 120.
348, "I regret exceedingly," *Ibid.*, p. 103.
348, "And besides," *Ibid.*, p. 49.
349, "It is to be considered," TJ, TJR, v. 3, p. 347.
349, "There is reason to believe," TJ, F, v. 7, p. 103.
349, "Every thing must give way," AH, S, v. 20, p. 377.
349, "Mr. Adams is President," *Ibid.*, pp. 515–16.
350, "By a firm adherence," GW, F, v. 34, p. 402.
350, "to be on friendly terms," *Ibid.*, p. 401.
350, "We are an Independent Nation," *Ibid.*, v. 35, p. 40.

XVIII

352, "Monroe's book," TJ, F, v. 7, p. 190.
352, "Colo. Monroe," GW, F, v. 36, p. 18.
352, "It would be impossible," TJ, F, v. 7, p. 166.
353, "a favorite nephew," GW, F, v. 36, p. 53, *fn.*
353, "nothing short of the Evidence," *Ibid.*, p. 182.
353, "prone to antipathies," TJ, TJR, v. 4, pp. 409–18.
354, "General Washington," *Ibid.*
355, "After I retired," *Ibid.*, p. 243.
355, "Attempts to injure those," GW, F, v. 36, p. 182.
355, "Mr. Adams whom he," TJ, TJR, v. 4, p. 4.
356, "He spoke of his *masters*," *Ibid.*, p. 171.
356, "then your secret," Cappon, p. 332.
357, "The storm thickens," GW, F, v. 36, p. 298, *fn.*
357, "The Opposers of Government," *Ibid.*, p. 306.
357, "Under the rose," *Ibid.*, p. 319.
357, "I should like," *Ibid.*, p. 273.
358, "There is one thing," *Ibid.*, p. 315.

358, "It was the ground on which," *Ibid.*, p. 455.
359, "Being senior to Colonel Hamilton," *Ibid.*, p. 325.
359, "My wish to put you first," *Ibid.*, p. 332.
359, "I confess," *Ibid.*, p. 394.
359, "I should have been," GW, S, v. 11, pp. 534–35.
360, "I rejoiced," AH, JCH, v. 6, pp. 373–74.
360, "I had thought," *Ibid.*
361, "I will endeavour," GW, F, v. 36. p. 395.
361, "It will be agreeable," AH, JCH, v. 6, p. 354.
361, "Delicacy, if matters become serious," GW, F, v. 36, p. 395.
361, "He finally agreed," GW, S, v. 11, p. 543.
362, "General Knox," JA, CFA, v. 8, p. 580.
362, "The original letter," AH, JCH, v. 6, p. 351.
362, "neither contain sentiments," JA, CFA, v. 8, pp. 587–88.
363, "In the last resort," AH, JCH, v. 6, p. 355.
363, "my mind is unalterably made up," *Ibid.*, p. 356.
363, "I cannot blame you," *Ibid.*
363, "Measures have been taken," *Ibid.*, p. 359.
363, "I have seen the correspondence," GW, F, v. 36, p. 452.
364, "I would have told you," *Ibid.*, pp. 454–62.
364, "departure in almost every other instance," *Ibid.*, p. 475.
365, "As I think I stand," *Ibid.*, p. 479.
365, "You will be at no loss," *Ibid.*, p. 464.
365, "The rough draught," *Ibid.*
365, "I some time ago," JA, CFA, v. 8, pp. 600–1.
365, "General Knox," GW, F, v. 36, p. 500.
365, "Enclosed is a copy," *Ibid.*, p. 502.
366, "If you must have an army," AH, JCH, v. 6, pp. 396–97.
366, "Evidently . . . kept secret," TJ, F, v. 7, p. 366.
367, "I have neither time nor inclination," AH, JCH, v. 6, pp. 396–97.
367, "it was agreed to reject," *Ibid.*, p. 400.
367, "I was surprized at the measure," GW, F, v. 37, p. 409.
367, "Stricken dumb," *Ibid.*, p. 428.
369, "I believe he expected," JA, S & A, p. 226.
369, "An insolent coxcomb," *Ibid.*, p. 48.
369, "Hamilton's project," *Ibid.*, p. 36.
369, "I ought to have said No," *Ibid.*, pp. 98–99.
370, "He felt weary," *Ibid.*, p. 226.
370, "I was no more at liberty," *Ibid.*, p. 99.
370, "His absence gives," GW, F, v. 37, p. 328.
370, "Should you decline," Morris, v. 3, pp. 123–24.
371, "Let me ask," GW, F, v. 37, p. 349.
371, "I was the *first*," *Ibid.*, p. 372.
371, "all fits that end," *Ibid.*, v. 36, p. 109, *fn.*
372, "had a hoarseness" and quotations which follow are from GW, Ford, v. 14, pp. 246–64.

377, "Perhaps the strongest feature," TJ, TJR, v. 4, p. 241.
378, "He is no lover of parade," Deane, v. 19, p. 62.
379, "My first wish," GW, F, v. 28, p. 202.
380, "Next to being strong," *Ibid.*, v. 10, p. 52.
380, "If the public believes," *Ibid.*, v. 13, p. 465.
380, "It is uncertain," Robin, p. 35.
380, "Men will not adopt," Jay, v. 3, p. 208.
381, "He was naturally," TJ, TJR, v. 4, p. 243.
381, "I have accustomed myself to judge," GW, F, v. 25, p. 415.

Bibliography
Papers and Direct Sources

Papers by or to Washington:

WASHINGTON, GEORGE. *The Diaries of George Washington,* ed. John C. Fitzpatrick. Boston: Houghton Mifflin, 1925, 4 v., *(GW,D)*.

_____.*George Washington's Rules of Civility,* ed. Moncure D. Conway. New York: United States Book Company, 1890, *(GW,R)*.

_____.*The Writings of George Washington,* ed. John C. Fitzpatrick. Washington, D.C.: Government Printing Office, 1933-44, *(GW,F)*.

_____.*The Writings of George Washington,* ed. Worthington C. Ford, New York, Putnam, 1889, 14 v., *(GW,Ford)*.

_____.*The Writings of George Washington,* ed. Jared Sparks. Boston: Russell, Odroine and Metcalf, 1834, 12 v., *(GW,S)*.

Letters to Washington, ed. Stanislaus Murray Hamilton. Boston: Houghton Mifflin, 1898, 5 v., *(GW,L)*.

Other Sources:

ADAMS, JOHN. *Adams Family Correspondence,* ed. Lyman H. Butterfield. Cambridge: Harvard University Press, 1963, 2 v., *(JA,AFC)*.

———. *The Adams-Jefferson Letters,* ed. Lester Cappon. New York: Clarion Books, 1971, *(Cappon).*

———. *Diaries and Autobiography of John Adams,* ed. Lyman H. Butterfield. Cambridge: Harvard University Press, 1963, 4 v., *(JA,AB).*

———. *Letters of John Adams, Addressed to His Wife,* ed. Charles Francis Adams. Boston: Little Brown, 1841, 2 v., *(JA,L).*

———. *The Political Writings of John Adams,* ed. George A. Peek, Jr. Indianapolis and New York: Bobbs Merrill, 1954, *(JA,Peek).*

———. *The Works of John Adams,* ed. Charles Francis Adams. Boston: Little Brown, 1851, 10 v., *(JA,CFA).*

The Spur of Fame, Dialogues of John Adams and Benjamin Rush, ed. John A. Schutz and Douglass Adair. Kingsport: Kingsport Press, 1966, *(S&A).*

ALLEN, ETHAN. *Narrative of Colonel Ethan Allen,* ed. Brooke Hindle. New York: Corinth Books, 1961.

ANDRÉ, JOHN. *Major André's Journal.* New York: N. Y. *Times* & Arno Press, 1963.

BERNARD, SIR FRANCIS. *The Barrington-Bernard Correspondence,* ed. Edward Channing and Archibald Cary Coolidge. Oxford: Oxford University Press, 1912.

BOUQUET, HENRI. *The Papers of Henri Bouquet,* ed. E. K. Stevens, Donald H. Kents and Autumn Leonard. Harrisburg: Pennsylvania Historical and Museum Commission, 1951.

BURKE, EDMUND. *The Correspondence of Edmund Burke,* ed. Lucy S. Sutherland. Cambridge and Chicago: Cambridge and the University of Chicago Press, 1960, 5 v., *(Burke,S).*

———. *Edmund Burke on the American Revolution,* ed. Elliot R. Barkan. New York: Harper Torchbooks, 1966, *(Burke,B).*

BURNETT, EDMUND C., ed., *Letters of the Members of the Continental Congress.* Washington: The Carnegie Institution, 1921-36, 8 v.

BURR, AARON. *Memoirs of Aaron Burr,* ed. Matthew L. Davis. New York: Harper & Brothers, 1836.

BYRD, WILLIAM. *History of the Dividing Line and Other Tracts,* ed. T.H. Wynne. Richmond, 1866, 2 v.

CLINTON, SIR HENRY. *The American Rebellion,* ed. William B. Willcox. New Haven: Yale University Press, 1954.

CUSTIS, GEORGE WASHINGTON PARKE. *Recollections and Private Memoirs of Washington.* New York: Derby & Jackson, 1860.

DINWIDDIE, ROBERT. *The Official Records of Robert Dinwiddie,* ed. R. A. Brock. Richmond: Virginia Historical Society Collections, 1936, 2 v.

FORBES, JOHN. *The Writings of General John Forbes,* ed. Alfred Proctor James. Menasha: Collegiate Press, 1938.

FRANKLIN, BENJAMIN. *The Works of Benjamin Franklin,* ed. John Bigelow. New York: Putnam, 1904, 12 v., *(BF,B)*

———. *The Papers of Benjamin Franklin,* ed. Leonard W. Labaree and others. New Haven: Yale University Press, 1959-71, (*BF,L*).

GAGE, THOMAS. *Correspondence of General Thomas Gage,* ed. Charles E. Carter. New Haven: Yale University Press, 1931-33, 2 v.

GATES, HORATIO. *Horatio Gates Correspondence.* New York: New-York Historical Society.

GEORGE III. *The Correspondence of George III,* ed. Sir John Fortescue. London: Macmillan, 1927-28, 6 v., (*GIII,F*).

———. *Correspondence of George III with Lord North,* ed. W. Bodham Donne. London: John Murray, 1867 2 v., (*GIII,Donne*).

———. *Letters of King George III,* ed. Bonamy Dobree. London: Cassell & Co. 1935, (*GIII,Dobree*).

GREENE, NATHANAEL. Nathanael Greene Papers, microfilm collection. New York: New York Public Library.

HAMILTON, ALEXANDER. *The Papers of Alexander Hamilton,* ed. Harold Styrett and others. New York: Columbia University Press, 1961-73, 18 v., (*AH,S*).

———. *The Works of Alexander Hamilton,* ed. John Church Hamilton. New York: John H. Trow, 1850, 6 v., (*AH,JCH*).

JAY, JOHN. *The Correspondence and Public Papers of John Jay,* ed. Henry F. Livingston. New York: Putnam, 1891, 4 v.

JEFFERSON, THOMAS. *The Complete Jefferson,* ed. Saul K. Padover. New York: Duell, Sloan and Pearce, 1943, (*TJ,P*).

———. *Memoirs, Correspondence and Private Papers of Thomas Jefferson,* ed. Thomas Jefferson Randolph. London: Colburn & Bentley, 1829, 4 v., (*TJ,TJR*).

———. *The Writings of Thomas Jefferson,* ed. Paul L. Ford. New York: Putnam, 1892-99, 10 v., (*TJ,F*).

KING, RUFUS. *The Life and Correspondence of Rufus King,* ed. Charles R. King. New York: Putnam, 1895, 6 v.

KNOX, HENRY. *Life and Correspondence of Henry Knox,* ed. F. S. Drake. Boston: S. G. Drake, 1873.

LAFAYETTE, MARQUIS DE. *Memoirs, Correspondence and Manuscripts of General Lafayette.* London: Saunders & Otley, 1839, 3 v.

LAURENS, JOHN. *The Army Correspondence of Colonel John Laurens.* New York: N. Y. Times & Arno Press, 1965.

LEE, CHARLES. *The Lee Papers.* New York: Collections of the New-York Historical Society, New York, 1872-75, 3 v.

MADISON, JAMES. *The Writings of James Madison,* ed. Henry Gaillard. New York: Putnam, 1906, 3 v., (*JM*).

MARSHALL, CHRISTOPHER. *The Diary of Christopher Marshall,* ed. William Duane. New York: N. Y. Times & Arno Press, 1969.

MARTIN, JOSEPH PLUMB. *The Adventures of a Revolutionary Soldier,* ed. George Scheer. New York: N. Y. Times & Arno Press, 1962.

MASON, GEORGE. *The Papers of George Mason,* ed. Robert A. Rutland. Chapel Hill: University of North Carolina Press, 1970, 3 v.

MONROE, JAMES. *The Writings of James Monroe*, ed. Stanislaus M. Hamilton. New York: Putnam, 1898, 4 v.

MORRIS, GOUVERNEUR. *The Life of Gouverneur Morris with Selections from His Correspondence*, ed. Jared Sparks. Boston: Gray & Bowen, 1832, 3 v.

OLIVER, PETER. *Origin & Progress of the American Rebellion*, ed. Douglass Adair & John A. Schutz. Stanford: Stanford University Press, 1967.

REED, JOSEPH. *Life and Correspondence of Joseph Reed*, ed. William B Reed. Philadelphia: Lindsay & Blakiston, 1847.

ROBIN, ABBE. *New Travels Through North America*. New York: N. Y. *Times* & Arno Press, 1969.

ROCHAMBEAU, COMTE DE. *Memoirs of the Marshall Count de Rochambeau*. New York: N. Y. *Times* & Arno Press, 1971.

RUSH, BENJAMIN. *The Letters of Benjamin Rush*, ed. Lyman H. Butterfield. Princeton: Princeton University Press, 1951.

SERLE, AMBROSE. *The American Journal of Ambrose Serle*. San Marino: The Huntington Library, 1840.

SMITH, JOSHUA HETT. *Narrative of the Death of Major André*. New York: N. Y. *Times* & Arno Press, 1971 (*Smith, Narrative*).

————. *Trial of Joshua Hett Smith for Complicity in the Conspiracy of Benedict Arnold and Major André*, ed. H. B. Dawson. Morrisania, New York, 1866, (*Smith, Trial*).

SPOTSWOOD, ALEXANDER. *The Official Letters of Alexander Spotswood*, ed. R. A. Brock. Richmond: Virginia Historical Society Collections, 1932, 2 v.

STEDMAN, CHARLES. *History of the Late War in America*. New York: N. Y. *Times* & Arno Press, 1965.

STIRLING, WILLIAM ALEXANDER. *The Life of William Alexander, Earl of Stirling, with Selections from His Correspondence*, ed. William Alexander Duer. New York: Wiley & Putnam, 1847.

SULLIVAN, JOHN. *The Sullivan Papers*. Concord: Concord, New Hampshire, Historical Society Publications, 1930-39.

TALLMADGE, BENJAMIN. *Memoir of Colonel Benjamin Tallmadge*. New York: N. Y. *Times* & Arno Press, 1967.

THACHER, JAMES. *Military Journal of the American Revolution*. New York: N. Y. *Times* & Arno Press, 1967.

TUDOR, JOHN. *Deacon Tudor's Diary*, ed. William Tudor. Boston: Wallace Spooner, 1896.

VON CLAUSEN, LUDWIG. *The Revolutionary Journal of Baron Ludwig von Clausen*, ed. Evelyn M. Ascomb. Chapel Hill: University of North Carolina Press, 1958.

WALPOLE, HORACE. *The Last Journals of Horace Walpole During the Reign of George III*, ed. A. Francis Steuart. London: Lane, 1910, 2 v., (*Walpole,J*).

The Letters of Horace Walpole, ed. Mrs. Paget Toynbee. Oxford: The Clarendon Press, 1904, 16 v., (*Walpole,L*).

_____. *Memoirs and Portraits,* ed. Matthew Hodgart. New York: Macmillan, 1963, (*Walpole,M*).

WAYNE, ANTHONY. *Anthony Wayne Correspondence.* New York: New York Public Library.

WILKINSON, JAMES. *Memoirs of My Own Time.* Philadelphia: Abraham Small. 1816.

Anthologies:

BELOFF, MAX. ed. *The Debate on the American Revolution.* London: Adam & Charles Black, 1960.

CHINARD, GILBERT. *George Washington as the French Knew Him.* Princeton: Princeton University Press, 1940.

COMMAGER, HENRY STEELE, and RICHARD B. MORRIS. *The Spirit of Seventy-Six.* Indianapolis and New York: Bobbs Merrill, 1958, (*C&M*).

CRARY, CATHERINE S.. *The Price of Loyalty.* New York: McGraw-Hill, 1973.

HAMILTON, CHARLES. *Braddock's Defeat.* Norman: The University of Oklahoma Press, 1959.

MOORE, FRANK. *The Diary of the American Revolution,* ed. John Anthony Scott. New York: Washington Square Press, 1968.

MORISON, SAMUEL ELIOT. *Sources and Documents Illustrating the American Revolution.* Oxford: Oxford University Press, 1965.

MUMBY, FRANK ARTHUR. *George III and the American Revolution.* London: Constable & Co., 1924.

RANKIN, HUGH F. *The American Revolution.* New York: Putnam, 1964.

SCHEER, GEORGE F., and HUGH F. RANKIN. *Rebels and Redcoats.* New York: World, 1957 (*S&R*).

WHEELER, RICHARD. *Voices of 1776.* New York: Crowell, 1972.

Other Books:

ADDISON, JOSEPH. *18th Century Plays,* ed. Ricardo Quintana. New York: Modern Library, 1952.

BEVERLEY, ROBERT. *The History and Present State of Virginia,* ed.

419

Louis B. Wright. Chapel Hill: University of North Carolina Press, 1947.

BONSAL, STEPHEN. *When the French Were Here.* Port Washington: Kennikat Press, 1968.

BRODIE, FAWN. *Thomas Jefferson, An Intimate History.* New York: Norton, 1974.

BROOKE, JOHN M. *The Chatham Administration.* Cambridge: Cambridge University Press, 1962.

CLELAND, HUGH. *George Washington in the Ohio Valley.* Pittsburgh: University of Pittsburgh Press, 1962.

CONWAY, MONCURE. *Barons of the Potomack and the Rappahannock.* New York: the Grolier Club, 1892.

DESMOND, ALICE CURTIS. *Martha Washington.* New York: Dodd, Mead, 1944.

DICKERSON, OLIVER MORTON. *Boston Under Military Rule.* Boston: Chapman & Grimes, 1936.

FLEMING, THOMAS J. *Beat the Last Drum.* New York: St. Martin's, 1963.

FREEMAN, DOUGLAS SOUTHALL. *George Washington.* New York: Scribner's, 1948, v.1-2.

HAMILTON, EDWARD P. *The French & Indian War.* New York: Doubleday, 1962, *(F&I)*.

HATCH, ALDEN. *The Byrds of Virginia.* New York: Holt Rinehart & Winston, 1969.

Historical Society of Pennsylvania Memoirs. Philadelphia: Lippincott, 1855, *(HSPM)*.

HOFSTADTER, RICHARD. *The American Political Tradition and the Men Who Made It.* New York: Knopf, 1948.

———. *Great Issues in American History.* New York, Vintage Books, 1958, v.1

JONES, HUGH. *The Present State of Virginia,* ed. Richard L. Morton. Chapel Hill: University of North Carolina Press, 1956.

KRAUS, MICHAEL. *The Atlantic Civilization.* Ithaca: Cornell University Press, 1966.

LARRABEE, HAROLD A. *Decision at the Chesapeake.* New York: Clarkson N. Potter, 1964.

Massachusetts Historical Society Collections. Boston, *(MHSC)*.

MCCARDELL, LEE. *Ill-Starred General.* Pittsburgh: University of Pittsburgh Press, 1958.

MILLER, JOHN, C. *Alexander Hamilton and the Growth of the New Nation.* New York: Harper Torchbooks, 1964, *(Miller, AH)*.

———. *Triumph of Freedom.* Boston: Atlantic-Little Brown, 1948, *(Miller, T of F)*.

MORISON, SAMUEL ELIOT. *The Oxford History of the American People.* Oxford: Oxford University Press, 1965.

MORRIS, RICHARD B. *The American Revolution.* New York: Van Nostrand Reinhold, 1955.

_____. *The Era of the American Revolution.* New York: Columbia University Press, 1939.

_____. *Seven Who Shaped Our Destinies.* New York: Harper & Row, 1974.

NAMIER, SIR LOUIS. *Personalities and Powers.* New York: Harper Torchbooks, 1965.

O'MEARA, WALTER. *Guns at the Forks.* Englewood Cliffs: Prentice-Hall, 1965.

PALMER, JOHN MACAULEY. *General von Steuben.* Port Washington: Kennikat Press, 1966.

PARKMAN, FRANCIS. *Montcalm and Wolfe.* New York: Collier Books, 1962.

PATTERSON, SAMUEL WHITE. *Horatio Gates, Defender of American Liberties.* New York: Columbia University Press, 1941.

Pennsylvania Magazine of History and Biography. (*PMHB*).

ROSSITER, CLINTON. *Alexander Hamilton and the Constitution.* New York: Harcourt Brace & World, 1964.

_____. *1787: The Grand Convention.* New York: Macmillan, 1966.

SCHACHNER, NATHAN. *Alexander Hamilton.* New York: A. H. Barnes & Co., 1961.

SMITH, GOLDWIN. *A History of England.* New York, Scribner's, 1969.

VAN DOREN, CARL. *Benjamin Franklin.* New York: Viking, 1938, (*VD,BF*).

_____. *The Secret History of the American Revolution.* New York: Viking, 1941, (*VD,SH*).

WARD, CHRISTOPHER. *The War of the Revolution.* New York: Macmillan, 1962, 2 v.

WAYLAND, JOHN W. *The Washingtons and Their Homes.* Staunton: McClure, 1944.

WRIGHT, LOUIS B. *The Atlantic Frontier.* New York: Knopf, 1947.

Index

423

431